One

Market

Under

God

One

Market

Under

God

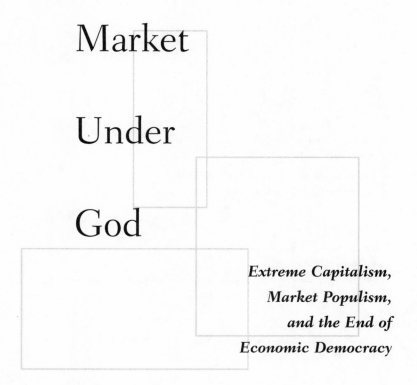

Extreme Capitalism,
Market Populism,
and the End of
Economic Democracy

Thomas Frank

Doubleday   New York London Toronto Sydney Auckland

PUBLISHED BY DOUBLEDAY
a division of Random House, Inc.
1540 Broadway, New York, New York 10036

DOUBLEDAY and the portrayal of an anchor with a dolphin
are trademarks of Doubleday, a division of
Random House, Inc.

Book design by Chris Welch

Library of Congress Cataloging-in-Publication Data
Frank, Thomas, 1965–
One market under God : extreme capitalism, market populism and the end of
economic democracy / by Thomas Frank.—1st ed.
p. cm.
Includes bibliographical references.
1. Marketing. 2. Capitalism. 3 Populism. 4. Kitsch. 5. Distributive justice. I. Title.
HF5415.F693 2000
330.12'2—dc21

00-031807

Portions of this book appeared in different form in *The Baffler, Harper's, Le Monde
Diplomatique,* the Chicago *Reader,* and *In These Times.*

ISBN 0-385-49503-X

Printed in the United States of America
November 2000
First Edition
10   9   8   7   6   5   4   3   2   1

In a time of faith, skepticism is the most intolerable of all insults.

—*Randolph Bourne,*
"The War and the Intellectuals"

Contents

Preface:
A Deadhead
in Davos

In February 1996, Congress passed the Telecommunications Act, a typical economic artifact of the Age of Clinton. While it inspired almost no debate in the nation at large, it was the object of hot controversy among the various broadcasting and telephone companies themselves, whose business it aimed to deregulate. Once the law's provisions had been agreed upon by lobbyists and legislators, its passage through Congress was assured by the generous donations that broadcasters had long made to legislators' reelection campaigns. Not that such inducements were wholly necessary to bring our representatives around. Deregulation was one of the central tenets of the free-market faith of the nineties, something that both President Clinton and the Republican Congress agreed was in the best interests of all. For them the Telecommunications Act was just another great push in the triumphant rollback of "big government" that had already been under way for fifteen years. As such, it was passed by a huge majority acting in the finest spirit of bipartisanship.

The new law removed certain long-standing restrictions on owner-ship of media properties, and after its passage the industry promptly embarked on a spree of buyouts and monopoly building, with tele-phone and cable systems merging and converging in a whirling tangle of free-market ebullience that continues to this day. More important, though, the Telecommunications Act cut the public out of the loop. The airwaves have always been public property; any thorough reorder-ing of the system of broadcast licensing should rightly have involved considerable public discussion over the country's media structure. But the new law closed off the prospect of such a troublesome and poten-tially embarrassing debate by simply giving away $70 billion worth of digital frequencies to existing broadcasters.[1]

A few isolated critics warned that the growing concentration of the in-formation industry constituted a threat to democracy. But according to the popular economic orthodoxy of the day, the exact opposite was the case: Real democracy was only possible when market forces had been liberated, when money was free to do its thing. What would ensure that broadcast-ers served the public was not congressional oversight or the meddling of some officious know-it-all regulator but the polls and focus groups and market research done by the broadcasters themselves. If we got lousy news or bad radio or crappy movies, we had only ourselves to blame.

The passage of the Telecommunications Act was thus one of those tableaux of greed, legislative turpitude, and transparently self-serving sophistry that American culture ordinarily delights in exposing and de-riding. It would have made rich material for a Lincoln Steffens or a Mark Twain. And yet the only really celebrated blast to break the si-lence was concerned not with the astronomically growing power of the telecoms and the broadcasters but with exactly the opposite: *Congress hadn't deregulated enough.* Government had no rights over markets whatsoever.

Announcing that it was time to "dump some tea in the virtual harbor," technology writer John Perry Barlow decried the passage of the Telecom Act by posting a fiery "Declaration of the Independence of Cyberspace." What had ticked Barlow off was not the virtual privatization of the airwaves but the "Communications Decency Act," a rider attached to the bill by religious conservatives that criminalized pornography on the Internet—and that was destined from the get-go to be struck down by the courts. But that hardly soothed Barlow, a former lyricist for the Grateful Dead, who proceeded to sound the tocsin of cyberlibertarianism.

"Governments of the Industrial World, you weary giants of flesh and steel," he ranted. "On behalf of the future, I ask you of the past to leave us alone." Even today Barlow's words blare from hundreds of websites,[2] reeking slightly of bongwater maybe, but standing proudly nonetheless as the ultimate statement of the principles of e-commerce, damning all governments as "tyrannies" with "no moral right to rule us," claiming to speak in the name of "liberty itself," reminding those interfering feds that they did not "create the wealth of our marketplaces," and hailing the dawn of a nearly flawless new democracy, a system so organically attuned to the popular will that it actually "grows itself through our collective actions." Standing up for this more perfect union, Barlow informed the governments of the world: "You are not welcome among us. You have no sovereignty where we gather."

The name of the place where Barlow and his colleagues gathered was given in the manifesto's final line: "Davos, Switzerland," the shrine of globalization where finance ministers and corporate executives gathered annually with the seers of "cyberspace" and the supplicant representatives of the Third World to reassure one another about the magic of markets and pep themselves up for another year of privatization, deregulation, phat stock returns, and austerity plans for the poor. What Barlow had transmitted to the world from the heights of Davos—ostensibly a populist manifesto on behalf of the humble people of "cyberspace"—was in fact a note-perfect expression of the imperatives of global business, made credible by the man's oft-remarked communion with the greatest shades of the hallowed sixties.

Deadheads in Davos: In a curious way, that's exactly what the nineties were all about. Barlow may have sounded like an alienated counterculturalist as he railed against the Telecom Act, but he essentially agreed with the suit-and-tie media execs on the big issue—that markets enjoyed some mystic, organic connection to the people while governments were fundamentally illegitimate. And in writing and posting the Internet's "Declaration of Independence" from among the central bankers and hedge fund managers in Davos, Barlow performed a feat of amazing cultural prescience. While insurgent democracy was the Web's sales pitch, its true value, as every American knew by the end of 1999, lay in the promise of undreamed-of riches from e-tailing, online brokerages, "B2B commerce," and dot-com stock schemes.

Barlow's proclamation was part of a larger shift in American culture. While the "New Economy" was teaching Americans to heed the words of the Deadhead in Davos, it was also teaching us that those patriotic blue-collar types who had served such a crucial symbolic role in the late sixties were in fact exactly the thick, robotic louts of countercultural legend. Hippies were whispering words of wisdom about deregulation, cyberspace, lower taxes, but the hardhats, American opinion leaders clucked, just didn't get it; they were missing out on the joy, the freedom, the sweet buzz of liberation. The old rivals had switched symbolic places. This new attitude became particularly apparent after union protests against the World Trade Organization's Seattle meeting in November 1999 caused the pundit class to turn as one for battle with the new national foe. Now, they told us, it was lovable outcasts like Bill Gates and his legion of tattooed-casual disciples who stood up for law and order—and it was union workers, once the rock-solid middle class hailed by Nixon and Reagan, who were the deluded, racist foot soldiers of protectionism.

Charles Krauthammer of *Time* magazine argued that while the blue-collar workers were once again turning their backs on the underprivileged, the market was picking up the banner of the "once colonized," generously helping "previously starving Third World peasants get their start." The influential *New York Times* columnist Thomas Friedman pointed out that the protesters' Seattle was far overshadowed by the hopeful Seattle of the Third World delegates to the WTO and the cool Seattle of Microsoft, the company that, like some sort of latter-day Beatles, had "captured the imagination of youth all over the world."[3] Economist Paul Krugman, flaying labor for its stance on free trade with China, compared American unionists to the architects of South African apartheid. Economist Jagdish Bhagwati, pounding labor for its anti-sweatshop activism, found pro-union college students so contemptible that he imagined they must have been brainwashed somehow. Labor unions were "misleading a few gullible undergraduates," he wrote, drumming bad ideas into the heads of "captive" students until these poor youngsters were driven to "chant on campuses" to secure their masters' ends.[4]

What is most fascinating here is the specific kind of brute that union supporters are said to be. They're not "Communists" or "philistines" as they were in the past—they're *automatons,* people lacking agency of their own, empty vessels filled with the will of others. In an op-ed piece that ran the day after the Seattle events, Thomas Friedman declared that unionists "have been duped by knaves like Pat Buchanan"; one newspaper editor in Canada even suggested that the protesters were puppets of exotic crazymen such as Osama bin Laden.[5] Treating workers in such a manner has obvious tactical advantages—it excuses one from taking their ideas seriously. But it also reflects one of the most basic assumptions of New Economy culture: Union workers are believed to be automatons because they act *outside the market.* For business and economic thinkers of the nineties, this was dangerous stuff. Only when people act within the marketplace, such thinkers told us, do they act rationally, choose rightly, and make their wishes known transparently. Only then could business give us what we wanted, cater to our freely expressed choices. Markets are where we are most fully human; markets are where we show that we have a soul. To protest *against* markets is to surrender one's very personhood, to put oneself outside the family of mankind.

This is why Bhagwati could claim that Phil Knight, the CEO of Nike, had conscientiously "taken a stand" when he fought union sympathizers on campus, but that those who criticized his use of sweat-shops were "captive to unions," incapable of thinking for themselves. This is why, in the culture of the nineties, CEOs were "leaders" and union chiefs were "bosses," regardless of the fact that unions are often democracies while corporations are almost always dictatorships. This is why it is thought to be an act of heroism to denounce government regulation from the heights of Davos but an act of cynicism to go on strike against new management strategies in Detroit. Similarly, this is why hipsters who work for software firms or ad agencies are enlight-ened, possibly holy, nonconformists while hipsters who march for en-vironmental issues are crazy or stupid. This is why workers who join unions are robots while workers who trade stocks online are getting in touch with their humanity. *We* are willing, interactive participants in the funky, individualistic, ever-changing web of market democracy; *they* simply hear and obey.

From Deadheads to Nobel-laureate economists, from paleoconserva-tives to New Democrats, American leaders in the nineties came to be-lieve that markets were a popular system, a far more democratic form of organization than (democratically elected) governments. This is the central premise of what I will call "market populism": That in addition to being mediums of exchange, markets were mediums of consent. Markets expressed the popular will more articulately and more mean-ingfully than did mere elections. Markets conferred democratic legiti-macy; markets were a friend of the little guy; markets brought down the pompous and the snooty; markets gave us what we wanted; mar-kets looked out for our interests.

Many of the individual components of the market populist consen-sus have been part of the cultural wallpaper for years. Hollywood and Madison Avenue have always insisted that their job is simply to mirror the public's wishes, and that movies or ad campaigns succeed or fail depending on how accurately they conform to public tastes. Similarly, spokesmen for the New York Stock Exchange have long argued that stock prices reflect public enthusiasm, that public trading of stocks is a basic component of democracy. And ever since William Randolph Hearst, newspaper tycoons have imagined themselves defenders of the common man.

But in the nineties these ideas became canonical, solidified into a new orthodoxy that anathematized all alternative ways of understanding democracy, history, and the rest of the world. Certainly one of the factors that made this efflorescence possible was the sudden demise of virtually all the historical foes of the American business community. Here at home, a Democratic president renounced his party's traditional faith in "big government" as a means of achieving economic justice, and organized labor, pounded by years of union busting and deindustrialization, slipped below 10 percent of the private-sector workforce. Overseas, Japan, OPEC, and the Soviet Union each faltered or collapsed completely. In Britain, the Labour Party abandoned its commitment to national control of industry, making that country once again safe for investment, and leftist parties elsewhere in Europe made similar gestures. In lesser economic powers from Indonesia to Argentina, the strict regimen imposed by Wall Street and the IMF ensured the same results: that capital would be free to move in and out, untroubled by the specter of nationalization, excessive regulation, or union troublemaking. Markets were in command, and market populism was what supplied them with the legitimacy required to rule.

Market populism is an idea riven by contradictions. It is the centerpiece of the new American consensus, but that consensus describes itself in terms of conflict, insurrection, even class war. It is screechingly democratic, and yet the formal institutions of democracy have never seemed more distant and irrelevant than under its aegis. It speaks passionately of economic fairness, and yet in the nineties the American economy elevated the rich and forgot about the poor with a decisiveness we hadn't seen since the 1920s. Market populism decries "elitism" while transforming CEOs as a class into one of the wealthiest elites of all time. It deplores hierarchy while making the corporation the most powerful institution on earth. It hails the empowerment of the individual and yet regards those who use that power to challenge markets as robotic stooges. It salutes choice and yet tells us the triumph of markets is inevitable.

Its most profound contradiction concerns human intelligence. Market populism imagines individuals as fully rational economic actors, totally capable of making their needs known in the marketplace and of looking out for their interests. As workers they are similarly wise, always rising to the occasion, muddling through, thinking outside the box, making wow, bargaining cannily with employers. The common people are a brilliant people indeed, and anyone who doubts this is guilty of a disgusting elitism. But take the people out of the market context, and suddenly they become fools. When it comes to people in government or academia, responding as they do to a different set of incentives, market populism lapses into a deep and vicious anti-intellectualism. Such figures cannot possibly understand the world of the market in all its mystery and complexity; just by trying to figure things out they commit acts of hubris and arrogance, inexcusable offenses against democracy. Some of the most prominent thinkers of market populism even assert that those who criticize business are motivated by a hostility to markets roughly equivalent to racism.

For all these contradictions, though, market populism is a surprisingly vital and durable doctrine. What allows it to survive its errors, I believe, is the way it has inoculated itself against its opposition. Market populism isn't social darwinism; it makes a place for the angry, the hungry, and the disenfranchised. It has a fully developed theory of class conflict; it welcomes creativity and rebellion; it smiles understandingly on those with a beef against the world. The market is broad enough and welcoming enough to contain all these within its bounds.

That is why I am not optimistic about certain of the high-profile schemes to challenge the global corporate order that well-meaning people have proposed in recent years. Several of these, as I point out in the chapters to come, actively affirm important elements of market populism. One group asserts that by focusing on the empowerment of the consumer, always cleverly remaking the messages of the world around them, we can see that the doings of business really don't matter. Another insists that, if media outlets could just use more polls and focus groups, democracy would bloom everywhere. Others speak of relearning the ways of "civility," as though markets would become friendlier—would stop forming monopolies and stop bidding wages down—once CEOs learned to behave themselves.

I believe that the key to reining in markets is to confront them from outside, to do exactly the sort of things that have so infuriated Bhagwati, Friedman, and the rest of the nation's op-ed writers in recent months. What we must have are not more focus groups or a new space where people can express themselves or etiquette lessons for executives but some countervailing power, some force that resists the imperatives of profit in the name of economic democracy. That is, after all, precisely what the original Populists had in mind.

This book makes use of a great many previous works of social theory, and I have tried to spell out my debts specifically at the appropriate points. Two texts, though, were particularly important to the overall project. Both had to do with issues of social class, a topic that is both omnipresent in American writing and yet weirdly neglected. Over the course of writing this book I was continually struck by the insightfulness of Barbara Ehrenreich's description of the dreams and fears of the American middle class. Sometimes I feel as though all of my writing is one long footnote to her 1989 book, *Fear of Falling*. A paper that *Newsday* editor Chris Lehmann gave at a 1998 conference on the future of left politics (and which appeared in shorter form later that year in *In These Times*[6]) impressed me powerfully with the extent to which the language of populist class revolt had degenerated into culture war nonsense while huge changes went on uncontested in the economic realm. I also owe Chris a debt of gratitude for reading over several of the book's chapters when they first appeared as essays in *The Baffler* magazine.

Many people helped me with research and directed me to useful stories. Foremost among them was Emily Vogt, my colleague at *The*

Baffler, who braved many a boring book on my behalf. My prose was dramatically improved by the timely intervention of George Hodak and David Mulcahey, and my grasp of economics was enhanced immeasurably by Wendy Edelberg and Doug Henwood. Greg Lane gave encouragement without which none of this would ever have been written. Andrew O'Hagan, who is, incidentally, one of the finest novelists of my generation, provided invaluable logistical assistance. My agent, Joe Spieler, and my editors, Gerry Howard and Geoff Mulligan, believed in this project even as the rest of the world was swept up in the millennial ecstasies of the "New Economy." My colleagues at *The Baffler* made it possible, offering constant support, forgiving my lapses, and pushing ahead despite my preoccupation. I also owe thanks to Jim Arndorfer, Rob Bingham, Tom Brown of Detroit, Edward Castleton, Nick Cohen, Zayd Dohrn, Jim Frederick, Tom Geoghegan, Josh Glenn, Eric Guthey, Serge Halimi, Mike Lenehan, Paul Maliszewski, Jim McNeill, Ben Metcalf, Will Mollard, Mike Newirth, Dan Peterman, Lars Stole, Michael Szalay, Michael Thomas, and Julie Wilgoren. For the many errors that undoubtedly follow I have only myself to blame.

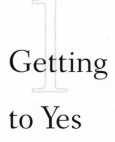

Getting to Yes

The Architecture of a New Consensus

American industry—the whole capitalist system—lives in the shadow of a volcano. That volcano is public opinion. It is in eruption. Within an incredibly short time it will destroy business or it will save it. —*PR man Carl Byoir, 1938*[1]

I am a revolutionary, as you may know.
—*John S. Reed, CEO of Citicorp, 1999*[2]

Let Us Build Us a Bill Gates

It was the age of the focus group, of the vox populi transformed into flesh, descended to earth and holding forth majestically in poll results, in town hall meetings, in brand loyalty demographics, in e-mail bulletin boards, in website hits, in browser traffic. The people's voice was heard at last, their verdict printed in a full-color chart on page one. The CEO was down from his boardroom and taking questions at the empowerment seminar; the senator was pointing out a family farmer right there in the audience; the first lady was on a "listening tour," the anchorman was keeping an anxious eye on the chat-room. The president himself was "putting people first"; was getting down at a "people's inaugural"; was honoring our values at "town meetings"; was wandering among us in a humble tour bus; was proving his affection for us with heroic feats of consumption—an endless succession of Big Macs, apple pies entire.

For all that, the formalities of democracy seemed to hold little charm for We the People in the 1990s. Election turnouts dwindled through the decade, hitting another humiliating new low every couple of years. Any cynic could tell you the reason why: Politics had once again become a sport of kings, with "soft money" and corporate contributions, spun into the pure gold of TV advertising, purchasing results for the billionaires' favorites as effectively as had the simple payoffs of the age of boodle. For those who could show us the money, to use one of the era's favorite expressions, there were vacancies in the Lincoln Bedroom, coffee klatches with the commander-in-chief, special subsidies of their very own. We voted less and less, and the much-discussed price tags of electoral victory soared like the NASDAQ.

Maybe the amounts our corporate friends were spending to court us should have been a source of national pride; maybe those massive sums constituted a sort of democratic triumph all by themselves. Certainly everything else that money touched in the nineties shined with a kind of populist glow. In the eighties, maybe, money had been an evil thing, a tool of demonic coke-snorting vanity, of hostile takeovers and S&L ripoffs. But something fundamental had changed since then, we were told: Our billionaires were no longer slave-driving martinets or pump-and-dump Wall Street manipulators. They were people's plutocrats, doing without tie and suit, chatting easily with the rank-and-file, building the new superstore just for us, seeing to it that the customer was served, wearing name tags on their work-shirts, pushing the stock prices up benevolently this time, making sure we all got to share in the profit-taking and that even the hindest hindmost got out with his or her percentage intact. These billionaires were autographing workers' hardhats out at the new plant in Coffeyville; they were stepping right up to the podium and reciting Beatles lyrics for the cameras; they were giddy with excitement; they were even allowing all people everywhere to enjoy life with them via their greatest gift of all—the World Wide Web. Maybe what our greatest popular social theorist, George Gilder, had said about them all those years ago was finally true: "It is the entrepreneurs who know the rules of the world and the laws of God."[3]

Or maybe Gilder didn't go far enough. Stay tuned for a while longer and you would see the populist entrepreneurs portrayed as something not far removed from the Almighty Himself. In a 1998 commercial for IBM's Lotus division that danced across TV screens to the tune of REM's Nietzschean anthem, "I Am Superman," great throngs of humanity were shown going nobly about their business while a tiny caption asked, "Who is everywhere?" In the response, IBM identified itself both with the great People and the name of God as revealed to Moses: The words "I Am" scrawled roughly on a piece of cardboard and held aloft from amid the madding crowd. The questions continued, running down the list from omnipresence to omniscience and omnipotence—"Who is aware?," "Who is powerful?"—while the hallowed scenes of entrepreneurial achievement pulsated by: an American business district, a Chinese garment factory, a microchip assembly room, and, finally, the seat of divine judgment itself, the trading floor of the New York Stock Exchange. "I can do anything," sang a winsome computer voice.

If there was something breathtaking about the presumption of this particular bit of corporate autodeification, this conflation of God, IBM, and the People, there was also something remarkably normal about it. Americans had already made best-sellers of books like *God Wants You to be Rich* and *Jesus, CEO*. The paintings of Thomas Kincade, the decade's greatest master of kitsch (and a man who actually trademarked a description of himself—"painter of light"), freely mixed heavy-handed religious symbolism with the accoutrements of great wealth, plunking Bible references down alongside glowing mansions and colorful gazebos. "The Market's Will Be Done" was the title Tom Peters, guru of gurus, chose for a chapter of his best-selling 1992 management book, while techno-ecstatic Kevin Kelly, whose 1994 book, *Out of Control*, was a sustained effort to confuse divinity with technology, referred quite confidently to a list of New Economy pointers he had come up with as "The Nine Laws of God." The heavens seemed even closer as the decade progressed and the surly bonds of the "Old Economy" slipped away. The publisher of *Fast Company,* a magazine dealing in the apotheosis of the new breed of corporate leaders, described his publication in 1999 as "a religion"; one Morgan Stanley analyst was routinely referred to in print as "the Internet Goddess" (her "embrace" of a company was described by one magazine as "a laying on of hands"); a much-discussed online operation matched "angel" investors with thankful startups in a cyber-space called "Heaven"; ads for the GoTo search engine showed Muslims at prayer and suggested that such a "loyal following" could be yours as well were you to patronize their product; and advertisements for Ericsson cellphones insisted that the product conferred powers of omnipresence: "You Are Everywhere."[4]

So pervasive did the business-as-God routine become that in 1999 the Merrill Lynch brokerage actually ran commercials seeking to correct an apparent heresy in the new faith. Reminding us that however wonderful computers might be they had still been constructed by Business Man in his own image, the brokerage admonished us to get our theology straight: we were to "admire machines" but "worship their inventors."[5]

This was something far beyond simply being "bullish on America." It was as though the good people of Merrill Lynch, IBM, and their fellow worshipers, standing at the millennium's end, could look back over the entire sweep of human struggle and see they themselves at its climax, its very peak. They were supermen, indeed, presiding over an era of historical advance so rapid, of change so profound, that it constituted nothing less than a "New Economy," a magic time in which the ancient laws of exchange, of supply and demand, had been repealed at last. From the rousing op-eds of *Wired* and *Forbes,* from CEO conference calls, from the bubbling announcements on CNBC, from the ecstatic babel of motivational seminars, came word of the miraculous advance: Through feats of sheer positive thinking, Business Man had overturned the principles of accounting, had smashed the barriers of price-to-earnings, had redrawn the map of competition, had thrown off the dead hand of the physical world! The country's gross national product, we exulted, weighed less than ever before! We dealt in ideas rather than things! And just as the laws of Newton had given way to those of the microchip, so scarcity itself, the curse of the material world, had been overcome once and for all. Not even the Fed could call the "New Economy" back to earth. We were, as one pop-economics title put it, *Living on Thin Air*.

The race was on to describe an achievement we believed to outrank any in human history, to hail the achievements of Business Man in the most grandiose possible terms. "Is this a great time or what?" asked a series of 1996 commercials for telecom giant MCI. "Let us celebrate an American triumph," thundered a Mort Zuckerman editorial early the next year in *US News & World Report*, a "triumph" based on the solid rock of pro-business political principle: "privatize, deregulate, and do not interfere with the market."[6] And as the logic of the "New Economy" spread over all things, the imperatives of Business Man inundated every other way of imagining the world. "Everything is now thought of as a business of a sort," wrote management theorist Charles Handy in 1994. "We are all 'in business' these days, be we doctor or priest, professor or charity-worker."[7] This was not just metaphor, either. As the Dow mounted higher and the startups soared, every avenue of inquiry found its appointed role in the new order. A 1999 story in an Internet trade journal instructed startup entrepreneurs on how to coax peak performances from a stable of nominally independent intellectuals, the sort of respected thinkers who could send a company's IPO through the ceiling by enthusing about it energetically enough. In addition to a venture capitalist (always referred to in such places as "VC") and a lawyer, entrepreneurs were advised to retain the services of a "pundit," a "journalist," and an "academic," manipulating each of these value-building experts by seeing to it that they understood the place of your enterprise in their own visions of the "New Economy" future. All the seers and eggheads of the world would have to puff in unison if your IPO was to net you the millions you desire.[8]

"New Economy" thinking expanded geographically as well. Just as Americans had once looked to Japan for the secrets of prosperity, now we demanded that other nations follow our lead. America's business thinkers confidently diagnosed the economic ailments of their competitors and announced their findings at one international summit after another: While in America business could proudly announce "I Am," in Europe and Japan it was "held back," as journalist Louis Uchitelle summarized the conventional thinking, "by uniform pay scales, strong unions, generous unemployment insurance, costly benefits, and anti-efficient regulations. . . ."[9] One memorable incident, at a meeting of economic policy-makers from the largest industrialized countries that was held in Denver in June 1997,

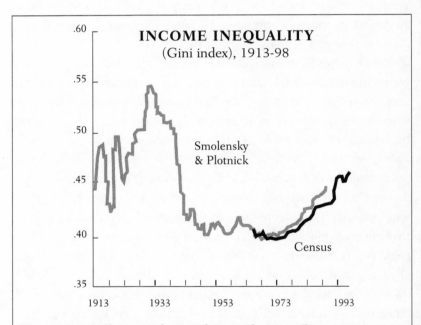

INCOME INEQUALITY
(Gini index), 1913-98

Smolensky & Plotnick

Census

Historic Gini coefficients in the United States. The Gini coefficient is a measurement of a population's income inequality on a scale of 0 to 1. A country with total equality of incomes would have a Gini coefficient of zero; a country with complete inequality (one person with everything; others with nothing) would score a 1. Most industrialized countries fall between .2 and .4. Figures derived from census data are shown going back to the late 1960s (when the U.S. achieved its greatest level of equality ever); figures from earlier eras are as estimated by economists Eugene Smolensky and Robert Plotnick in their 1992 paper, "Inequality and Poverty in the United States: 1900 to 1990," University of California, Berkeley, Graduate School of Public Policy, Work Paper #193. Chart courtesy of Doug Henwood.

signaled the new mood. President Clinton and Larry Summers, then deputy secretary of the treasury, seized the occasion to tell the world about the miraculous new American way. They handed out pairs of cowboy boots and proceeded to entertain the foreigners with what the *Financial Times* called a steady diet of "effusive self-praise" spiced with occasional "harsh words . . . for the rigidities of French and European markets." Don your boots and down with France![10]

Many statistical measures could be used to compare the triumphs of "New Economy" America to the floundering old economies of Europe and Japan: American productivity was up (at least it was in the second half of 1999), American growth was up, American stock markets were way, way, way up. Perhaps the most important markers of American uniqueness, though, were the different ways in which this "New Economy" chose to dole out the benefits of prosperity to different social classes. For the majority of American workers, wages through the nineties either fell or barely kept pace with inflation.[11] But for top corporate executives these really were years in which to stand up and say "I Am." According to *Business Week* magazine, CEO compensation during the decade went from 85 times more than what average blue-collar employees received in 1990 to some *four hundred and seventy-five times* what blue collar workers received in 1999. In Japan, meanwhile, that multiple stood at about 11 times and in Britain, the country most enamored of New Economy principles after the US itself, only 24 times.[12] And these were average numbers, remember. Some chief executives did far better: In 1997, Jack Welch, the much-revered CEO of General Electric, was paid some 1,400 times the average wage earned by his blue-collar workers in the US—and 9,571 times the average wage earned by Mexican industrial workers, who made up an increasing percentage of the GE workforce as production was moved to the region just across the border.[13]

What was true for CEOs was also true for the social class to which they belonged. The wealth of America's most privileged ballooned during the age of Clinton. Thanks to the feats of the Dow, the country's richest 1 percent found themselves happily holding an estimated 40.1

percent of the country's wealth in 1997, up from 35.7 percent in 1989 (and from only 20.5 percent in 1979). By the third year of the Man from Hope's first term, the country's next richest 9 percent were the proud owners of 33.3 percent of the nation's wealth.[14] Measured according to the more comprehensive standard of inequality known as the "Gini Index," the US was achieving levels of wealth polarization both unique among industrialized nations and, according to economics writer Doug Henwood, not seen on these shores since the 1920s.[15]

But what made the new draughts of wealth especially sweet was the exclusion of the bulk of the population from the boom times. This was most definitely not a matter of bad luck: While the inevitable trickle-down had its predictable effects (booming service industries, great innovation in luxury products, the return of servants to the homes of the rich), many of the usual mechanisms that allowed workers to participate in boom economies had been shut down. For the boldest American thinkers this was an integral part of the "New Economy," one of the things that made it "new." Stock markets, now enthroned as the judge of all economic value, massively rewarded those companies and those CEOs most ruthlessly committed to laying off great swathes of their workforce. Or take the nation's productivity figures, of which so much was made in the late nineties. Before the nineties, productivity had been a meaningful measure precisely because it signified real economic advances for the entire population. Growing productivity was, in fact, just about the only condition under which neoclassical economics was willing to acknowledge that wage increases were justified. But while productivity numbers in the final years of the decade grew at rates not seen since the 1960s, what put them on the front page and made them the subject of breathless commentary in *Wired* and on CNBC was that this connection to higher wages no longer seemed to exist. Wages remained stagnant *even while productivity increased;* the advances were funneled directly into stock prices. This was the reason productivity announcements in the late nineties were greeted with such jubilation: The people who got richer as workers became more productive were stockholders.[16]

Just as critical was the belief among "New Economy" economists and journalists that rising wages were by definition a form of inflation—the one thing that could conceivably dim the luster of the new millions. And as inflation was the declared mortal enemy of national economic policy, rising wages had to be constrained by any means necessary. Fortunately, one of the hallmarks of the "New Economy" was a vastly enhanced arsenal of techniques for keeping wages down. With labor unions already enfeebled by years of political assault, even run-of-the-mill CEOs found they were capable of performing such celebrated tricks as the old hire-back-the-downsized-as-temps routine.[17] And with tariff barriers lowered, with communications technology dramatically improved, and with a vast multitude of union-free regions beckoning, American managers found they only needed to raise the subject of relocation in order to restore that much-desired "flexibility" and "discipline" to a demanding workforce. At the national level interest rates could be manipulated and immigration policies modulated to suit the needs of particular industries and even particular employers. And, of course, one should not discount the influence of prisons, which helped both to maintain the appearance of reasonable unemployment rates and to further discipline a troublesome working class.[18] The results were gratifying indeed: Even at the height of the boom in 1998 and 1999, with unemployment at historic lows and with Merrill Lynch warning us against worshiping the wrong "New Economy" deity, wage growth dropped precipitously.[19]

For "New Economy" ideologues, though, such trends sparked no regrets. The free market, they believed, had its own built-in devices for social redress. The new order created so much opportunity for individuals to get ahead, to leave their old lives for the instant plutocracy of Silicon Valley, that the misfortunes of broad groups, while sad, paled in insignificance. Unfortunately, the promise of vastly enhanced class mobility in the "New Economy" turned out to be another myth, easily exploded by a systematic appraisal of the data. When economists measured mobility over the period 1986–91 they found that, in comparison with low-paid workers in European countries, American workers actually enjoyed slightly *less* class mobility, not more.[20]

But who was counting? Americans in the nineties seemed to love the rich. The robber barons of old with their miserly, ground-out fortunes, had always had to confront a hostile, suspicious world. But now it was "Who Wants to Marry a Multimillionaire?" And, hell, who didn't? This plutocracy was cool! They were flooding into bohemian neighborhoods like San Francisco's Mission District, chatting with the guys in the band, and working on their poetry in Starbucks; they were going it alone with their millions and their out-of-wedlock child; they were abjuring stodgy ties and suits for 24/7 casual; they were leaping on their trampolines, typing out a few last lines on the laptop before paragliding, riding their bicycles to work, listening to Steppenwolf while they traded, drinking beer in the office, moshing at the Motley Crue show, startling the board members with their streetwise remarks, roaring down the freeway in their Lamborghinis, snowboarding in Crested, racing their jetskis by the platform at Cannes and splashing all the uptight French people.

And when they weren't being cool, they were being just like us, only more so. One of the most treasured fantasies of the decade was that of the hardworking billionaire, the no-nonsense businessman whose pragmatic ways weren't ruined by his massive wealth. Both Bill Gates and Warren Buffett had legendary appetites for hamburgers, the food of the common man. Both men were said to work way excessive hours. The none too subtle implication, of course, was that these men deserved their riches. They were rich because they had somehow done the labor of a million other men, created all manner of good things in direct proportion to their reward. From this attitude flowed, as financial journalist Michael Lewis put it in 1995, a "righteous indignation toward the claims of the unrich." The slightly more subtle implication was that the rich and the poor had somehow exchanged class positions (at least for purposes of moral righteousness), a cliché that one found repeated in management literature as well as "radical" showplaces like *Wired*. "The rich, the former leisure class, are becoming the new overworked," that magazine declared in a series of late-nineties manifestos. "And those who used to be considered the working class are becoming the new leisure class."[21]

We cheered as a late-decade series of IPOs (supported, one assumes, by the correct amounts of pundit, journalist, and academic cheerleading) propelled a host of lovable and photogenic new stars into the plutocratic firmament. We marveled at the sassy attitude of the one who had made her millions without finishing college; we guffawed at the boyish workplace hijinx of the one who had built his startup from a dorm room; we nodded knowingly at the one whose mountainous achievement began in a search for that irony item nonpareil, the discarded Pez dispenser; we overflowed with emotion when told the story of the one who had driven across the country chasing the American dream, who had filled his office with secondhand furniture, who had earned the love of his warehouse workers. Every day we tuned in to CNBC to see how they had fared on the "CEO Wealth-Meter," a scoreboard that computed each one's net worth based on the day's market movements. We even derided the millionaires whose fortunes were considered to be so grand in past decades and gloried in the superiority—in raw dollar terms, adjusted for inflation, as a percentage of GNP, however you cared to slice it—of the fortunes of *our* millionaires, our silicon geniuses and IPO kids.[22] Economist Lester Thurow enlivened his 1999 book, *Building WEALTH,* with this ode to riches:

> Great wealth allows individuals to place their footprints in the sands of time. . . .
>
> Political influence can be quietly bought. Campaign contributions effectively give the wealthy more than one vote. . . .
>
> Wealth ultimately is the way the score is kept in capitalism. . . .
>
> Those with great wealth are important, to be courted. They are deserving of respect and demand deference. They are the winners.
>
> Wealth has always been important in the personal pecking order, but it has become increasingly the only dimension by which personal worth is measured. It is the only game to play if you want to

prove your mettle. It is the big leagues. If you do not play there, by definition you are second rate.[23]

Towering over them all was the great Bill Gates, a man who in 1999 owned as much as 40 percent of the American population put together. However we might complain about Microsoft products and curse the company's name, there always remained a certain fascination for this figure who had so finally altered the way we thought of money. He was a homely nerd, we imagined, not some plundering robber baron. He dressed in humble chinos and sweaters, not stiff suits. He built corporate "campuses," not skyscrapers. And he was, after all, *our* billionaire, *our* Rockefeller. His success was our success, and we whiled away the hours marveling at how many aircraft carriers he could afford or at the measures he took to keep the public away from his wedding on the privately owned Hawaiian island of Lanai. Because "the world's wealthiest man is once again an American," wrote Thurow, it was appropriate to exult that, "It is the best of times for America," that "America is back!"[24] We spoke of him as though We the People had built him, had knowingly piled up our treasure at his feet, and we thrilled to news of his philanthropy, of his faintly creepy Seattle chateau as we would to the deeds of our own relatives. We stuck with him even when that bummer antitrust suit befell him: The *Wall Street Journal* polled us and found that Americans wanted the government to just leave the boy billionaire alone; a *Time* magazine item on the sad event pleaded with the chief federal prosecutor to "cut a deal and let's [sic] get back to making bucks."[25]

All of which marked a fairly radical historical shift. According to the old "consensus" ideas developed in academia in the decades after World War II, the distinguishing feature of American civilization was its great and evenly distributed wealth. Consensus intellectuals of the 1950s wrote fondly about the "People of Plenty," about the "Affluent Society," imagining America as a land whose social problems arose not from deprivation but from abundance. From Henry Ford to the United Auto Workers our economic leaders imagined America as the land of the universal middle class; Richard Nixon used the panorama of goods available to even the lowliest American worker as evidence of the righteousness of our battle with Communism. Ours was a nation of homeowners and two-car garages, American writers told us, where bus drivers and sewer workers were distinguished from their white-collar neighbors by manners and tastes, not by income. And while endless consumption might not make much aesthetic or philosophical sense, the huge and widespread demand of all Americans for new cars, suburban homes, refrigerators, and stereo systems was thought to be the secret of our global preeminence. Shared abundance was not just a nice thing; it was virtually the definition of America.

But as the "New Economy" sent us on our way back into what strategist Edward Luttwak called a "Victorian pattern of income distribution," a system without any structural need for a well-paid blue-collar class, pundits discarded the ideology of abundance as though it had never existed. Now they looked into our past and saw precisely the opposite: Our tolerance for vast inequalities of wealth was what made us who we were. In an influential but strangely misinformed British study of our excellent American ways and how they might be imported into the UK, it was noted both that "the US is surely the land of grotesque inequality" and also that this was just part of our national character, something we simply "accept," abiding extremes of wealth and poverty with an admirable tolerance that the author projected into our remotest past.[26] One can hardly blame a foreign observer for misreading American culture so wildly, though, since everywhere one looked in late-nineties America, the same story was being sung to the skies. In enthusing over a 1999 study that purported to measure international levels of "entrepreneurship" and also to prove that this quality contributed mightily to a country's growth (naturally, the US ranked number one by this measurement), the *Wall Street Journal* focused on the study's finding that "entrepreneurial societies have *and accept* higher levels of income disparity." Once it was our rage for economic democracy that was thought to yield such spectacular growth, putting a

Model T in every garage: Now it was our tolerance for plutocracy that made things go. For Lester Thurow, the economist who saw such national glory in the building of Bill Gates, we were a people "comfortable with inequalities," a people for whom the obscene concentration of wealth that appeared in recent years was somehow an expression of our easygoing national virtue, since it never caused "anyone of importance to suggest that Americans ought to change the system."[27]

And just as a friendly pundit boosts his best for some kid's startup IPO, Thurow followed this up by suggesting that a good way of measuring a country's health was simply to ask: How many billionaires did it have? Thus America was said to be enjoying the "best of times" because "American billionaires number in the hundreds." The folly of the Asian nations, meanwhile, was nailed down by the observation that "what had been forty-one Japanese billionaires fell to only nine at the most recent count." Then there was "the case of the missing European billionaires," which reflected an even more profound national-economic foolhardiness. To persuade readers that they should welcome cultural and economic "disequilibrium," Thurow confided that such a state was an environment "where billionaires could emerge." The logic could be taken much farther: One could easily posit a billionaires-to-earnings ratio and conclude that by far the most laudable economic endeavors in all of history are the launching of Internet IPOs and the founding of sales organizations on the Amway model.[28]

Having piled up such a prodigious amount of the stuff that makes life worth living at the feet of Bill Gates, having raised him and his fellow billionaires above all men and all things, we Americans, in the great narrative of the nineties, saw that it was good and decided to remake utterly both our society and the outside world so that this wondrous operation might be repeated again and again. Unfortunately, the price of building billionaires was very high: To get a country on the billionaire scoreboard its citizens must do nothing less than, as Thurow repeatedly chanted, "destroy the old." Only when we have smashed our culture, our institutions, our assumptions, our sense of pastness generally, will we have made it possible for billionaires to walk among us, to appear on our TVs and announce, "I Am."

Consensus and the Legitimacy Problem

It is the argument of this book that "destroying the old" and making the world safe for billionaires has been as much a cultural and political operation as an economic one. Consider for a minute the factors—weak trade unions, a declining regulatory apparatus, and the outright repeal of the welfare state under presidents Reagan and Clinton—that distinguish the United States, with its "New Economy," from the other industrialized nations. Aside from the technological advances of recent years (which may or may not live up to the world-historical importance we routinely ascribe to them), very little of the "New Economy" is new. What the term describes is not some novel state of human affairs but the final accomplishment of the long-standing agenda of the nation's richest class. Industries come and industries go, but what has most changed about America in the nineties is the way we think about industries, about economies. Once Americans imagined that economic democracy meant a reasonable standard of living for all—that freedom was only meaningful once poverty and powerlessness had been overcome. Today, however, American opinion leaders seem generally convinced that democracy and the free market are simply identical. There is precious little that is new about this idea, either: For nearly a century, equating the market with democracy was the familiar defense of any corporation in trouble with union or government; it was the standard-issue patter of corporate lobbyists like the National Association of Manufacturers. What is "new" is this idea's triumph over all its rivals; the determination of American leaders to extend it to all the world; the general belief among opinion-makers that there is something natural, something divine, something inherently democratic about markets. A better term for the "New Economy" might simply be "consensus."

Writing a history of an intellectual consensus sometimes feels like a patently un-American undertaking. Even to assert that consensus exists is to challenge one of our fondest notions of ourselves. If there's anything that defines us as a people, we believe, it's our diversity, our differentness, our nonconformity, our frontier individualism. In the nineties this rage for differentness became such an orthodox bit of "New Economy" theory that it was transformed into one of those quasi-economic "laws" that the computer industry so loved to toss about. As the awestruck British writer Geoff Mulgan summarized what he called "Kao's law," "the power of creativity rises exponentially with the diversity and divergence of those connected into a network." America had done the fantastic things it had, Mulgan continued, because it had chosen "dissonant" voices over "consensus."[29] Back home in the land where theorists sought to make nonconformity into a universal economic "law," our most valuable corporations led us in elaborate sponsored fantasies about "changing everything" and "thinking different"; even the notorious utility conglomerate Enron, a high-profile donor to *both* political parties, was running TV commercials celebrating the subversive power of those who "ask why," which was said to be "the chosen word of the nonconformist."[30]

But however nineties America professed to love differentness, there was in fact less difference in certain reaches of the nation's public sphere than there had ever been in its history. It was a decade of many spectacular avant-gardes, to be sure. And yet however we celebrated our ethnic diversity or the dynamic variety of the Internet, America was in the grip of an intellectual consensus every bit as ironclad as that of the 1950s. In a manner largely unprecedented in the twentieth century, leaders of American opinion were in basic agreement on the role of business in American life. Daniel Yergin, a great celebrator of the laissez-faire way, called the new conviction that government had almost no legitimate place in economic affairs the "market consensus"; in international monetary dealings it was referred to as the "Washington consensus." Luttwak exaggerates only slightly when he remarks that, "At present, almost all elite Americans, with corporate chiefs and fashion-

able economists in the lead, are utterly convinced that they have discovered the winning formula for economic success—the only formula—good for every country, rich or poor, good for all individuals
willing and able to heed the message, and, of course, good for elite
Americans: PRIVATIZATION + DEREGULATION + GLOBALIZA-
TION = TURBO-CAPITALISM = PROSPERITY." As a description of
attitudes among computer and Internet elites this statement was clearly
correct. In 1998 "virtual reality" pioneer Jaron Lanier looked back at the
preceding five years and marveled at how "the libertarian view of capitalism has become so exalted among tech types and bright young people that it isn't even contested anymore—it is just the common air we
breathe." A little later that year Thomas Friedman, the *New York Times*
columnist whose beat was "explaining globalization," found occasion to
express his own wonderment at the accomplishment of the same intellectual goal among people who would ordinarily be inclined toward
some kind of role for government in the economy—those left behind by
the "New Economy," he gloated, no longer had any political recourse at
all! While once "people thought" there were ways to order human affairs
other than the free market, those options just no longer existed. "I don't
think there will be an alternative ideology this time around," Friedman
wrote. "There are none."[31]

In the world of politics, certainly, Friedman's assessment was an accurate one. Here the nineties were the age of the great agreement, as
leaders of left parties in the US and the UK accommodated themselves
to the free market faiths of their predecessors, Reagan and Thatcher.
As both Clinton and Tony Blair made spectacular public renunciations
of their parties' historic principles, the opposition literally ceased to oppose. In the service of the market and to safeguard its supposedly endless array of choice, they ensured that voters would have no choice at
all over the larger direction their nations took. Americans traded their
long tradition of electoral democracy for the democracy of the supermarket, where all brands are created equal and endowed by their creators with all sorts of extremeness and diversity.

One useful way to understand the consensus of the nineties is to revive a notion from the consensus of the fifties. John Kenneth Galbraith, who still reigned in the 1990s as the bête noir of the conservative mind, had once proposed that American capitalism worked the way it did not because of competition, but because corporate America was faced with a variety of "countervailing forces," mainly a strong labor movement and an interventionist state. By the end of the nineties, with "big government" having surrendered and labor prostrate, Galbraith's formula no longer applied. In matters cultural an analogous scenario was unfolding. Where corporate visions of the one true way had previously been balanced or at least tempered by rival visionaries from academia and journalism, the corporate way no longer had to undergo serious challenges. You could see the sense of universal agreement in the late-decade fad for serial delivery of advertising slogans, that technique in which a montage of people from all races and walks of life are shown reading the same script of hope and optimism, singing "We are the champions" for a company called Agillion or marveling at the godlike attributes of the Internet for Cisco. One of the popular management tracts of mid-decade got the new state of affairs exactly right with its title: *The Boundaryless Organization.*

I should repeat before proceeding that by "consensus" I do not mean "complacency," or "conformity," or "universal sameness." The nineties were obviously not a time in which everyone agreed, or in which conflict ceased to exist, in which difference was stamped out, or in which the attitudes of the fifties were somehow revived. On the contrary, one of the curious minor themes of the nineties consensus was a tendency to compare our advanced, diversity-tolerant, liberated selves to the soul-starved, conformity-driven, tech-deprived people of the fifties. Just as the authors of popular management tracts loved to linger on how much more computing power could be found in, say, their new staplers than in all the Univacs and Sabre jets of the Korean War, so Americans lined up to make a hit of *Pleasantville,* a 1998 movie which juxtaposed the tiredest clichés about the conformity and colorlessness of the fifties with the smuggest of affirmations for our present-day liberation and enlightenment. The film imagined that the patriarchy of the fifties was so offended by the rise of coolness that it brought the equivalent of racial persecution to bear on the hip, yet steadfastly refused to question the corporate order itself. On the contrary, one of the great lessons taught by *Pleasantville*'s time-traveling teenagers (in this case, to the robotic proprietor of a hamburger stand) is the superiority of nineties-style flexible production to the regimented management techniques of the past.

Similarly, Bill Clinton and British Prime Minister Tony Blair, the two individuals most responsible for choking off dissent in the Anglophone world, loudly celebrated diversity and multiculturalism even as they enshrined the market as the mono-logic of state; both men understood their move to the right not as a capitulation but as an exciting "new politics," the pursuit of a novel "third way," even as a new "New Deal" (Blair's term for his welfare-to-work program). In the consensus of the nineties sameness cohabited quite comfortably with blaring, boastful extremeness, with hyper-outrageous youth cultures, and with an ever-rising tide of sponsored obscenity.

The American historian Richard Hofstadter once observed of his country's past that "conflict and consensus require each other and are bound up in a kind of dialectic of their own."[32] Never was this more true than in the nineties. Our pride in our diversity played off our scorn for the square; our fury at the "liberal elites" sat easily next to the constant pseudo-provocations of MTV; and the partisans of both positions were easily brought together under the grand umbrella of the Market. The "New Economy" consensus united right-wing libertarian think-tankers and left-wing academic literary scholars; former Communists and management theorists; Republican culture warriors setting out to save "family values" from the marauding of the counterculture and New Labour, going into battle against "the forces of conservatism." More generally, it was a consensus that shamelessly swiped the righteousness of genuine social movements—one of the more disheartening commercial fads of the nineties was the tendency to compare a given company's products to the civil rights movement—always imagining them as object lessons in the struggle of the corporation to be free from onerous state tyranny.

Continually balancing glamorous conflict—chaos, revolution—with the imperatives of the market, the consensus of the nineties was anything but complacent and soothing. Its most farsighted architects understood it as an ongoing battle for the public mind, a cultural offensive that lived in constant danger of self-contradiction, of coming apart, of unraveling overnight. It was a struggle to establish the legitimacy of the free-market order by grounding it in something decidedly un-conservative; it was a consensus based not on obedience to God or deference to great men but on the volatile new idea that social conflict affirmed the principles of the market.

"Legitimacy" was the actual word used in 1998 by business journalists Daniel Yergin and Joseph Stanislaw to describe what was needed to keep what they call the "market consensus" from unraveling. Having described how business had conquered the "commanding heights" of the economy from government and labor, the writers suggested that there was also a cultural "commanding heights" that had yet to be mastered.

> A system that takes the pursuit of self-interest and profit as its guiding light does not necessarily satisfy the yearning in the human soul for belief and some higher meaning beyond materialism. In the Spanish Civil War in the late 1930s, Republican soldiers are said to have died with the word *Stalin* on their lips. Their idealized vision of Soviet communism, however misguided, provided justification for their ultimate sacrifice. Few people would die with the words *free markets* on their lips.

A "consensus" had been achieved among economists, politicians, and business elites, yes. But publics everywhere, as described by Yergin and Stanislaw (to whom we shall return shortly), had never really been brought on board. Paying no mind to the truth as revealed by libertarian economists such as Friedrich Hayek and Milton Friedman, publics continued to persecute entrepreneurs, to side with unions, and (most gallingly) to express doubts about the deeds of Thatcher and Reagan. Business had beaten government, but if it wanted to stay on top it would have to rededicate itself to the cultural battle, to persuading the public that markets represented something greater than simple greed.[33]

This problem of public doubt comes up again and again in the literature of the new consensus. Just as business thinkers tend to see "socialism" in every jot of regulation and every electoral maneuver of the Democratic Party, they perceive disaster for capitalism itself lurking in even the most harmless-sounding skepticism. Usually this problem is described with the class poles reversed: It's not that capitalists need us to believe in order to preserve their piles; it's that we must believe if we are to prosper. George Gilder spelled the problem out this way in his best-selling 1981 book, *Wealth and Poverty*. The world is plagued not so much by poverty, he wrote, as by a rampant "suspicion of wealth," a willful refusal to believe in the market's magic that one could find in every sneer and snippet of social criticism. As faith constitutes the very "foundation of capitalism," Gilder was able to attribute just about every economic disorder to an excess of criticism, to an insufficient respect for entrepreneurs. "Everywhere these ideas prevail," he wrote, "poverty persists and spreads."[34]

The problem of public doubt would also come into widespread use as a device for blame-evasion. When stock markets tanked, when companies blundered, when economies slumped, responsibility for the nastiness could be sloughed off on those who did not have faith in the market, on those who had criticized capitalism. A remarkable example of this logic in action was a 1997 editorial in *Forbes ASAP* (a magazine actually started to showcase the writing of George Gilder) that urged readers to "get ready to defend the free market." Throwing together the perfidy of critics, the glory of the Internet, and the horror of France into a gigantic preemptive *j'accuse,* the essay suggested that those who badmouthed the market were sending the world straight into depression and—yes—war!

You may ask: Why the yap about capitalism's critics? What's this got to do with computers, software, and the Net?

Everything, actually. Computers, software, and the Net now run the economy. Moreover, they throw free enterprise into warp speed. Without mercy or remorse, they slice through decaying business models, defensive managers . . . they humiliate economies like France's. They quickly reallocate capital to the bold; they elevate the industrious; they reward lifelong learners.

Which country has benefited the most from this? Hint: It's the same place where joblessness is down, wealth is rising and spreading, human life spans are up, etc., etc.

Seems obvious, but the grand argument is not yet won. And since it is not, *this* set of bad things could happen: America loses its heart in the race to apply the new digital tools . . . catches the French disease . . . becomes obsessed with income gaps and job protection . . . seeks a "Third Way" . . . submits to zero-growth fatalism . . . elects a class-warrior president . . . bans encryption and e-cash . . . attempts a "social justice" surtax on Net use . . . triggers a spiral . . . downward . . . downward . . . to Depression . . . trade wars . . . jingoism . . . tough talk . . . saber rattling . . . "incidents" . . . War. . . .[35]

Computers, software, and the Net may "run the economy," smashing obstacles "without mercy or remorse," but if anything went wrong, the editor of *Forbes ASAP* wanted you to know that computers, software, and the Net would not be responsible. That would be the burden of those on the other side of the "grand argument," those who, like the hated French, worry about inequality and jobs.

Whether the consequence of losing that "grand argument" was described as a lack of legitimacy for the corporate order or as depression, and whether it was expressed in the sensible tones of Daniel Yergin or the mad self-righteousness of *Forbes ASAP*, the importance of business's cultural battle cannot be overstated. This book is the story of how that argument was joined and won in the 1990s, of how the American corporate community went about winning the legitimacy it so covets, persuading the world that the laissez-faire way was not only the best and the inevitable way, but the one most committed to the will and the interests of the people. This is a study of business culture—of the literature of Wall Street, of management theory, of the conventions of marketing and advertising—and of the ways in which business ideas were reflected in the broader culture. It has little to do with the actual economics of production and exchange and offers no advice that might help the reader to pick a NASDAQ ten-bagger, say, or rebrand a line of detergent or footwear. It evaluates its subject matter not in terms of its practical usefulness (this management theory seems to work better than that one) but in terms of its ideology: The way Wall Street spokesmen presented the bull market as a device of popular empowerment; the parallels that management theorists always seemed to find between their ideas and those of liberal democracy. It is above all the history of market populism: its origins, its coalescence in the thought of certain business writers, its concentration in the worldview of certain industries (Internet theorists, for example, seem to be particularly fervent market populists), its rise to orthodoxy under Newt Gingrich and then with the seemingly less partisan dawning of the "New Economy," and its consequences for American culture and American democracy.

From Culture War to Market Populism

Those accustomed to thinking of the United States as a monolithically "capitalist" nation might be surprised at the suggestion that business has ever had to struggle to achieve legitimacy here. And yet broad public consent for free-market principles has never been an easy thing to achieve. Not only does the logic of competition ensure that individual businesses will forever seek to smash each other's public image, but at certain points in the last hundred years the credibility of the corporate order itself has collapsed disastrously: From the 1890s until World War II the free-market system, with its extremes of wealth and poverty, came under fire repeatedly for its offenses against democracy; on several occasions it seemed to lose its very ability to provide the American people with the necessities of life. Not only was the free market patently unfair, a growing number of Americans believed, it wasn't even doing its job. With its reputation in ruins after the stock market crash of 1929 and the banking crises of the early thirties, business was forced to submit to round after round of regulation and oversight; with labor unions finally legitimized by the 1935 Wagner Act and with government no longer willing to help break strikes, business was forced to bargain with its workers collectively and, eventually, pay them the wages and benefits that we now associate with middle-class life. Speaking in the broadest terms, both developments served to democratize American economic life, to build the affluent society celebrated by the "consensus" thinkers of the 1950s. Thus it was that even in a country like ours, where welfare provisions have always been the least generous of any industrialized nation and where nationalization of industries has (except in wartime) never been a serious political option, the stakes in the contest between business, labor, and government remained massive. Winning the "commanding heights" of legitimacy could eventually save businesses and the business class billions lost to taxes, wages, and regulation; it could also help to shift corporate profits away from workers and tax collectors and back to where free market theory always asserted that they belonged: in the pockets of stockholders. In countries like Britain, where the welfare state consumes a much larger percentage of corporate profits and where nationalization was until recently a very real threat, the stakes of the "grand argument" are even larger. And whatever one might think of the radical charge that big business, big government, and big labor simply learned to share the power of an imperialistic nation in those years, the fact remains that US business leaders continued to curse the New Deal (the servants of J. P. Morgan, Jr. had to remove all pictures of FDR from a newspaper before Morgan would read it), to regard government and labor with considerable hostility, to resent the regime that had been pressed down on them in the thirties, and to exploit every opportunity to beat back their enemies and regain the legitimacy they lost on that October day in 1929.

Unfortunately for them, the corporate cause has never been very popular. The conservative politicians who are the heroes of the market order—the people who transferred power from government to business—were never able to win elections on that basis alone. Not even the inflation of the 1970s, the event routinely identified by "New Economy" enthusiasts as the straw that broke the back of the liberal order, ever really turned the public finally against the labor movement, social security, or the regulatory state established by the New Deal. In fact both Reagan and Clinton found it useful to present themselves as inheritors of the Roosevelt mantle, not as the undoers of his legacy. What beat the left in America wasn't inflation and uppity workers, it was the culture war. Starting with the Nixon campaign in 1968 and continuing up through the Gingrich years, the American right paid the bills by handing out favors to business, but it won elections by provoking, organizing, and riding a massive populist backlash against the social and cultural changes of the 1960s.

To speak of pro-corporate populism is to raise one of the great political enigmas of the last thirty years. Historically populism was a rebellion *against* the corporate order, a political tongue reserved by definition for the non-rich and the non-powerful. As historian Michael Kazin summarizes it, populism* contrasts an immensely idealistic conception of the nation and the common people with visions of a malevolent, scheming elite. As the "common people" were once easily defined as the working class and the "elite" as the owners and managers of industry, populism first arose as the vernacular of a series of insurgent labor movements (the Farmers' Alliance, the CIO). Populism was the American language of social class.

But beginning in 1968 this primal set piece of American democracy seemed to change its stripes. The war between classes had somehow re-

---

*Spelled with a lower-case "p," populism refers to a language and a set of symbols. With an upper-case "P" it refers to the specific movement associated with the Farmers' Alliance and the People's Party in the late nineteenth century, where many of these characteristics first emerged.

versed polarity: It was now a conflict in which the patriotic, blue-collar "silent majority" (along with their employers) faced off against a new elite, the "liberal establishment" and its spoiled, flag-burning children. This new ruling class—a motley assembly of liberal journalists, liberal academics, liberal foundation employees, liberal politicians, and the shadowy powers of Hollywood—earned the people's wrath not by exploiting workers or ripping off family farmers, but by showing contemptuous disregard for the wisdom and the values of average Americans. The backlash erected an entire new social hierarchy according to which the "normal Americans" were at the bottom as usual—but the people at the top weren't the millionaires or the owners, they were those sneering kids who dodged the draft, along with their liberal parents and the various minorities and criminals those parents seemed so determined to pamper. Enunciated memorably in the speeches of Spiro Agnew and in the movies of Clint Eastwood, backlash populism proved immensely powerful, and for thirty years American politics seemed mired in the same imagery and cultural questions, with right-wing populists forever reminding "normal Americans" of the hideous world that the "establishment" had built, a place where blasphemous intellectuals violated the principles of "Americanism" at every opportunity, a place of busing and crime in the streets, of unimaginable cultural depravity, of epidemic disrespect for men in uniform, of judges gone soft on crime and politicians gone soft on communism. The backlash became a fixture of the American scene as our never-subsiding mad-as-hellness elected wave after wave of conservative politicians who warred on the liberal media, the welfare queens, and the "countercultural McGoverniks."

The thirty-year backlash brought us Ronald Reagan's rollback of government power as well as Gingrich's outright shutdown of 1995. But for all its accomplishments it never constituted a thorough endorsement of the free market or of laissez-faire politics. Barbara Ehrenreich, one of its most astute chroniclers, points out that the backlash always hinged on a particular appeal to working-class voters, a handful of whom were roped into the Republican coalition with talk of patriotism, culture war, and family values. Both Reagan and Nixon spoke fondly of blue-collar "middle America" even as they kicked its ass, and George Wallace, in some ways the most ferocious backlash figure of all, was an out-and-out liberal on economic issues. Appealing to class anger worked for Republicans as long as it was restricted to cultural issues; when economic matters came up the culture-war compound grew unstable very quickly. Lee Atwater, an adviser to Presidents Reagan and Bush, warned his colleagues in 1984 that their new blue-collar constituents were "liberal on economics," and that without culture wars to distract them "populists were left with no compelling reason to vote Republican." As if to warn his colleagues to stay away from the stuff, Pat Buchanan, one of the inventors of the backlash strategy, spent the mid-1990s using the language of populism to embarrass his fellow Republicans for their pro-business politics.[36]

In 1988, George Bush managed to win the presidency by spreading alarm about flag-burning, a nonexistent threat that older voters remembered with horror from twenty years before. This was not a trick that could be repeated too many more times. Even though the culture wars reached their polarized and outrageous peak in the decade that followed—with all the shootouts between survivalists and the ATF, the bombing of abortion clinics and government buildings, the brief notoriety of gun shows and right-wing militias, as well as with Pat Buchanan's 1992 declaration of war, the righteous fury of the congressional "freshmen" of 1994, and the impeachment of the president—they also began visibly to subside. It was during the impeachment proceedings that the backlash, clearly overextended and running now on little more than thirty-year-old rage, reached a state of obvious exhaustion. The public was slipping away. In the battle of the focus groups the president was winning easily. Nobody seemed to care anymore about the betrayal of the bureaucrats, about the secular humanists' designs on family values, about the Panama Canal giveaway, about flag-burning kids from the rich suburbs, or even about the communistic professors, trashing the great books and blaming America first. In their desperation the backlashers finally turned on the public itself, lamenting that the dream of a "moral majority" had foundered and declaring that maybe the common people didn't deserve such noble defenders after all. Paul Weyrich, one of the most prominent leaders of the family values movement of the seventies, eighties, and nineties, used the failure of impeachment as an opportunity to declare that the right had lost the culture war, that "the United States is very close to becoming a state totally dominated by an alien ideology"—an ideology that Weyrich proceeded to identify as "Cultural Marxism." Clearly something new was needed in the race for legitimacy. Clearly some new constellation of symbols and words had to replace the ebbing tides of backlash.

Stay tuned to the impeachment show for a little while and you could see signs of the transition for yourself. While the House of Representatives was taking the historic vote to impeach the president, CNN broke for a commercial and we beheld the mythic deeds of a heroic young entrepreneur, a shaggy-haired leader of some tech startup who is assisted in his feats of "New Economy" derring-do by the Arthur Andersen consultancy. As a can-do businessman, this character's attitudes toward the free market almost certainly mirror those of the bitter, suited, and pomaded men who were exacting their revenge on the sixties down in Washington. But he has about as much use for culture wars or churchgoing hardhats as he does for steel mills and Lawrence Welk: We rock enthusiastically as the tale of his heroism is told to the pounding beat of Iggy Pop's "Lust for Life"; we gawk as he rides his bike to work, as he chats easily with a very pregnant coworker. He's a man of the people, to be sure—the commercial includes a shot of little kids on a school bus staring at him with admiration—but he hardly needs any blue-collar signifiers to establish that. We know he's against elitism because he permits such a free-form office, wears casual clothes, doesn't get pissed off when an employee goes zooming by on a skateboard, eats pizza and spontaneously plays nerf basketball during meetings with his fellow heroes.

Or consider the version of populism proposed by *Newsweek* magazine a year later in a cover story marking the end of the twentieth century: "Fanfare for the Common Man." The story's title came from a Depression standby (a 1942 piece by Aaron Copland) and the writing recalls the militant populism of that era. Looking back on the events of the "people's century," it occurred to the story's author that for once in the human experience "ordinary folks changed history." To nail it down he singled out a succession of popular heroes who changed things: Suffragettes, feminists, the antiwar and civil rights activists, and, finally, "the entrepreneurs"—this last group illustrated with a drawing of Bill Gates. But while hailing the richest man in the world as a champion of the common people, the author took pains to point out that the New Deal wasn't as wonderful as everyone thought it was. The other hero of the thirties, the labor movement, was not mentioned in the story at all.[37]

This may seem egregious but it was hardly atypical. Wherever one looked in the nineties entrepreneurs were occupying the ideological space once filled by the noble sons of toil. It was businessmen who were sounding off against the arrogance of elites, railing against the privilege of old money, protesting false expertise, and waging relentless, idealistic war on the principle of hierarchy wherever it could be found. They were market populists, adherents of a powerful new political mythology that had arisen from the ruins of the thirty-year backlash. Their fundamental faith was a simple one: The market and the people—both of them understood as grand principles of social life rather than particulars—were essentially one and the same. By its very nature the market was democratic, perfectly expressing the popular will through the machinery of supply and demand, poll and focus group, superstore and Internet. In fact, the market was *more* democratic than any of the formal institutions of democracy—elections, legislatures, government. The market was a community. The market was infinitely diverse, permitting without prejudice the articulation of any and all tastes and preferences. Most importantly of all, the market was militant about its democracy. It had no place for snobs, for hierarchies, for elitism, for pretense, and it would fight these things by its very nature.

As *Newsweek* columnist Robert Samuelson said of the stock market in 1998, "the Market 'R' Us."[38] Whatever the appearances, the market *by definition* acted always in our interests, on our behalf, against our enemies. This is how the New York Stock Exchange, long a nest of privilege, could be understood in the 1990s as a house of the people; how any kind of niche marketing could be passed off as a revolutionary expression—an empowerment, even—of the demographic at which it was aimed.

Market populism was just the thing for a social order requiring constant doses of legitimacy. Taking as fact the notion that business gives people what they want, market populism proceeds to build all manner of populist fantasies: Of businessmen as public servants; of industrial and cultural production as a simple reflection of popular desire, of the box office as a voting booth. By consuming the fruits of industry we the people are *endorsing* the industrial system, voting for it in a plebiscite far more democratic than a mere election.

And as business leaders melded themselves theoretically with the people, they found powerful new weapons with which to win their "grand argument" with those who sought to regulate or control any aspect of private enterprise. Since markets express the will of the people, virtually any criticism of business could be described as an act of despicable contempt for the common man. This was an argument that would unite such disparate characters as the Gingrich right, who would use it against those who found fault with the market, and Howard Stern, who would use it against the critics of his tastelessness; it would permit both Hollywood executives and cultural studies scholars to shoot down critics of virtually any culture product as snobs out of touch with the tastes of the common people.

The idea that criticism of the market's workings was automatically "elitist" became one of the most familiar airs in the "New Economy" repertoire. According to market populism, elites were no longer those who, say, spent their weekends at Club Med or watched sporting events from a skybox or fired half their workforce and shipped the factory south. Since the rich—particularly the new rich—were the chosen of the market, they were in fact the very emblem of democratic modesty, humble adepts of the popular will. It was entrepreneurs, as the *Newsweek* story had it, for whom the nation sounded its "Fanfare for the Common Man"; elitists were the people on the other side of the equation, the labor unions and Keynesians who believed that society could be organized in any way other than the market way. Since what the market did—no matter how whimsical, irrational, or harmful—was the will of the people, any scheme to operate outside of its auspices or control its ravages was by definition a dangerous artifice, the hubris of false expertise. Don't think about how to fix things, the new populists would counsel. Surrender your arrogant egotism and humbly heed what the market whispers.

This fantasy of the market as an antielitist machine made the most sense when couched in the dynamite language of social class. Businessmen and Republican politicians have always protested the use of "class war" by their critics on the left; during the nineties, though, they happily used the tactic themselves, depicting the workings of the market as a kind of permanent social revolution in which daring entrepreneurs were endlessly toppling fatcats and snatching away the millions of the lazy rich kids. The "New Economy" was a narrative of class warfare as much as anything else: Wherever its dynamic new logic touched down, old money was said to quake and falter. The markers of inherited wealth were being superseded by more extreme tastes; operagoing CEOs were giving way to those who wore goatees and fancied the deffer rhymes of the street; the scions of ancient banking families were finding their smug selves wiped out by the new jack trading of a working-class kid; the arrogant stockbrokers of old were being humiliated by the online day-traders; the buttoned-down whip-cracking bosses were getting fired by the corporate "change agents"; the white men of the world were getting their asses kicked by the women, the Asians, the Africans, the Hispanics.

Market populism encompasses such familiar set pieces as Rupert Murdoch's endless efforts to cast himself as a man of the people beset by cartoon snobs like the British aristocracy. Or Detroit's long-running use of the simple fact that Americans like cars to depict even the most practical and technical criticisms of the auto industry (seat belts, airbags, fuel efficiency, etc.) as loathsome expressions of a joyless elite.[39] Market populism can also claim a good number of economic blunders, as well. When the public first began to sour on the gigantic American cars of the fifties, according to culture critic John Keats,

"Detroit decided there really weren't any problems, after all, and that the criticism was nothing but a lot of nittering and nattering emanating from a few aesthetes and intellectuals from the effete East—from the kind of people who drove Volkswagens and read highbrow magazines just to show off."⁴⁰

In the nineties these fantasies flowered spectacularly. Not only was the "New Economy," that vision of the market unbound, believed to be crushing the privilege of inherited wealth, but it was also said to constitute a standing refutation of the learning of traditional elites. Its stock market valuations, so puzzling to economists and old brokerage hands, were crystal-clear to the little guy. Its productivity increases may not have been visible to those using the traditional tools of expert evaluation, but they were as plain as day to the common man, sitting in his humble cubicle. "New Economy" companies were doing without entire layers of experts and bureaucrats; they were turning their backs on standard methods of teaching and learning; they were tearing up the carefully designed flowcharts and job descriptions of old. Sometimes the conflict of markets with authority went even further. When the Dow Industrials fell but the NASDAQ soared in early 2000, market populist commentators asserted that the "New Economy" was not only incomprehensible to elites, it was beyond their power to rein in. The people were in control at last, and all the Man's bureaucrats could never restore his power.

Here, market populism owes much to its backlash predecessor. Backlash populism had envisioned a scheming "liberal elite" bent on "social engineering," a clique of experts who thought they knew what was best for us—busing, integration, the coddling of criminals, coexistence with Communism. Market populism simply shifted the inflection: Now the crime of the elite was not so much an arrogance in matters of values but in matters economic. Still those elitists thought they were better than the people, but now their arrogance was revealed by their passion to raise the minimum wage, to regulate, oversee, redistribute, and tax.

There would be critical differences between market populism and the earlier politics of the backlash, of course. While the backlash had been proudly square (think of "Okie from Muskogee"), market populism was cool. Far from despising the sixties, it broadcast its fantasies to the tune of a hundred psychedelic hits. Its leading think tanks were rumored to pay princely sums to young people who could bring some smattering of rock 'n' roll street cred to the market's cause. And believing in the market rather than God, it had little need for the Christian right and the Moral Majority. It dropped the ugly race-baiting of the previous right-wing dispensation, choosing instead to imagine the market as a champion of the downtrodden Others of the planet, speaking their more authentic truths to our corrupt, degraded power. Market populism generally failed to get worked up about the persecution of Vietnam vets (it even enjoyed equating new-style investment bankers with the Viet Cong); it abandoned the "family values" of Ronald Reagan; it gave not a damn for the traditional role of women or even of children. The more that entered the workforce the merrier.

This change has proven difficult for many to grasp. For writers schooled in the culture wars, the most important conflict in America was and will forever be the one between the hip and the square, the flag-burning and the church-going, the hippie and the suit. But as the nineties progressed, as the Deadhead made his pronouncements from Davos, as jeans replaced suits in the offices of America, and as the ultra-hip culture of cyberspace became the culture of the corporation generally, business increasingly imagined itself on the other side of the equation.

Consider the career of Stewart Brand, another frequent *Wired* contributor who first came to prominence as one of Ken Kesey's Merry Pranksters, then published the famous *Whole Earth Catalog,* then did important early Internet work—and then co-founded the Global Business Network, a hot consultancy that has thought big thoughts for Royal Dutch/Shell, Xerox, and Hewlett Packard. " 'Do your own thing' easily translated into 'Start your own business,' " Brand remembered for readers of *Time* magazine in 1995. "Reviled" by the middle American "establishment," Brand's brand of hippies got their revenge on the squares by going into business. Consider the parallel career of the Unix operating system as imagined by a 1999 IBM ad: From a

"Child of the '60s," it became a "Campus Radical in the '70s," and finally a "Capitalist in the '90s." Or consider the historical vision of Tom Freston, the longtime CEO of MTV, who recently told the *Wall Street Journal* about what the sixties meant to him and his industry:

> I wasn't a child of the '60s in the classic way. . . . I wasn't a hippie or a political radical. But I was there . . . and the '60s in some ways were a prelude for the [pop culture] industry. In the '60s you got a sense that new things were possible. You got a sense that nonconformity was something not to be feared, but something to be revered. . . . It was the first time there was a real sense of generational consciousness . . . and we basically built the business around that issue, around generational unity.[40]

So routine and matter-of-fact did the connection between counterculture and "New Economy" eventually become that even the government of Singapore was reported in 1999 to be making official efforts to cultivate nonconformity and ignite a youth culture.[41]

The shifting corporate attitude toward the sixties and insurgent youth culture must seem, to those accustomed to the alignments of the culture wars, like a fairly massive change. Intellectually, though, the transition from the backlash to the New Economy proved a surprisingly easy one. The symbols may have changed, but the ideas flowed smoothly from the ultra-patriotic Reagan era into the Ecstasy-popping days of market populism.

George Gilder, the writer who would eventually emerge as one of market populism's most prominent theorists (as well as a major beneficiary of those elite-defying late-nineties stock valuations), first came to prominence as one of the Reagan administration's house intellectuals. Gilder's 1981 book, *Wealth and Poverty*, might someday be seen as the bedrock of "New Economy" thinking, but it was mostly devoted to pounding home the standard backlash notions of the day: that the poor were poor because they were bad people who had turned their backs on family values; that racism was an insignificant factor in the fate of the black population; that most social problems in America could actually be attributed to liberalism and to the "socialists" who were everywhere in government and academy; that "hedonism" and the other surviving elements of the counterculture were markers of a social breakdown. These would be embarrassing if not poisonous suggestions to the market populists of our own day. And yet another equally zany Gilder idea would resonate powerfully in the late nineties: that entrepreneurship is a form of class war. Entrepreneurs, whom Gilder admired so much that he dedicated a later book to their virtual deification, were both society's "greatest benefactors" and yet also the "victims of some of society's greatest brutalities," despised and always in danger of physical persecution by "the mob." And who stirred up that mob? None other than the very rich, the people of inherited *but declining* wealth whom, Gilder imagined, controlled "the media and the foundations, the universities and the government," from where they spread a vile "sense of defeat." The real class war, then, was between righteous new money, the entrepreneurs who created wealth, and bitter frustrated old money, the resentful heirs of the great fortunes who, having "mastered the art of communication," proceeded to manipulate the single-parent, slum-dwelling poor. Gilder was thus able to build the stereotype of the "limousine liberal" into an entire theory of American civilization. "The war against the rich thus continues in the world's wealthiest country," Gilder steamed. "It is a campaign now led and inspired by the declining rich, to arouse the currently poor against the insurgently successful business classes." And though Gilder was willing to assert that racism was no longer important in America, he did not hesitate to use it metaphorically to describe how these rich liberals did their cynical work: "Hatred of producers of wealth still flourishes," he wrote, "and has become, in fact, the racism of the intelligentsia."[43]

Gilder was, in those days, no populist. He frankly acknowledged that what he called "progress" was "ineluctably elitist," since it "makes the rich richer." But he also understood markets as a "cornucopia of choice" so elaborate they put the two-party "democracy" of our public institutions to shame.[44] Gilder's views were seconded by Friedrich Hayek, the Austrian economist who provided market populism with some of its basic myths. In his most famous work, *The Road to Serfdom* (1944), he had memorably equated British-style socialism with the Nazi obscenity; in his 1988 book, *The Fatal Conceit,* he asserted that businessmen were in fact the victims of elite prejudice. In the grip of a primitive, irrational fear of trade, snobbish antimarket types have from time immemorial "thrust [merchants] outside the established hierarchy of status and respect." The men of commerce were not only subject to ostracism and superstitious dread, but were in fact the *real* victims of the social hierarchy, "almost a class of untouchables" in one country. The persecution of the businessman by "the scribe" is thus a tragic constant of human existence, unchanged from ancient times to our own, as unvarying and universal as the principles of the market themselves. Even now, Hayek sputters in one remarkable passage, "intellectuals" who treat economics with a "general disdain" are preventing the world from "comprehending the order on which the nourishment of the existing multitudes of human beings depends." Maybe those liberal college professors *are* keeping you from riches, after all.[45]

Hayek may be dear to the hearts of a certain breed of corporate autocrat, the sort of guy who finds it easier to get through the day by imagining himself the target of a vast conspiracy, marked for death by the eggheads simply for daring to fill out forms or produce boxes at such a fantastic rate. And it is exactly this sort of corporate true believer on whom we will focus in the chapters to come. But before we consider the business world's conversion to market populism and the thinkers who made it possible, it is important to recall that corporate autocrats were not always so sanguine about the People or even about democracy. A hundred or so years ago, in fact, they were far more likely to understand the advent of popular democracy as a titanic threat. In those days, corporate America stood both at the zenith of its power and the low ebb of its popular appeal. Its leaders were hardly populists; they were men of unbelievable economic power and a staggering arrogance: William Vanderbilt damned the public; John D. Rockefeller claimed that "God gave me my money"; and, in what must rank as the most astonishing statement of corporate hubris ever, mine operator

George Baer used these immortal words to address the issues of a 1902 coal strike: "The rights and interests of the laboring man will be protected and cared for—not by the labor agitators, but by the Christian men to whom God in his infinite wisdom has given the control of the property interests of this country." When that "laboring man" developed the nerve to deviate from the politics of "the property interests of this country," the voices of progress could take on a savagely misanthropic tone. The classic example remains William Allen White's bitterly sarcastic 1896 essay, "What's the Matter with Kansas?" Originally dashed off in a fit of rage at the Populist politics that were chasing the "moneyed man" from the state, White's jeremiad was picked up and reprinted by newspapers from coast to coast, becoming the signature Republican document from the great electoral battle of that year.

> Whoop it up for the ragged trousers; put the lazy, greasy fizzle who can't pay his debts on the altar, and bow down and worship him. Let the state ideal be high. What we need is not the respect of our fellow men, but the chance to get something for nothing.[46]

Not surprisingly, neither statements of the divine right of capital nor of angry contempt for the common man did much to allay the growing industrial discontent of the age. Sure, the Populists were beaten in 1896, and Kansas was once again made safe for habitation by the respectable, but within a few years corporate interests were under siege again. The power of capital to extract what it chose from its labor force was being challenged in vast industrial strikes and by groups like the incomprehensibly hostile IWW; muckraking journalists were launching assault after assault on standard corporate practices and the business heroes of the age; antitrust laws were calling into question the rights of property themselves; and nearly every popular politician of the day seemed to build his reputation by sounding off against the "conspirators of Wall Street" and the "industrial feudalism" of the age. A colossal confrontation between money and democracy was coming rapidly to a head.

Enter public relations. As Stuart Ewen describes the situation in his

1996 history of the profession, PR was born when a new generation of conservative intellectuals, horrified by the elitism and intransigence of the business class, argued that something had to change. "Corporate postures of arrogance and secrecy [were] leading toward a dreadful and inevitable social conflagration," Ewen writes, and the young thinkers rushed to offer their services as defusers of the mounting crisis. Democracy could not be beaten with a few cruel words and a squad of hired goons; it was advancing irresistibly, and from now on capital's public pronouncements would have to be managed as closely as were workers on the shop floor. As Ivy Lee, one of the nation's first PR men, told a group of executives in 1916, "The crowd is in the saddle, the people are on the job, and we must take consideration of that fact, whether we like it or not."[47] The great debate over the problems of mass democracy would continue well into the 1920s, with various partisans of business civilization stepping forward to express doubt about the ability of the people to govern themselves, but for corporate America as a whole the debate was over. Companies would present themselves not as hideous snobs but as considerate neighbors, kindly folk in awe of the goodness of the people.

The battle began in earnest during the Great Depression, when corporate America again became the target of popular outrage. Muckraking journalism was revived with a vengeance; the CIO began its epic organizing campaign, and a new administration in Washington promised renewed waves of investigation, antitrust enforcement, unemployment insurance, and regulation. Accompanying each of these was a renewed cultural offensive, an aggressively populist "documentary style" that focused on the everyday life of average (and sometimes very poor) people—and which seemed calculated to give the lie to the prosperity talk of the corporate world. Business thinkers grew desperate during the thirties; many sincerely believed that capitalism faced a mortal threat in the person of FDR. Before long, though, they rallied to the challenge. As Ewen tells the story, corporate America finally realized that to stave off the threat posed by economic democracy, it would have to establish its own democratic credentials in as forceful a manner as possible: Corporate America would have to "claim the social values of the New Deal as their own"; it would, as one PR man put it, have to "learn the language of the people."[48] Populism was too important to be left to the populists.

Amid the massive wave of strikes after World War II, American business leaders had reason to expect the unfinished business of the thirties to be resumed before long. Much chastened by their drubbing in the Depression years, they took elaborate precautions to ensure that economic populism never took the same form again. As one PR man told the executives of Standard Oil of New Jersey (later Exxon), business would have to alter fundamentally the way it explained itself: "Identify yourself not with bondholders, . . . Wall Street, but with labor, *with Americans.*" Naturally, the aesthetic tool that business chose to accomplish this task was the very documentary style that had so offended executives ten years earlier. In 1943 the corporation soon to be known as Exxon hired Roy Stryker, the man who had directed the government's photography project during the thirties, to launch a PR campaign of its own. Stryker, the son of Populist parents who had despised Standard Oil above all other corporations, seems to have been genuinely puzzled by the company's interest in his art. As Ewen points out, though, their goals were in fact quite direct. The soon-to-be Exxon wanted to combat its reputation for "cold-bloodedness," and New Deal populism was exactly the way to do it.[49]

Public relations populism, along with the new people-friendly styles of factory management and soothing slogans of the post-crash stock exchange, served as an effective temporary counter to the populism of Roosevelt. Nice talk about the goodness of the American people fit well in the age of the postwar consensus, as corporate America bowed to the pressure of unions and liberal government. But it was hardly an ideology of the free market triumphant, of the people rising up to defend their corporations from the onslaught of the elites. It would only become that with the turbocharged theorizing of figures like Gilder and Hayek, and in the context of our own noisily populist age.

Just Plain Bill

One of the first important works of political analysis to appear in the nineties predicted that the new decade would see an explosion of thirties-style hostility toward corporate America. Kevin Phillips, the writer who had so famously anticipated the backlash politics that kept the GOP in power for thirty years after 1968, argued in his 1990 book, *The Politics of Rich and Poor,* that the country's tide of outrage was now ready to flow the other way. After a decade of Reaganite politics in which the nation's wealth had been shifted—obviously, spectacularly, and with great fanfare—into the bank accounts of "Upper America," Phillips claimed that the public had had enough. Working Americans no longer wanted to hear about yuppies, entrepreneurs, and buyout artists; they would no longer stand for the rampant deindustrialization of their cities and the obscene enrichment of Wall Street sharks like Henry Kravis.

> Vivid grass-roots trends fleshed out the official statistics: *Wealth within the United States had been changing hands, regions, vocations, economic sectors and income strata with a vengeance.* Magazines ran endless surveys of the new mega-fortunes, and of the lesser but soaring compensation packages of investment bankers and corporate chief executives. The clumsiest television producer could film the pain in boarded-up Iowa farm towns, empty Ohio steel mills and city parks full of homeless drifters—or show the BMW-thronged streets of Connecticut suburbia, retooling export plants and West Coast port cities flush with the profits of unloading and transshipping Japanese cars and Korean color televisions. Few observers doubted the rich were getting richer, while the poor were fulfilling their half of the cliché.[50]

Phillips believed that the stage was set for a populist revolt following the script of the 1890s and 1930s. Voters were outraged by what markets had done to their world during the eighties; with the proper leadership they would soon move to adjust the imbalance.

And indeed, the nineties saw a spectacular revival of the language of social class. No, there were no mass movements along the lines of the Farmers' Alliance or the CIO; no, the rich never got soaked; and no, the sagging voter turnouts of the eighties never revived. But to scan the surfaces of what Americans said, watched, and read in the nineties one might easily believe that the people were on the march once again, that the authorities were being challenged, that the unfair distinctions of class and expertise and even of taste were being discredited like never before. Snobbery, arrogance, and pedantry—widely understood in the nineties as the telltale sins of elitism—rapidly ascended the register of moral vices, outranking such peccadilloes of the past as envy and avarice. Hierarchy became a universal enemy, a sinful principle that had to be rooted out and destroyed wherever it worked its evil logic. *Time* magazine contributor William Henry has written that he became aware of this new moral climate sometime in 1992, when "it dawned on me that the term 'elitist' . . . has come to rival if not outstrip 'racist' as the foremost catchall pejorative of our times."[51]

For Henry, as for so many others of his profession, the new populism registered merely as a call to arms for the culture wars, where he proceeded to add his cranky sniping to the already massive barrage of denunciation raining down on "political correctness." Henry believed that the demonizing of "elitism" he was noticing everywhere constituted a genuine threat to everything from capitalist meritocracy to the classics of Western civilization. Had he looked a little closer, he might have noticed that the cultural populism that so worried him was in fact a product of the elites themselves. In politics a new breed of hacks had learned to win elections by couching their mountebankery in populist terms. George Bush scarfed pork rinds and, as advised by Lee Atwater, posed memorably with an electric guitar. Bill Clinton wolfed more credible junk foods, gave us a "cabinet that looked like America," launched one "national dialogue" after another, and, as advised by Dick Morris, gloried in the favorite pseudo-interactive format of the day, the "town meeting." Both presidents worked to continue the deregulatory thrust of the Reagan administration and to roll back the legacies of the thirties and sixties, with Clinton achieving the milestone repeals of the Glass-Steagall Act and the AFDC program and giving the business community its long-sought "free-trade" deals with Mexico and China. And if two procorporate populists weren't enough, nineties voters could also choose Ross Perot, a billionaire "outsider" who bounced onto the national stage complete with a grassroots movement he had built in his garage.

Despite Clinton's early posturing as a friend of labor, most of the new breed of populists were distinctly right wing. The elections of 1994 transformed Newt Gingrich, easily the decade's most emblematic populist figure, from a typical complainer about Washington into a nationally celebrated prophet of a truly strange sort of capitalist egalitarianism. And however little it did by way of legislation, the Republican Congress that Gingrich led was remarkable for its ferociously populist understanding of the GOP mission, powered by a gang of supposedly uncorruptible "freshmen" who were determined to do nothing less than "shut it down" if they didn't get their way. Nor did Gingrich's fall after three years as speaker of the house signal the decline of the new populist style: On the contrary, it left the nation in the hands of less visionary but even more pugnacious elite-baiters like Tom DeLay and Dick Armey. Meanwhile, the state governments to whom the Republican Congress so wished to devolve power were being led by a new crop of populist governors like Wisconsin's Tommy Thompson, an aggressive champion of the right of corporations to relocate (to his state, of course) who fancied himself both the heir of the La Follette tradition and such an unsurpassed friend of the common man that he titled his 1996 memoirs *Power to the People*.

Backing it all up was the much-discussed AM radio uprising of the early nineties, which looked enough like a non-staged popular movement to make it all seem plausible. On the commercially undesirable AM frequencies, average people in vast numbers were tuning in to hear angry commentators flay the liberal elite—and what's more, these listeners were themselves participating in the flaying, phoning in to voice their own anger with the bureaucrat know-it-alls, the tax-and-spenders, the politically correct, the Marxist professors, the beneficiaries of affirmative action, and the welfare queens. Rush Limbaugh, a radio populist so effective that the revolutionary Congress of 1994 made him an honorary member, may have spent much of his airtime detailing Clinton's many scandals, but as he explained it his true mission was war against "elitism" generally—against wrongful authority, false expertise, and class arrogance. "Liberals fear me," he once wrote, because "I represent middle America's growing rejection of the elites." Limbaugh could be very specific about who made him mad. In addition to the liberal media conspirators who so haunted the imagination of nineties populism, Limbaugh extended his list of "so-called 'professionals' and 'experts' " to include "the medical elites, the sociology elites, the education elites, the legal elites, the science elites . . . and the ideas this bunch promotes through the media." In contrast to the "arrogance" of these elites, Limbaugh offered his own humility before public tastes. While *their* social programs revealed a contemptuous desire to use "all Americans as their guinea pigs," and while *they* wanted only to "grab even more power and control over the lives of individuals," Rush wanted merely to "let the marketplace rule," to let each of us "think for yourselves." His success, as he repeatedly reminded listeners, was due to the fact that he respected us and that we responded by tuning in.[52]

Not that the directors of the liberal cultural establishment were ready to confess to any charges of "elitism," of course. On the contrary: The makers of our official public culture were just as enamored of the People's majesty as were the congressional fire-eaters so determined to defund them. Take, for example, the "Favorite Poem Project," an all too typical artifact of the Age of Clinton. Directed by poet laureate Robert Pinsky and funded by foundations great and small, it was an effort to record one thousand Americans of all ages, regions, ethnicities, and "professions" (what you and I might call "classes") as they read their favorite poems. Clearly inspired by the documentary impulse of the thirties, the project's planners described it as a way to take a once-high-brow form back to the People, to free poetry from the tyrannical authority of "academic heaviness," to put the common man in charge, to honor the tastes of the average American, "to listen," as Pinsky himself put it, "to the American audience. . . ."[53]

It is difficult to look back over the populist fireworks of the 1990s with any emotion more charitable than exhaustion. While the culture warriors loudly assailed each other's elitism, the public whose wisdom and empowerment and back-talking they so proudly hailed was going through the least populist economic developments since the 1920s. Salutes to the wisdom and historical agency of the People may have become a mandatory element of everything from art criticism to AM radio conspiracy theorizing, but all through the nineties the public itself seemed to shrink ever further from any actual embrace of democratic power. And while contemporary populism arose after a period of wealth-concentration and corporate evildoing similar to the one that ignited the original Populist revolt, the populism of our time served not to overturn but to acclimate. It may have made tasteful use of thirties stylings—the people on the march, the gorgeous mosaic of differentness, the great virtue of the common folk—but it had nothing but assent for the repeal and rollback of the social and economic order the thirties' social movements gave birth to. It was a populism of acquiescence in which endless salutes to the people's power covered the people's growing powerlessness; in which constant talk of popular wisdom served mainly to justify the ever-widening gap between rich and poor. It was a thirties without the New Deal; all Capra, no CIO.

Sources of the New Faith

In his 1995 book, *The Populist Persuasion,* Kazin traces the language of populism to its earliest roots and concludes by remarking on the simultaneous pervasiveness of populism in the 1990s and the disappearance of its traditional concerns from national politics and media. Nineties journalists, for example, had no trouble making the usual genuflections before middle America and its supposed virtues, but they had ceased to understand "the ethical link between labor . . . and the creation of wealth that had been at the core of populist language" since the beginning. And although Bill Clinton, impressed by a mass of focus group data, adopted a populist style for the 1992 election, Kazin argues that the logic behind his shift was descended more from the thinking of advertising men than from the agrarians of 1890.

> This was a populism that saw no need for organized movements from below to support and extend its achievements. Like the copywriters for Hewlett-Packard and Banana Republic, Democratic campaigners were trying to pitch populism to a certain segment of the national market. But, in politics as in any sales effort, the consumers could always select a competing product or simply decline to buy any goods at all.[54]

Kazin's analogy was a telling one. For those in the nineties who took populism seriously enough actually to bother theorizing it (as opposed simply to firing off scattershot charges of "elitism"), it was becoming a doctrine much better suited to the needs of commerce—and only dimly related to the language of class revolt of the 1890s and 1930s.

Jeffrey Bell, a former aide to Ronald Reagan and Jack Kemp, published *Populism and Elitism,* his contribution to the literature, in 1992. This stalwart of the backlash argued that *real* populism was something quite different than what everyone had always thought it to be: In fact it had nothing to do with questions of relative wealth and even less with the policy proposals of the actual Populists of the 1890s. The term "populism," Bell wrote, was actually a moral abstraction. It referred to a particularly optimistic attitude concerning "people's ability to make decisions about their lives," as he put it. "Elitism," meanwhile, was a term correctly applied to those who believe in "the decision-making ability of one or more elites, acting on behalf of other people." Having spelled this out on the first page of the book, Bell proceeded to feed in the raw data of recent American politics and spit out some interesting results: Ronald Reagan, whose deregulatory and tax-reducing fervor could be portrayed as faith in the public's ability to manage their own money, came out a populist; while Michael Dukakis, along with anyone else who believed in regulation, was an elitist. Bell's book was tiresome and confusing but his clever inversion device—capable of transforming the traditional instruments of left populism into the rankest form of elitism—would prove extremely useful to those determined to extend the deregulatory and low-wage agenda. Take the problem of growing corporate power and ever-more-concentrated wealth: Any effort to reverse these phenomena, what Bell called "managing toward equality," would of necessity require "some kind of elite to do the managing," and was therefore not populist but elitist! Real populists were by definition *not* concerned about the gulf between rich and poor, since they knew that equality always exists already, "that it is innate in human beings."[55] Thus the true solution to the problem of elitism, redefined as the moral offense given by experts, snobs, know-it-alls, and the politically correct, was ever more deregulation and tax cutting. As the upper-case "p" Populists of the 1890s, who called for government ownership of the railroads as well as the establishment of the income tax, posed an insuperable obstacle for Bell's theory, he mentioned them as infrequently as he could, and always in a fairly roundabout fashion. He ignored the labor movement almost entirely.

Bell's book was not original in any particular way,[56] and yet it possessed an undeniable power. By throwing together all these prejudices in one place Bell managed to formulate what would become one of the most powerful ideas of the decade in a fairly succinct fashion. In a chapter outlining "economic populism" (you know, "optimism about people's ability to make economic decisions") he proposed that what it meant to believe in the people was to believe in Adam Smith's free market. In fact, the people and the market were connected so closely that Bell was able to scan political figures of the last two centuries and nimbly pick out "populists" from "elitists" based on whether or not they supported free trade, minimal taxes, laissez-faire government, absolute property rights, and the gold standard. (For those who are confused, all of these are said to be markers of "populist" sentiment, thereby making the 1890s Populists themselves "elitists" on all counts.)

Bell's formulation was not an entirely novel one: As we have seen, elements of what would become market populism had already emerged in corporate public relations and in the persecution fantasies of thinkers like Gilder and Hayek. But Bell's book, published in a climate of hostility toward "elites" so ferocious and abstract that it reminded one of attitudes toward Communists in the 1950s, was the first to bring all these elements together.

The language of market populism became particularly noticeable after the landmark Republican electoral triumph of 1994. A collection of conservative essays, published in the flush of victory under the jaunty title *Backward and Upward*, took great pains to distance the new breed of conservatives from the things with which the right had long been associated—order, deference, the past, "family values"— and to proclaim instead the new gospel: That democracy was closely related to the holy acts of buying and selling, and that those who try to control the market are therefore setting themselves against nothing less than the almighty will of the people themselves. Robert L. Bartley, editor of the *Wall Street Journal,* had news for those conservatives still stuck on the idea of the nation. "The world is ruled not by politicians but by markets," he wrote. "National governments will evolve toward something like state governments today: Each will have its own industrial development program to show why it has the best business and investment climate." Those who truly believe in democracy must learn never to "fight the marketplace, but listen to what it is telling us," must abandon their fanciful ties to the past and throw themselves headlong into the whirling currents of market whim. As for those who do "try to fight the marketplace," Bartley's coauthors had a ready response: They were not only wrong but elitist, arrogant, in the grip of wild delusions of grandeur. In one essay these meddlers with the market, this new "liberal elite," were said to believe "that they are philosopher-kings . . . that the people simply cannot be trusted; that they are incapable of just and fair self-government; that left to their own devices, their society will be racist, sexist, homophobic, and inequitable—and the liberal elite know how to fix things." Believing that things can be fixed is, in some way, an offense to popular sovereignty. And in a contribution that shows why he became the Beltway superstar of the nineties, Fred Barnes found an allegory for this new line of populist reasoning in the glorious churn of the traffic jam. Barnes told readers that he liked to drive, speculated about how offensive this must be to the politically correct, who wanted to force everyone to stop driving, but he liked to do it anyway—and so did everyone else, for that matter—and so there! In the isolation of his car, Barnes heard echoes of the vox populi: Driving was a matter of individual "freedom, convenience, and flexibility." Mass transit, though, was an elitists' dream: The planners knew where it was best for you to go, and some "expert" somewhere was always directing the traffic. For Barnes it's the people's way all the way, "even if that means inching to work on congested highways."[57]

Even more revealing of the market populist consensus was the curious mid-decade mania among conservatives for describing the operations of government in the supposedly more democratic language of business. Journalist John Fund wrote in the immediate aftermath of the 1994 elections that if government "were a consumer product on a store shelf, it would be removed for being defective and sued for false advertising." Give the people of America *real* democracy—the democracy of the competitive marketplace: "They want to be treated as customers, not constituents." Among campaigning politicians the language of marketplace democracy was no less incendiary. The Republicans' "Contract with America" announced that the public could now decline to reelect officials just as they might fire a disobedient employee (a power they seemed to think was denied to us before). Ross Perot suggested that we could solve our problems if only we could learn to think about government like a business. So great a fuss did he make over a document entitled "The Annual Report of the United States" (its genius insight: discuss the relationship of government and public as though it were a business and its shareholders!) that he launched its author, Meredith Bagby, on to a career as a CNN financial correspondent and all-around chronicler of her generation's contributions to the corporate world.[58]

For Texas congressman Ron Paul (a former Libertarian elected as a Republican), the market populist equation was so self-evident that he asked Congress to repeal antitrust law on the simple grounds that "bigness in a free market is only achieved by the vote of consumers." Corporations are the product of a democratic process far more sensitive and sophisticated than elections; by definition corporate behavior reflects popular consent. Compared to the market, in fact, government just plain sucks. The marketplace, at least, yields up "profits for stockholders" and happiness for consumers while the actual institutions of democracy—the various branches of government—are staffed with what Paul called "little men filled with envy . . . capable of producing nothing."[59]

In Britain, a country whose politicians have embraced the logic of the focus group and the religion of the Market with an affection that could be off-putting even to the most enthusiastic Americans, New Labour politicians made even more brazen statements about the democracy of the marketplace. Stanley Greenberg, a pollster for both Bill Clinton and Tony Blair (the latter perhaps being the only man in the English-speaking world to regard the former as a figure of great historical significance), was quoted by *Observer* columnist Nick Cohen in 1999 describing polling, focus-grouping, and the other arts of marketing as "part of the democratization of modern elections." Peter Mandelson, New Labour's frightening spinmeister, declared that these same tools were bringing "the era of pure representative democracy . . . to an end."[60] Blair and co. may be aping the soft populism of Clinton when they speak of their "Third Way," their "People's Budget," and their "People's Princess." But when they are called to task by journalists like Cohen over the collection of privatization, deregulation, and sweetheart deals that make up their industrial policy, they fall back mechanically on the criticism-as-elitism patter that they can only have learned from the American right. As Cohen continues, "When you attack them, you are accused by the elite movers and Third Way shakers of being a 'liberal elitist' even though you have no chance of getting near power because you suffer from the crushing disability of not being a big businessman. We thus have an elite that embraces populism and forces the most degraded aspects of equally elitist corporations' populist diet and journalism on everyone's children but their own—while branding its principled critics as modern aristocrats."[61]

The figure who propelled market populism to center stage was Newt Gingrich, in whose person was combined a Jacobin fervor for "revolution" and a faith in the goodness of business so guileless that he would fantasize about achieving a "consumer-directed government" and once recommended that policy-makers settle the big questions by simply asking "our major multinational corporations" what they would have us do.[62] Gingrich's rise to prominence after the 1994 elections took the world by surprise: Suddenly one of the most powerful country's most powerful figures was this true believer in management theory, in the bizarre futurism of Alvin Toffler, in the Internet, and in the looming obsolescence of all previous history. At first the world gasped, then it mocked, and within a few years Gingrich had fallen prey to the very "old" politics he had always derided. However pathetic he would one day seem, though, Gingrich undeniably changed our culture, opened the floodgates of respectability to a new style and even a new species of market messianism. A man who seriously believed that unfettered free enterprise would save the world, Gingrich insisted on recasting the confrontation of the masses and the classes in terms of their relative attitudes toward business. In *To Renew America,* his 1995 statement of principles, he posited a "democratic entrepreneurism" in which Americans from any social class could "invent their own future"—a spirit that he claimed was lacking in Europe, where "inventions often remained the province of the wealthy and the aristocratic." What's holding the people back is the "credentialing of the professions" and the cynical bad-mouthing of businessmen by the "elite." So deeply did Gingrich believe in this weird class conflict—in which Business Man squared off against the experts, professionals, bureaucrats, and politicians—that he actually declared the "so-called business cycle" itself to be a mere fabrication of expertise-mongering Federal Reserve economists.[63]

But according to market populism the political is a realm of hopeless and unavoidable corruption. The corporate world is where the people's work is done, where the real power resides, and so it seems only natural that the new idea's greatest theorists arose from business rather than politics.

A Great Time
or What

Market Populism Explains Itself

That elite is most successful which can claim the heartiest
allegiance of the fickle crowd; can present itself as most "in
touch" with popular concerns; can anticipate the tides and
pulses of opinion; can, in short, be the least apparently
"elitist."   —*Christopher Hitchens, 1999*[1]

Do rich people deserve more space than the rest of us? Was
technology meant to improve their lives alone? Do the stars
shine for their eyes only? Introducing the Special Edition of
Century 2000. It's the first limited edition that isn't limited to
the rich. . . . A luxury car for everyone.
                              —*Advertisement for the Buick Century, 1999*

Great Books

There was a time—and not all that long ago, either—when the suggestion that business was merely a more perfect version of democracy
would have been greeted with a national horselaugh. Far from hailing
Business Man as a revolutionary genius and a leveler of the social
classes, Americans in the Depression years tended to regard prominent
CEOs as irresponsible puffers of an unsustainable bubble. The most
despised profession of all in the thirties was investment banking. And
among the many individual banks that vied in those years for the grand
title of most hated was the National City Bank of New York. In the

twenties National City had been the largest commercial bank in the country, and its president, Charles Mitchell, had been one of the most celebrated personalities of the bull market. While run-of-the-mill bank officers liked to fancy themselves gentlemen of probity and responsible conservatism, Mitchell was an unreconstructed salesman, a flashy, aggressive promoter of bonds, stocks, and faith in what was then called "the New Era" of finance. Employing an army of salesmen who pushed securities on the general public, Mitchell transformed National City into what Wall Street historian Charles Geisst calls a "financial department store." Today Mitchell would probably be hailed as an "evangelist" or as an "empowerer" of the common man; he liked to style himself a "manufacturer," dreaming up new equities and persuading governments in South America and Eastern Europe to issue bonds that National City's sales force could then palm off on a middle America grown ravenous for speculation. No one hyped that grandest of bull markets more enthusiastically: From his position atop the nation's greatest bank, he announced that stocks were "as safe as bonds" (one of many Mitchellisms that would be repeated in the nineties); only weeks before the crash he maintained that "market values have a sound basis in the general prosperity." And when the Federal Reserve tried to curb margin buying and deflate the bubble in early 1929, Mitchell single-handedly thwarted their plans, sending the market spiking up again—to great popular acclaim. To Bruce Barton, the twenties adman who famously described Jesus as an unusually effective businessman, Mitchell's techniques were nothing less than "revolutionary."[2]

But as the market crashed and Mitchell's Peruvian bonds drifted inevitably toward worthlessness, a different sort of populism took hold of the American mind, and Mitchell became a public villain almost overnight. At the Pecora hearings, a senate inquiry held in the early thirties that investigated the causes of the bull market and the crash, it was revealed that Mitchell had been doing extensive trading in his own bank's stock. Humiliated and under fire from newspapers as well as from Franklin Roosevelt himself, Mitchell finally resigned from National City in 1933. The Glass-Steagall Act, which would regulate banks and infuriate bankers until the great bull market of our own time, was passed a few months later in response to National City's escapades during the twenties.[3]

It was not until fifty years later, with the charismatic Walter Wriston occupying Mitchell's old position atop the nation's largest bank (renamed Citibank in the seventies), that the banking industry would be ready to fight the cultural battle again, to pick up where Mitchell had left off and claim the ideological high ground of populism. Mitchell himself was discreetly omitted from the emerging narrative, of course, but otherwise it was as if a page had been lifted from the annals of jazz age finance. The hero this time was Wriston, and the journalist was Joseph Nocera, author of the 1994 book *A Piece of the Action,* but the plot was the same: Wriston was a great benefactor of the common people, leading them in their long struggle for financial liberation because he (a) rebelled against the "gentlemanly culture" of banking; (b) made lots of loans to Third World governments; and (c) oriented Citibank towards sales, filling it with "marketing" people who "understood that bank accounts could be thought of as 'product lines' and peddled like breakfast cereal." Nocera also points out, with admiration, that Wriston was unusually peeved by the provisions of the Glass-Steagall Act, that he took up the banking industry's war on that law with special relish. Other journalists might have hailed Wriston as a banker among bankers, shouldering the political burdens of his industry with exceptional skill; or they might have reasoned that Wriston almost *had* to take up antigovernment politics with vigor, as it was his bank that had been most responsible for the disasters that precipitated Glass-Steagall. But for Nocera the war on banking regulation was something considerably more noble. By blasting Glass-Steagall, Wriston became a hero of what Nocera calls the "money revolution," a powerful ally of the "middle class" in its glorious pursuit of an ever-greater percentage.[4]

If anything, Wriston himself probably regarded Nocera's cheering as a little lukewarm. According to his own thoughts on the subject, which he published in 1992, the bankers' eternal war with government and regulation is nothing less than the cause of human freedom itself.

Wriston's book, *The Twilight of Sovereignty,* deserves recognition as one of the landmark texts of the nineties, not merely because literate books by bankers are such a rarity, but because it helped launch so many of the market-populist ideas that would be orthodoxy by century's end. To read *The Twilight of Sovereignty* for the first time eight years after its original publication, one feels a creepy sort of ideological deja vu: There seems to be a cliché or tired tale on just about every page. This is not because Wriston was unoriginal but because so many of the points he made in the book—his phrases, his anecdotes, his goofy historical "proofs"—were rehashed and recycled and recited so many times during the decade. *The Twilight of Sovereignty* is the sacred text that launched a thousand shibboleths. It is mentioned or its author name-checked wherever "New Economy" reading lists are assembled; and it is thanks to Wriston that Americans of the late nineties didn't simply laugh when they were told that the Internet negates Social Security, high taxes for the rich, or antitrust enforcement.

The Twilight of Sovereignty is also noteworthy as one of the texts, along with George Gilder's *Microcosm* (to which we shall come presently), that led the right out of the dead end of backlash. True, Wriston did run over many of the usual right-wing[5] obsessions—taking pains to smear the sixties antiwar movement, to accuse the media of left-wing bias, and to equate government regulation in America and Britain with communism—but he had a much grander rhetorical maneuver in mind than simply squalling about the great books or political correctness. The balance of power in the eternal conflict between industry and meddling feds had been irreversibly altered, Wriston argued: Technology itself had wandered in and "changed everything," had launched an "information revolution" as all-transforming as the Industrial Revolution had been, and had in the process made all efforts to regulate industry as outmoded as the sundial. Markets would be the real ruler in the nineties, forcing upon every government everywhere the same laissez-faire policies for which the Republican Party, USA, had fought for so many years. "Capital will go where it is wanted and stay where it is well treated," Wriston announced. "It will flee from manipulation or onerous regulation of its value or use, and no government power can restrain it for long."[6] The big-government jig that, coincidentally, Citibank had done so much to begin in the first place, was up at last.

The global triumph of markets, in Wriston's telling, was not simply a victory for Citibank or for Wriston's cronies sitting up in business class and hassling the flight attendants: It was in fact the final triumph of democracy itself. "Markets are voting machines; they function by taking referenda," Wriston wrote. Markets are "global plebiscites" that pass democratic judgment day and night, that "conduct a running tally on what the world thinks of a government's diplomatic, fiscal, and monetary policies." Markets are giving the "Power to the People," a slo-gan that Wriston proudly rescues from its misuse by the hated pro-testers of the sixties.[7]

In particular, "information" is said to militate by its very nature against dictatorship of any kind. In an ideological homily that would become so orthodox by the end of the decade that it would color much of the foreign affairs reporting to appear in the US, Wriston recites how the VCR brought down Marcos, how the cassette tape brought down the Shah, and how TV destroyed Communism. So wondrous are these devices' democratic properties, in fact, that when people watch TV they are actually "voting" for the laissez-faire way, "for Madonna and Benetton, Pepsi and Prince—but also for democracy, free expres-sion, free markets, and free movement of people and money." Culture warriors might huff about Madonna's bad values, but Wriston saw the light: To watch the "material girl" prance was to do nothing less than endorse the steel industry's efforts (much lauded in the book) to es-cape regulation and unionization, to authorize Wriston's own legendary attacks on Glass-Steagall. In fact, so compelling was the freedom the market offered that Wriston could confidently predict a day when the bankers' war became People's War, when even the proletariat would "fight to reduce government power over the corporations for which they work, organizations far more democratic, collegial, and tolerant than distant state bureaucracies."[8]

In other passages this far-off corporate utopia is already a done deal.

Wherever markets go they undermine the elitism and arrogance of the mighty. For Wriston this moral fable is true at such a fundamental level that, he notes with glee, "government economists" who "used to be pretty sure what made economies work" can no longer even measure what is going on in the world. Deprived of the swagger of certainty that they developed in the 1930s (at the expense of Citibank), the experts do not understand the information age and can no longer plan or regulate: "You cannot fine-tune what you cannot measure." In the information revolution the hubris of regulation must end: Governments must learn humility before the eternal principles of the market, must learn "modesty," must "know that they do not know."[9]

These were the ideas that, echoed and amplified by a million magazine articles and a string of influential books, would inflate the great economic bubble of the late nineties. Although Wriston does not use the term "New Economy," all the telltale faiths are here: The invocation of technological and economic "change" so massive, so earth-shaking, and so all-enriching that there is no way to understand it rationally; an awestruck reverence for "the market" and its inevitable triumph; a matching contempt for "government" and its futile efforts to resist; and, most importantly of all, an ecstatic confusion of markets with democracy, markets with people, markets with empowerment, and markets with the globe itself. Each of these ideas had been floating around on the fringes of corporate and right-wing thought for years (as Wriston's endnotes make clear); now they were coming together into a market populist juggernaut that, before the decade was up, would sweep all before it. It is somehow fitting that so much of the hot air that would buoy the nineties was puffed by a successor of Charles Mitchell, the greatest of the bulls of the twenties; it is even more appropriate that cyber-ecstaticism, the signature literary tradition of the decade, would arise from the political struggles of the commercial banking industry.

Between the books by Wriston and Jeffrey Bell, both published in 1992, most of the ideas and symbols that would make up market populism were out in the open. Both of these writers, along with Gingrich,

Limbaugh, and the cast of management thinkers and investment advisers whose stories make up this book, had subjective interests in arguing that market forces, if left scrupulously untouched by regulators and unions, would automatically act out the people's will. The new consensus seems to have followed the same trajectory across the board: Market populism began in nearly all of its varieties as an ideology of business, as a PR scheme for this industry or that, as a simple management tactic, as a dream of the media conglomerates, as an official slogan of the New York Stock Exchange. What makes it worth studying, though, is its recent triumph in the larger world of American culture, the process by which even non-bankers, non-CEOs, and non-Republicans learned to accept the logic of the market as a functional equivalent of democracy.

The most powerful symbolic weapon in the arsenal of market populism was the astonishing new information technology of the decade, to which all manner of cosmic significance could be attributed and from which no end of lessons could be drawn. Kevin Kelly, a former editor of the countercultural standby *Whole Earth Review,* became in the nineties one of the most eager finders of such significance, both in *Wired,* the magazine where he merged countercultural tastes with the hardest of free market faiths, and in *Out of Control,* his sweeping 1994 examination of the distinction between living things and the ever-cooler products of various high-tech researchers. As one might expect, Kelly's goal was to break that distinction down, to show how man-made objects were becoming ever more like biological things. Along the way, of course, he had to settle on a definition of biological things that would permit such a conclusion, and what he came up with was *networks.* In nature, as in the coming robotic world, everything is connected to everything else; knowledge and power are distributed; relationships are so complex that individuals can't possibly fathom the whole.

The obvious inspiration for Kelly's definition was the Internet, and *Out of Control* anticipated the gathering Internet mania with uncanny prescience. But Kelly's "neo-biological" metaphor had even more far-reaching ramifications when applied to the realm of economics. Here the analogue for the network being was the market as theorized by Hayek, and in one memorable passage Kelly equated a scientist's theories for robot design, the behavior of "complex organisms of any kind," and the free market, all of them as one in utilizing the timeless, anti-hierarchical principles of distributed intelligence. And if the logic of markets was equivalent to the humble yet transcendent logic of nature, the great offender against righteousness was that same meddling, taxing, regulating big government that had annoyed great bankers and small-town merchants since time immemorial. Kelly duly offered up all sorts of schemes for obsoleting government functions, and excitedly reported on a conference of hackers and libertarians in which "encryption" technology was settled upon as the silver bullet for destroying government power in just about every way.[10]

This is not to say that Kelly, the confirmed counterculturalist, was acting as a shill for the great bankers and small-town merchants whose ideological position he seemed to have adopted. Heaven forbid! In fact, and along with many other market populists of the decade, he vigorously shook his fist at the hierarchical corporate powers of the world and declared that the networking logic of nature (and of the market) would "truly revolutionize almost every business." What Kelly meant by "revolution," though, was not common ownership or even a more democratic distribution of wealth, but an increasing reliance on "outsourcing" by companies that had figured out they no longer required a massive, vertically integrated operation. Why anyone other than shareholders should celebrate this development—"outsourcing" as a thinly veiled strategy for union busting was in fact one of the few labor controversies of the decade to make newspaper front pages, especially during a short but painful strike at General Motors in 1998—is not discussed: Kelly seems to find the simple fact of decentralized production mind-bogglingly cool, tantalizing readers with the tale of one company buying its parts from another company, and then hiring someone else to do its advertising. Similarly, Kelly predicted that moving from hard currency to electronic money would somehow "break the monopoly of financial Brahmins," a fantasy that would recur throughout the nineties, but never with much of an explanation. (Were we all just supposed to get free money? Had these "financial Brahmins" been hoarding greenbacks in their vaults?) But who needed an explanation? Once the divine logic of the network had been fully embraced by the corporate world, hierarchies would just *have* to tumble; people would *have* to be empowered. Kelly offered the parable of Benetton, where, through the intercession of an accelerated production system, "the cash registers, not fashion mavens, choose the hues of the season." We would get to choose the colors, and the companies themselves, duly chopped down and speeded up, would become *living things,* in the manner of another enlightened clothes manufacturer that Kelly referred to as an "economic superorganism."[11]

We can also observe a contradiction running throughout Kelly's ecstatic evocation of the networked world. Kelly affirmed the goodness and smartness and empowerment of the regular people, arguing along with just about every other market populist that computers and the Internet would soon transfer power in great tranches on down to the common man. On the other hand, though, he emphasized the people's inability to understand the economic whole. We were part of a "hive mind," more akin to a swarm of bees than a collection of rational, thinking persons. We were smart, but not smart enough to be able to order the world in any successful way. The key was to *surrender control,* an imperative Kelly repeats like a mantra throughout the book, to realize that the big things are simply beyond us. The way we will finally and correctly learn to understand "network economics," he writes, is through a "new spiritualism." Appliances and even clothes may learn to talk to one another, to do miraculous things, but we humans must realize our limitations and embrace the laissez-faire way as we would a religion.[12]

Such theories of the "New Economy" future gave rise to equally fantastic visions of the past. In 1997, Peter Schwartz, a leading "futurist," took to the pages of *Wired* magazine, where Kelly was executive editor, to describe the present as though he were looking back from the enlightened year 2020, from which vantage point his social vision was perfect and the meaning of contemporary events became clear. It was quite obvious, the seer wrote, that what was going on back in 1997 was neither bubble nor mania, but in fact a "long boom," an economic expansion without end that would eventually "solve" just about every known social problem, from poverty to the environment. The appeal of such a literary tactic—and the quality that made Schwartz's "long boom" theorizing such a staple of nineties optimism—was that it mustered the gravitas of history and inevitability for the corporate deeds of just a few weeks before. Thus the present-day economists' failure to verify the massive computer-driven productivity growth that Schwartz *knew* to be taking place* was simply due to their use of soon-to-be-laughable "industrial-age" standards; as a result, "reengineering" or "downsizing," while controversial in 1997, is "in fact" simply the inevitable corporate advance towards "the smaller, more versatile economic units of the coming era"; and thus Reagan and Thatcher's regime of "busting unions" (Schwartz's term), privatization, and "dismantling the welfare state" could at last be correctly understood as "the formula that eventually leads toward the new economy."[14]

But "let them eat future" has its weaknesses as a rallying cry, and fortunately Schwartz was able to make out the glorious figure of Democracy leading the advance of history right by Inevitability's side. "Interactive technologies" were not only permitting all sorts of fabulous downsizings, they were spawning "radically new forms of participatory democracy on a scale never imagined." And since not only "our market economy" but "our ecosystem" work best when "diversity is truly valued," the "New Economy" would also soon be smashing racism, routing sexism. In fact, in the year of Our Market 2020 "many young people"—oh, you idealistic kids!—"say that the end of the nation-state is in sight." Markets and multiculturalism: So well did they go together that Schwartz actually

---

*The stagnation in productivity growth that persisted through much of the nineties remained a particularly annoying problem for "New Economy" evangelists, and in the literature of market populism one repeatedly comes across denunciations of "the experts" for their failure to apprehend the true gains that the common people simply *know* to exist.[13]

blames the Great Depression on ugly, intolerant nationalism; so genetic are they that he elevates "openness" to a universal principle of life, dictating our behavior in both the corporate and political worlds: "Open, good. Closed, bad. Tattoo it on your forehead. Apply it to technology standards, to business strategies, to philosophies of life. It's the winning concept for individuals, for nations, for the global community in the years ahead." Open minds, evidently, require open shops.

And as if global peace and democracy weren't enough, Schwartz also spies Patriotism at the head of the advancing legions of history. As the US is the place where "the free market economy and democracy" were first understood to be one and inseparable, ours is naturally "the first country to transition to the new economy," whither everyone else was forced to follow. It seems more likely, though, that what historians of the future will actually find in this bizarre form of self-justification is little more than the computer industry's desire to see other people's money "transition" into hefty first-day pops for the thousand IPOs that this kind of "radical optimism" made possible.[15]

But in the heady days of the late nineties there was no stopping the ecstatic testifying of the free market faithful. In 1998 Pulitzer Prize–winning business writer Daniel Yergin and his colleague Joseph Stanislaw would supplement Schwartz's pseudo-history with what appeared to be the real thing: *The Commanding Heights,* their grand and glorious story of how it was that the market way triumphed over all the world. It was a book that only the mad celebrationism of the time could produce: By adopting the most sweeping, most generalized sort of historical analysis, Yergin and Stanislaw put across the very, very specific conclusion that the "market consensus" we enjoy right here, right now, is the highest pinnacle of human development. They take as their subject the experience of the entire world during the entire twentieth century, thus permitting them to pick and choose from an almost unlimited array of events, ideas, and personalities. Thus framed, it is perhaps not surprising that the story turns out to be such an inspirational one, that each country of the world follows the same trajectory, flirting dangerously with the bad ideas of regulation, national ownership, and outright socialism—and then coming around magnificently to the good old market.

Most of the elements of the emerging master narrative are included. Labor unions are, virtually without exception, portrayed as quasi-criminal organizations that exist only to impede, frustrate, and stifle the workings of the market. Financial markets are said to "vote constantly on countries' fiscal policies." Until the big turnaround engineered by Margaret Thatcher, a person Yergin reveres without restraint, "entrepreneurs" were said to be a persecuted and despised class, while the logic of markets was a thing unknown among national leaders and entirely extinct in the UK.[16]

Each of these notions could be dismissed as simple attempts to pass off decades of GOP propaganda as objective history. But Yergin and Stanislaw go far beyond these: Their central narrative device seems actually to have been drawn from the speeches of Joseph McCarthy. The history of the twentieth century can be understood as a great battle between ideas, Yergin and Stanislaw argue, between faith in markets on the one hand and faith in government on the other. And when Yergin and Stanislaw speak of "government" they mean *all* government: democratic, Stalinist, whatever. Any effort to tame markets is thus tainted with totalitarianism. While we may have believed that the Cold War between the US and the Soviet Union was the epitome of this "Manichaean contest," in fact it was never so simple. Communism was only the most radical expression of a misguided faith in government that Yergin and Stanislaw trace to every country on the planet—even America. As they put it, "Marxism and communism not only constituted a competitive model to market societies but also shaped the terms of the global debate, weighting it toward a powerful role for the state even within capitalist systems." The American regulatory state and the European welfare states are only a slightly lighter shade of red; the commissar is cousin to the OSHA bureaucrat. Yergin and Stanislaw seem to find the influence of Communism almost everywhere people turn their backs on the market: In the British Labour Party and trade union movement, in the Third World, people were mesmerized by the Soviet Union's successes. Yet when it finally became clear that Soviet industry was hardly the behemoth everyone believed it to be, "the result was a vast discrediting of central planning, state intervention, and state ownership." Similarly, the fall of the Berlin Wall, easily the decade's favorite historical reference, represents for Yergin and Stanislaw not merely the collapse of a despicable dictatorship but proof that governments *everywhere,* dictatorships or not, must surrender to the market: "As communism was the most extreme form of state economic control, its demise signaled an enormous shift—from state control to market consensus." With the dismantling of the Berlin Wall, the New Deal in America was finished as well, and Clinton's famous recognition of the end of "big government" made the surrender complete.[17]

To be fair, Yergin and Stanislaw can hardly be blamed with pioneering this sort of latter-day red-baiting. Walter Wriston had used the same reasoning in *Twilight of Sovereignty,* ludicrously identifying Karl Marx as the great founding thinker of big government and glibly eliding the difference between the Soviet Union and American regulators: Both were simply "governments," after all, driven by the natural impulse of all "government" everywhere to "impose rules and exact payments."[18] The fall of the Berlin Wall was somehow thought to discredit the regulators that hounded Citibank all those years. Neither Wriston nor Yergin and Stanislaw, it should be noted, invoked the hobgoblins of treason and subversion that accompanied earlier waves of red-baiting; all of them adduced the connection between communism and American liberals as if it were a self-evident matter of the historical record. Then again, neither really had to do much more than that: After fifty years of Cold War, of Soviets as national enemies on a level with the Nazis, establishing their opponents as somehow related to the beast was more than enough.

The public thinker of the nineties who was fondest of making his points by casual comparison between the Red menace and whatever was impeding the "New Economy" this week was Thomas Friedman, the *New York Times* columnist. For Friedman the fall of the Berlin Wall was not just a landmark historical event, it was an analogy applicable almost everywhere. As that wall fell, Friedman would write, so were other walls falling all the time: The walls that restricted the salaries of major-league athletes, for example, or the walls that kept "information" at a company's uppermost levels. It sounded neat on the surface, and we're all against "walls." But the Berlin Wall wasn't just any old wall: It was the preeminent symbol of the world's most dangerous and mur- derous dictatorship. When Friedman declared that, as fell the Berlin Wall, so must also fall protective tariffs or the militancy of Brazilian workers, he wasn't simply railing against barriers in a general sense: He was comparing tariffs and worker militancy to the most detested regime of all, implying that tariffs or worker militancy had some subtle thing in common with the monstrous practices of the Soviets.[19] And Friedman seemed to go out of his way to apply the analogy to organized labor. In a December 1999 op-ed, he compared the destruction of the Berlin Wall to the "Internet revolution" on the grounds that the latter was stripping power (power to regulate "capital flow," that is) from "governments and unions."[20] One would think that the labor move- ment's own ferocious anticommunism campaigns in the 1940s and its stout patriotism during the Cold War—in which it persisted almost to the point of self-destruction during Vietnam—had long since put this kind of analogy off-limits. But not for Friedman, who with every pass- ing month in the late nineties seemed to become more convinced that trade unions were some kind of sinister dictatorship-in-waiting, always craving "more walls," befouling the pristine streets of Bill Gates's Seat- tle, and bankrolling the opposition to the new global order.[21] He has charged union members with being "afraid of the future" and accused longshoremen of harboring a pathological hostility to turtles. He has also declared that "the most important thing" President Reagan ever did "was break the 1981 air traffic controllers' strike"—because that "helped break the hold of organized labor over the US economy," in turn "spurring the information revolution," a statement it's hard to re- peat with a straight face.[22]

I do not mean to suggest that Friedman is an opponent of democracy or an enemy of working people. On the contrary, what makes his writing such a touchstone for our times was the way he mixed an enthusiasm for markets and the smashing of wages with passionate cheers for democracy and statements of deep concern for the workers of the (rest of the) world. The equation of democracy and laissez-faire principles was so automatic for him that it seems whatever the market touched, it liberated, it democratized. Every time an American union was busted a worker somewhere cried out for joy.

Friedman was in some ways the very embodiment of market populism at flood tide. As the intellectual life of the decade came to resemble a race among popular financial commentators to win for themselves, through a sort of cosmic optimism about all things dotcom, the title of most enthusiastic pundit, Friedman was the blue-ribbon boy. He wrote as though his thoughts were somehow pegged to the insanely rising Dow, as though each advance on Wall Street was a go-ahead for a new round of superlatives and hyperbole. Friedman topped them all: Yergin, Kelly, Schwartz, Wriston, or even the cyber-ecstatics at *Wired* magazine.

In 1999, Friedman organized a number of his *Times* columns into a book to which he gave the portentous-sounding title *The Lexus and the Olive Tree*. The book's ostensible purpose was to help readers "understand globalization," which apparently meant hammering into our heads the notion that "globalization" (meaning, of course, free markets) was the end object of human civilization, that "globalization" was lovable and trustworthy, that "globalization" would make us rich, set us free, and generally elevate everything and everyone everywhere.

Friedman set about his subject in the usual manner, seeking to prove that the global triumph of free-market capitalism had brought democracy to the peoples of the world. He told of the "democratization of technology," in which we would all get computers and telephones; he marveled at the "democratization of finance," in which we would all get to invest in whatever we wanted; he described a miraculous "democratization of information," in which we would get more TV channels than ever before. All of these forces had combined to bring down the mighty and subvert top-down hierarchies of all kinds, he asserted, citing (like Wriston) a list of former dictatorships that had been laid low by the humble VCR, TV, and Internet. This last, of course, was something of a market-populist wonder-worker, an institution that Friedman found to be both the most democratic on earth as well as the very "model of perfect competition."[23]

Lexus was a millennial work in the fullest sense of the word, with each of the various fad ideas of the nineties pushed to the point of world-ending gloriosity. When the subject was countries other than the US, Friedman asked readers to imagine these nations' humiliation at the hands of what he called "the Electronic Herd," otherwise known as buyers of securities, and invented all manner of pithy putdowns that this "herd" might deliver as it rolled out of a country that had been insufficiently attentive to the imperatives of the market. In one chapter he imagined the nations of the world spread out before him like so many stock listings in the daily newspaper; he recommended that we "buy" some and "sell" others. Or take democracy itself, that greatest good thing of all. As it turned out it was mainly a matter of money: "It's one dollar, one vote," a system in which the market and corporate interests rightly and naturally get to dictate to everyone else. Thus, even as Friedman whooped it up for diversity and the empowerment of the People, he took pains to warn us that the real boss, the market, would not tolerate any sort of political japery beyond its very narrow spectrum of permissible beliefs. No country that wished to participate in the global gloriosity would be allowed to regulate its industries or provide for its unfortunates beyond what Friedman deemed appropriate; their "political choices get reduced to Pepsi or Coke—to slight nuances of taste, slight nuances of policy . . . but never any major deviation from the core golden rules." He even described the various punishments that the wrong sort of voting would bring down on a country, as investors "stampede away" and stock markets crash.[24]

None of which should really worry Friedman's readers back home in the US, for ours is the country in whose image markets quite naturally wished to remake the world. In a closing chapter Friedman asked readers to wonder with him at how "a visionary geo-architect" (i.e., God) would go about designing the ultimate nation, how He would insist that it had "the most flexible labor market in the world," how He would ensure that bosses were tolerant of whatever rebellious and zany lifestyle accessories white-collar people used to signify their creativity, but also (and only a few sentences away) how He would be sure to let those same bosses "hire and fire *workers* with relative ease."[25] The point here wasn't to reiterate the traditional patriotism of the age of affluence—fruited plains, hand of Providence, etc.—but to affirm that what's best about America, what most pleases the Almighty, are those very particular things celebrated in recent management theory. While IBM was going on the airwaves to proclaim "I Am," Friedman was virtually asking us to imagine that God was somehow behind the reengineering programs at AT&T or GE, that God stood in solidarity with strikebreakers everywhere, that it was God who told American managers to outsource the job, to initiate "change" programs, to send the entire payroll out into the parking lot one fine morning and hire half of them back as temps.

Not surprisingly, Friedman's book was littered with quotes from many of the same madly triumphalist commercials for brokerage houses and software manufacturers that I refer to in these pages—not as examples of corporate myth-making, but as particularly compelling, particularly truthful bits of soothsaying which he evaluated only by appending his fervent amens. Nor did his reverence for market culture stop there: He also informed readers that his analytic abilities were patterned after the thinking of hedge fund managers. He even called his method of cultural reasoning "arbitrage." His collected works constitute a veritable dictionary of the market-populist myths of the age, awesome in its inclusiveness: Enthusiasm for the "rebranding" of Britain, pointless ponderings about the physical weight of each country's GNP, facile equating of Great Society America with the Soviet Union. Each of them is preposterous in its own way, but thrown together they make a truly dispiriting impression, a feeling akin to the first time I heard Newt Gingrich speak publicly and it began to dawn on me that *this is what the ruling class calls thinking,* that this handful of pathetic, palpably untrue prejudices are all they have to guide them as they shuttle back and forth between the State Department and the big think tanks, discussing what they mean to do with us and how they plan to dispose of our country.

All the Cats Join In

There is a point in the life of ideas when they become natural, when they are accepted so universally that their history, the struggles that produced them, are forgotten as though they never happened. Although the sequence of events in which this transformation takes place remains obscure, by the mid-1990s market populism was clearly on its way to becoming naturalized. The faith that had begun life in a hundred small-town chambers of commerce, in the Depression-panicked councils of the National Association of Manufacturers, in the reactionary fantasies of the banking industry, was becoming accepted wisdom across the spectrum of journalistic opinion. Leftoid rock critics, family-values Christians, and just about everyone in between seemed to find what they wanted in the magic of markets. Markets were serving all tastes; they were humiliating the pretentious; they were permitting good art to triumph over bad; they were extinguishing discrimination; they were making everyone rich. The depth of market populism's penetration is perhaps best judged by the casualness with which certain journalists threw it around in the latter part of the decade. It appeared in the writing of Michael Lewis, who went from assailing the culture of Wall Street in *Liar's Poker* to describing the struggle between "aristocratic values" and "market values" for readers of the *New York Times Magazine* in 1997. "Hostility to the market," it seemed, could be best understood as a form of elitist hostility to the people, but fortunately "only two classes of citizens" still practiced "antimarket snobbery": artists and aristocrats. This was an odd conclusion indeed in a country with no aristocracy but an enormous labor movement that was still formally committed, even in its most conciliatory moments, to reining in the market. But, as we shall see, ideology often made such troublesome facts invisible. To question the market was to be a snob. Or worse: Martin Wolf of the *Financial Times* insisted in a 1997 debate on the merits of "globalization" that dissent against the new global order arose from a "hatred of markets" so "pathological" that it was analogous to racism. Sometimes the intellectual gymnastics associated with market populism could become quite spectacular. When the *Wall Street Journal* editoralized in September 1999 in favor of industry-specific relaxations of immigration law which would allow certain high-tech companies "greater freedom . . . to import skilled immigrants" and keep costs low, the paper chose to pound the measure's opponents—people already working in those high-tech fields—by accusing them of foul class snobbery *toward themselves:* "It was always a slur on American workers that their employability depended on closing our markets to foreigners."[26]

Market populism was always at its fiercest when it was being used to counter some criticism of industry practice or defend free-market policy. The general principle on such occasions was a constant assertion of invisible majorities: Since market populism insisted that the people were always on the side of the market, a true believer had only to search until he could come up with a group somewhere on whose behalf he could posture. Thus the anti-WTO protests in Seattle in December 1999 were met with a uniform declaration, mouthed by American newspaper columnists as well as WTO officials, that free trade was something akin to humanitarian work, a mission undertaken by the rich countries to better the station and ease the suffering of the poor countries and the vast majority of the world's population—a calculus that neatly put protesters at the very top of the class pyramid, "standing," as the *Wall Street Journal* so memorably put it, "atop the prone bodies of people who hunger for the fruits of free trade."[27] And thus was a 1998 speech by Hillary Clinton warning against the values of consumerism rebutted by economist Stanley Lebergott on the op-ed page of the *New York Times,* who pointed out that the consumer culture, and by extension the free market generally, was itself the righteous collective product of the people themselves. "Who creates this 'consumer-driven culture' but 270 million Americans?" he asked. Taking an indignant swipe at the carping snobbery of the "best and the brightest," Lebergott asserted that criticism of business is in fact criticism of "other consumers," and that simply by participating in American life—by driving "a 1-ton car to the theater" or by "accumulat[ing] books and newspapers printed on million-dollar presses"—we authorize whatever it is that the market chooses to do.[28]

This little melodrama of marketplace democracy and the intolerable snobbishness of critics could be adapted to just about any corporate situation. During the Microsoft antitrust trial of 1999—an episode that was virtually the Dreyfus affair of the American business class, to judge by the impassioned editorializing and accusations of unfair persecution that surrounded it—the *Wall Street Journal* repeatedly accused the Justice Department, that nest of commerce-hating elitists, of acting to advance "special interests" and against the will of "consumers," who were said to love Microsoft as only an imaginary, idealized public can do. At a rate of about once a month the paper ran op-ed stories depicting the Microsoft trial as so massively illegitimate, the machinations of Microsoft's enemies so villainous, the officeholding ambitions of the prosecutors so blatant, that the proceeding was an offense against democracy itself—which moral fable it spiced up with an occasional news story about average people who became millionaires by buying and holding Microsoft shares. At its most sweeping, the *Journal's* populism portrayed antitrust itself as an elitist device used by hateful politicians "to promote the interests of the few at the expense of the many." And when the verdict finally came down in November 1999, the paper regretted that Microsoft had not adopted the editors' fire-breathing populist line as fully as it might have done: "Microsoft should have argued that we have a monopoly because our customers want us to have one."[29]

Market populism was also useful in the late-nineties battle over genetically modified (GM) foods. In the US, of course, there was no battle. Largely lacking institutions for popular participation in economic decision-making, we had no choice but to do as the corporations bade us, and GM foods entered the commodity stream without incident. In Europe, though, massive popular outrage caused big problems for particular companies. Monsanto, whose ever-ascending profitability had once been perceived as a sure thing (thanks to their invention of a "terminator" gene that would require farmers to come back to the company every year for new seed), soon faced the very real threat of being locked out of the European market altogether. Dissent had to be controlled, and market populism was the obvious tool for doing so. It alone could explain the triumph of GM foods in America without public debate as a triumph for democracy, and yet depict the debates over the subject in Europe as expressions of rampant elitism. First, genetically engineered crops were said to constitute a heroic solution to world hunger, another grand humanitarian corporate gesture on behalf of the silent billions.[30] Second, it was pointed out that the opponents of GM foods were also a heavily subsidized "special interest" who produced what all Americans know to be snob products: expensive cheeses, pâté, endive. In other words, they were farmers—European farmers. Looking for an ideal elitist whose opposition to GM crops could be portrayed as an aristocratic affectation and thus used to tarnish the entire movement, one *Wall Street Journal* editorialist hit the jackpot—Prince Charles, an outspoken opponent of the new technology. "Oh well," the writer sneered, "he probably doesn't need the money improved productivity would yield. . . ."[31] But in Europe the market-populist campaign mounted by Monsanto fell flat. As one British observer put it, "In the States, PR works. Over here, it's seen as a species of corporate lying." Still, even as the company retreated it stuck carefully to the script. In October 1999, Monsanto's CEO spoke to a conference in London and confessed—not to the grandiose will to monopoly that the "terminator" gene clearly implied, but to "condescension," "arrogance," a failure to "listen."[32]

The scheming-elites melodrama of market populism was played out most successfully in reporting about the progress that the American-style "New Economy" was making in other countries. Michael Lewis, for whom the conflict between markets and aristocratic, expertise-wielding elitists seemed to be a dialectic of nearly universal applicability, used it to explain the Asian meltdown of 1997–98 for readers of the *New York Times Magazine*. Looking for a bright side to the story, Lewis wrote that even if businesses and lives were being ruined, at least the values of the market (and of America) were being sternly reinforced. Where the Asians had gone wrong, what they had done to precipitate the savage rebuke of the international financier community, was to fail to internalize the principles of market populism. They had placed their "faith in elites," by which Lewis meant central planners and top-down managers: "Elites rather than markets had determined who got capital, and therefore who was allowed to succeed in business." But the market is a jealous god, and in Lewis's quasi-spiritualist telling of the Asian collapse it simply would not tolerate such hubris any longer. The only thing that could save the Asians now, he asserted, was a healthy dose of cultural nonconformity and a political revolt against elites, a "shareholder rebellion" along the same ultra-democratic lines that had brought on the rage for downsizing back here at home.[33]

Not all elites were bad, though. "I accept free markets," remarked a Korean professor of finance who served as Lewis's Asian protagonist. "There is only one way to organize an economy, and it will dominate the world." Strangely, Lewis quotes this statement in a long passage hailing the professor not as a would-be dictator, making the trains run on time and snapping his country back into discipline, but as a "radical," plotting with American mutual fund managers in a "free market revolt" that has "the deliciously illicit feel of a conspiracy against established authority."[34]

Lewis himself, though, was hardly "rebelling" by interpreting events in Asia in this manner. By the late nineties the market-populist uprising that was turning traditional Asian elites on their ear had become something of a journalistic orthodoxy. Once the land of "crony capitalism," Asia was now said to be rebuilding itself as a people's continent. When a 1999 Chinese telecommunications reform handed control of certain wires from government to private businessmen, for example, the *Wall Street Journal* described the transition as a "populist" deed, even though it had been spurred by what it called "a Western-style media campaign" mounted by "bureaucrats and academics." And while Indonesians were having trouble making their transition to political democracy, the *Journal* optimistically noted that "polo populism is thriving here": People from even the lowest orders were getting together on weekends to flout social convention and take the polo fields back from the snobs.[35]

If Asia was in the grip of a market populist revolt, making itself ever more like the US, certain countries in Europe—true to the aristocratic, arrogant stereotype that every American schoolboy knows—were thought to be heading the opposite direction. As the hosannas rose higher for the American way in the mid-nineties, and as the American corporate order emerged as the model for all men and all nations, American pundits and journalists became increasingly concerned with establishing the perfidy of France, a land where labor unions remained powerful and the welfare state was still largely intact. Edward Luttwak points out that the French elections of 1997 actually addressed the issues of the "New Economy" far more specifically than is customary in American politics. "After an exceptionally informative election campaign," Luttwak writes, "devoid of moralistic posturings on abortion or drugs, in which no accusations of sexual peccadilloes were traded, and which instead amounted to an accelerated course in today's brutal economic realities," French voters chose to halt the course of privatization and deregulation upon which the government had embarked.[36] As with genetically modified crops, American voters never had that choice. But to read American journalistic accounts of events in France, what was going on was not democracy but the exact opposite: Elitism, inexcusable snobbery, racism even. So emphatic did the chorus of Gallophobic invective become in 1997 (we have seen several examples of it already) that it began to seem as though some blue-ribbon committee had chosen France to succeed the Soviet Union as the avatar of economic and cultural error, the rhetorical straw man to set the peanut gallery hooting and hissing. Roger Cohen, a European correspondent of the *New York Times* enumerated in February 1997 the many ways in which the French were out of step: They didn't understand the Internet, they didn't like America, and they still clung to what Cohen called a "highly centralized system" in which elitist "technocrats" ran everything and labor unions were far, far too powerful. By October of that year, with France having voted "no" on the "New Economy," Cohen was ready to pronounce the ultimate judgment on this vexing nation: "France has set itself up as perhaps the nearest thing the United States has to a serious ideological rival in the last decade of the 20th century," he wrote.[37]

Instead of rejecting wealth polarization or the spread of poverty, what France was doing, as one writer put it, was trying "to preserve its cherished ideas of Frenchness." With a few details about the rise of the xenophobic politician Jean-Marie Le Pen, the story almost wrote itself. Since free markets are by definition the same as democracy, any effort to restrict them is an act of unpardonable pretentiousness, of arrogant disregard for the Will of the People. And for such times the French make a perfect enemy, since they have always figured in the American imagination as grade-A snobs. Even the most casual followers of the news in America know that France is a country that restricts American movies, periodically tries to stamp out English-derived words, and feels it must educate kindergartners about traditional French cuisine. They are a stubborn people swimming mulishly against the current both culturally and economically, American pundits maintain; they are ruled by a martinet government that prevents people from riding the ecstatic waves of commerce; and they are a nation of uptight killjoys bent on ruining the sweet American buzz that everyone else is getting into. Whether the French person in question was a rude waiter mocking your request for ketchup, a skiier turning up his nose at snowboarders, or a social planner seeking to soften the blows of the global economy, they were all one and the same for American observers, and the nifty possibility of mixing stereotype with economic crusading was too great for the culture-warriors of the new global order to resist.

By the end of the century it would be hard to flick a channel-changer without hearing some slur regarding the French. Insinuations of French pigheadedness found their way into a corporate pep rally broadcast by NPR. A *New Republic* editorial laughed at their "obtuse and suicidal" politics—"so perfectly French." An angry essay by the editor of the *Wall Street Journal Europe* identified a gap between bitter, anti-American French "elites" and the pro-market French "people," and quoted senior American diplomats as saying "we don't trust the French." By the year 2000, the paper was doing everything short of calling for war. An op-ed piece that appeared in March of that year actually declared that, thanks to the country's strong unions and stable bureaucracies, contemporary France was far closer to "the soviet utopia" than the Russia of the Bolsheviks. A few months later the *Journal*'s American edition printed the letter of an eager graduate student tracing the depredations of the Khmer Rouge to that slough of elitist theory, "French café society."[38]

But by far the most significant American persecutor of France was the *New York Times,* where reporters joined columnists in banging out a steady if sometimes far-fetched anti-Gallic drumbeat. Virtually every week in 1997 there was some memorable image or hilarious French foul-up to report: The French intellectual, say, who was found writing a dissertation on the impact of the Internet—with a pen! Or that great photo of a French cabinet minister staring at a computer—with an astonished look on his face!

Thomas Friedman, the paper's free-market Savonarola, laid down the terms of the conflict between global democracy and French arrogance in a February 1997 column. The problem with France was something that anyone who's watched a James Dean movie or a lifetime of car commercials knows instinctively to abhor. "The French system rewards people for their capacity to follow the path laid out for them," a friendly "expert" told Friedman; meanwhile the American system taught people "to rebel." The French disease, in other words, was not just a case of economic error; it was the familiar American melodrama of rebel versus bureaucrat, the people versus the intellectuals. In this contest there could be no question which side is in the right. And to announce that right, the ever-explosive Friedman rolled out the world-historical heavy artillery, the kind of verbiage we hadn't seen since the early days of the Cold War: France, land of unions and welfare, was doing nothing less than "play(ing) footsy with the enemies of America, who are often the enemies of modernity."[39]

Friedman was only building on the foundation constructed by Roger Cohen, whose reporting from Paris repeatedly fell back on the darkest American stereotypes about French arrogance and snobbery. For Cohen, the French don't just have problems; every economic move they make can be traced to their objectionable cultural traits. Their "hankering for grandeur," their "excessive pretensions," their "notion of occupying a position close to the center of the world," all these facets of national vanity prevented them from embracing the exciting multicultural future; the need to "nourish" the "French ego" made it difficult to predict which silly political scheme they would vote into power next. Deluded by Charles de Gaulle's "certain idea of France," it was a country that "sits in concrete," a place of "internal paralysis" that felt "threatened by innovation," where entrepreneurship was strongly discouraged, where "technocrats . . . appear overtaken by the global economy" and unions, "parading the rags of an exhausted socialist dream, . . . seem equally fossilized."[40]

But while any effort to control the market was automatically vain, certain swashbuckling French businessmen earned Cohen's approbation. There was the software baron who was reported to have antagonized "the Paris establishment" with egalitarian ideas he picked up at Stanford such as "promote a shareholding culture" and "think marketing." Then there was the little parable of Chateau d'Yquem, a vineyard embroiled in an ownership controversy between two people, one of whom "represents the soil; the other the market." Guess which characteristics go with which: While "the market" is a "restless entrepreneur" whose upstart ways make him a dealer in "bruised egos," "the soil" is matched up with a vainglorious aristocrat, a daft son of luxury who Cohen finds musing poignantly on a stopped clock.[41]

The other side of the story, which Cohen told with some excitement, was the glorious and irresistible progress of American mass culture through the French cultural heartland, an advance that Cohen apparently believed to reflect the will of the people in all its global-marketed majesty. Under a photo of roller skaters leaping and stunting before the Eiffel Tower, Cohen hailed the irrepressible youth of France, enthusiastic participants in the global market, daringly consuming the latest American youth-culture products despite the warnings of their anti-American elders. "The reversed baseball cap, basketball shoes, American movies and music," he wrote, "these are the frame of reference of a majority of French kids. The anti-Americanism glibly wheeled out by intellectuals and politicians finds little echo among ordinary French people." The kids, like the people generally, know where it's at: The Top-40 charts record the people's will as well as the popularity of the Backstreet Boys, and there is nothing the arrogant intellectuals can do about it.[42]

In pressing this interpretative scheme down on French politics, though, Cohen produced some very curious ideological results. Since suspicion of the market is tantamount to ethnic arrogance, the one French figure that Cohen's reporting rendered in strong relief was the racist and xenophobic Jean-Marie Le Pen, for whom, he wrote, the French "mood . . . provides a perfect feeding ground." For Cohen, Le Pen was the inevitable figure of the moment, the perfect reactionary for this backward-looking country. Other politicians come off as Le Pens minus the racism, or Le Pens minus the Europhobia; all elections were described as victories of some degree for Le Pen's party, the National Front. So urgent and convincing was Cohen's obsession with Le Pen that readers must have felt confused when they read that, in fact, the National Front did not win the elections, that Le Pen did not hold national office. (A few years later Cohen applied the same reasoning to the rise of Austrian neo-fascist Jörg Haider, again suggesting that racist politicians somehow expressed the arrogant determination of European elites to resist the global market. Again, though, Cohen was wrong: While Haider might oppose immigration, he is otherwise a staunch friend of business and the market, and is even described by other reporters as a kind of Alpine Thatcherist.)[43]

About French socialist leader Lionel Jospin, the man who was actually elected prime minister, Cohen had quite little to say. Clearly regarding him as the product of the same retrograde antimarket feeling that produced Le Pen, Cohen simply dismissed him as a less interesting but still glib wheeler out of anti-Americanism, just another incorrigible produced by this vainglorious desire to stand up to market forces. Reporting on Jospin's effort to reduce the French workweek, Cohen quoted a contemptuous economist at the Smith-Barney investment house: "The problem with these ideas is that they preserve the fantasy that this is the direction in which to go."[44]

To be sure, France has a host of thorny, chronic problems to deal with—high unemployment, public debt, and so on. But this was a style of reporting that seemed designed less to get at the essence of a country's politics than to spin a morality tale for readers back home. It was the news from abroad transformed into a market fable as polished as a TV commercial for a computer manufacturer, a vision of rebellious youth versus sclerotic order as melodramatic as the collective paid daydreams of Nike, Reebok, Pepsi, Coke, and Sprite. As such it fit the emerging consensus perfectly. While our great corporations were depicting themselves as the ultimate expression of democracy, and while our bankers and stockbrokers were seeking to fill the role once played by such folk as tillers of the soil and builders of cars, our journalists saw to it that they had a host of easily hated snobs against which to define themselves. By contrast, America's overlords were looking folksier all the time.

Stealth Reactionaries

If France was the great enemy of market populism, a solidly rooted place where rampant cultural elitism led to regulation, welfare spending, and even national ownership, cyberspace was its direct opposite, the promised land of the free market. It didn't have to be that, of course: The interpretations that could have been applied to this new-found-land might have been as polymorphous and diverse as the vast waves of differentness that it is routinely said to have unleashed. And yet, since the moment the Internet was noticed by the mainstream media in 1995, it has filled a single and exclusive position in political economy: a sort of cosmic affirmation of the principles of market populism. "Think of the Internet as an economic-freedom metaphor for our time," wrote bull-market economist Lawrence Kudlow in August 1999.[45] "The Internet empowers ordinary people and disempowers government." And we were only too glad to do as Kudlow instructed us, to think of it in precisely this way. In fact, so closely did the Internet and market populism become linked in the public mind that whenever a pundit or journalist mentioned the Web, one braced oneself for some windy pontification about flexibility, or the infinite mobility of capital, or the total and unappealable obsolescence of labor, government, and any other enemy of the free-market enterprise.

For this vision of the Internet as laissez-faire incarnate we have George Gilder to thank, that same theorist of the backlash with which our story began. Now neither Gilder nor any other individual can be held entirely responsible for what the Internet has become, of course, or for the identity that has been pinned on it so effectively. But Gilder's post-eighties career—his trajectory from supply-side champion to cover boy of the "radical" magazine *Wired*—is in many ways emblematic of the evolution of market populism.

With Reagan finally departed from the White House and the backlash sentiments he had done so much to popularize on the wane, Gilder appears to have been one of the first to give up on culture war, to realize that railing against a counterculture of twenty years before and wagging his finger at irresponsible minorities could only carry the free market so far. In the late eighties this reactionary's reactionary seemed to undergo a thorough transformation, abandoning his former fondness for sprawling disquisitions on the grandest themes of all and remaking himself as a humble business journalist, a tyro at the feet of the great entrepreneurs of Silicon Valley. To be sure, there is ideology aplenty in Gilder's landmark 1989 book *Microcosm*. But now it was couched in the story of a particular industry—the microchip business—rather than stated overtly; now the ideology seemed to emerge as a natural consequence of the technology being discussed rather than from the random floating anger of betrayed patriots. Gilder's reporting in *Microcosm* is competent, even compelling. But the book's most important achievement was as a work of political persuasion. So firmly did Gilder weld computers to free-market politics that no one since has been able to pry them apart.

At the center of Gilder's—soon to be the entire world's—conception of the personal computer was a vision of class conflict. In his backlash days Gilder had written about an elemental clash between heroic entrepreneurs (i.e., Newt Gingrich's "normal Americans") and the despicable scions of existing fortunes who were also, and quite mysteriously, identical to bureaucracy, to government, and to the mass media (i.e., the "liberal elite"). In the microchip industry Gilder found a powerful illustration of this strange struggle, only now the normal Americans weren't quite so normal. In this most important capitalist arena, established prestige counted for naught. "The United States did not enter the microcosm through the portals of the Ivy League, with Brooks Brothers suits, gentleman Cs, and warbling society wives," he wrote. On the contrary: This was the people's technology. In one of the most remarkable market populist passages ever published Gilder extolled the ordinariness of his new heroes:

Few people who think they are in already can summon the energies to break in. From immigrants and outcasts, street toughs and science wonks, nerds and boffins, the bearded and the beer-bellied, the tacky and uptight, and sometimes weird, the born again and born yesterday, with Adam's apples bobbing, psyches throbbing and acne galore, the fraternity of the pizza breakfast, the Ferrari dream, the silicon truth, the midnight modem, and the seventy-hour week, from dirt farms and redneck shanties, trailer parks and Levittowns, in a rainbow parade of all colors and wavelengths, of the hyperneat and the sty high, the crewcut and khaki, the pony-tailed and punk, accented from Britain and Madras, from Israel and Malaya, from Paris and Parris Island, from Iowa and Havana, from Brooklyn and

Boise and Belgrade and Vienna and Vietnam, from the coarse fanaticism and desperation, ambition and hunger, genius and sweat of the outsider, the downtrodden, the banished, and the bullied come most of the progress in the world and in Silicon Valley.

Gilder worked hard to play up the lowliness of the microchip's friends, imagining them on the receiving end of the *New York Times*'s terrible snobbery or being rejected at the senior prom. As he also wanted there to be no doubt about the microchip's doubters, he linked them both to the elitist upper classes and to Marxism, a devilish doctrine that mysteriously united the smugness of old money and the smugness of false experts.[46]

The social rank of the microchip's makers turned out, in Gilder's telling, to be an uncannily precise indicator of what the microchip did. Those experts, those sniffing nabobs, and those wielders of traditional power had good reason to fear and despise this tiny device, because it threatened to smash the social system that kept them so well-fed and haughty. The "law of the microcosm," Gilder wrote at several different points in the book, was that all hierarchies everywhere were finished: "Rather than pushing decisions up through the hierarchy, the power of microelectronics pulls them remorselessly down to the individual." Everywhere that the microchip laid its silicon finger, there freedom blossomed. This would especially be true of Gilder's old enemy, "government," a word that he, like Yergin and Wriston, used to describe everything from Stalinist dictatorships to our own democracy. While the logic of "government" ended in the hideous hierarchy Gilder symbolized with images of Brooks-clad blue bloods snubbing some poor kid from Levittown, the logic of the microchip would bring "the revolt of the venturers against all forms of tyranny." The microchip would make laissez-faire economics mandatory once and for all, freeing us finally from the fetters of the feds.[47]

The microchip was not only the enemy of government tyranny and social snobbery: In *Life After Television*, which Gilder published just a few years later, he extended his populist revolt to the culture industry as well. Armed with a new "law" he had dreamed up that could over-awe just about anything (now it was the "law of the telecosm," according to which the "total value" of computers in a network is really, really big), Gilder again called for the final destruction of all kinds of cultural hierarchy. Now it was those top-down TV broadcasters who were doomed, as the telecosm went about "moving authority from elites and establishments to creators and customers."[48] This time Gilder's target was a more traditionally populist one: the old-line networks and film studios (newspapers, for some reason, are predicted to survive) which, Gilder asserts, have controlled our national culture for so long.* We the People were to be fantastically empowered, no longer staring dully at our "idiot boxes" but participating in making our own culture inter-actively. Along the way, though, some of us were becoming vastly more empowered than others. The heroes of Gilder's populism are men of colossal fortunes and arcane financial manipulation: Bill Gates, Andy Grove, John Malone, Michael Milken. It is a populism that, even as it allows us to choose from more entertainment than ever before, serves to transfer the wealth of the nation upward in a gigantic heave-ho.

The market, freed up by the microchip, will take down all hierar-chies and disperse all clusters of concentrated power: This would soon become a profoundly influential idea. That is, it would become an in-fluential idea once it had been separated from Gilder the person. Gilder's backlash background made him a figure of some embarass-ment to even the most committed Internet boosters, people with little use for the Christian right or any of Gilder's other former con-stituents.[49] Although Gilder would continue to cover the industry and offer influential predictions from the pages of *Forbes ASAP,* the maga-

---

*In making this critique Gilder entered into a fairly massive contradiction of his usual market populism. Not only was he now embracing the TV-as-manipulator critique that conservatives generally shun and deride, he was announcing that consuming a product—or watching a TV show—really *wasn't* the same as voting for it after all. Hav-ing spent years trumpeting the democracy of markets, Gilder seemed here to be ad-mitting that markets weren't democratic at all before the advent of the microchip.

zine started as his very own "editorial pulpit," he remained a hopeless square, still photographed always in a tie even into the late nineties and refusing ever to disavow his now deeply unfashionable ideas about feminism and minorities (he did make some progress on a rapprochement with the counterculture).[50]

But in other showplaces of Internet ideology Gilder's populism was being successfully grafted onto a different "people" altogether: the libertarian hipster, the Republican Deadhead, the rock 'n' rolling millionaire, the dope-smoking stockbroker. Although you can find such figures in full cry almost anywhere on the Web, we will for sake of brevity focus first on Jon Katz, the veteran journalist who wrote media criticism for the computer industry magazine *Wired*. Katz took to the work with considerable ferocity, pounding the "old media" with a piercingly populist critique. The signal failing of American journalism, according to Katz, was its "arrogance and elitism," a charge he lifted directly from the backlash playbook (remember Limbaugh's war on "media elites") but which he updated with the now-standard patter about the democracy of listening. Referring to *The New Yorker*, he wrote, "This clearly seems like a publication that doesn't relish the idea of hearing from too many of the foul-mouthed and unschooled masses. Its objective is to talk, not listen." The term "elitism," as he used it, designated not the owning class but a certain attitude towards the people and towards popular intelligence. Thus the "elitism" of "the Pundits," a group for whom Katz reserved his most venomous attacks, was established by the assertion that "they accused you of being civically dumb, apathetic, and ignorant." But such contempt for the public mind, Katz assured us, could never take place on the Net, this "new, democratic, many-to-many model of communication." So effervescently populist is this new medium that almost anything or anybody associated with it comes off as a friend of the People.[51]

Katz's most important turn on the national stage came in December 1997, when he announced from the pages of *Wired* that the Web, this hyper democratic medium, had given birth to a powerful new voting bloc ("digital citizens") who would soon be forcing their intensely laissez-faire politics on the nation. The idea that the Internet was libertarian by nature and would transform people to suit its pro-market views had been proposed first by Gilder and would by the end of the nineties become something of an accepted bit of journalistic wisdom, but Katz's story was the turning point, the journalistic place where the ascendency of market populism over backlash populism was made concrete by the pseudo-science of polling. The story went like this: *Wired,* acting in conjunction with stockbrokerage house Merrill Lynch, had commissioned a study of the attitudes of technology users from the famous conservative pollster Frank Luntz, and Katz had been tapped to reveal the findings to the public. Not surprisingly, those who used e-mail, cell phones, beepers, laptops, and had a computer at their homes—the "digital citizens"—were found to "worship free markets," to believe that companies were more important than government, and to accept certain of the hot ideas of contemporary management theory. To this Katz added a few of his own characteristic populist flourishes: The "digital citizen's" love for markets did not simply indicate that he or she wished to stay at the top of the American class system, because he or she was deeply hostile to "rigidly formalized authority." In fact, these market-worshipping Internet users were "startlingly close to the Jeffersonian ideal." Naturally, those who opposed the pro-corporate beliefs of this hot new demographic were dismissed as "political and intellectual elites," tired relics of the old system who "remind [Katz] of the hoary old men in the Kremlin . . . during the dying days of communism. . . ."[52]

But it was left to Frank Luntz himself, writing in a sidebar to Katz's screed, to drop the biggest bomb. These "digital citizens," with their overpowering "faith in business and technology," represented nothing less than "the future." They were the "most politically important demographic group of our era," and politicians with a mind to winning elections "shouldn't even dream of talking to them about the past." Thus did the new order announce its arrival a year before the culture wars finally burned themselves out in the insane melodrama of impeachment: A new constituency for the free market had arrived just in time to supplant the old constituency for the free market. And this time it was having none of the nostalgia of the older variety. It didn't care about the lost fifties. It didn't care about family values. All it wanted was the government off its back—and off the back of the bankers, the manufacturers, and the e-traders, while they were at it.[53]

In *Wired* itself hipness, and the free-market politics to which the Web was wedding it, came together in a mixture of boastful "radicalism" and an almost deranged optimism. The magazine's fifth anniversary issue showed this stealth-reactionary style at its most blaring: Someone from the libertarian Cato Institute declaring the lifespan of *Wired* to be the "five greatest years for humanity" ever; software designer Jaron Lanier announcing that "we are witnessing the most productive, intelligent, and optimistic example of youthful rebellion in the history of the world"; Gilder himself stating matter-of-factly, "The last five years have seen . . . the final overthrow of the tyranny of matter"; and an editorial broadside booming, "In this economy, our ability to create wealth is not bound by physical limits, but by our ability to come up with new ideas—in other words, it's unlimited." All of which sat easily side by side with more ordinary corporate salivating: Walter Wriston opining that the power of "government" is being reduced and the institution is in danger of being replaced—not by Citibank, but by "everybody"; a *Wired* editor instructing us to think of the state as just another "medium, a way of expressing the popular will," and as such subject to supercession (or "disintermediation," a favorite expression of that year) by the Internet; and someone from the libertarian magazine *Reason* who's come up with yet another inventive way to compare government regulators to racists and Communists. But what made *Wired* so effective were the layers and layers of knowing, future-wise "radicalism." *Wired* didn't just give us the wisdom of bankers, but the wisdom of bankers—and photos of the radical, mysterious Burning Man festival! Calls for deregulation—and a story admiring the "heavy-duty, radically defiant, street-level" hippies of St. Petersburg, Russia! Salutes to "open markets"—and pictures of cartoon characters farting mischievously, great gusts of brown wind puffing from their little pixellated anuses![54]

These things are amusing, and they are sometimes so ephemeral it is difficult to imagine that they have any significance at all. But they matter. It is worth examining the way business talks about itself, the fantasies it spins, the role it writes for itself in our lives. It is important to pay attention when CEOs tell the world they would rather surf than pray, show up at work in Speedos rather than suits, hang out in Goa rather than Newport, listen to Stone Temple Pilots rather than Sibelius. It is not important, however, in the way they imagine it is, and for many Americans it is understandably difficult to care very much whether the guy who owns their company is a defender of family values or a rave kid. But culture isn't set off from life in a realm all its own, and the culture of business in particular has massive consequences for the way the rest of us live. Consider the notion of the "New Economy" with which the last chapter began. While there are of course genuine economic changes underway in America (as there have always been), this idea is in large part not about economies at all but about ways of thinking about economies. It's a set of beliefs (importantly, beliefs first enunciated by Ronald Reagan)[55] that, once enacted into public policy, has permitted an upward transfer of wealth unprecedented in our lifetimes; it's a collection of symbols and narratives that understand the resulting wealth polarization as a form of populism, as an expression of the people's will.

And yet the "New Economy" is a fraud. Tom Friedman's formula, "one dollar, one vote," is not the same thing as universal suffrage, as the complex, hard-won array of rights that most Americans understand as their political heritage. Nor does it mitigate the obscenity of wealth polarization one whit when the richest people ever in history tell us they are "listening" to us, that theirs are "interactive" fortunes, or that they have unusual tastes and work particularly hard. Markets may look like democracy, in that we are all involved in their making, but they are fundamentally not democratic. We did not vote for Bill Gates; we didn't all sit down one day and agree that we should only use his operating system and we should pay for it just however much he thinks is right. We do not go off to our jobs checking telephone lines or making cold calls or driving a forklift every morning because this is what we want to do; we do it because we have to, because it is the only way we can afford food, shelter, and medicine. The logic of business is coercion, monopoly, and the destruction of the weak, not "choice" or "service" or universal affluence.

"Democracies prefer markets but markets do not prefer democracies," writes political scientist Benjamin Barber in *Jihad vs. McWorld*, one of the most thoughtful recent books on the new capitalism. "Having created the conditions that make markets possible, democracy must also do all the things that markets undo or cannot do."[56] Markets are interested in profits and profits only; service, quality, and general affluence are different functions altogether. The universal, democratic prosperity that Americans now look back to with such nostalgia was achieved only by a colossal reining in of markets, by the gargantuan effort of mass, popular organizations like labor unions and of the people themselves, working through a series of democratically elected governments not daunted by the myths of the market.

The same thinkers who lead us in believing that all government is essentially equivalent to the Soviet dictatorship have a word for the argument that I make in these pages: They call it "cynicism." One comes across denunciations of this "cynicism" constantly: from the promoters of the new civility, from public journalists, from advertising executives, from "futurists," from management theorists, from stock market gurus.[57] The correct intellectual posture, they admonish, is the simple faith of childhood. Children of the most exaggerated guilelessness turn up everywhere in the corporate speech of the nineties, hailing the glory of the Internet, announcing corporate mergers, staring awestruck at new computers, clarifying the bounds of history, explaining the fantastic surge of the Dow, and raising their winsome voices to proclaim the unanswerable new management logic that showed—as all previous management logics had also shown—just why it was that labor must submit to capital. The masters of the "New Economy" may fancy themselves an exalted race of divinities, but they counsel the rest of us to become as little children before the market.

The Democracy Bubble

> It does not redeem the situation that these kings and chiefs
> of industry are not chosen upon the hereditary principle
> (sometimes, alas! they are) but are men who have risen by
> their own capacity, sometimes from utter obscurity, with the
> freedom of self-assertion which should characterize a free so-
> ciety. Their power is none the less arbitrary and irresponsible
> when obtained. That a peasant may become king does not
> render the kingdom democratic.   —*Woodrow Wilson, 1910*

Year 1 in the Republic of Al

The Dow Jones Industrial Average finally crossed the 10,000 mark in
March 1999, a figure so incomprehensibly great that it was anyone's
guess what it signified. The leaders of American opinion reacted as
though we had achieved some heroic national goal, as though, through
some colossal feat of collective optimism, we had entered at long last
into the promised land of riches for all. On television the endless
rounds of triumphal self-congratulation paused for a nasty rebuke to
the very idea of financial authority, brought to you by the online brokerage E*Trade, a company that prospered as magnificently as any
from the record-breaking run-up: "Your investments helped pay for this
dream house," declared a snide voice-over. "Unfortunately, it belongs to
your broker." And behold: There was the scoundrel himself, dressed in

a fine suit and climbing out of a Rolls Royce with a haughty-looking woman on his arm. Go ahead and believe it, this sponsor cajoled: Wall Street is just as corrupt, as elitist, and as contemptuous toward its clients as you've always suspected. Later commercials in the series proposed an opposite but equally malevolent stereotype: Broker as buffoon, cramming himself into the subway every morning and making pathetic cold calls to uninterested strangers. Either way you wanted none of it: You would have no more intermediaries between you and the national ATM machine in downtown Manhattan. You wanted to plug yourself in directly to the source of the millions, subvert the hierarchy of financial authority once and for all. "Now the power is in your hands."

In the rival series of investment fairy tales broadcast by the Discover online brokerage (a curious corporate hybrid of Sears and J. P. Morgan), a cast of rude, dismissive executives, yawning and scowling, were getting well-deserved payback at the hands of an array of humble everymen. Again the tables of traditional workplace authority were rudely overturned by the miracle of online investing: The tow truck drivers, hippies, grandmas, and bartenders to whom the hateful company men had so condescended were revealed to be Midases in disguise who, with a little help from the Discover system, now owned their own countries, sailed yachts, hobnobbed with royalty, and performed corporate buyouts—all while clinging to their humble, unpretentious ways and appearances just for fun. And oh, how the suits squirmed as their social order was turned upside down![1]

In the commercials for *his* online brokerage, Charles Schwab appeared in honest black-and-white, informing viewers in his down-home way how his service worked, how it cut through the usual Wall Street song and dance, how you could now look up information from your own home. "It's the final step in demystification," he said quite evenly. "This Internet stuff is about freedom. You're in control." To illustrate the point, other Schwab commercials paraded before viewers a cast of regular people (their names were given as "Howard," "Rick," and "Marion") who shared, in what looked like documentary footage, their matter-of-fact relationship with the market—the ways they used Schwab-dot-com to follow prices, how they bought on the dips, how they now performed all sorts of once-arcane financial operations completely on their own. To underscore the implication that the stock market was all about Rick's and Marion's power, not Charlie Schwab's, other spots showed his non-hotshot, non-threatening brokers in action, one of whom was actually blind.

In another of the great stock market parables of that golden year, the Ricks and Marions of the world were imagined in a far more insurgent light. Here the common people were shown smashing their way into the stock exchange, breaking down its pretentious doors, pouring through its marble corridors, smashing the visitors' gallery windows and sending a rain of shards down on the money changers in the pit—all to an insurgent worldbeat tune. As it turned out, this glimpse of the People triumphant in revolution—one of the only times, in that century of red-hunting and labor-warring, that Americans had been encouraged by one of the great broadcasting networks to understand such imagery in a positive light—was brought to you not by the IWW but by Datek, still another online trading house. What the people were overthrowing was not capitalism itself but merely the senseless "wall" that the voice-over claimed always "stood between you and serious trading."[2]

Exactly! As the century spun to an end it occurred to more and more of the market's biggest boosters that "revolution" was precisely what was going on here. Thus the owners of *Individual Investor* magazine decided in late 1999 that the thing to do to promote their entry into the already crowded field of personal finance serials was to send gangs of costumed guerrillas dressed in berets and armbands around Manhattan to pass out copies of an "Investment Manifesto" hailing the "inalienable right" of "every man and woman . . . to make money—and lots of it."[3]

Meanwhile, the National Association of Real Estate Investment Trusts ran ads in print and on TV in which a casually dressed father and his young son capered around the towering office blocks of a big city. "Do we own all this, Dad?" queried the tot. "In a way we do," answered his father. This land is their land—not because they have bought it outright, like Al, the country-owning tow truck driver in the Discover spots, but in a more populist, Woody Guthrie sort of way: Because they have invested in REITs.[4]

Not to be outdone by such heavy-handed 1930s-style imagery, J. P. Morgan, the very personification of Wall Street's former power and arrogance, filled its ads with hyper-realistic black-and-white close-ups of its employees, many of them nonwhite or nonmale. Literally putting a face on the secretive WASP redoubt of financial legend, the ads sought to establish that Morgan brokers, like Schwab brokers, were a humble lot. "I will take my clients seriously," read one. "And myself, less so."[5] The ads even gave the names and e-mail addresses of the Morgan employees in question, a remarkable move for a firm whose principal had once been so uninterested in serving members of the general public that he boasted to Congress that he didn't even put the company's name on its outside door.

Faced with this universal embrace of its original populist campaign against Wall Street, E*Trade tried to push the trope even further: The changes in American investing habits that had brought it such success were in fact nothing less than a social "revolution," an uprising comparable to the civil rights and feminist movements. In its 1999 annual report, entitled "From One Revolution to the Next," E*Trade used photos of black passengers sitting in the back of a bus ("1964: They Said Equality Was Only For Some of Us") and pre-emancipated white women sitting in the hilarious hair dryers of the 1960s ("1973: They Said Women Would Never Break Through the Glass Ceiling") to establish itself as the rightful inheritor of the spirit of "revolution." The brokerage firm made it clear that the enemy to be overthrown on *its* sector of the front was social class: Next to a photo of a suit and a row of doric columns a page of text proclaimed, "They said there are 'the haves' and the 'have-nots.' " But E*Trade, that socialist of the stock exchange, was changing all that: "In the 21st century it's about leveling the playing field and democratizing individual personal financial services." The company's CEO concluded this exercise in pseudo-radical chest-thumping with this funky rallying cry: "Bodacious! The revolution continues."[6]

Whatever mysterious forces were propelling the market in that witheringly hot summer of 1999, the crafters of its public facade seemed to agree that what was really happening was the arrival, at long last, of economic democracy. While the world of finance had once been a stronghold of WASP privilege, an engine of elite enrichment, journalist and PR man alike agreed that it had now been transformed utterly, been opened to all. This bull market was the Götterdämmerung of the ruling class, the final victory of the common people over their former overlords. Usually this "democratization" was spoken of as a sort of social uprising, a final routing of the snobbish old guard culture of Wall Street. Sometimes it was said to be the market itself that had worked these changes, that had humiliated the suits, that had handed out whole islands to auto mechanics, that had permitted little old ladies to cavort with kings. Sometimes "democratization" was described as a demographic phenomenon, a reflection of the vast percentage of the nation's population now entrusting their savings to the market. Although the figures varied depending on the source and the requirements at hand, whether it was a whopping 60 percent, a still-staggering 40 percent, or a feeble 20 percent, it was a figure that exerted the same awesome power over the popular imagination of the 1990s that the percentage of the population under thirty had in the 1960s: It was said to demonstrate a vast sea change in American thinking about money and business, a mounting tidal wave that one either surfed or succumbed to.[7]

Your Share of America

However bodacious the E*Trade "revolution" might have seemed to the company's CEO, the notion of a democratized Wall Street was not a novel development, unique to the 1990s. Like Henry Ford "democratizing" the automobile or Coca-Cola bringing Tab to the masses, the investment industry has always had an obvious financial interest in encouraging the general public to entrust it with our savings. Mass participation in securities markets always brings, at the very least, increased demand for stocks and hence ascending prices, not to mention the commissions that brokers charge for their services.

Less often remarked is the industry's—and the wider business community's—*ideological* interest in the democratization of Wall Street. Every historical movement to rein in Wall Street; every argument for regulating or otherwise controlling American business has taken as its starting point the imperatives of democracy. Financial practices, reformers have charged again and again, stand in flagrant violation of our common values of justice, equality, and universal representation. In the nineties, though, the narrative of populist Wall Street seemed to prove the exact opposite: Popular *participation* in the stock market amounted to popular *sanction* of both the processes of the exchange and the corporations whose shares were traded. When pundits spoke of the stock market having been "democratized," they implied that the market now functioned like a democracy; that the market represented the people, that it acted on the people's behalf, that it spoke in the vox populi. Markets were not merely organs of exchange, they were a never-ending election that had, in Thomas Friedman's phrase, "turned the whole world into a parliamentary system," a place where people "vote every hour, every day through their mutual funds, their pension funds, their brokers, and, more and more, from their own basements via the internet."[8] The NYSE, once the locus of elite power, had become a national town meeting, its daily tickings up or down as much an expression of the people's will as of economic well-being. The bull market of the nineties was to be nothing less than the People's Market, a combination voting booth and prosperity machine for the common man.

So just as efficient market theory holds that stock markets process economic data quickly and flawlessly, American commentators came to believe that stock markets perform pretty much the same operation with the general will, endlessly adjusting and modifying themselves in conformity with the vast and otherwise enigmatic popular mind. Public participation in the stock market, then, was evidence of that most ardently desired ideological objective of all: popular consent to the deeds of American business. Thus it was the miracle of the Dow that provided the evangelists of the New Economy with one of their most potent economic arguments. Second only to the fall of Communism as "proof" of the historical correctness of the corporate way, the ever-ascending Dow was what put the self-assured swagger in the "New Economy" consensus, what permitted Bill Clinton and his allies to declare that they alone could see the path of democratic righteousness, what put the seal of public approval on the politics of privatization, deregulation, deunionization, and the downgrading of the welfare state. Partisans of the new corporate order the world over pointed to the performance of the American stock markets the way politicians point to the "mandate" given them by landslide electoral victories. The ever-rising Dow was the ideological trump card that allowed the faithful to dismiss doubters with an almost mathematical certainty: After all, the naysayers said what they did when it was still at 7000, or even when it stood at a mere 5000.[9]

It was also the market's spectacular deeds that propelled so many of the myths and fad notions of the nineties. If we needed the vapid pseudo-philosophy of Suze Orman to help us deal with our riches, it was because our investments had been compounding so nicely of late. If our boss had "moved our cheese" down to the unemployment line, he had probably done so in order to enhance the value of his own shares in the company. If there was a boom in the construction of suburban mansions, a steady increase in the price of cigars or yachts, it was due to the magical goings-on at the blessed intersection of Broad and Wall.

Wall Street itself had even better reasons to understand public participation as "democratization." As symbol and as a real center of American capitalism, the financial industry has both the most to lose from a resurgence of antibusiness sentiment and the most to gain from the

ideological victory of market populism. For a hundred years the financial industry had been the chief target of populist reformers of all
kinds; for sixty years banks, brokers, and exchanges have labored at
least partially under the regulations those earlier populists proposed.
And Wall Street has never forgotten the melodrama of crash, arrogance, and New Deal reform that gave birth to those regulations. To
this day Wall Street leaders see the possibility of a revived New Deal
spirit around every corner; they fight not merely to keep the interfering
liberals out of power, but to keep order in their own house, to ensure
that the public relations debacle of 1929–32 is never repeated. This is
why so much of the bull market culture of the nineties reads like a long
gloss on the experience of the 1930s, like a subconscious battle with
the memory of the Depression.

That the literature of the financial industry is animated by an ongoing need to preempt criticism and suppress doubt can be seen in even
the most quotidian documents. In the aftermath of various revelations
of unsavory practices by day-trading firms in August 1999, for example,
the *Wall Street Journal* editorialized in favor of stringent self-policing
lest the "politicians . . . descend in force to impose regulations that
could hamstring the markets and shut down the good times for everybody." As a warning of what could come "if businessmen don't do their
own dirty laundry," the *Journal* referred explicitly to the hated Glass-
Steagall banking law, passed amid the revelations of the early thirties.[10]
It didn't matter that years of spectacular gains had largely drowned out
such criticism or that the Glass-Steagall act itself was about to be repealed: the war went on.

Fearing that a replay of the Glass-Steagall catastrophe lurks forever
just offstage, Wall Street leaders take any opportunity to turn the populist tables, to identify themselves with the tastes, mores, and aspirations of the vast American middle. This was the greatest promise of the
"democratization" of the nineties: If the interests of the Street had
once been identified with the arrogance of J. P. Morgan, now the industry was one with the people. Again, a workaday example drawn
from the *Wall Street Journal* editorial page, in this case a March 1996

denunciation of a proposed increase in capital gains taxes as a delusion of "the reactionary left" on the grounds that it posited a class divide between average people and financiers—or between "Wall Street and Main Street," to use what would become one of the decade's favorite phrases—that no longer existed "in the decade of the mutual fund pension." After all, the newspaper pointed out (without benefit of evidence), "Wall Street's junk bond demons created Main Street's jobs."[11] According to the new populism, it was the market that spoke for the people, and the would-be taxers, regulators, and critics of Wall Street who were the elitists.

And if you pushed the notion of "democratization" a little—took some chances, transgressed some boundaries—you could imagine much more than that. Just as the irresistible power of the "New Economy" was said to be forcing the US to raze the welfare state, the new, more public orientation of the stock market could be summoned forth as evidence of the new capitalism's social beneficence. In fact, there was a real ideological diversity to stocks. If you thought about them just right, it seemed, you could imagine stocks as a substitute for pretty nearly every aspect of the social order of the thirties, as American business's answer to the New Deal, complete with the cultural trimmings.

Before we proceed, however, let us be clear about the stock market's actual contributions to economic democracy in the United States. However widely dispersed stock ownership may have become in recent years, the vast majority of shares are still held by the wealthy. It is this simple, incontestable fact of American life that, more than almost anything else, has permitted the massive skewing of wealth distribution in the last two decades. Stocks are the economic engine that has generally made the rich so very much richer than the rest of us, first through the bull market of the eighties and then through the bull market of the nineties. There is no controversy or secrecy about these facts: Even an economist as partial to the "New Economy" as Lester Thurow acknowledges that America's widening inequality can be attributed directly to the rising stock market. A full 86 percent of the market's advances in the last four years of the bull market, he points out, went to the wealthiest 10 percent of the population. The majority of the population, not owning any stock, shared in the great money handout not at all.[12] The booming stock market of the nineties did not democratize wealth; it concentrated wealth.

Nor did stock prices reflect the growing prosperity of middle America. On the contrary, throughout the nineties stock prices consistently rallied on news that wages were lagging. The opposite was also true: Reports of even marginal wage increases were sufficient throughout the duration of the People's Market to send the Dow into terrible fits and faints. And while millions of average white- and blue-collar workers (including this author) saw their pension plans, 401(k)s, and IRAs appreciate nicely thanks to the deeds of the Dow, this hardly made up for the weak performance of wages. After all, workers can hardly be expected to own shares if they can't afford them. And even if everything went well—the market continued to perform so miraculously and all of us picked stocks that went up—the resulting gains would only ensure a few years of secure retirement in the distant future, not ease in the here-and-now.

As for the notion of representation through stockholding, it is important to remember that "one dollar, one vote" is the definition of plutocracy, not democracy. While it is true that even the smallest of shareholders is entitled to attend companies' annual meetings and help themselves to the free radishes and nonalcoholic beer dispensed there, their votes are, in almost all cases, woefully insignificant in comparison to the massive clout wielded by institutional investors. In the case of mutual funds and pension plans, the instruments most frequently cited for their democratizing effects, individuals have even less of a voice. The voting is done for them—and by law, in the case of certain union pensions—by the manager of their plan or mutual fund.

Regardless of how we think about stocks or exactly how we kneel during our prayers to Wall Street, the nine years (as of this writing) of the last bull market only worsened what was already a spectacularly

backward distribution of national wealth. Any claim that mass participation in the market has in some way brought economic democracy to
the United States is false in a prima facie sense.

But this is a book about the faiths and beliefs of business, and in
this strictly cultural sense the notion of economic democracy through
investing has proven not only durable but irresistible. As a faith, as a
simple, abiding belief, market populism is capable of answering all
doubts and silencing all doubters. Take those stagnant-to-declining
real wages of American workers, for example. The market doesn't rally
upon hearing bad news just because it's perverse or because brokers
enjoy the spectacle of human suffering. In point of fact, according to
the reigning pop-economic theorists of recent years, the stock market
is very much part of the problem here: A central principle of "New
Economy" thought is that corporate growth and productivity gains in
the new era have been rightfully severed from wage increases and
handed over instead to top management and shareholders. And, since
the redistributionist policies of "big government" are now as impermis-
sible as labor organizing, stocks of necessity have become the sole legitimate avenue for the redistribution of wealth. In other eras such an
arrangement would have seemed an obvious earmark of a badly mal-
functioning economic system, a system designed to funnel everything
into the pockets of the already wealthy, since that's who owns most of
the stock.

But toss the idea of an ongoing financial "democratization" into the
mix, and presto: Now the lopsided transformation of productivity gains
into shareholder value is an earmark of *fairness*—because those shareholders are us! Sure, workers here and there are going down, but most
of us, through the miracle of stocks, are on our way up. Furthermore,
ownership of stock among workers themselves, it was sometimes argued, more than made up for the decade's stagnant wages. Workers'
portfolios would surge in exact proportion to every management depre-
dation! Line workers and organization men alike would get rich even as
they were fired! What capital took away with one hand, it was reasoned, it gave back with the other—and with interest.

This idea of stock prices compensating for lost or stagnant wages has long been a favorite ideological hobbyhorse of the corporate right, implying as it did that wealth was created not on the factory floor but on Wall Street and that workers only shared in it through the grace of their options-granting CEO. But as the NASDAQ proceeded from triumph to triumph, economists and politicians of both parties came around to this curious notion, imagining that we had somehow wandered into a sort of free-market magic kingdom, where ever-ascending stock prices could be relied upon to solve just about any social problem. Now we could have it all: We could slash away at the welfare state, hobble the unions, downsize the workforce, send the factories to Mexico—*and no one would get hurt!*

Naturally the idea was first sailed out for public viewing in the aftermath of a serious public relations crisis for Wall Street. One fine day in January 1996, AT&T announced it was cutting forty thousand white-collar jobs from its workforce; in response Wall Street turned cartwheels of joy, sending the company's price north and personally enriching the company's CEO, Robert Allen, by some five million dollars. The connection of the two events was impossible to overlook, as was its meaning: What's bad for workers is good for Wall Street. Within days the company was up to its neck in old economy-style vituperation from press and politicians alike. Then a golden voice rang through the din, promoting a simple and "purely capitalist" solution to "this heartless cycle": "Let Them Eat Stock," proclaimed one James Cramer from the cover of *The New Republic.* "Just give the laid-off employees stock options," suggested Cramer, a hedge fund manager by trade who in his spare time dispensed investment advice on TV and in magazines, and "let them participate in the stock appreciation that their firings caused." There was, of course, no question as to whether AT&T was in the right in what it had done: "the need to be competitive" justified all. It's just that such brusque doings opened the door to cranks and naysayers who could potentially make things hot for Wall Street. Buttressing his argument with some neat numbers proving that, given enough options, the downsized could soon be—yes—*millionaires,*

Cramer foresaw huge benefits for all. Options would not only make everyone rich, they were wonder-working cynicism-abatement devices. Significantly, Cramer noted that no company then offered such a "stock option severance plan." But the principle was the thing, and in principle one could not hold the stock market responsible; in principle the interests of all parties concerned could be fairly met without recourse to such market-hostile tools as government or unions.[13]

And in ideology all one requires is principle. Thus it turned out to be a short walk indeed from Cramer's modest proposal to a generalized belief in the possibility of real social redress through stocks—as though stock ownership by workers was something that actually took place on a huge scale, something that happened all the time. After all, since anyone could buy stocks, we had only ourselves to blame if we didn't share in the joy. The argument was an extremely flexible one, capable of materializing in nearly any circumstance. In a November 1999 think-piece addressing the problem of union workers angered by international trade agreements that made no provision for labor rights, a *New York Times* writer found that they suffered from "confusion" since even as they protested, their 401(k)s were "spiking upward" due to "ever-freer trade."[14] To Lester Thurow, the answer to massive and growing inequality was not to redistribute wealth or reorganize the economy but to "widen the skill base" so that anyone could "work for entrepreneurial companies" and thus have access to stock options.[15] For lesser bull market rhapsodists the difference between "could" and "is" simply disappeared in the blissful haze. Egalitarian options were peeking out of every pocket. The cover of the July 1999 issue of *Money* carried a photo of a long line of diverse, smiling workers—a familiar populist archetype—under the caption, "The employees of Actuate all get valuable stock options." Inside, the magazine enthused about how options "are winding up in the shirt pockets of employees with blue collars, plaid collars and, increasingly, no collars at all" (this last being especially significant since the only option beneficiary the article profiled was a "software engineer" who dreams of millionairehood while mountain biking). By decade's end the myth of the wage/stock tradeoff was so widely accepted that its truest believers were able to present it as a historical principle, as our final payoff for enduring all those years of deindustrialization and downsizing. In a January 2000 *Wall Street Journal* feature story on how the good times were filtering down to the heartland folks of Akron, Ohio—a Rust Belt town hit hard by the capital flight of the seventies and eighties—the soaring stock market was asserted to have gone "a long way in supplanting the insecurity of the 1980s, when the whole notion of employment for life was shattered, with something else: a sense of well-being." Yes, their factories had closed—but just look at them now! The *Journal* found a blue-collar Akron resident who played golf! And an entrepreneur who drove a *Mercedes!*[16] Who needed government when they had options?

It may have been fun to imagine what these enchanted options could do in the service of economic democracy, but in point of fact their powers were almost always directed the other way. Options did not bring about some sort of "New Economy" egalitarianism; they were one of the greatest causes of the ever widening income gap. It was options that inflated the take-home pay of CEOs to a staggering 475 times what their average line-worker made; it was options that made downsizing, outsourcing, and union-busting so profitable. When options *were* given out to employees—a common enough practice in Silicon Valley by decade's end—they often came in lieu of wages, thus permitting firms to conceal their payroll expenses and artificially inflate the price of their shares, pumping the bubble still further.[17] Options were a tool of wealth concentration, a bridge straight to the nineteenth century.

And yet the bull market faithful found it next to impossible to talk about options in this way. Only one interpretation, one explanatory framework seemed to be permissible when speaking of investing or finance—the onward march of democracy. Anything could be made to fit—the popularity of day-trading, the growth of the mutual fund industry, the demise of Barings bank, the collapse of the Thai currency. The bubble being blown on Wall Street was an ideological one as much as it was anything else, with succeeding interpretations constantly heightening the rhetoric of populist glory being heaped on the exchange. It was an "investing revolution." It was all about "empowerment."

And there were incredible prizes to be won as long as the democracy bubble continued to swell, as the notion of Wall Street as an alternative to democratic government became more and more plausible. Maybe the Glass-Steagall Act could finally be repealed; maybe the SEC could finally be grounded; maybe antitrust could finally be halted. And, most enticingly of all, maybe Social Security could at last be "privatized" in accordance with the right-wing fantasy of long standing. True, it would be a staggering historical reversal for Democrats—the party that had traditionally campaigned against the "economic royalists" of Wall Street and that had encumbered the financial industry with the various hated reforms of the 1930s—to consider such a scheme, but actually seeing it through would require an even more substantial change of image on Wall Street's part. In order to claim the massive "windfall"[18] that Social Security would represent, Wall Street would have to convince the nation that it was worthy of the charge, that it was as public-minded and considerate of the little fellow as Franklin Roosevelt himself had been. Although one mutual fund company actually attempted this directly—showing footage of FDR signing the Social Security Act in 1935 and proclaiming, "Today, we're picking up where he left off"[19]—most chose a warmer, vaguer route, showing us heroic tableaux of hardy midwesterners buying and holding amid the Nebraska corn, of World War II vets day-trading from their suburban rec rooms, of athletes talking like insiders, of church ladies phoning in their questions to the commentator on CNBC; of mom and pop posting their very own fire-breathing defenses of Microsoft on the boards at Silicon Investor. This was a boom driven by democracy itself, a boom of infinite possibilities, a boom that could never end.

As the true believers began to see that the bull market stretched out before them to the furthest horizon, they began also to notice that it had been around for an unusually long time—that it was in fact very close to being a *permanent* bull market. For the technically inclined the boom's starting date was March 1991, making it the longest bull market on record. But in the latter years of the decade the long bull market began to take on even more awesome attributes. Endless stock market prosperity was a "new paradigm," not simply a bull market, and the faithful now saw it stretching all the way back to 1982, uninterrupted by the crash of 1987 or the disruptions during the Gulf War, reaching generously back to shower its blessings on old Ronald Reagan himself—the patron saint of CEO enrichment, bogus populism, and the union-free workplace.[20] After all, if the Dow could grow from 3,000 to 12,000, why couldn't it be eighteen years old instead of nine?

Ah, they were gorgeous dreams indeed, these rosy fantasies of the People and their Dow. And it was this notion of market democracy, amplified by the repetition of thousands of journalists in hundreds of books and magazines, by the words of the hopeful in online chatrooms, as much as any mundane factor like greed or earnings or growth, that propelled the averages up and up, on through the limits of the old bull markets, on into democratic ecstasies unknown and uncharted. This was a magic boom, a romp that grew back into the past even as it ascended into the heavens, a frolic that defied the very rules of unemployment and "wage inflation," as workers—charmed too, no doubt, by the ubiquitous upward curve—virtuously refused to demand higher wages. It was prosperity as an act of populist faith, a People's boom driven by memories of Capra movies and Norman Rockwell paintings, by pureness of heart and steadfastness of faith.

The Madness of Crowds

It pleased financial commentators of the 1990s to believe that the "democratization" of Wall Street was a unique, even an epochal, plate-shifting development. In fact, mass public enthusiasm for stocks has been a recurring feature of American life since the earliest days of American industry. Here is how Henry Adams, writing in 1870, described the Civil War speculative boom:

By means of this simple and smooth [investment] machinery, which differs in no essential respect from the processes of roulette or *rouge-et-noir,* the whole nation flung itself into the Stock Exchange, until the "outsiders," as they were called, in opposition to the regular brokers . . . represented nothing less than the entire population of the American Republic. Every one speculated, and for a time every one speculated successfully.[21]

As public enthusiasm can contribute mightily to prices, Wall Street has great interests in encouraging it, in enlisting the savings of the millions. It is thus, in addition to being a place of rigorous fiscal calculation and economic realpolitik, a land of obsessive optimism, of nonstop PR, of mass salesmanship. In *The Great Crash,* John Kenneth Galbraith observed that manic bull markets require not just sound numbers but relentless "incantation," a veritable army of pundits and PR men to engage the public in a "process of reassurance."[22]

It is this requirement that brings on one of the most ironic aspects of Wall Street culture: its intermittent but torrid love affair with the language of populism. For the original Populists and their successors, of course, Wall Street had always been the locus of the greatest financial evil of them all, the faceless "money power" that senselessly and arrogantly brought boom or bust, flush times or despair, prosperity or ruin to industries, businessmen, and workers alike. Wall Street was what the common people had to rally *against.* But Wall Street has continually worked to turn the language of populism around, to identify itself as a responsible organ of the popular will. Charles Merrill, for example, understood the mission of the great brokerage that he founded in 1940 as "bringing Main Street to Wall Street."[23] According to the slogan adopted by the New York Stock Exchange in the 1950s, investing allowed you to "Own your share of America."

But the best-known antecedent of the People's Market of the nineties was the boom of the 1920s. "Antecedent," though, is too weak a word: The parallels between that bull market and this one are so painfully clear that all the overheated market populism of recent years

sometimes seems like a permanent feature of the American imagination, present always just beneath the surface and ready to flow forth at
the slightest hint of prolonged good times. Like the People's Market of
recent years, the bull market of the twenties was said to be a democratic phenomenon, one in which an unprecedented proportion of the population was participating.[24] Friendly economists, then as now, spoke of
permanent prosperity and a "New Era" of industrial organization and
economic democracy. (While financial writers of the nineties generally
preferred the phrases "New Economy" or "New Paradigm," the very
term "New Era" actually came briefly into fashion again in 1999 as they
searched for a fresh neologism.)[25] The New Era, like our own New
Economy, was powered by an unshakable faith in the long-term return
of common stocks and by sudden manias for companies whose business
had to do with new communications technologies.[26] Like the boom of
the nineties, that of the twenties boasted a cast of popular financial heroes, ethnic outsiders like Joseph Kennedy, Mike Meehan, and Bernard
Baruch, who served as symbolic confirmation that Wall Street was no
longer an exclusive precinct of the traditional ruling class. In the 1920s,
as now, prominent Democrats lent the market populist credibility with
their enthusiastic boosting: In the nineties we had Bill Clinton and Andrew Tobias, treasurer of the Democratic National Committee and author of the humorous value-investing manual *The Only Investment
Guide You'll Ever Need.* In the twenties it was New York governor Al
Smith and financier John J. Raskob, who took time off from his duties
as Democratic national chairman to participate in some of the wackier
stock market japes of the day, and to send the nation into a giddy paroxysm of joy when he proposed, in June 1929, to set up a colossal mutual
fund that would, as one account put it, "give working people the same
chance that the rich banker has of profiting by the rise in values of the
common stocks of America's most successful corporations." When
Raskob addressed readers of *Ladies' Home Journal* a few months later (in
a soon-to-be notorious article titled "Everybody Ought to be Rich"), he
explicitly described his plan to permit even the lowliest to "secure their
share in the nation's business" as an alternative to "socialistic" solutions

to the problem of wealth inequality. Through the miracle of the mutual fund, Wall Street could make the welfare state unnecessary.[27]

Before two months were out, Raskob's market populism would be little more than a cruel joke. Before five years had passed, his party had not only embraced the "socialistic" measures he had warned against, but had actually passed legislation outlawing many of the stock market practices from which he and his colleagues had benefited so hand-somely. As Raskob drifted off into the land of far-right politics, found-ing the American Liberty League and inveighing endlessly against the New Deal, his Wall Street populism was replaced by the populism of Roosevelt, which would remain enshrined as national economic com-mon sense until it was pushed aside in the 1990s.

John Brooks' famous account of the twenties boom, *Once in Gol-conda,* is essentially a study of the rise and fall of Wall Street populism. Brooks gives the idea its due: He leaves no doubt, for example, that the New York Stock Exchange was, immediately after World War I, a place of "arbitrary and arrogant mood" accustomed to "explaining itself to the public in terms so patently preposterous as to seem to express con-tempt." Even worse, it was a "private club" filled with "consummate snobs" and overseen by the exclusively WASP partners of the House of Morgan. As these figures were challenged by the new breed of public-minded bankers and brokers, though, the Street gradually lost its elit-ist image. Or, more precisely, elitism was democratized, made available to all. The crowds of small investors who would show up on Wall Street during the later 1920s, Brooks writes, had:

> come to feel a sense of belonging there; the scars on [J. P.] Morgan's [inflicted by a 1920 bombing attack] are their scars and the grave of Hamilton in Trinity Churchyard is theirs. . . . The most change-re-sistant of institutions, the urban club, has gone democratic on Wall Street; luncheon clubs, most of them no more than six months old, are everywhere, ranging from fancy cafes to one-arm counters in bare rooms, and membership is just a matter of knowing some-body—anybody—and paying a fee.

For a moment, at least, the middle class (as one commentator in the 1990s would put it) had joined the money class, had embraced the symbols, heroes, and values of aristocratic politics. But this was democracy as a promotional trick: The real thing, Brooks insists, came only in the penitent aftermath of the Great Crash.[28]

Even in the thirties, though, market populism didn't die out altogether: It was merely transformed into a defensive device. If the stock market is a democratic institution, a transparent representation of public desire, then its leaders can hardly be held responsible for its ups and downs. Thus, when congressmen investigating the causes of the Depression asked NYSE president Richard Whitney to explain the late bull market, he passed the buck on to the general public, telling his interlocutors to "ask the one hundred and twenty-three million people of the United States."[29] To examine the workings of the market was to do nothing less than to second-guess the wisdom of the people.

For about twenty years after the 1929 crash, though, it was the other populism that colored commentary on Wall Street, consistently pointing to the elitist tastes and attitudes of the financiers as evidence of their unfitness to rule. Thurman Arnold sardonically debunked what he called *The Folklore of Capitalism* while Matthew Josephson's slash-and-burn book *The Robber Barons* portrayed Wall Street as the site of a colossal national mulcting. Perhaps a better demonstration of the depth of anti-Wall Street feeling is found in the writing of Frederick Lewis Allen, one of the greatest masters of American middlebrow. Once a sunny chronicler of the American pageant, Allen concluded in his popular 1935 financial history, *The Lords of Creation,* that financial markets served mainly to enrich the already wealthy, to divide the country into "economic strata," and to fund the sumptuous pastimes of an American "aristocracy," whose frivolities he described in lurid detail. Allen filled the book with photos of financiers behind bars or arriving to be interrogated by congressmen. After narrating J. P. Morgan's appearance before the Pujo committee in 1913, he described the great man in these terms:

He was a Bourbon, contemptuous of democratic processes: a believer in the manifest destiny of aristocrats like himself to enjoy and
distribute the fruits of industry. The financial methods which he
sponsored did much . . . to widen the gulf between rich and poor; to
levy, as it were, a heavy Wall Street tax upon the production of goods,
a tax sometimes too heavy to be borne.[30]

The impression of Wall Street as an aristocratic fortress was strength-
ened by the Pecora investigation of 1933, when the country learned
the dimensions of the Morgan bank's exclusivity and its open-handed-
ness toward society's masters; the related idea of Wall Street as an assortment of upper-class imbeciles sprinkled liberally with criminals
also received ample confirmation. By 1940 even humorous treatments
of Wall Street like Fred Schwed's memoir, *Where Are the Customers'
Yachts?*, could take this latter characterization as proved. The Depression left investment bankers, in the assessment of historian Charles
Geisst, "the most hated professional group in the country."[31]

There can be little doubt that the populists of the thirties had a
point. Even as the Morgan Bank determined the fate of the country's
industry (even, according to the findings of the Senate's Nye committee on war profiteering, dragging the US into World War I), it remained
completely aloof from the public, taking deposits from and doing business with only those it deemed proper. Wall Street's leading personalities in those years were snobs in the classic sense, perfectly capable of
expressing a Hamiltonian contempt for the public mind. Galbraith recalls one 1929 volume, by Princeton professor and bull market promoter Joseph Stagg Lawrence, which understood any doubts federal
officials had about the stock exchange as merely the resentment of the
uncouth, "a bias 'founded upon a clash of interests and a moral and intellectual antipathy between the wealthy, cultured, and conservative
settlements on the seacoast (including Wall Street) and the poverty-
stricken, illiterate, and radical pioneer communities of the interior.' "[32]

Not even the experience of the Depression cured Wall Street of its
habitual haughtiness. Although the servants and mansions and polo

ponies disappeared (especially after hyper-aristocratic NYSE president Richard Whitney was sent to prison for embezzlement), the disdain for the public remained long afterward. In the boom of the 1960s, a period of soaring idealism about "the people" generally, Wall Street figures continued to speak scornfully of the mass mind. The financial journalist "Adam Smith," whose best-selling 1967 book *The Money Game* remains an amusing account of those frenetic years, used the notion of psychological combat between genius financiers and a herd-like public to give his book narrative continuity. The simplest "indicator" used by Wall Street honchos, he wrote, was to "find out what the average investor, or the little investor, is doing. Then you do just the opposite. The sophisticates never feel comfortable unless they can be reassured that relatively uninformed investors are going the other way with some conviction." The "little people," the "public," in other words, "are always wrong."[33] For the assorted brokers, fund managers, and traders that "Smith" followed, small investors were blundering chumps whose enthusiasm for any particular issue was a clear signal to those in the know that it was time to get out. He even described fund managers paying regular visits to Merrill Lynch, then the leader of Wall Street democracy, in order to use its clients' moves as a contraindicator. Such "sophisticates," according to "Smith," were avid fans of the deeply antidemocratic turn-of-the-century social psychologist Gustave Le Bon, whose contribution to Western letters was the notion that, given the proper techniques, the public mind could be easily manipulated. They were even more partial to a curious book called *Extraordinary Popular Delusions and the Madness of Crowds,* written by one Charles Mackay in the 1840s but which only began to find a mass audience during the conformophobic years of the 1960s and 1970s. With its tales of Dutch tulip mania and other memorable financial bubbles, the book served to provide the sanction of the ages for Wall Street's disdainful take on the public mind. The introduction to the 1980 edition, for example, comments with tory scorn on the absurdity of various fads and popular dances of the seventies and even blames a "panicked" public for the banking collapse of the 1930s.[34]

As late as the eighties, Wall Street's ingrained contempt for the public ensured that thirties-style populist outrage would continue to erupt periodically, summoned forth by movies like *Wall Street* and journalistic coverage of the era's various financial scandals: leveraged buyouts, junk bonds, insider trading, the 1987 stock market crash, the collapse of the savings and loan industry. Along the way, though, the populist tradition had changed in a very curious manner. "Smith" wrote of the corporate shenanigans he saw everywhere in the sixties with an undeniable admiration: Those who successfully outsmarted the public were otherworldly geniuses, figureheads for a new kind of acquisitiveness. This Machiavellian turn would become even more pronounced in the 1980s. True, financial writers would still emphasize the malevolence and greed of Wall Street insiders and the relative weakness, foolishness, and insignificance of the average citizens who were their customers. But they also put a perverse twist on the old populist moralism, doting on the financial power of the Henry Kravises and John Gutfreunds rather than deploring it, marveling at the ingenuity with which they broke up beloved companies and smashed trusted brand names. For all the revulsion expressed by books like *Liar's Poker* and *Barbarians at the Gate,* the dominant note was starstruck wonderment at these "masters of the universe," at their millions and their manses, at their Gulfstream jets and Mercedes cars, at the high quality of the sex and luxuries they enjoyed. Occasional digressions to consider those shafted by the pros served only to heighten this sense, to establish just how satisfying it was to bring misfortune to some dope on the phone. The more monstrous the manipulation the merrier.

But as the traditional critics of the financial industry were adopting this more worldly approach, Wall Street was picking up the banner of the common people and advancing against itself. The transition from the coke-and-limo Wall Street of the eighties to the earnest, neighborly Wall Street that we know today can be seen quite clearly in the Treasury bond scandal that engulfed Salomon Brothers in the early nineties. Thanks to the revelations of *Liar's Poker,* Salomon was then

regarded as the very incarnation of the sinister Wall Street of the eighties; its misdeeds provoked Congressional hearings that threatened to
become another Pujo or Pecora investigation. But according to financial journalist Roger Lowenstein, the brokerage's real sin was that it
had acted as "the picture of Wall Street arrogance—and arrogance,
more than any specific crime, is what turned the public's stomach."[35]
This is precisely true. Whatever the specific issues at hand, American
criticism of the financial industry has always lingered on this particular venal quality: J. P. Morgan's yacht; the banquets and effete sports
enjoyed by the Astors, the Belmonts, the Du Ponts; the Go-Go traders
scoffing at the clients of Merrill Lynch. This focus on the problem of
"arrogance" would also turn out to be the critical tradition's undoing.
As it happened, what resolved the Salomon scandal was not a populist
assault on Wall Street by politicians but a populist assault on Wall
Street by Wall Street itself. Saintly commoner Warren Buffett, the
Omaha-based billionaire known for his folksy habits, materialized in
1991 to buy Salomon Brothers, end the moral depravity that critics
seemed to think the company harbored, and steer it back into the
warm mainstream of democratic values. "Gordon Gekko and Sherman
McCoy are alive and well on Wall Street," thundered one congressman
during the Salomon hearings in September 1991. "Mr. Buffett . . . get
in there and kick some butt."[36] What was required was not federal oversight, but a shift in public image: Arrogant Wall Street was being replaced by down-home Wall Street. Surely a new age was at hand.

No one was aware at that time that the greatest bull market in the
nation's history had just gotten under way, but the flamboyant pseudo-
populism that would power it to the colossal heights of 1999 was already filling the air. If the boom of the eighties was one of greed,
insiders, and malevolent yuppies, that of the nineties would be altogether different: A bull market that granted the worst suspicions of the
thirties-style populists and that presented itself as the solution to
upper-class arrogance. What emerged, by the middle of the 1990s, was
a curious but ideologically potent cultural hybrid bringing together the
antiauthoritarian strains of traditional populism with the most ortho-

dox faiths of classical economics. Wall Street would accommodate itself to the language (if not the ideas) of its critics, would invent a vision of the nation's banks, stock exchanges, and mutual funds as instruments of the common weal more representative and less corrupt than any government could ever be. The nineties would see a melding of the populisms of the twenties and the thirties. An issue of *Forbes* that appeared in December 1999 actually put Raskob's infamous words, "Everyone Ought to Be Rich," in gigantic type on its cover, arguing that the market of the nineties had vindicated the mis-timed optimism of that great hero of the people. In an advertisement inside, the T. Rowe Price mutual fund company positioned itself as the true successor of Franklin D. Roosevelt and Social Security.[37] This was the bull market of the people, their long alienation from Wall Street over at last, voting with their dollars and deliberating with all the majesty attributed to them in commercials for Chrysler cars. For the financial industry itself market populism would demand certain departures from the past—they could no longer openly despise Roosevelt, nor could they speak of "extraordinary popular delusions"[38]—but the potential rewards were astronomical: Not only could the ranks of investors, customers, and simple suckers be expanded massively, but the financial industry could finally achieve that most coveted object of corporate desire—it could become *normal.*

Mutual, Omaha

Among the founding faiths of the People's Market was the notion that mutual funds were somehow rearranging the landscape of social class. In theory, at least, this made a certain amount of sense: If everything worked right, mutual funds could make the "genius" of the hot stock picker available to just about anyone. But before the 1990s serious market observers rarely considered mutual funds to be implements of democracy. In his account of Wall Street in the 1960s, *The Go-Go Years,* John Brooks maintained that "the high-performance funds of that era were obviously unfair if not illegal," simply because the reputations of their closely observed "gunslinger" managers made any pick an automatic winner as the millions rushed to follow their lead.[39] Writing of the same period, "Adam Smith" describes the owner of Fidelity, the nation's largest mutual fund company, not only as a fan of the noxious social theories of Gustave Le Bon but as a social conservative of the most stalwart sort, a Harvard-educated brahmin and a member of the Union League Club.[40] And in the aftermath of the 1929 crash, of course, the masterminds of the big mutual funds (at the time called "investment trusts") were regarded as the greatest public thieves of all.

Much of the change in the image of the mutual fund—and, by extension, in the image of the stock market generally—can be attributed to Peter Lynch of Fidelity's Magellan Fund, the man who still holds the title of all-time greatest fund manager some ten years after his retirement. His unbroken string of successful annual returns made him a public figure in the late 1980s and early 90s, as much a celebrity "gunslinger" as his predecessors had been in the 1960s. And his celebrity in turn made Magellan the largest mutual fund of them all, the vehicle of choice for average Americans interested in dabbling in the market. Lynch's celebrity was of a different moral kind than his predecessors, however: One admirer describes him as "relentlessly normal," a man of "deeply middle-class instincts and tastes—which is perhaps why the middle class felt so comfortable with him as its designated stock picker."[41] Lynch is said to be humble, not arrogant. Unlike his Union-Leaguer boss, Lynch was no brahmin. He graduated from Boston College rather than Harvard, appears publicly in crooked glasses and poorly chosen clothes, and recounts in his books the many hours he spends not in the stuffy confines of the Union League Club but amid the crowds at various shopping malls and fast-food restaurants.

Lynch's investing strategy, as he outlined it in his books *One Up on Wall Street* (1989) and *Beating the Street* (1993), reflected this everyman public persona and inverted the fundamental public-as-dope theorizing of generations of his predecessors. He begins *One Up on Wall*

Street with this populist blast against expertise: "Stop listening to professionals! . . . Any normal person using the customary three percent of the brain can pick stocks just as well, if not better, than the average Wall Street expert." Instead of complex analysis he proposes the "power of common knowledge," in which it is one's *averageness* that determines one's success in the market. Lynch writes about people who discovered stock market "ten-baggers" (his folksy term for a stock that has appreciated to ten times the purchase price) by contemplating products or brands in the grocery store, at the shopping center, in the food court, at work, and literally in the backyard. He tells of all manner of average people who "beat the Street," regaling readers with tales of stock-picking firemen, small-town North Carolinians, seventh-graders, and again and again returning to the often-overlooked wisdom of housewives. And even though the Lynch name is indelibly associated with mutual funds, the greatest financial institution in his telling seems to be the local investment club, where a group of friends and neighbors do their own research and invest faithfully on a regular schedule, regardless of the financial weather.[42]

The stock-picking strategy that emerges from all this averageness is, simply, to buy shares in brand names. And the key to identifying the brands in which to invest is being an alert consumer. Many of the stock-stories that make up Lynch's books arise from everyday encounters with products, chain stores, or middlebrow restaurants, where a good consuming experience convinces Lynch to take the relationship one step further. So thoroughly intermingled are everyday consuming and stock-picking that Lynch even describes a trip to the local mall not as browsing but as "fundamental analysis on the intriguing lineup of potential investments, arranged side by side for the convenience of stock shoppers."[43] It is no coincidence that Lynch's investing heroes, the housewives and the seventh-graders, are among the demographics most heavily targeted by national marketers. By the middle of the 1990s this would be a stock-picking strategy in such widespread use that it couldn't help but succeed, at least for a time, as millions of

Lynchites across the land snapped up shares in the same familiar consumer brands and retail chains.

Lynch also celebrated personal thriftiness and wise buying as natural traits of the savvy investor. This is a theme that would run throughout the populist investment literature of the nineties, and that would lead to one of its most basic contradictions: As consumers, Lynch advises us to be skeptics, to keep an eagle eye on price and quality, always saving money in order to sock it away in the market. But as stock-pickers we are to be intensely brand-conscious, always on the lookout for those brand names (Coca-Cola, Gillette) that have most successfully persuaded Americans to pay premiums for ordinary goods. As consumers we scoff at ads, drink off-brand cola, and save our pennies; as investors we put our money on the most irrational achievements of Madison Avenue. Here, as in so many other places in the elaborate philosophical castle of market populism, everything comes back to the brand, to the adman's ability to persuade our fellow citizens that this soda carries with it the aura of authenticity; that this sneaker is revolution incarnate. *We* are never fooled; *everyone else,* though, is a TV-watching, ad-believing dope.

Perhaps it is not a surprise, then, that for all Lynch's celebration of the wise consumer there is a distinct anti-intellectualism to his thinking. Channeling averageness is the essence of his strategy, and the best stock-pickers, in his accounting, always turn out to be those with the least affected, most "normal" tastes of all. The foolish "experts" of Wall Street, meanwhile, are in thrall to all manner of empty financial scholasticism. "There seems to be an unwritten rule on Wall Street," Lynch sighs. "If you don't understand it, then put your life savings into it. Shun the enterprise around the corner, which can at least be observed, and seek out the one that manufactures an incomprehensible product." The sin of Wall Street is intellectual arrogance in its most highfalutin form. Financial analysts will actually "sit around and debate whether a stock is going up," Lynch writes incredulously, "as if the financial muse will give them the answer, instead of checking the company." For us, though, it's level-headed empiricism, and an almost infantile simplicity: "Never invest in any idea you can't illustrate with a crayon."[44]

It is Wall Street that is in the grip of extraordinary delusions. The stout "normal" person stands pat with his neighborhood investment club while the effete financiers of Manhattan, driven by imaginary fears and wild superstitions, panic and flee. "It's the amateurs who are prudent and the professionals who are flighty," Lynch insists, inverting the ancient financial mantra. "The public is the comforting and stabilizing factor." Such a formulation leads Lynch inevitably to a curious sort of populist jingoism, melding the egghead-baiting of the 1950s with the anticapitalist broadsides of the 1930s—and all in the service of better stock market returns. Lynch describes, for example, an annual *Barron's* roundtable discussion, where, year after year and regardless of what's actually going on outside, leading brokers and fund managers wax "negative" about market, nation, and world. Average folk, meanwhile, are said to succeed because they "keep the faith" in the people and their corporations, making those monthly contributions to the investment club kitty and continuing to believe "that America is a nation of hardworking and inventive people," that "people will continue to get up in the morning and put their pants on one leg at a time, and that the corporations that make the pants will turn a profit for the shareholders." Looking for a metaphor for Wall Street error, Lynch quite naturally settles on . . . the French, those notorious believers in the welfare state, consumers of luxury foods, and snubbers of American culture.[45]

An equally important early symbol of the People's Market was the above-mentioned Warren Buffett, the famous "oracle of Omaha." By the 1990s, Buffett had been something of an idol on Wall Street for many years, a powerful and even occasionally ruthless player during the now-unfashionable lucre-glutted eighties. In accounts dating from that period, his singular investing strategy and parsimonious personal habits were treated as curiosities, if not weird eccentricities. But in the nineties, Buffett studies changed. Now he became an investment deity for the general public, the subject of four biographies, one financial how-to book, and a collection of down-home Buffett homilies. In fact,

Buffett's public persona has changed little since he first rose to prominence among investors in the 1950s; what made him suddenly seem so timely in the 1990s—apart from an ever-rising net worth that would eventually make him one of the wealthiest individuals on earth—were the country's changing ideas of what it meant to be a capitalist. Now the aspects of Buffett's life and stock-picking strategy that had struck observers as strange were thought to be normal, the very characteristics most worthy of admiration and emulation.

Accounts of Buffett written in the 1990s seem to focus quite obsessively on his down-home averageness. Despite his vast wealth, he is said never to have upgraded his plebeian tastes. A typical Buffett-story will point out that he has lived on the same middle-class block in Omaha since the 1950s, that he has an apparently bottomless hunger for hamburgers and thirst for Cherry Coke, that he wears rumpled clothes and plain plastic spectacles, that his personal routine includes endless visits to the same Omaha steak restaurant and jewelry store. He shuns the posh trappings of the executive lifestyle. He drives his own car (a Lincoln). He is thought to unite in one person, as one biographer put it, the financial genius of J. P. Morgan and the down-home wit of Will Rogers.[46] Although he learned stock-picking from Ben Graham, the legendary Wall Street figure, he is universally portrayed as an industry outsider, a quintessential midwesterner overflowing with all the simplicity, honesty, friendliness, and other assorted virtues that the word "heartland" implies. Even studies of his investing strategy refer to him as "Warren." All of which detail is supposed to supply much, much more than simple human interest: If we are to judge the stock market by its implied attitudes toward the average people, then these are significant facts indeed. If "arrogance" is the sin of the financier, then here is walking proof that the charge no longer applies.

Buffett's stock-picking technique, at least as it is explained by his admirers, is also a thing of humility and averageness. It involves identifying businesses whose "intrinsic value" has been underestimated by the market, buying heavily into them, and sitting on the shares not just for the long haul, but "forever." Buffett clearly understands his version of value investing as something very close to actually producing wealth—which allows him easily to turn the traditional populist disdain for the speculator on *other* market players—the architects of LBOs in particular. As he told an audience in 1988,

> Now when you read about Boone Pickens and Jimmy Goldsmith and the crew, they talk about creating value for shareholders. They aren't *creating* value—they are transferring it from society to shareholders. That may be a good or bad thing but it isn't creating value—it's not like Henry Ford developing the car or Ray Kroc figuring out how to deliver hamburgers better than anyone else. . . .

It is a strange thing to hear undiluted producerism of this sort from a man whose greatest claim to fame is his knack for buying cheap and selling dear, who has a pronounced fondness for owning monopolies, and who also had a hand in some of the biggest buyouts of the eighties, but that contradiction is easily trumped by the irony of Buffett, who has led thousands of investors to lives of coupon-clipping ease, snarling routinely at the "superrich" and declaring himself opposed in principle to the very idea of inherited wealth. Not only has he refused to ensconce his family in the splendor to which his riches would ordinarily entitle them, but in one 1980 newspaper article, cited by Buffett's biographer Roger Lowenstein, he assailed the idle rich in terms updated only slightly from the populist jeremiads of the century before.

> The latter-day Du Ponts . . . had "contributed very little, if anything, to society while claiming a great many times their pro rata share of its output." With a typically egalitarian flair, Buffett noted that the Du Ponts "might believe themselves perceptive in noting the debilitating effects of food stamps for the poor" but were themselves living off a "boundless" supply of "privately funded food stamps."

Like Peter Lynch, Buffett invests exclusively in industries he "understands." He has a soft spot for marquee brands and corporations with a populist streak of their own (Coca-Cola and Gannett, for example). And, as with Lynch, there is a certain anti-intellectualism to his stock-picking. As Lowenstein describes his greatest moment—buying massively when everybody else was selling in the early 1970s—Buffett's good fortune arose directly from his refusal or inability to consider the broader global picture, a landscape of oil embargos, regional wars, and social upheaval that terrified most Wall Street regulars. Buffett kept the faith in America while the pointy-headed pantywaists turned tail and fled. In keeping with the populist narrative, Lowenstein even manages to shade Buffett's faith in securities during those dark days with a touch of the backlash sentiment of the seventies, imagining his hero as the victim of Wall Street's anti-American cynics, who "greeted with a snicker" anyone who did his patriotic duty and continued to believe "that stocks represented the country's earning power."[47]

None of this is to say that Buffett or Lynch caused, masterminded, or instigated the long bull market of the 1990s. In fact, Lynch retired from Magellan in 1990 and the floundering of Buffett's investments in the late nineties was widely noted. But both men served as symbolic figureheads of the People's Market: Buffett as an inspiration to millions of individual investors who accepted his populist image, bought books like *Buffettology,* and aped his every financial move; Lynch as the author of two best-sellers, a columnist for *Worth* magazine, a regular commentator on the CNBC financial network, and, of course, a fixture of Fidelity advertising. The two seemed to hover everywhere in the gigantic investment literature of the decade, in words and in images, their folksy stock-picking wisdom translated into millions of individual portfolios.

Thus the modest beginnings of the democracy bubble: Not only *ought* everybody to be rich, *only* everybody can be rich.

"We" Get "Ours"

Statistically the bull market got its start in March 1991, but it was not until 1993 that the financial commentator community was ready to inaugurate the new paradigm, to declare that massive popular participation in the stock market was both driving up prices and signaling a great rapprochement between the people and Wall Street. Economic democracy was finally at hand, the observers proclaimed, but not by the actions of any of its usual historical protagonists—government or labor unions. Yes, the people were coming at last to claim what rightfully belonged to them, to smash the barriers of social class and halt the scoffing of the arrogant plutocrats, but they were doing it entirely through mutual funds, or investment clubs, or online chat-rooms, or day-trading.

An early indicator of the new public attitude was the cataract of cash that began to flow into mutual funds in the early 1990s. The *Wall Street Journal* estimated in 1994 that some $523 billion had poured into mutual funds between 1991 and 1993, more than in all the years since 1939 put together. These funds, it further conjectured, had bought some 50 percent of all new stock issues in that period and were thus the single greatest force driving the market up.[48] In 1988, according to the mutual fund lobbying group, the Investment Company Institute, some 22.2 million American households owned mutual funds; by 1996 that number had increased to 36.8 million, and by 1999 it had doubled, reaching 48.4 million. The number of stock mutual funds ballooned during that same period, tripling from 1,011 in 1988 to some 3,101 in 1998.[49] More important still was the moral quality of mutual funds. If the characteristic Wall Street institution of the eighties was the slash and burn LBO operation, mutuals were, almost by definition, the moral opposite. Advertised as stable, long-term investments, they were Buffettesque buy-and-holders almost by their very nature. Mutuals rendered the mysteries and tempests of Wall Street safe for average Americans who had no interest in fielding calls from brokers or minding their investments day by day. They transformed the stock market's ups and downs into an almost bland consumer experience.

There was also a corresponding boom in the literature of personal finance. *Money* magazine, the longtime leader of the field, had been published by Time-Life since 1972. *Kiplinger's Personal Finance,* its staid competitor, had been around since 1947. In 1992, though, the ranks of personal-finance magazines doubled with the launch of *Smart-Money,* a Dow Jones product, and *Worth,* a publication of none other than Fidelity Investments, the nation's largest mutual fund company. With their upscale production values and almost instant rise to circulations in the hundreds of thousands, the two new magazines seemed to signal a broad public enthusiasm for the arcana of investing. *Money* had already claimed a secure hold on the most desirable demographic territory of personal finance journalism, endlessly saluting the wisdom and decency of the middlebrow audience, laying it on thick and earnest in the classic Luce style. *Worth,* meanwhile, derived its appeal from regular columns by Peter Lynch, tossing off pearls of populist wisdom from behind a shopping cart, and a handful of more flamboyant moneymen like Jim Rogers, who offered investment tips he had dreamt up in the saddle of his motorcycle as he wandered the highways of the world. Simultaneously exotic and mundane, *Worth* was mainly distinguished by an obsession with the luxurious trappings of semi-big money, of the kind supposedly coming within reach of the average white-collar man. This was the magazine to pick up to learn about the "Richest Towns in America," to read a salivating account of all the big new mansions being built by all the big new millionaires. *SmartMoney,* meanwhile, brought attitude to the pushing of mutual funds. The point here wasn't merely investment tips, but investment tips that only the cool people knew about. Simultaneously populist and elitist, *Smart-Money* addressed its hundreds of thousands of readers in the well-known tones of the hip insider. Its trademark innovation was expanding the simple, uninflected adulation enjoyed by certain mutual fund managers into the full range of the celebrity experience. Mutual fund managers could fail as well as succeed, and when it wasn't running fawning profiles of this year's most successful hotshots, it was detailing the painful downhill slide of those whose shots had grown cold.[50] The magazines' most important contribution to the field, though, was to blur the line between PR and news reporting. In the twenties, stock market manipulators had routinely paid reporters to help them bull a particular issue; in *SmartMoney* and *Worth* (which operated under a perennial conflict-of-interest shadow due to its relationship with Fidelity) the brokers simply did the job themselves under the guise of sharing with readers the excitement of the trading floor. The most notable of this new breed of financial writer was James J. Cramer, who, though hounded by a conflict-of-interest scandal of his own, contributed to both new magazines, developing in them his peculiarly manic, macho style of dispatch from the ever-advancing Wall Street front.[51]

Before long the changes underway began to impress themselves on financial commentators of established wisdom and discernment, and the first of what would prove to be an exceedingly long series of hymns, hosannahs, and praise-God-almightys began to pour forth from the organs of cultural and financial orthodoxy: The People and Wall Street had come together at last! As fell the Berlin Wall, so had fallen that nasty, un-American idea of social class! Economic democracy was at hand. The financial historian Ron Chernow was among the first to announce that the era of what he called "democratic investing" had arrived. Once upon a time "a social hierarchy governed financial markets," he wrote in a much-noted August 1993 article in the *Wall Street Journal.* Our "social betters" used to get out when the common people got in. But something fundamental had changed: The small investors had now been in for several years, and the market only went up and up. The soaring popularity of the mutual fund was, in particular, a sign that equality had trumped hierarchy. "Never before in American history have so many middle-class people enjoyed something at least faintly resembling the 'private banking' available to the rich," he wrote. Something dramatic had changed, and Chernow naturally chose the language of social democracy to describe it: "The financial services industry is decreasingly segregated by class."[52]

This new narrative of democracy through investing was nailed down by the spectacular news, appearing just about wherever newspapers were published in December 1995, that one Anne Scheiber, a New

Yorker who had died at the age of 101, had over the course of some fifty years turned a five-thousand-dollar investment into a portfolio worth $22 million. She did it, it was said, without any advice from brokers and entirely by the same buy-and-hold strategy as Warren Buffett, investing mainly in companies with established brand names: Coca-Cola, PepsiCo, Loews, Paramount, and Capital Cities/ABC. Scheiber appeared to have lived a miserly, unhappy life. But newspaper accounts found rich cosmic justice in the fact that she had once worked for (and been sorely mistreated by) the IRS, imagining her great wealth as a sort of revenge on that most hated of government agencies. And then there was the anti-expertise lesson that nobody missed: As the *Times* of London put it, the "moral" of the story was "that anyone can become fabulously wealthy from the market if they are sensible, methodical and, above all, patient."[53]

Before too long the "democratization" of the stock market was one of the hottest ideas in the world of journalism, bringing with it some appropriately bizarre proclamations of millennial change. The author of a June 1996 *Business Week* cover story claimed to see in the recent "flood of money into equities" (mainly in the form of mutual funds) "a transfer of wealth from the corporation to the individual." And if that wasn't enough, the very social hierarchy of Wall Street was also said to have been stood on its head: Now "the big market gains are going to the little guys." Three months later the *Wall Street Journal* began a series of front-page stories entitled "A Common Market—The Public's Zeal to Invest," in which the many avenues of public participation were explored and celebrated. The first installment, penned by Roger Lowenstein, the erstwhile biographer of Warren Buffett, described a man actually named Joe Smith (Lowenstein notes redundantly that he is "an Everyman for the '90s") giving a lecture on investing to an audience at a public library that is decorated, Lowenstein observed significantly, with a "mural of an 18th Century town meeting." In December of that year the *New York Times Magazine* carried a cover story on a day in the life of a mutual fund manager, one Michael DiCarlo of the John Hancock Special Equities Fund. Although a hero of Olympian proportions, this DiCarlo, it is noted, is a real regular guy, a rags-to-riches child of the working class—a rock 'n' rolling, State-U educated "son of an Italian immigrant cement mason," to be precise. Nor do his activities constitute some sort of class treason: By managing a mutual fund, it is noted, DiCarlo is helping out all manner of "plumbers and electricians" who have come to Wall Street with their quotidian financial problems. Naturally he is compared to Peter Lynch. And naturally he is described as a relentless optimist. Asked to comment on the naysaying of some slick Morgan Stanley type, the Boston-based DiCarlo responds, "I haven't seen nothing out there I can't beat."[54]

Ideological fantasies of this kind rarely appear without a ready-made history, a story of arduous but inevitable progress toward the incredible achievement we enjoy in the present. And the brand new narrative of the People's Market was no exception. In the fall of 1994, Joseph Nocera, the financial journalist whose portrait of Walter Wriston was mentioned above, published *A Piece of the Action: How the Middle Class Joined the Money Class,* an account of the rise of all the various consumer financial instruments of the previous thirty years—credit cards, money market accounts, mutual funds. For Nocera, each and every one marked yet another advance for the common man, another step toward "financial democracy," another opportunity for "the middle class" to use "all the financial tools that had previously been available only to the rich." At the end of that long road, naturally, lay the bull market of the 1990s, which differed from all other booms, Nocera asserted (the 1920s boom was considered only in passing), in that it was enriching the regular people rather than the bloated aristocrats of Wall Street. Nocera never offered much of a definition of the "middle class," but still he claimed for it an inherent and awesome virtuosity. The result was a work of populist pretension so grand that much of it was actually written in the first person plural, like *USA Today* editorials or the Constitution. "We" were said to "shop for investments," to "stand back and watch in admiration" as our hero Peter Lynch piled up money for us, to have spent the last twenty years "participating in nothing less than a money revolution." Jimmy Carter? "We booted him out of office." The inflation of the 1970s? "It scared us, this inflation; it scared us terribly, and it changed us."[55]

Beneath this glorious tale of "our" long, arduous march to the present lay a fairly standard financial history. Nocera's innovation was to describe each mass-market success by a bank or brokerage as a victory for a democratic "revolution." Thus Merrill Lynch is an early hero because of its network of branch offices, its massive publicity campaign for the stock market, and its introduction of the cash management account, which offered bank-like services with a slightly higher rate of interest. But in 1975, Merrill made the fatal error of raising brokerage commissions when the logic of the mass market (and "the money revolution") dictated that they be lowered, and in Nocera's telling they instantly lost their position in the vanguard of economic democracy to the even more populist Charles Schwab & Co., which offered steeply discounted trades.

But here, as in so many market populist texts, it is the repugnant elitism of the old-time financial industry and the rise of the more democratic new generation that is the really important narrative. Nocera's populist financiers were mirror images of "Adam Smith's": Instead of scoffing at the crowd they affirmed the wisdom of the People. Old-line bankers, for example, are said to have denied the People their rightful percentage out of "snobbery" or "arrogance," both qualities being eventually overcome by the Bank of America, which was founded by an ethnic outsider, a true "populist entrepreneur." The New York Stock Exchange of twenty years ago is described as "snobbish," a "cartel" that answered its critics with "arrogant conceit." Traditional authority figures—journalists, congressmen, and the like—are said to doubt (snobbishly, arrogantly) the intelligence of the people, to seek to protect "us" from ourselves. It was the old-style financiers who suffer from "Delusions and Madness," as one chapter title put it.[56]

On the other side were the people's financiers whose quiet, noble determination to let "us" control "our" own lives made them fantastically rich. Joseph Williams, for example, one of the inventors of the credit card, is said to have been motivated by a "passionate belief in the goodness of the common man." Peter Lynch, too, is said to be among the faithful, remaining "steadfast in his belief that the rest of us could do as well in the market as he had done." And since the bull market of the nineties was a fairly direct expression of the needs and desires of the middle class, the way one interpreted its prospects served as a handy indicator of one's commitment to democracy itself: One could either "worry that the 'unsophisticated' small investor would panic at the first sign of trouble and bring the whole thing tumbling down," or "one could applaud it, seeing it as a democratic trend in a democratic society. . . ." Not only were elitists bad people, but their snobbishness had led them to miss out altogether on the wondrous profit-taking of recent years. The bull market of the nineties was such a grassroots affair, Nocera insists, that the establishment newspapers didn't even *notice* it until "Main Street" had run the Dow up for two whole years. And even though this was a book about the inventors of popular financial instruments, Nocera refuses to let that elite focus detract from the agency of his real subject: We the People. Sure, a guy at Merrill Lynch *invented* the cash management account, and sure, a guy at Fidelity *introduced* the notion of mutual funds to the mass public, but the real actor here was the holy middle class itself, whose demand for each new financial product essentially amounted to authorship. Thus the curious phrase Nocera repeats throughout the book (with modifications to fit the topic under discussion), in which event X or product Y is said to have brought the "middle class" to the collective "realization" that it "was going to have to take control of its own financial future." The implication, of course, was one of all-American responsibleness, of a national coming-of-age. It all sounded very nice. But by far the biggest beneficiary of these developments wasn't the middle class, but Wall Street itself, transformed through this fantasy of popular consent into the only true and proper instrument of social security. For pure, unadulterated, up-with-people smarminess it would be hard to top one of Nocera's conclusions on the way the "new investors," desperate for percentage, found a friend in the market:

It wasn't that they were "unsophisticated"; their market behavior since the crash [of 1987] should have put that one to rest. Nor was it that they failed to appreciate the potential benefits the new world had created for them. They understood those benefits completely. . . . Thus did they salt away funds for retirement, and move money around to get a higher return. Thus did they jump into risky and exotic foreign funds with some of their money—and put other funds into conservative bond and asset allocation funds. Thus did they subscribe to newsletters and pore over the stock tables each day. Thus did they take control, as they knew they had to.[57]

All that's missing is a dust jacket illustration by Norman Rockwell: "Mr. Smith Reads the Business Section."

The notion of the "middle class" somehow "taking control" of Wall Street may be a little dotty, but it's hard to disagree with the underlying aspiration for a democratic economy, a financial system that responds to the needs of the people. Traditionally, of course, the institution by which the middle class has "taken control" has not been the mutual fund or the discount brokerage, but the labor union, which has a proven historical track record for democratizing the distribution of wealth. Unfortunately, Nocera had no interest in seeing the *working class* join the "money class"; in fact, when it came to unions, he had nothing but scorn. What unions brought was not economic democracy but *inflation,* the great bogeyman of his beloved "middle class." In establishing this point Nocera made it clear that unions, as representatives of "the lucky few," were fundamentally not "us"; in fact, they were basically indistinguishable from all the arrogant bankers and others who denied "us" our rightful percentage in the first place. "Whenever a union chief won a demand that his members receive wage increases exceeding the cost of living," he wrote in a chapter on the economic climate of the 1970s, "his action made inflation worse for all of us, who had to bear the cost of those higher wages for the lucky few." (This reasoning, which would become commonplace in the nineties, seemed never to apply to those whose stock market winnings exceeded the cost of living—or to those whose stocks went up while other peoples' fell.) Before long Nocera was equating union contract negotiation with the doings of OPEC, and describing Ronald Reagan's smashing of the air traffic controllers union in 1981 as an anti-inflationary masterstroke.[58]

For all his celebration of the little guy, Nocera saw progress only in the terms of corporate America. Granted, he was no friend of the House of Morgan or the old-fashioned Wall Street club members—but then, according to the club members' advertising in the nineties, neither were they. The real "establishment" villain was, as always, the federal government, with its senseless "Depression-era" bank regulations, now transformed through the magic of market populism from thorn-in-the-side of the big banks to intolerable restraint on the ceaseless efforts of the "middle class" to get their just percentage. Nocera's celebration of the "money revolution," published at about the same time the "Republican revolution" swept the Gingrich Congress into power, encapsulated the ideological tenor of the decade: Smash the unions and deregulate everywhere—but do it in the name of the People. Evidently the "middle class" had not only "joined the money class," "we" had absorbed its politics as well.

Meet John Doe, Arbitrageur

As the People's Market continued its march—the Dow Jones Industrial Average hitting 4,000 in February 1995, 6,000 in October 1996, 8,000 in July 1997—the nation seemed to develop a bottomless appetite for tales of market swashbuckling by just about everyone *except* the Gordon Gekkos, Henry Kravises, and J. P. Morgans of the past. Regular people became the secret journalistic ingredient for virtually any story relating to the stock market, and reporters fanned out across the nation in search of exotic averageness: a guy in Texas who watched CNBC; people who owned stock and lived in Providence, Rhode Island; people who invested from *Akron,* even. The *Wall Street Journal* ran stories on hot mutual funds based in non-elite places like

Knoxville, Tennessee ("This is one place where Main Street really does beat Wall Street") and on the non-flashy tastes and lifestyles of an assortment of down-home millionaires ("The Rich Aren't So Different After All"). This latter subject became something of a journalistic boom all its own as a wave of rags-to-riches mania swept the land. In July 1996 the *Reader's Digest,* ever the master of the middlebrow sensibility, ran "You Can Make a Million," a feature story detailing the rise to plutocracy of a number of average folks, all of whom made their piles by regularly investing small amounts of money in stocks and mutual funds and holding them forever. Thriftiness was now a staple element of such stories, with *Reader's Digest* describing its worthy millionaires as folks more at home "popping corn instead of champagne corks."[59]

The greatest eulogists of the democracy of riches were Thomas J. Stanley and William D. Danko, the authors of a rambling 1996 best-seller (it was still on paperback best-seller lists four years later) that combined the focus groups and homespun analysis so beloved of market populism with an unbearably unctuous reverence for people of "high net worth." But what distinguishes *The Millionaire Next Door* from run-of-the-mill "Lifestyles of the Rich and Famous" palaver is its insistence that the vast majority of wealthy Americans are, in fact, humble, frugal, self-made people. The authors' heroes turn down gifts of Rolls Royces, they live in blue-collar neighborhoods, they drink Budweiser instead of wine. And the only real social conflict taking place in America is the showdown between these salt-of-the-earth millionaires and the high-living, conspicuous-consuming, Ivy League, showoff millionaires (and, of course, their psychological cousins in the working class, who insist on spending rather than saving). In the book's liveliest passages, a series of populist millionaires best a bunch of these noxious nabobs of privilege. There's "Bubba Richards," a mobile home dealer, a man of massive personal net worth, vs. "James H. Ford II," an establishment attorney who has wasted his substance on luxury cars, fine suits, and country clubs. There's the hilarious situation that ensues after a man shows up to a focus group session with "gold bracelets" and "an expensive-looking diamond-encrusted watch" and commences to boast of the number of celebrities who live in his neighborhood, but whose "confidence seemed to deteriorate" as he is forced to spend "three hours . . . talking with eight wiser men. . . ." Then there is poor "Toddy," an acquaintance of the authors, who went to prep school and Princeton and liked to talk about the financial deeds of his ancestors and his ancient WASP lineage. Eventually "Toddy's" company is bought out by some Russian immigrant parvenu, permitting Stanley and Danko to dilate with fondness about the coming day when the "Toddys" of the world are "extinct."

The Millionaire Next Door may be filled with questionable science and repulsive ethnic stereotyping, but as ideology it is a masterpiece. Amid all their fawning at the feet of the rich, Stanley and Danko have come up with nothing less than a full-fledged rewriting of social conflict. Just as for George Gilder, all of history was a struggle between old money and new, between the people they call "PAWs" and "UAWs" ("prodigious accumulators of wealth" and "under accumulators of wealth," respectively). And the difference between these fundamental groups is not so much money but morality: PAWs are humble, thrifty, and wise, while UAWs (who, as their name suggests, populate the working class as well as the money class) are effete, boastful, and profligate. Of course they also have very different ideas about the wisdom of the People—in this case, very different faiths in the average person's ability to get rich. As the authors put it, "people of modest backgrounds who believe that only the wealthy produce millionaires are predetermined to remain non-affluent."[60]

Thus was the backlash theorizing of Hayek and Gilder transformed into one of the most pervasive cultural motifs of the nineties: The notion that the displacing of one batch of millionaires by another is in some way "revolutionary," that it somehow constitutes economic democracy all by itself. And also one of the era's most enduring figures: The self-righteous parvenu; the nouveau-riche as Lenin. The language of social class was becoming yet another dialect of market-speak. The most savage caricatures of the rich invented by Thorstein Veblen were finally permissible in the literature of Wall Street popularizing, but with Veblen's radical politics carefully omitted. Money, as it turns out, is sufficiently revolutionary in itself to push those bad old conspicuous-consuming millionaires into their graves.

As did so many of the important texts of the People's Market, *The Millionaire Next Door* took a militantly Calvinist attitude toward consumption. Saving and investing are ends in themselves, evidence of moral virtue, while spending is empty dissipation. Luxury goods are a particular mark of shame, and the authors repeatedly run over a list of items that brand one as a scattergoods UAW: foreign cars, good wine (scotch whiskey is, for some reason, exempt from their judgment), expensive watches, expensive clothes, large houses, jewelry, foreign travel, and private schools (and also, mysteriously, any association with nonprofit organizations). Nor did one pile up money in order to pass it on to one's descendants—"economic outpatient care" of this kind is actually the subject of two excoriating chapters. The Lynchian problem concerning brands was thus pushed to an even more painful contradiction: The prosperity of the virtuous, humble, investing PAW actually depended on the brand-addled foolishness of the rest of the world—and on the deeply undemocratic belief that the rest of the world were prevented by their very moral nature from ever figuring this out. The outer limit of Stanley and Danko's populism, then, was the promise that an occasional regular guy could sometimes join the captains of industry in plundering the world.

One of the most memorable—and in some ways, one of the most pathetic—episodes in this Dow-driven popular faith in the accumulation skills of the average was the media storm over the Beardstown Ladies, an investment club from central Illinois whose members seemed, for a few years, to personify the jes' folks values that were thought to be replacing the cutthroat mores of establishment Wall Street. The Ladies first captured the attention of the national media in 1991, when CBS sent a crew prospecting for investment clubs in the Midwest and found exactly the sort of heartland schlock they were no doubt looking for: A collection of stock-picking grannies who acted out their roles so perfectly they might have been sent from central casting.

True, the Ladies' portfolio did boast an extraordinary annual return (or, rather, it seemed to: their figures were later revealed to be greatly exaggerated), but particular stock picks were not the main point of all the publicity. In fact, the investment advice included in the Ladies' 1994 *Common-Sense Investment Guide* is quite rudimentary, covering such topics as what stocks are and how they are listed in the newspaper. More important by far was the Beardstown episode as a moral fable, a sweetly touching testimonial to the accessibility of the stock market. The Ladies seemed to prove that even society's feeblest, and poorest-informed—superannuated widows from the ever-innocent small-town Midwest—could beat the "self-important MBAs" of "New York, or Zurich, or Tokyo," as their book's introduction puts it. The pages that follow are filled with little parables of small-town wit and wisdom: recipes, recollections of the Depression, and a story in which a vice president of an insurance giant visits nearby Peoria, Illinois, the mythic landscape of corporate populism, where he learns (first from one of the Ladies and then through his own experience) to stop scoffing and love Wal-Mart. In return the Ladies showered their own affection on Wall Street. If, as Roland Marchand claims in *Creating the Corporate Soul*, the long-term cultural project of corporate America is to become more fully human, the Beardstown Ladies played an important part in the saga, becoming loving grandmas of the companies whose stock they bought and (of course) held. As one of them put it, "We're all hyped up about McDonald's and PepsiCo. You feel like you're acquainted with them when you follow their stock."[61]

The Beardstown episode also threw into high relief the working of a new logic of corporate culture: The enthusiasm of traditional outsiders was much more meaningful than that of the usual Wall Street crowd. Clearly it was worth more, on some imaginary scale of ideological merit, for residents of some midwestern burg to declare their faith in stocks and their love for corporate America than for New Yorkers to do the same. Thus when the Beardstown Ladies were finally pushed from the investment club throne, it was almost a requirement of the genre that their successor hail from an even more remote locale. And sure enough, it turned out to be the Klondike Club of Buffalo, Wyoming, described by *Money* magazine as "ordinary citizens in a tiny western town," a place of "big skies, frigid winters, and a hardscrabble economy that breeds both self-reliance and a we're-all-in-this-together kind of fellowship."[62] Similarly, the words of those who had lived through the Depression (like many of the Beardstown Ladies) were worth more than those of people who grew up in the 1960s. Farmers, ranchers, and westerners generally, forever associated in the popular mind with the original Populist uprising, outweighed businessmen. The stock market interests of leftists yielded greater publicity dividends than those of Republicans.[63] When Jesse Jackson seemed to have been converted to the gospel of Wall Street in 1998 (Jackson proposed both more investment in poor areas and the launching of church-based investment clubs), all the buttons were pushed at once.

There was often thought to be a different moral quality to the way the new crop of average folks invested as well. In each of the investment fables cited above—from the next-door millionaires to the oft-cited strategies of Warren Buffett—investing was treated almost as an act of faith. Nocera asserted that the small investors were distinguished by their steadfastness during crashes, standing pat while the smart money fled. Charles Schwab commercials gave us Rick and Marion, taking a break from their vacation to buy when they heard the market was down.

And the stocks the everyman investors bought—heck! Those, too, were humble, honest, unpretentious. If the bull market of the sixties is remembered by "swinging" issues like Ling-Temco-Vought or Control Data, the People's Market of the nineties was dominated by shares that conformed to Peter Lynch's "common knowledge" imperative. All across the country, in small-town investment clubs and online chat groups, "normal" people were looking around, noting the same big-name brands, and buying the same things: Wal-Mart, Coca-Cola, Pepsi, McDonald's, Gannett, Home Depot, Rubbermaid, Chrysler.

Companies they knew about. Companies they understood. Companies that never high-hatted them, companies that took them seriously. Best of all, market populism *worked:* As millions of populist investors, using populist brokers, put their money in the same handful of populist companies, the share prices of those companies (and, in the case of Charles Schwab, those populist brokers) went through the roof.

Even the motives of the new investors were said to be so humble, so honest. The People's Market was driven not by greed, nor by a corrupt hunger for luxury goods, but by the everyday requirements of averageness. Think of the Merrill Lynch ads of mid-decade, which speak not of speculation but exhort readers who "may not be able to count on a large inheritance" to "take control of your future" in order "to buy a home, send the kids to college and retire comfortably." Think of the "millionaire next door's" demonic asceticism, his absolute refusal to buy luxury goods. Think of superstar fund manager Michael DiCarlo's summary of the transition from the eighties, when "we bought every toy known to mankind," to the responsible nineties, when "we started looking at things that would require long-term financial planning, like our children's college tuition and our own retirement. All of a sudden we went from a nation of conspicuous consumers to a nation kicking up the saving and investment rate." Think of Joseph Nocera's responsible middle class, rolling up their sleeves and taking over the stock market "as they knew they had to":

> The market had become an integral facet of their lives. It held money for their children's college tuition, money to get them through an emergency, money for that great vacation they were saving for, money for retirement.

Or of Peter Lynch, the People's broker, who was "stopped . . . in the street" after his retirement, according to Nocera, just so people could "thank him for making it possible for them to send a child to college, or put an addition on their home."[64]

It is not a coincidence that each of these necessities—pensions, shelter, education—were things Americans had once sought to ensure through union activity or government intervention, things that Americans once believed were theirs simply by virtue of being citizens, things that could and should be available to everyone in a democratic society.

I Want My
NYSE

Corporations are slower than we are. We're modern capitalist
mavericks. We're shattering the old broker universe.
> —*Commercial for Suretrade online brokerage, 1999*

The stock market is a money machine. . . .
> —*James Glassman and Kevin Hassett,* Dow 36,000 *(1999)*

They were all very pleasant fantasies, those small town grandmas, those
lonely westerners, those millionaires moving in next door. They were
also corny in the extreme. The Norman Rockwell imagery of the early
People's Market—small investors earnestly talking mutual funds at
town meetings in public libraries—was vulnerable to the free-floating
public cynicism that had become, by the mid-nineties, the chief worry
of the nation's theoreticians of middlebrow. The ongoing crisis of "civility," Americans' refusal to believe, threatened the financial industry just
as it did the advertising industry, the music industry, and journalism,
and it, too, would have to find some more wised-up, worldly way of ap-
proaching the mass public.

The solution proved remarkably easy to find. After all, for the big
thinkers of market populism, the demographic with by far the greatest

significance was Generation X, the recently "discovered" group whose mysterious tastes were causing attitude upgrades all across the culture industry as existing models were retrofitted with new slang and sounds. For Wall Street, Generation X had particularly great strategic importance. Not only were members of this group the very kids on whose behalf "we," the middle class, had so arduously pursued percentage, but they were the only mass constituency anyone could come up with that could conceivably have a subjective interest in privatizing Social Security, Wall Street's biggest public policy interest in recent years (and an issue on which the industry was willing to spend virtually any sum). The logic went like this: So great are the numbers of baby boomers who will start retiring in the early twenty-first century that they will place an intolerable tax on the generation just behind them, who will be required to pay the Social Security bill for their elders. Unfortunately, the looming Social Security "crisis" that began to inform every journalistic account of "Generation X" to appear after about 1994 was largely imaginary.[1] But again, ideological need far outweighed facts. And thus was born perhaps the most curious set of bull market myths and symbols of them all.

"There's something just a little odd about the idea of people in their twenties obsessing over retirement," journalist Josh Mason has pointed out. "I have no idea what I'll be doing in 4 years, let alone in 40." And yet to read any of the position papers and calls for reform generated in the mid-nineties by Third Millennium, Generation X's very own self-proclaimed advocacy organization, this was the issue that young people cared about more than any other. What did Generation X want? The privatization of Social Security. Third Millennium was ostensibly "bipartisan," of course (any lobbying group planning on doing business must be), but in practice it tended to march in step with Wall Street PR campaigns, insisting over and over again that Congress somehow permit or require taxpayers to invest their FICA money in equities. In fact, the relationship between Wall Street and this voice of Gen-X went much deeper than that. In a 1995 statement of Third Millennium principle, Richard Thau, the organization's executive director, called

for "leaders on Wall Street" to "invest" in a PR blitz on behalf of a partial privatization plan, asserting that with proper backing from the
moneymen, "a thunderous chorus . . . would ensue. The political
winds would then shift sufficiently to pass Kerrey-Simpson [a then-
current legislative bill], thereby reaping a windfall for investors and
shoring up our outdated national retirement system."[2] Although Thau
makes a point of publicly complaining that Wall Street failed to rally to
his call, Third Millennium has since enjoyed the generous assistance
of Oppenheimer Mutual Funds as it goes about its various generational
PR jobs.[3] And while the group ostensibly speaks for an entire generation, its "board of directors" might be more accurately described as a
cross-section of young Wall Street: It lists one CNN financial correspondent (and former Morgan Stanley analyst), one MSNBC correspondent (and member of the Eastside Conservative Club), one
corporate tax lawyer, one brokerage executive, one accountant, one insurance industry executive, one business school student (and child of
a state governor), one representative of the right-wing foundation community, one consultant, and a dot-com employee.[4]

Other than its resumé-waving strain of generational messianism,[5]
Third Millennium's single notable contribution to American political
life was a simple marketing trick that it managed to transform into journalistic orthodoxy sometime in mid-decade. It seems Third Millennium (with the help of Frank Luntz, who we last encountered
theorizing "digital citizens" for *Wired* magazine) took a poll which
found that Gen-Xers were less likely to "believe" in Social Security
than in UFOs. The organization followed this up with polls comparing
the faith of young people in Social Security to their faith in the
longevity of General Hospital, to betting on the Super Bowl, to almost
any pop-cult inanity the Millennialists cared to dream up. They were,
naturally, polls designed more to persuade than to describe. This snide
juxtaposition of once-sacred social issues with mindless pop culture
was just the right way to desecrate what remained of the New Deal
public religion. So endlessly cited and so triumphantly displayed were
these polls that before long they were established as the ineluctable

terms of debate, the hard "data" that every newspaper account of the matter had to include. "In its infinite repetition," as journalist Rick Perlstein has put it, "the UFO statistic . . . moved mountains in instilling a popular defeatism" about Social Security.[6]

Thus, after sixty years of direct political assault from the far right it was Gen-X sarcasm that blew the first hole in the walls of the New Deal citadel. Irony did what Reagan couldn't—and Wall Street sat up and took notice. Nothing punctured the airy pretensions of the welfare state, the Third Millennium episode seemed to prove, better than the dumb-shit pop-cult language of youth. The high-minded legacy of the hated FDR was being driven from the field by the moronic chant of *as if.*[7]

It made the perfect launching pad for the next ideological skyrocket of the People's Market. The chroniclers of American affluence had discovered—and in the most improbable demographic locale—what sounded like the ideal new language for talking about the market. And in the process, the earnest, ultra-square culture of investing was being transformed into something that seemed very different: The image of the small investor as jaded, knowing hipster. In some ways, of course, the hipster-as-investor would embrace certain well-established tenets of the People's Market: Suspicion of financial authority and of establishment Wall Street, for example. But hipsters were neither buy-and-hold grandmas or mutual fund-minded family men: They were fundamentally in the know, tuned in to most fleeting trends, and ready to trade on a moment's notice. What emerged as the decade wore on was a curious hybrid of "Adam Smith's" Nietzschean traders and Peter Lynch's everyman-as-expert: Everyman as his own cigar-chomping, commodity-broking, devil-take-the-hindmost asshole, hovering over the office computer (fuck the boss!) to spread rumors on the Raging Bull message boards and scalp the gains on E*Trade, all the while listening to the scabrous rantings of Limp Bizkit, cultivating a goatee, and dreaming about Xtreme sports. Generation X and stocks, it now seemed, went together like Kurt and Courtney.

And always the Third Millennium Social Security "finding" lurked in the background—Wall Street's own pet version of the inevitability maneuver that served the writers of management literature and new economy social theory so well. If the demise of Social Security is inevitable (and only suckers believe it isn't), then get used to it and stop wasting time trying to save it. When the online magazine *Salon* published an appreciation of the "baby bulls" in April 1998, the young investors' well-known "lack of confidence in the Social Security system" became the historical explanation for their speculative enthusiasm. Another factor, though, was the bull market itself, which was now—just five years since Ron Chernow had announced the arrival of the People's Boom—being described as a historical phenomenon as permanent as the Cold War, a "fact of life" for "Generation X." Gone forever were the images of Gen-X alienation and unemployment; now they were a generation for whom "investing in the stock market is just good sense"; a demographic represented by the article's handful of youngsters who had parlayed tiny stakes into fantastic winnings. The Gen-X narrative, as set forth by *Salon* (and as echoed across the financial-journalism landscape), incorporated crucial elements of the standard myth of the People's Market: Just like the Beardstown Ladies or Anne Scheiber, the young investors don't "fit the mold of the sleek Wall Street investor"; they are to be commended for their sensible, down-to-earth goals (they're worried about their retirement, duh); and although their investing style is said to be "aggressive," as it turns out they practice the same brand-name strategy as everyone else (stocks mentioned in the article include IBM, Nike, the Gap, and Procter & Gamble). But the Gen-X investment narrative also includes curious new additions to the tale: One young investor recounted how he was ostracized for his acquisitiveness while at college; others imagined speculation as a way to avoid working at a hated job. *Worth* and *Esquire* columnist Ken Kurson, who was often quoted as a leading authority on Generation X, spoke of investing as a way of accumulating "fuck-you money," funds that would allow workers to turn the tables on the boss. Playing the stock market had always had patriotic overtones; this exciting new generation was conferring upon it an even more far-fetched aura: investing as social conflict, the NASDAQ as a tool of workplace revolution.[8]

The author of the *Salon* story, writing in early 1998, had any number of authorities on the investing practices of Generation X to choose from. By then the financial-journalism scene was being routinely crisscrossed by a number of barnstorming spokesmen for Generation X, each of them more aggressively bullish than the last. Their charge, though, wasn't so much to provide useful financial advice as it was to give the ideology of the market a much needed "attitude" infusion. Ken Kurson, for example, had been a punk rocker and zine publisher before moving on to *Worth* and *Esquire*. But the most shameless panderer to Wall Street's bottomless hunger for the hip was one Jonathan Hoenig, author of the 1999 book *Greed is Good,* columnist for *P.O.V.* magazine, commentator on NPR, market reporter for a Chicago TV station, and purveyor of a manic, blustering verbal style. Hoenig got his start publishing his own personal finance zine, *Capitalist Pig,* in which he dispensed rudimentary advice to a small circle of readers. The attraction here wasn't the quality of the tips: it was the very idea of samizdat financial advice, of investing as an underground culture all its own.

In *Greed is Good* he runs through the usual round of Third Millennium–inspired hysterics about Social Security, issues standard warnings against carrying credit card debt, and spends several pages debunking advertising and consuming in general—better to save your money and invest it. The various investment devices themselves are discussed only at the most elementary level. What has allowed Hoenig to win the "voice of finance for Generation X" title (bestowed on him by *Forbes* magazine) is not his stock-picking ability but the curious way in which he declares his love for the market. *Greed is Good* is awash in ironic pop-culture references and smart-ass asides. To illustrate how bond funds work, Hoenig asks us to imagine the various characters from *Happy Days* pooling their funds and getting Fonzie to manage the pile. He calls the exchange "a mosh pit of finance" and comforts readers with the knowledge that investing "is simpler than a *Scooby-Doo* storyline." Similar references to *Good Times, The Love Boat, Charles in Charge, The A-Team, The Brady Bunch, Star Trek, The Jeffersons,* and to the movie career of John Travolta punctuate the book. Here, clearly is a man who has mastered the language of the young.[9]

As with so many of the others examined here though, Hoenig's stock-picking takes a distant second to his ideology spinning, to his musings about capitalism as the greatest of social orders and the chosen way of the people. This is what has won him the plaudits of the *New York Times, Forbes,* and the *Wall Street Journal.* And it must be admitted that, if nothing else, as ideologue Hoenig has a certain panache and ingenuity. Start with the name he chose for his zine, radio show, and *P.O.V.* column: "capitalist pig." His point isn't that capitalists are evil creatures, but just the opposite: The true capitalist—he who is one with money in his heart, not just in the fickle tastes of the moment—is an object of unfair persecution and ostracism, the ultimate "White Negro." Why? Because the true capitalist threatens what Hoenig calls "the establishment," "the Man," the soulless, affected "yuppies." The true capitalist is the ultimate social revolutionary, at once a man of the people and a rule-breaking outsider.

In other words, Hoenig seems to have been gulled by one of the nation's longest-running intellectual hoaxes: He has confused money with class. He starts off *Greed is Good* proclaiming bizarrely that it is somehow "taboo" to do what he is about to do, that is, "talk about being interested in money." More importantly, Hoenig insists that this taboo only afflicts the "affluent": Regular guys like himself seem to have no problem talking about money—hell, Hoenig recalls at one point how he "spoke of mutual funds between bong hits" and riled some "affluent" friends. As it turns out, these suburban milquetoasts can't stand to address the dreaded subject because money has the power to turn the system that supports them upside down. And it's not just them. Hoenig blasts just about every aspect of economic life. He recalls the despised counter job he once held at Starbucks, he heaps obloquy on the yuppies, who accumulated for all the wrong reasons, he rails against traditional "business broadcasting" for being "boorish and boring," and even warns against the ways of "the Man." And money is the "life-affirming" thing that will set it all straight. As Hoenig puts it in his typically swaggering (and yet entirely unoriginal) way, workers will "discover it's much easier to give your boss the finger when you've got a few grand stashed somewhere for safekeeping."[10]

Finance, then, is subversion. From this preposterous premise flows all manner of imaginary heroics. As its curious title suggests, *Greed is Good* imagines itself as a thoroughly transgressive volume, one designed to strike a blow against the yuppies, the bluenose enforcers of social taboos, and the wealthy establishment all at once—and just by talking about mutual funds! Admitting daringly that "most of the establishment will probably hate" the book "because it doesn't look like anything they've ever seen," Hoenig clues us in to what's really going on in the world beyond our rosy suburban confines:

> A dramatic shout is being heard in America these days. *It's the voice of new money.* It's young people who are determined to be themselves.

New money and being yourself: It's the George Gilder model of social conflict—righteous new money vs. snooty old—only spiced up in this telling with a few tired slogans from the sixties, as filtered through decades of TV commercials. "Success has to be measured by each of us individually," Hoenig declares, "on our own well-considered terms, not by the material trinkets we can afford to amass." So disgusted are we by the materialism of our wealthy elders that we must break with them altogether and become . . . wealthy![11]

In the course of my life I have come across only two or three people who were genuinely interested both in rebel subcultures and in trading stocks. But whether the stereotype was true to life or not, it met nearly every one of the critical cultural needs of the financial industry in the late nineties, and before long it was appearing everywhere in industry discourse. Commercials for the Ameritrade online brokerage began to feature a trading enthusiast named "Stewart," whose outré sideburns and elaborately cropped and dyed hair testified to his coolness. In case viewers didn't realize how rebellious Stewart was, the commercials included shots of oldsters horrified by his capricious doings. As one spot opens he is shown running off images of his face on the office photocopier, a gesture so unambiguously antiauthoritarian that when the boss, in a rumpled gray suit, calls Stewart into his office, we are sure the defiant one is going to be punished. But no: The boss has opened an Ameritrade account and merely asks the assistance of the market-savvy Stewart as he makes his first stock purchase. (The hipster persuades him to buy shares in Kmart, retailer to the square masses.) "Do you feel the excitement?" Stewart asks archly, breaking into an ironic-funky dance. "You're ridin' the wave of the future, my man!" Ameritrade not only offers cheap trades, it brings the generations together as well, uniting them in a common enthusiasm for buying low and selling high. Stewart invites the older man to a party; he takes his leave with the words, "Happy trading. Rock on."

An even more telling barometer of the way investment culture changed in the late nineties was the metamorphosis of *Money* magazine. A publication of Time Inc. and the biggest entry in the personal finance category, *Money* had always been impossibly square and pathetically earnest. One of the most reliably populist supporters of the individual investor, it reveled in Gannett-like opinion polls and pie charts, amusing the people with news of themselves. It tended to address its middle-class readers in the first person plural. And it nearly always portrayed its little-guy heroes as members of a properly functioning middle-class family. Even a 1991 story about the "twenty-somethings" focused on Xers who were married and with children. *Money* was also irrepressibly patriotic. A special 1991 issue that aimed to compare the standards of living in the US to those of all other nations addressed itself specifically to the backlash sentiments of old, invoking none other than John Wayne in the first sentence and acknowledging readers' fears about national decline after "we retreated from Vietnam." The goal here, though, was not to enflame those fears but to assuage them, to find facts that would prove "reassuring." And sure enough, the editors of *Money* duly discovered that the US still ranked first among nations. In an accompanying story the magazine reaffirmed the most saccharine elements of the Horatio Alger myth: the US as a land of explosive opportunity, a place where "your dreams are within your grasp," ever so unlike the "class-conscious societies of Europe and Asia" where "success is like royalty: you must be born to it." What's more, the news for the middle class seemed always to be good news. Considering, in 1992, the undeniable fact that the middle class was shrinking, *Money* insisted that this was because so many were "*climbing* the income ladder, not sliding down it." The magazine's most overtly populist moments were drenched in Capra-esque treacle: Think of the 1991 story in which the magazine's editor recounted how he "delivered your mail to Washington" ("When you roar," the editor applauded his readers, "the whole country hears you") and which was illustrated with a photo of said editor wagging a finger at a congressional committee.[12]

By 1998 slushy homilies like these wouldn't play anymore, not even in Peoria. As the kids of its subscribers declared their allegiance to alternative nation and as its own pages filled with the abrasive, disturbing ads of the online brokerages, *Money* finally got attitude and began speaking for a middle class that believed more in money than in the verities of John Wayne. Now the magazine wondered about the investment portfolios of people like Joan Jett, who appeared in the August 1999 issue in all her dyed, pierced, and tattooed glory (not that her stock-picking strategy differed in any significant way from that of the non-tattooed: "I choose companies I see in everyday life," she told the magazine, among them Starbucks, Boeing, IBM, FedEx, and Disney). It compared one fund manager to Puff Daddy and referred to another as the "king of extreme investing." It used mildly unsettling illustrations: Stock listings projected on a man's naked body, a pile of glass eyeballs, photos of superstar fund managers distorted in such an edgy manner they would be at home on a punk rock CD cover. The new

Money also ran mildly discomfiting stories, stories about how much more the richest people on earth have than the poorest, stories cautioning readers against being tricked by all the scams and deceptions out there, stories about stocks that *Money* had recommended that then tanked. Horrifying stories, like the one about a Japanese family who lost everything in that country's long, bitter recession. Debunking stories, usually from columnists like Jason Zweig and the bearish James Grant. Stories with huge doses of sarcasm about subjects that used to be so dear to *Money*'s middle-class heart—such as America's advantages over the rest of the world. ("Used to be, the U.S. colonized the minds of kids worldwide via Mickey Mouse and Sesame Street," a writer spat in the March 2000 issue, but now our own kids "are prey" to *their* mass-cult offerings.) *Money* even found high schoolers with a stake in the market, noting how they fine-tuned their portfolios while listening to Tupac and doting on their conservative cool.[13]

The Web Changes a Few Things

And then along came the Internet, showing up like a long-awaited market populist messiah. By the time it emerged into the mainstream of American life in 1995, of course, the People's boom was already well under way. But the Internet, like Generation X, fit the fantasy of economic democracy through stock ownership so perfectly that it seemed like confirmation from on high. Now, it was argued, anyone could do their own research, could keep an eye on their portfolio, could place their own trades. So profoundly had the new device leveled the playing field that the people wouldn't even have to stick with the buy-and-hold model of Lynch and Buffett: They could now become self-reliant day-traders all on their own, each one communing with their brands in their own way.

Again James J. Cramer helped to spell out the new consensus faith. Writing in *Worth* magazine in May 1997, Cramer insisted that, thanks to the "overall empowerment of the individual stock picker" through the information available on the Internet, "the small investor has never been in such good shape." "Good shape" was just the start of it. Cramer asserted that given this new equality of information and the flexibility of the amateur investor (professional fund managers were constrained by all sorts of institutional rules and practices), the small-timer should be wiping the floors with the bloated institutional player. Consequently, Cramer advised readers to abandon mutual funds and take up stock-picking themselves—and if not for the money, then for the freedom: "It's never been this easy to have control over your own monetary destiny." Sure, guys had been talking about financial democracy for almost a decade now, but this time it was here for real.[14]

But while the Web did indeed bring a vast expansion of talk and commentary, at a rate of millions of words per day, and while it noticeably upped the nation's attitude quotient, it challenged the prevailing notion of the People's Market not at all. On the contrary, the Web almost instantly became the familiar vehicle of cultural populism it remains today, a place where anybody could thumb their nose at authority. It permitted the replacing of middle-American types like the Beardstown Ladies with a different sort of populist subject, the day-trader, but even this new "extreme investor" retained the same transcendental humility as before. Successful day-trading, advised one 1999 description of the phenomenon, required an abandonment of egotism and arrogance, "a certain wisdom, a Zen-like sense of [one's] own insignificance in the face of the market."[15] In issues of personal finance, the transition to the Web served to amplify the small investor's darkest suspicions about the Wall Street establishment, to foster an ever-escalating competition to believe the worst. Web discourse was like *Consumer Reports* with an extremely bad attitude: The world was out to rip you off, and only suckers doubted it. It was both hardened and innocent at the same time, and for all its skepticism it sent the notion of the People's Market soaring. And with that idea went so much else: Prices, of course, but also (and ironically) the larger fantasy of the unification of popular and corporate interests. If the Web achieved anything even close to the millennial hopes of its promoters, it was in its final blurring of the line between the People and corporate America.

Cultural entrepreneurs saw the potential of the Internet immediately, and any number of investment-oriented websites were quickly established. Among the first to capture the public imagination with investment advice, interactive stock discussion boards, and an early version of the wiseass tone that would soon be the Internet's greatest gift to civilization was the site on America Online known as The Motley Fool. Operated and filled with content by twentysomething brothers David and Tom Gardner, The Motley Fool came online in 1994, offering pretty much the same sort of anti-expertise riffs one found in the works of Peter Lynch, the how-to tips of the Beardstown Ladies, and the thrift-obsessions of *The Millionaire Next Door*. Before long the brothers Gardner discovered something even better than dispensing personal financial advice: the wonder of mass two-way communication, or, as they put it, the "grassroots revolution" of interactivity. (They have also described it as a "subversive movement" and a parallel of the Protestant Reformation.) On the Motley Fool website, anyone who cared to log on was able to share their thoughts on different companies and to expand on the investment prospects they saw in each. "Average people," not experts, were talking to each other about corporate America: Pretty wonderful stuff indeed. According to the Motleys, this broker-free conversation, bringing in as it did all manner of unusual information and privileged perspectives, actually gave "little-guy investors" a considerable advantage not only over older methods of investment research but over the Wall Street experts themselves.[16]

From this epiphany the Motleys proceeded to build a media empire in miniature. They have published four books as of this writing, host a regular radio show, and claim to operate the "world's most popular online financial site." The secret ingredient to all their success is an undiluted, 180-proof market populism mixed with the brothers' trademark witty asides and snide interjections. For *the Motleys despise Wall Street*.

In their 1998 book, *You Have More Than You Think,* they charged that money, a naturally "universal, commonplace" thing, had been cruelly monopolized by "an exclusive ruling class of 'financial professionals.' " But "America gets more democratic and egalitarian with every passing day," the brothers insist, and they are here to bring down the people's will on the world of investing. In their utter certainty that anyone can manage a portfolio as well as anyone else, the Motleys have taken as their mission the overthrow and final destruction of this "ruling class," to whom they apply virtually any enemy-of-democracy epithet that's handy, comparing them to an "elite clergy," mocking their "marbled mansions," describing them as an "entrenched establishment," noting how commissions allow your broker to "detail his DeLorean."[17]

Where the Beardstown Ladies offered recipes as evidence of their down-homeness, the Motleys offer a full-blown carnivalesque mythology all their own, a fantasy of the world of Wall Street expertise turned upside down. They and their followers call themselves "Fools" as a way of tweaking Wall Street's traditional contempt for the small investor. Meanwhile the "Wise," a.k.a. the bankers, stockbrokers, and fund managers of the Old Economy, replete with their "expensive suits and gold cufflinks," are said to "prey on ignorance and fear." Like just about every other ideologue of the nineties business world, the Motleys believe that the greatest error of the past, the Man's most heinous sin, is his belief in—and ability to profit from—public stupidity. "The financial world does not want you to educate yourself," the Motleys insist in one of their collections of ho-hum saving-and-investing advice. "It hates the idea that you might actually read this stuff." But don't get carried away with this assault on investment propriety: All we need to overthrow this system is more information, and the Motleys have made it their job to tell you how to find it. Poring over data, doing your own research, as advised by Buffett, Lynch, the Ladies, and just about everyone else, here takes on an odd new attribute: Reading the NYSE listings is a subversive act! So is saving, so is not playing the lottery, so is facing down a salesman, and so is just about any other bit of thrifty behavior, all of which gives the Motleys' website its weird feel of a cross between the IWW songbook and "Hints from Heloise." Here is how one participant, having adopted the Motleys' Fools-against-the-world lexicon, described a few years ago his insistence on driving the same car for a long time: "Recently I watched the odometer on the Foolmobile flip 200,000 miles. Oh my! That's not what you're supposed to do. I've been told time and again that I shouldn't keep a car with that many miles; it isn't wise. Of course, the people who tell me *that* are generally car salespeople, and they seem to recommend getting a new car at whatever miles are currently on my odometer."[18] Dare to struggle, dare to save!

Investors need information, and the most crucial item of information is the disposition of the popular mind. For admen and politicians it is found through focus groups, but for populist investors the correct tool is, of course, the Internet. In a 1999 disquisition on "The Spirit of Foolishness," one of the Motleys' cast of writers informed readers that "large numbers in the return column" spring from democratic principle rather than any particular approach, from "paying no mind to the Wise gooroos who speak in magazines and on TV, listening instead to a national audience in the open forum provided by this incredible medium." The Web has opened the logic of the focus group to everyone, and anyone can profit from the insights, provided they *believe:* Believe in the wrongness of authority, in "not taking yourself too seriously, and always maintaining your humility."[19] Big returns await him who is down with the people.

But what does it mean in practical terms to believe in the people? Like just about every other prominent investment adviser in the nineties, the Motleys counsel their followers to invest in "businesses that have built a global consumer brand." "Dominant brand" is point number one in one of the Motleys' stock-picking systems; an online explanation of the strategy hailed in particular those brands that had "mindshare," that had "burrowed a small home into your cerebellum." Not surprisingly, the Motleys endorse as stock picks the same names chosen by just about everyone else in that brand-mad decade: Coca-

Cola, Microsoft, Nike, Gillette, Pepsi, Wal-Mart, Disney, Gannett. Again the brand is the thing, the mystery substance that distinguishes winners from losers, that props up market value as well as market share, earnings, and just about everything else. To believe in the people means to believe in their brands.[20]

Again, though, the inherent contradictions of market populism rise to the surface. Advertising, as the great temple of consumption and credit buying, is naturally a central target of any program for increased thriftiness. For someone like "capitalist pig" Jonathan Hoenig, advertising is the hellish opposite of the true path of investing, the siren song luring his generation to its financial doom. The Motleys share this perspective, heaping derision on "misleading" financial advertisements in one book and bemoaning the way advertising leads consumers to play the lottery in another. But advertising also happens to be the bricks and mortar of brands. Were the entire world to be converted to Folly (or Lynchdom, or Pigdom, or move to Beardstown), cut back on its senseless consuming, and begin to question the absurd claims of advertising, the share prices might soar for a while, but ultimately the blue-chip brands would collapse in short order. Clearly the Motleys think such a scenario could never come to pass: The vast majority of us will continue to listen to the Wise, will kindly permit advertising to burrow into our cerebellum. *This* aspect of business-as-usual will never change.

On paper the Motleys were partial to the brand-based, buy-and-hold investment strategies of the early nineties. But the particular stock-trading escapade with which they will forever be identified was the feverish 1995–96 speculative bubble in shares of Iomega, the manufacturer of Zip drives for personal computers. In their first book the Motleys offer up an early, triumphant account of the Iomega episode as an illustration of the way all investing will be done in the fabulous future. In the very early stages, after the Zip drive had been invented but while there were still doubts about the company's manufacturing capacity, investors from across the land, mistrusting main-

stream news accounts of the company, started doing their own leg-
work on Iomega and posted their findings on the Motley Fool website.
As a result, readers of The Motley Fool knew more about Iomega
sooner than any "Wall Street analyst or firm." Writing in 1995, the
brothers Gardner offered this as evidence of the Web's ability to utterly turn the world of traditional hierarchy upside down: "Thanks to
online communication, it is now little-guy investors—not huge brokerage firms—who hold the most valuable cards." Meanwhile, Iomega
was on its way up from two dollars a share to an eventual high of
$330.75, which it reached in May 1996. All along the path of the
stock's astonishing advance—and its precipitous drop soon thereafter—the Motleys were the subject of a good old-fashioned media
frenzy, as part of which it was suggested both that their community of
contributors were dealing in inside information and that they were
heedlessly puffing a mass mania. In the Fools' considerably more
humble 1998 account of the Iomega episode, they make fewer grand
claims for the online "revolution" and insist instead that they were
merely following their unchanging principles: Iomega made a good
product, and "the stock market rewards great brand names and consistently strong growth in profits."[21]

"Great brand names" is the key here. However modest the two chief
Fools' goals had been, out on the Motley Fool discussion boards their
vision of investing as town meeting had come more to resemble a focus group that had consumed way too much complimentary coffee.
Iomega bulls and bears, each under their colorful pseudonyms, had
transformed a discussion of the Zip drive and the company's fiscal
wherewithal into a vicious free-for-all over the nature of the brand. The
"Iomegans," as they called themselves, were much more than what the
admen refer to as "core users": They were brand loyalists of the most
fanatical tendency, partying at annual shareholder meetings, shouting
down the doubters, declaring their undying love for all things Iomega,
interpreting bad news for their company as hostile propaganda, un-
masking the naysayers and informing on them to their employers. The
Iomega bears, for their part, played the opposite role, developing an in-

explicable hostility for the company and taking obvious pleasure in announcing bad news to the faithful.[22]

News accounts of the episode expressed alarm at the stream of rumor and falsehood that was obviously driving the price of Iomega, but the lesson for committed market populists (like the brothers Fool themselves and writers for publications like *Business Week* and *Fortune*) was encouraging. Average folks were now able to talk back to the professionals, to spread their own rumors the way insiders had always done, and even to take terrible revenge on the Wise—most notably in the case of the unfortunate Wall Street firms who shorted Iomega on the theory that the public was always wrong. This was a mania that for once worked the other way, that left the insiders holding the bag. In addition it was the first open glimpse of that most majestic of democratic processes: *The people were making their brands.*

By 1997, the traditional mass media had observed so many stock prices bubble and burst due to "online hype" that the phenomenon had largely dropped from the front pages. But the transformation in the People's Market was more lasting. The Motleys may talk of Buffett and Lynch, of solid brands and buying for the long run, but the lesson their Website taught was that brands could be built and wrecked overnight, and that anybody could make it happen. The dream of universal access to information had become one of everyman as insider. Since broker-free, discounted trading had become widely available online in 1998, and since ticker prices, newswires, and even rumor wires could be viewed online, now anyone could trade like the insiders, taking profits from minute-to-minute fluctuations rather than the long, responsible haul. Now anyone could start his own rumors and commit his own forgeries. Now anyone could stay one step ahead of the deluded public, the foolish crowd.

And Zig a Zig Ah!

Nothing could stop the People's Market as it rolled through 1998 and 1999: Not the destruction of the once-celebrated Asian economies by international currency speculators; not the warnings of economic experts, whose comments we had learned to disregard way back in '91 and '92; not the spectacle of the poor, deluded Russians, their naive free-market hopes squashed like yesterday's Coke can; not the Old Economy–style collapse and the Old Economy–style bailout of the Long Term Capital Management hedge fund, not even news footage of crazed day-traders gunning down their former comrades-in-speculation. Let the elitist naysayers gnash their teeth: The people were in the saddle now, and we Americans *believed* in the market, like we believed in apple pie, in Chevrolet, in rock 'n' roll, in ourselves. We the People had caught a glimpse of ourselves in the mirror of the market, had seen and recognized our own hunger for percentage, and we hymned our own genius as we sent the prices mounting steadily upward.

Of course there were gradual changes, just as there were slight modifications in the way the market was explained to a worshipful public. By 1999 we were officially inhabiting a "New Economy," after all, and some alterations were in order. For example, the blue-chip brands had changed, gone from populist retailers and populist manufacturers to populist revolutionaries, to the companies that were turning the Old Economy on its ear and thereby making people's power possible— which is to say Internet portals, computer manufacturers, and online brokers: AOL, Schwab, E*Trade, Intel. Now we were logging on to Schwab.com and investing in Schwab; using AOL to log on to E*Trade and investing in both AOL and E*Trade. The logic was circular but no one could deny that it worked.

New optimists were constantly bubbling up, flickering briefly across the national culture and assuring us, based on this or that newly discovered economic calculus, not only that the market had much, much further to go but that those who doubted it were doubting the people themselves. One of the most remarkable of the late bulls was James Glassman, a *Washington Post* columnist whose optimism was as inflated as the market itself: When the Dow stood at 10,000, he declared in the pages of the *Wall Street Journal* (and then from the pages of the *Atlantic Monthly* and then in a book titled, simply, *Dow 36,000*) that it should rightly be standing at 36,000. He arrived at this extraordinary conclusion not through some hazy belief in "progress" but through a militant faith in popular enlightenment. The people, also known as "small investors," were becoming "calmer and smarter," realizing that, if one invested for the long haul, then stocks were no riskier than bonds. All the market was doing, then, was reflecting this new found wisdom and pricing stocks accordingly—that is, running them up to some three-and-a-half times what they were when Glassman went public with his discovery. High stock prices, he insisted, reflected "not [the people's] nuttiness but their sanity." Naturally Glassman phrased his discovery as a sort of culture war in miniature, with small investors, in all their wisdom, being *"rationally* exuberant" while the "experts" and the preening Wall Street "establishment" sought to slow their drive to the top by "accusing them of being screwy."[23] For Glassman, the stock market reflected the wisdom of the people so reliably that it acted as a quasi-divine dispenser of moral justice, humbling the proud and elevating the modest. Since the stock market represented, as he and his coauthor Kevin Hassett put it in their 1999 opus, *Dow 36,000,* the "collective judgment" of "millions of people around the world," it was foolhardy in the extreme for a single individual to think he could "outsmart" it. "Respect the market," they intoned. Doing the opposite, showing "a kind of know-it-all hubris, is what leads to disaster, not just in personal life, but in the stock market." The arrogant, the expert, the snobbish, the didactic, were all doomed once the market was free to stride the earth as it saw fit.[24]

For others, 36,000 was a piker's number. The people wouldn't rest until their Dow hit 50,000! That was the figure insisted on by corporate economist Lawrence Kudlow when his turn came on the *Wall Street Journal's* op-ed page. Kudlow insisted in March 1999 on understanding the market as the site of a titanic struggle between the freedom-loving people and the "experts," a class of "economic and investment gurus" who *since all the way back in 1982* "have preached pessimism." Writing again in August, only days after certain prominent Fed spokesmen had expressed reservations about the bull market,

Kudlow angrily responded with a vision of the people rising to "confront" this snobbish, pessimistic "economic establishment," lifting themselves as one in defense of their Dow. Kudlow evoked the scene in stirring thirties populist fashion, picturing "a tidal wave of opposition from the shareholders, farmers, seniors, homeowners, Web site operators, venture capitalists, small-business men and others who make up the new investor class." All of us—even farmers and seniors, those stalwarts of New Deal imagery—are now as one in the marketplace, and by putting money in the market we have endorsed Kudlow's vision of the universe. "These asset owners know that markets, not governments, create wealth. They will not permit new tax, monetary, trade and regulatory obstacles to impede free enterprise."[25]

Delusional though this stuff may have been, market populism was slowly becoming a functioning element of the market itself. Ideology, it seemed, was an investment-grade substance all on its own. So predictably did any hint of popular participation inflate share prices that in 1999 the stock split itself—an early-twentieth-century reform designed to make shares more affordable for small investors—actually became for some a powerful inducement to buy. It didn't matter, really, that technically the post-split shares were supposed to be worth the same as the old share, since the act of faith itself was enough to make share prices increase, thus *making* splits a reliable indicator and bringing in more buyers every time one was announced. A June 1999 issue of *Money* magazine announced the appearance of beepers that would notify anyone anywhere that a company had decided to split its shares (now if only we could invest in the company that made those beepers!). Elsewhere in the same issue an editorial gamely entitled "Hooray, U.S.A." used the relative rarity of stock-splitting in Europe as evidence that "European capitalism," unlike the American variety, "is organized to benefit a wealthy elite."[26]

This was the climate in which Joseph Nocera returned, with great fanfare, to the scene of his earlier triumph. So widely were we now participating in the stock market, he declared in the October 11, 1999, issue of *Fortune* magazine, that owning Americans now constituted a proud "Trader Nation" all their own, a phrase emblazoned on the magazine's cover just above text announcing, "It's more than a bull gone mad. It's a new set of rules." Like Tom Friedman's tales of the final democratization of everything by the Internet, this tale of the final democratization of everything by the Internet (illustrated with images of revolutionary fists clutching computer mouses while a Wall Street sign is pulled down in the background) began by invoking a TV commercial for an online brokerage. And an introduction to Nocera's article written by another *Fortune* reporter proclaimed the tenets of market populism as baldly as anything produced during the decade:

> What we have here is nothing short of a revolution. Power that for generations lay with a few thousand white males on a small island in New York City is now being seized by Everyman and Everywoman. In fact, it's no overstatement to suggest that this movement from Wall Street to Main Street is one of the most significant socioeconomic trends of the past few decades. It's not only changing the way we invest, it's changing the way we work and live too. And it's sure as hell rocking the boat on Wall Street.[27]

Nocera, for his part, followed the market populist script to the sentimental letter. He revisited his hometown of Providence, R.I., marveled at how many people in that quaint and unpretentious locale had money in the market, and captured them talking about business so quaintly and unpretentiously that corporate doings might be mistaken for sports. They cheered for their favorite companies, they cursed at the ones that let them down; they hissed the bad CEOs and confided confidently about the good ones. These all-American characters turned out to be astonishingly virtuous investors as well, refusing to panic and run (like a certain bunch of white males on a small island in New York City), providing for one another's prosperity through their faithful contributions to 401(k) plans. In return, the stock market had been damned neighborly to lovable, unpretentious Providence, building it a nice Nordstrom's in the new mall. Once again, Nocera discovered that the People's Market seemed to have abolished social class. Gaping at the (utterly unremarkable) fact that the owner of a commercial cleaning business had money in the market, Nocera declared, grandly, "You can't judge a man's portfolio by the clothes on his back or by his profession. Not anymore."

And winging above it all were the leaping, soaring Internet shares, the primary objects of a speculative bubble that, by century's end, dwarfed any in human history. As this is where the story of the People's Market turns ugly, let me acknowledge that most of the journalists, magazines, newspapers, and websites discussed here routinely warned investors that Internet shares were overpriced; that their valuations didn't make sense according to the usual rules of investing; that speculators could get burned easily. But those scattered notes of caution were far overpowered by a decade of promotional hype, of talk about the "third industrial revolution," the "information superhighway," the abolition of distance, the glories of cyberspace, the magic of communication "mind to mind," the technology that "changed everything," the place where the "old rules" no longer applied, where the inevitabilities of Moore's Law, of Metcalfe's Law, of Gilder's Law ensured that hundred-bagger appreciations would continue to fall from the heavens. Who cared if the experts doubted? Hadn't the central lesson of market populism and of the great bull market itself been that the experts knew nothing? This "New Economy" thing, they were saying on CNBC, had broken free from terrestrial understanding altogether! Right there in the *Wall Street Journal* a "strategist" from Morgan Stanley was announcing that not even interest rate hikes could bring the "New Economy" stocks back to earth![28] Nor could the brief cautionary notes at the bottom of the ads hope to counterbalance what had been, after all, a long and concerted PR effort by the nation's largest computer, software, and telecommunications corporations; the president, vice president, and speaker of the House; the director of the MIT Media Lab; the right-wing foundations and think tanks; and virtually every newspaper columnist in the land. The entire American establishment with the exception of the military had puffed for this one all together. No effort had been spared to convince Americans that the Internet was something close, in miraculous effect as well as capacity for salvation, to a democratic second coming.

This is not to deny the very tangible changes the Internet brought: By 1999, Internet brokerages were servicing some ten million accounts, up from seven million the year before (and up from none only four years before).[29] Mutual funds, the early hero of the People's Market, had fallen from favor as the notion of every man his own broker caught on and individual investors used online brokerages to build their own portfolios. Value investing, the populist favorite of the early nineties, yielded such poor returns in 1999 and 2000—even as the "New Economy" rained free money down on its true believers—that at least one prominent value fund manager, in his frustration, gave up the business altogether. Even Buffett's magic touch seemed to wear off as Berkshire Hathaway lost nearly half of its market value in 1999 and the first few months of 2000.[30] Had any of the buy-and-hold faithful still been holding Procter & Gamble, the greatest brand-stock of them all, on March 8, 2000, they would have seen their investment lose nearly a third of its value in one day. The trade-off from the brand fad to the Internet fad could be quite direct. Everywhere reporters looked, investors seemed to be dumping their funds and whiling away the hours at work following their stakes in AOL, DoubleClick, E*Trade, and Inktomi.[31]

Full-service brokerages were hit hardest of all. After years of vilification in investment guides, online screeds, and TV commercials, they began to succumb. On June 1, 1999, Merrill Lynch, the nation's largest brokerage firm, ran up the white flag, announcing that it, too, would finally offer discounted stock trading over the Internet. Within days the announcement had been woven seamlessly into Wall Street's new narrative: This was a triumph of nothing less than popular democracy, an ideological homecoming for the firm that had begun life promoting itself as the bridge between Main Street and Wall Street.

Merrill itself was only too happy to agree. By June 9 the firm was running huge two-page spreads in the *Wall Street Journal* describing the decision as a "merger" of "Merrill Lynch, You & Co.," a grassroots reworking of the corporation that was said to be so thorough and so public-minded that "you" can be said actually to have "designed" the company's various "initiatives." Amid quotations from Charles Merrill, the original market populist, the company declared that, after fifty years, it had entered "phase two" of its business. By November, Merrill Lynch was running television commercials imagining itself as the hotly debated subject of a "town meeting," that most abused of populist clichés.

By the summer of 1999, though, even the hardest core of the efficient-market faithful could be heard speaking of bubbles. Others fought back, standing by to reassure us with the comforting banalities of inevitability and "change." Thus Andy Kessler, a Silicon Valley investment banker who appeared on the *Wall Street Journal* op-ed page in July to calm the occasional gusts of panic, conjured up images of an economy where the overpowering logic of the Internet had obsoleted all old standards of measurement and understanding, where things work when "no one is in charge," where smart companies give things away, where massive losses in the ledger books are a sign of corporate health, and where the cool people will do anything for more stock options: "Nobody wants cash; it's too final." Currency, Kessler reminds us, is backed by the government, while "Internet paper, on the other hand, is backed by smart entrepreneurs who work like dogs through the night to change the world." Just to nail it down, Kessler tosses in the usual reference to inevitability: "This is where the world, and all of us, are headed."[32] So get used to it—and buy those Internet shares!

In the world of advertising the Internet-as-messiah barrage never slackened. And to listen to the nonstop bubble-talk on CNBC, where even the darkest days offered silver linings, the naysaying to which Kessler responded might as well have been issued by *Pravda,* so easily was it tuned out. One commercial in particular that ran during those months seemed to capture the swaggeringly optimistic tenor of those

days: a low-budget spot for Suretrade, one of many new online brokerages, that I saw for the first time just a few months after the Clinton
administration rescued the millionaire directors of Long Term Capital
Management. In the world according to Suretrade, however, all that
mattered was individual initiative and moral disdain for such Old
Economy gestures, attributes that the People's Market is said to reward
generously. Behold as Generation X declares its independence: "We're
not relying on the government," announces a young black woman with
dreads. "We're not relying on the company," sneers a white guy with a
spiky do. "We're not relying on a big fat inheritance," scoffs a young
man with a hint of an Indian accent. How, then, do these salty young
unbelievers plan to make their way in the world? The answer is delivered by a matter-of-fact fellow in glasses. "We trade online." "We're
betting on ourselves," explains a confident-sounding white woman.
This was self-help and financial responsibility, circa 1999. So far had
the notion of a People's Market advanced that "we," Nocera's beloved
middle class, had actually been delivered from the necessity of working. All we had to do was sneer at the government and the Old Economy, and money would just fill "our" pockets, delivered by the Market
that we built.

Taken just a tad less literally, the commercial was eerily accurate.
There *were* any number of hip youngsters whose net worth had been
so immeasurably enhanced by online trading that, truly, they no longer
had any need of parents, corporation, or even nation. These were the
young e-barons, the people's plutocrats, who accumulated such staggering piles as the century drew to a close. They had done it not by rap-
ing the Erie, by pushing the Great Northern on through to the Pacific,
by implementing the Bessemer process, but by inventing brands,
brands that joined in the people's anthem to themselves, brands that
were "interactive," brands that could actually show us in all our us-ness
to ourselves. Each successful dot-com was a sort of meta-brand, a
company that existed primarily as an idea, as a distillation of some aspect of market populism. There was no longer any need to show earnings: The People would build these companies themselves, by

contributing their dollars and their sacred brand loyalty. There was no need to wrest an industry or even a living from the earth; we would create the wealth by acclamation. We the People *were* betting on ourselves.

In Priceline.com, the vendor of discount airline tickets whose shares we bid up to the point where its market capitalization was twice that of United Airlines, we saw the very apotheosis of consumer empowerment. In print the company's founder hailed himself as a corporate explorer of the Lewis and Clark variety; others saluted him as a "New Age Edison," inventing and actually patenting a "buyer-driven" business model. We believed, and we made him a multibillionaire, propelled him in the course of one trading day from obscurity to being one of the richest men on the planet.[33] In the company's omnipresent ads, lovable ham William Shatner promised, simply, that his employer would one day be "big, really big." We believed, and we made it so.[34]

In eBay.com, the all-purpose online auction mart that we raised overnight to the size of an Exxon, we thought we glimpsed the primal democracy of the marketplace, the Norman Rockwell–style swap meet without end. "Having corporations just cram more products down people's throats doesn't seem like a lot of fun," says the company's "libertarian" founder. "I really wanted to give the individual power to be a producer as well." Not only did it enrich everyday Americans pursuing their humble, everyday hobbies, but it was a bona fide "community."[35] Newspaper accounts of the company's IPO emphasized the telling anecdote in which competing groups of investment bankers, told to bring something they had purchased on eBay to an initial meeting, were easily sorted out when one brought expensive French wines (grrr!) and lost out to the gang that showed up with bits of the common people's culture like Beanie Babies and a board game from the seventies.[36] In its early days eBay even featured online help dispensed by a rustic character from Vermont or somewhere—surely that was worth an additional hundred million! We believed—oh, we *believed!*—and we made it so.

And in Amazon.com, the "borderless" online bookstore that we pumped up into the most grotesquely overcapitalized company on earth, we perceived the very incarnation of democratic business practice, "the world's most customer-centric company." Not only did *Time's* December 1999 hagiography of the company hail its methods as a glorious "dotcommunism," but it offered us the unimaginable class-smashing spectacle of man-of-the-people CEO Jeff Bezos autographing his employees' hardhats! And if selling tax-free books wasn't enough, both Bezos and his laughing millionaire employees were reported to have extraordinarily grand, people-friendly goals for their future careers as philanthropists.[37] Could we afford not to believe?

In our belief that the expertise of the past was but effete elitism, we charged ahead regardless of the traditional measurements. And in an ecstasy of self-love We the People were making economic history: In June 1999, eBay was trading for 3,991 times earnings while Amazon and Priceline had ratios that were infinite, since they had no earnings at all. And for this there was no precedent in the entire experience of the world.[38]

As for the young Turks of interactivity themselves, the ones that We the People had elevated to the uppermost ranks of the *Fortune* world's wealthiest list, one could not say that we had chosen poorly. In fact these fabulous figures were walking embodiments of everything the "New Economy" celebrated—and even before the riches descended on them. The People's Market was all about helping out the kids, providing for their futures, wasn't it? And these *were* the kids, boy billionaires with baby faces. It had all been about innovation, about breaking the rules, about overturning workplace hierarchy, hadn't it? And the kids were *all* that: the ones who we had been told (sometimes in exactly these words) to worship, the smart ones that we should never talk down to, the genius ones who were making us and our machines and our language and our very thoughts hopelessly obsolete. It was as though, having been convinced of these things after a decade of market populist incantation, we moved frantically to make it so in fact. It was as though we had gone through all those years of bull market thriftiness and patriotism and faith just to get to this moment, to arrive at this bizarre consummation, to make these kids rich beyond the imaginings of history, to channel the savings of all those World War II vets and those nurses and those sheet metal workers and all those tired engineers—still believers in those old Jeffersonian myths, after all these years—into their young, Xtreme pockets, to elevate these golden beings, this glorious progeny of the American century, above all the rest of the world.

Thus did rumors of righteous teenybopper millionaires make their way across the land in late 1999. Hanging by my desk is a postcard advertisement for Forbes.com that I picked up in a "cigar bar." "College quitting, credit card maxing, $23 million stock option owning RE-TIREE," it reads, over a picture of a close-cropped and heavily lip-sticked Gen-Xer mugging ironically for the camera. On my TV is Treasury Secretary Lawrence Summers, celebrating the incredible opportunity of the new economy by pointing out that "entrepreneurs may raise their first $100 million before buying their first suits."[39]

For the *Wall Street Journal,* at least, there was something deeply gratifying about the whole spectacle. In March 1999 one of the paper's reporters attended a party given to celebrate the uncanny ascension of the stock price of TheGlobe.com, a company whose business was not described. The reporter strained to get the mood of the "hip Soho nightspot" just right: Dancers in "gold-sequined bikinis" gyrated for the young men's pleasure while a "five-piece funk band" supplied musical credibility. The newly bemillioned wore nametags identifying them by their employer's ticker symbol and talked about the robust appreciation of their stock options. There was to be no mistake about their outrageousness: As the article's title puts it, they were "Risk Takers," for whom the "System is No Longer Sacred." But what system was it that the edgy, unpredictable Generation X sneered at? Certainly not that of the NASDAQ, which had proven itself a worthy social order indeed. No, these young hipsters, though they were but twenty-eight, twenty-nine, and thirty years of age, informed the reporter that they *no longer believed in Social Security!* One of them, flush with cash from one of the most remarkable speculative bubbles in human history, even declared that Social Security was "a little like a Ponzi scheme." The reporter recited the obligatory poll result—all the cool people think Social Security will soon be gone—and added his own twist: "For many, it's good riddance." Once so threatening to the corporate imagination, these young hipsters—their minds changed by stock market success—were now presented as the strongest possible endorsement of the *Journal*'s way of thinking.[40] Surely a new world (a *globe-dot-com!*) was being born here, a Wall Street world that knew nothing but bull markets and the beneficence of the trading floor. Surely God's in his heaven, all's right with the world!

In retrospect one can't help but feel that the young skeptics of TheGlobe.com would have been better advised to turn their doubt on targets closer to home. TheGlobe.com itself turned out to be a rich case study in Internet hype as personal enrichment scheme. Promoted as that most coveted object of market populist desire, an "online community," it went through what was then the most successful IPO in history in December 1998, going from nine dollars to ninety-seven dollars in a day. But as investors got acquainted with the site's leaden content, its share price began to plummet. In response the company sent TheGlobe.com's two teen-idol founders parading promiscuously through the nation's fashion and young-lifestyle magazines, paving the way for a secondary stock offering. And, evidently, for a big sell-off by the young company's main backer, the seasoned business veteran Michael Egan, who was able to dump 2.5 million TheGlobe.com shares when they were trading at twenty dollars. As a writer for *Fortune* put it months later, "$30 million has effectively gone from investors' wallets into Egan's own."[41]

They weren't all young and Xtreme, of course. And in some ways the most telling episode of the dot-com boom was the transformation of James J. Cramer—not from square to hip, but from investment commentator into investment proper. In 1996 Cramer had launched a financial publication of his own, an online magazine called TheStreet.com. Before two and a half years had passed Cramer took his new venture public. And the bull market that Cramer had done so much to promote over the years smiled graciously on its loyal son: One day after the IPO, TheStreet.com was capitalized at $1.42 billion while the value of Cramer's own holdings hit $216 million.[42]

Cramer is not a railroad builder. He is not an oil man. He is not even a tow truck driver. He is, of course, the same all-purpose market populist with which our story began, a fund manager become journalist who has hyped and puffed and pumped and bulled on every medium known to man. Cramer and his followers like to emphasize his real investing experience as a way of distinguishing him from full-time financial journalists, but ultimately Cramer was to profit far more from the ideological services he rendered the People's Market than from any bit of trading or buy-and-holding. From his first rise to prominence with the boom in personal finance magazines, Cramer seemed to have at least a finger in each of the bull market's greatest ideological turning points. It was Cramer who touted stocks that his fund held in the pages of *SmartMoney* in 1995 and thus generated one of the defining controversies of nineties financial journalism—a controversy he ended by pinning the inevitable "arrogant" label on his critics ("for they simply don't trust the common sense and intelligence of their readers").[43] It was Cramer who first aired the preposterous notion, from the cover of *The New Republic* (owned and edited by the co-founder of TheStreet.com, Martin Peretz), that stock could replace the various economic tools of the welfare state. It was Cramer who sang the Web as equalizer in the pages of *Worth* in 1997, and Cramer who called the move from consumer brands to technology brands in 1997, pushing Intel, Cisco, Microsoft, Sun Systems, and Hewlett-Packard over Coca-Cola or Gillette.[44] It was Cramer who wrote a story called, simply, "Yeah, Day Traders!" for *Time* magazine in May 1999, in which readers were informed that the Internet had virtually eliminated the advantages held by "me and my fellow professionals" and that "there has never been a better time to attempt to trade for a living."[45] It was Cramer who kept up a steady chant of support for amateur investors throughout the bull market, ready to sing their victories, their wisdom in whatever the key of the day—proclaiming, for example after the vanquishing of the Y2K bug, that as "the pros got it wrong," and as the individual investor had kept the faith, "You have to love a game where the amateurs beat the pants off the professionals." And it was Cramer who reigned throughout the later years of the decade as the manic, word-gushing face of the People's Market—on CNBC, in *SmartMoney,* in *Time,* on the Web—a veritable symbol of "the democratization of investing," as one magazine profile put it.[46]

For the hip investment commentators of the late bull market it was Cramer, not Lynch or Buffett, who reigned as the ultimate role model. Hoenig called him a "mentor" while Kurson, who wrote a *Salon* story defending Cramer against various journalistic critics, celebrated him as the very incarnation of that ideal figure of the overheated late-nineties imagination, the speculator as a populist rebel, or, as Kurson put it, the "type that has always irked those who like to think they control the public's imagination and heroes." The qualities that so enable Cramer to save the public from being manipulated by these monstrous elites, according to Kurson, are that he's "loud, smart, outspoken, opinionated and rich."[47]

Cramer himself preferred the Lynchian average-guy stereotype over the rebel hero version, impressing his unfamiliarity with "buzz" thusly upon an interviewer from the *New York Press:* "I'm a schlubby guy who goes home to his wife and kids in New Jersey." And like Peter Lynch, the early hero of the People's Market, Cramer is an ace stock-picker. But while the public was invited actually to allow Lynch to manage their money, Cramer merely gives them tips, advising them to do the actual investing themselves. Both men are populist celebrities, both appear in advertisements, in magazines, and on TV. But Cramer's unbelievable omnipresence in the end made him something quite different from Lynch: Cramer became a brand, the walking and incessantly talking personification of wiseass investor optimism. "Cramer" doesn't just signify a particular bundle of stock picks but a certain attitude about the market and the world. "Cramer" is the hipsters tearing down the doors of the Exchange to a funky dance hall beat, the day-traders running circles around the institutional investors, the Illinois farm wives whipping the pros. And Cramer the man seems to have understood his transfiguration, to have understood that it was democracy itself pumping the bubble, that our traditional faith in the wisdom of the common man had somehow been transferred onto the market, and from there onto him, the man who had done more than anyone else to bolster this market's credibility—financially, politically, and socially.

Cramer was a lively writer but his real genius was in cultural alchemy, his understanding that the Internet permitted him to violate traditional barriers—not merely those separating speculator from journalist, but those between investment ideologue and investment itself. The brilliance of TheStreet.com is not as a journalistic showplace (it has been solid here, if unremarkable), but as an instrument for ideological speculation. Cramer gave Americans a way to put their money down on nothing less than the fortunes of "the street" itself. If it is true, as Ken Kurson maintains, that Cramer confronts illegitimate authority simply by being "rich," then those who bought shares in TheStreet.com were taking sides in Cramer's war, working to ensure that the price of Cramer's shares remained high (I hate my boss—better do what I can to keep Cramer rich), expressing their wish for the market to continue on its ever-ascending path.

Somehow, though, things never quite worked out like the market's great theorists had planned. TheStreet.com hit its all-time high (a little over seventy) on its very first day of trading, on a feverish Tuesday in May 1999. From there it set out on the long downhill road to the land of true humility, to the lowly environs of six.

And the story was the same almost wherever one looked in the dotcom firmament. We the People clamored for more shares in these miracles of democratic interactivity, more shares to make us rich beyond the dreams of history's wisest men, and the great brokerages and investment bankers were only too happy to oblige, underwriting IPO after IPO. And as so many of those shares sank toward worthlessness, it quickly became clear that the ones who actually profited from the "democratization" of Wall Street were those same elite brokerages and exclusive investment bankers that we had supposedly been rebelling against all along. With their millions in underwriting fees they were the true winners of the great bull market's endgame—they and the dazzling assortment of con artists, bucket shop crooks, mafia figures, and two-bit yeggs who emerged from the woodwork in the late nineties, hearing in the populist call a once-in-a-lifetime opportunity to fleece the suckers. The People's Market was turning into a hustler's jubilee.

For the hustlers of ideology the bull market worked similar wonders. While "we" never quite "joined the money class" in terms of wages or security, everywhere one turned in the nineties there was some parable of regular people coming around to the money class's way of understanding the world: Grandmothers in Illinois realizing that the market was the true path to social security all along; regular joes in Detroit figuring out that the union was the wrong way to go; workers everywhere counting on tomorrow's fluctuations to make up for the fact that their boss was such an asshole about wages, that their market-driven health-care plan was worthless, that under no circumstances could they afford to send the kid to college. We were learning that past performance was never, ever, a guarantee of future anything; that if the market insisted it was time to burn our factories and sew microchips into our collars we would just have to do it. We were learning to accept the market as the arbiter of all things: To bow before what it chose to do to our cities, our industries, our lives—so long as that little lift continued in our 401(k)s. In one great patriotic auto-da-fé we were sending the work of decades up in smoke— send the jobs south! put our neighbor on a twelve-hour shift! smash the downtown merchants!—whatever it took to keep the market smiling.

We tried not to think about what would happen when the worm turned, when the hive mind flopped from buy to sell. Having hocked the apparatus of economic democracy in order to take our turn at the roulette wheel, we would have nothing to fall back on, and we would wonder hopelessly if Warren Buffett would ride to the rescue one more time, get us all out from under the plummeting hulk of yesterday's brands.

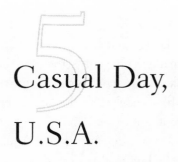

Casual Day, U.S.A.

Management's 1930s

> It's just not cool to make things anymore.
> —*Management consultant Ron Nicol, 1999*[1]

He Bag Production

That a "revolution" of some unspecified nature had stormed the world of business was, by the end of the nineties, one of the truisms of the age. Even if one had no idea what the "revolution" happened to entail, one was seldom out of earshot of its various bold pronouncements and manifestos. Business sang its rebellious new mood with full-page ads in every daily newspaper in the country; business hymned its new-found insurgency with beautifully choreographed pageants during the commercial time-out; business announced its insurrectionary intent from the sides of passing buses and the dead space in the corner of the web page. Business wanted us all to know: It had changed. It had become cool. It had become sensitive, youthful, soulful. It had learned to dance, to sing. Business was no longer wearing pinstripes or tuning in

170

to the old boys' network. In decades previous, perhaps, business had rewarded the well-born and the pompous, but now everything was different. In the nineties business was a truth-device; a friend of humanity; a powerful warrior for global democracy; a righteous enemy of pretense and falsehood. Business had declared war on the American ruling class, on the very idea of social hierarchy. Business had set out to destroy business itself, at least as it used to be practiced in the old days.

Plenty of average Americans, having considerable personal experience with the way the corporation worked, could easily have made their own contributions to the national conversation about the nature of the "business revolution." They could have pointed out that the most noticeable change that swept through the workplaces of the late eighties and nineties was the diverging fortunes of top management and everyone else; that the workplace was becoming ever more arbitrary; that they increasingly worked under an omnipresent threat of instant termination; that regardless of how they toiled they seemed always to be losing ground—and that during the same period CEOs and top management had virtually transcended the realm of work altogether, had achieved a sort of superhuman state from which they made oracular pronouncements and collected rewards on a scale beyond imagining. Were they given to dark humor, these average Americans might also mention that during the same period certain white-collar workers seemed to develop a strange fondness for the weird, mystical, almost crazy slogans of management theory, putting the stuff on company walls, on desks, on pencils; listening to it on tape while they exercised; tuning it in on their car radios while they drove from meeting to meeting.

But one of the things that made the "business revolution" so revolutionary was that, even during the hyper-populist nineties, such doubts were only rarely heard in the national arena. Only business could afford to run commercials on prime time, and in the nineties business seemed increasingly determined to use that advantage to share its thoughts on the nature of enterprise, of office life, of hierarchy, of multiculturalism, of globalization, of "change."

Thus in 1996, NASDAQ superstar MCI supplemented its usual talk about cheap long-distance service with a commercial announcing what sounded like the second coming. Against a screeching alternative-rock soundtrack and a rapidly flickering montage of small children and nonwhite adults, MCI invited the television audience to make believe that the various oppressions troubling the nineties soul had been magically abolished: "there is no race" (little girl crossing out the word "race"); "there are no genders" (two women sit in front of a computer); "there are no infirmities" (teenage girl doing sign language).* It's not true of the world we live in, of course, but it is true of the excellent, freedom-maximizing alternate universe imagined by the communications industry. The meek really will inherit the earth, and MCI will be there to hand them the keys. As the company's new slogan asked, "Is this a great time or what?"

For Nortel Networks, another telecom firm that had been working miracles on the stock market in 1998 and '99, it was such a great time that CEOs had morphed into rock stars. The nineties had become the sixties; the square hierarchs of old were on the run, and when our new-style CEOs stepped to the podium to give what would once have been some canned corporate speech, the words that came out of their mouth were these: "Here come old flattop, he come groovin' up slowly." The camera moved to show us executives and shareholders from all walks of life and in all corners of Business Man's ten-year-old world—on public phones, in taxis, in boardrooms and office suites—first shocked at and then *getting it,* rejoicing over the words of the switched-on leader. The wandering point of view descended gradually through the social ranks, going from observers in a posh executive dining room to a traveler in an exclusive-looking airport lounge, coming finally to rest amongst the company's blue-collar workers, identifiable by their

---

*Deaf children were one of the great clichés of the "business revolution." They appeared conspicuously in advertisements for Merrill Lynch, Nortel Networks, Enron, Sprint, and Cisco Systems, becoming by decade's end a symbol of the Internet's power to overcome disability.

hardhats, who were so overjoyed to discover the big man's cool that they played along to the well-known Beatles tune with air guitars.[2]

Others revolutionaries favored more revolutionary imagery. Clenched fists seemed to erupt defiantly from ads and article illustrations wherever the new order was being discussed. *Wired* magazine offered an eleven-page story on various "Corporate Rebels" illustrated with vibrant knock-offs of Stalin-era Soviet art. For others guillotines did the trick, or images of statues being torn down by the righteous masses. But we can only hope that the limit of the fantasy was reached by software maker Oracle, which ran a commercial during the 1998 Super Bowl comparing itself to the Khmer Rouge, who were shown herding refugees before them and firing their AKs as they ushered in the new era. While the ad did little to inform the public about what Oracle made or sold, it left no doubt about the market's victory over every other form of human organization. This was Year Zero of the Business Revolution: Pol Pot was in the boardroom and the mundane stuff of history was being finally rubbed out.

Advertisements like these were only the most visible aspect of the business revolution. While they were bombastic, they were also trite, the final, hundredth iteration of ideas, theories, and metaphors that had been circulating in the world of the corporation for ten years already. What ended with Oracle's weird homage to the Khmer Rouge began with that body of literature known as management theory, a perennially best-selling genre where celebrity thinkers ponder the problems facing business and its loyal upper-level executives. Management literature is the wellspring of nearly every element of the corporate ideology: It is the source of the metaphors and buzzwords that fill the ads, the annual reports, and the various public presentations that the rest of the world sees; it gives businesspeople their jargon, their concerns, their personal aspirations. Above all, it explains the ways of the mighty so they might be better honored, better imitated by us the lowly.

The first important artifact of business thought to announce that a "management revolution" was underway was *Thriving on Chaos*, the 1987 book by mega-consultant Tom Peters; in 1989, Doubleday launched its Currency line, under which imprint many of the most important contributions to business-revolutionary thought, like *The Fifth Discipline* and *The One to One Future*, would be published; within a few years the Harvard Business School had entered the game as well, giving the genre intellectual prestige and becoming the only academic press to show up regularly in best-seller lists. By the mid-nineties the business revolution even had its own magazine, *Fast Company*, whose premiere editorial was a self-proclaimed "manifesto" hailing the final destruction of "fifty years of received wisdom on the fundamentals of work and competition," and whose increasingly ad-packed pages profiled the various iconoclasts whose bold deeds were said to be redefining the world of production and exchange. *Fast Company's* overnight success in turn spawned an entire new category of extreme management magazines, each one more radical than the last: *Red Herring, Business 2.0, Revolution.* Along the way the business revolution tossed off curiosities like books of management poetry, leadership prayers, corporate mysticism, and even whole cities that adopted the theories of a prominent self-help guru.[3] A chain of mall-based stores called Successories (its first retail outlet opened in 1991) peddled office detritus emblazoned with the gee-whiz slogans of the revolution.

At the same time, the corporate anxiety to "change" in accordance with some management theory or other could sometimes reach a truly remarkable pitch of desperation. One example, cited in 1997 by prominent management theorists Sumantra Ghoshal and Christopher Bartlett, rings with a distinct organizational pathos:

> In the aftermath of a major restructuring, the new CEO embarked on a series of visioning retreats. One outcome was a senior management-endorsed definition of the company's core competencies that was then handed to a task force to recommend how they might be more effectively developed and managed. Meanwhile, the newly appointed chief knowledge officer launched an initiative to help the company become a more effective learning organization. And in a separate but contemporaneous initiative, consultants were called in to help design a reengineering program.[4]

One definition of the "business revolution," then, would be the remarkable flowering of management thinking that took place in the nineties. While the "culture wars" put the traditional humanities and social sciences under a cloud, the business schools and MBA programs where management theory was taught prospered and expanded, growing both at home and abroad as American business schools began offering "executive MBAs" to the credential-hungry executives of other lands. The field developed its own celebrities: the respected British sage Charles Handy, delivering his fatherly homilies on the BBC; Peter Senge, for whom business advice was a way of attuning oneself to the cosmic rhythms of the universe; and Tom Peters, whose ever louder, ever more outrageous style reflected the continuing fascination that cultural rebellion exerted over the corporate mind. And despite its pronounced anti-intellectualism, management literature began in the nineties to accrete the devices of scholarly legitimacy, as management writers learned to pick up each others' ideas and buzzwords, as they developed a professional language all their own, as they invented grand theories of history, science, and progress—and as they found those theories taken seriously in the highest counsels of state and industry.

Even as management theory enjoyed its greatest boom in history, though, it was constantly dogged by accusations of "faddishness." There was a persistent suspicion that the great gurus were in fact clever charlatans preying on a gullible public. Gurus were the butt of jokes; their highfalutin phrases were mocked in TV commercials; and the foolish managers who fell for their palaver were a constant target in *Dilbert*. Even a showplace of management theory like *Fast Company* was capable of running an occasional "Consultant Debunking Unit" in which the contents of popular books of theory were disparagingly summarized. After studying dozens of executives who had implemented some management theory or other, John Micklethwait and Adrian Wooldridge, the business journalists who have written most thoughtfully about the astonishing growth of the theory industry, reported in 1996 that even in the conversation of "those who have fired thousands in the name of one of these theories . . . sooner or later, in virtually every case, the word 'bullshit' appears."[5]

"Bullshit" was certainly the word that sprang to my own mind on that day when I flipped through my first book of management theory— Tom Peters' eight-hundred-page 1992 opus, *Liberation Management.* Peters' zanier 1997 book, *The Circle of Innovation,* struck me as bullshit on wheels. "Bullshit" was also my response when I sat amongst an audience of hundreds of paying businessmen and heard a "futurist" tell how Hegel, whom he had evidently confused with Francis Fukuyama, so long ago predicted liberal democracy's victory over fascism and communism. He also described the rich personal friendship of John Locke and Adam Smith and pronounced on the complete and laughable irrelevance of Newtonian physics now that all of Einstein's theories were "laws." Anybody who has had any experience with the management theory industry can tell similar stories: of quotes and dates wildly misplaced, of an alarming and misinformed credulity about science, of anecdotes that prove nothing, of patently absurd syllogisms, of meaningless diagrams and homemade master narratives.

Remarkably, however, management theorists pretty much take this criticism in stride. In the massive 1982 bestseller, *In Search of Excellence,* which established management writing as a popular genre, Tom Peters and Robert Waterman took pains to distance their own work from the "silly excesses" of previous management theory, even singling out for scorn a company that "went off the deep end" and adopted theory after theory. Since then Peters has made a practice of starting each book by acknowledging that his previous volumes either didn't go far enough or were outright wrong.[6] Theorist Richard Pascale opened his 1990 contribution to the genre by addressing the problem of theory fads. " 'Managerial techniques' are a packaged goods industry," he wrote; they zip across the consciousness of executives in such profusion that the only result is "superficiality." Pascale's admission soon became an element of consultant common sense.[7] Many if not all of the books that I will discuss in this chapter include some sort of confession along Pascale's lines: Theorists either find in the failure of earlier management theories good reasons to embrace the new management idea they are proposing, or they attribute the failure to slipshod execution on the part of the executive/reader, a lack of thoroughness which the new proposal will help to remedy. *Other* gurus produce fads and empty buzzwords; *this* guru produces the genuine item. Until now you've been *talking* empowerment and disintermediation; this guru will give you the true path to *accomplishing* them. So natural has this become to readers that Scott Adams, the creator of *Dilbert,* is able to present himself both as an acerbic critic of consultant-speak and as a true believer in the bona fide new corporate philosophies. Thus in one recent episode his cartoon character distinguishes between a "visionary idea," the "energizing force that gave [him] strength to work," and the similar-sounding theory proposed by his foolish boss, an "unimaginative retread of an idea that has been widely discredited."[8]

Clearly the "business revolution" is absurd in many ways. In what by rights should be the hardest-headed corner of American life, one encounters PhD-bearing experts on "aura," full-blown astrologies of "leadership" and "creativity," theories of art and learning so elementary they could have been lifted from the back of cereal boxes, and responsible adults devoted utterly to self-awareness tracts originally written for teenagers. Still, it will not do simply to dismiss the "business revolution" by laughing at its weirder manifestations, at the crazy panorama of white-collar men getting uninhibited, getting tattoos, getting in touch with the rhythms of the universe, getting into extreme sports, or comparing themselves to Che Guevara. Yes, the business revolution is hilarious, but it is also deadly serious. Its members may spend their weekends howling at the moon, but on business days they are helping shape the world in which the rest of us live. In fact, with the decline of unions and the rollback of government, executives as a class now have more power than at any time since the 1920s. Their beliefs may be patently wrong; their world of ideas may be little more than superstition; the people who have so captured their attention may be charlatans preying on the desperate and the credulous; their institutions of higher learning may be processing plants for the faking of intellectual authority; but the authority they enjoy remains terrifyingly absolute nonetheless.

Nor is it really useful to measure management theory along the pragmatic lines suggested by most of its critics. In fact it doesn't really matter whether management theory comes in "fads" or whether the advice of Guru X yields better product quality than that of Guru Y. The management theory of the nineties was consistently more about the nature of the corporation than about improving its processes or products. The real object of the "revolutionary" management theory of recent years was not efficiency or excellence or even empowerment, but a far more abstract goal: the political and social *legitimacy* of the corporation. By the nineties the problems of efficiency and production had long since been solved; the wars against the working class had largely been won; even the state had been harried back into its laissez-faire cage. But how could things be kept that way? How was the corporation to prove itself a worthy ruler, a power that the people would happily obey, a sovereign for whose betterment we would toil and maybe even die? These, not the mundane questions of shop-floor efficiency, were the burning issues of the "business revolution."

Certain management theorists of the nineties made this point explicitly. Ghoshal and Bartlett, who are business professors in Britain and the US respectively, acknowledge in *The Individualized Corporation* that "corporations have emerged as perhaps the most influential institution of modern society." But they proceed to warn readers that corporations were regarded with "deep suspicion" in Europe and that even in America waves of downsizing and the attendant bad publicity were threatening to turn managers into "one of the least trusted constituents of society." Corporations must take immediate measures to protect their place in society, to combat this incipient popular anger. After all,

> The clear lesson from history is that institutions decline when they lose their social legitimacy. This is what happened to the monarchy, to organized religion, and to the state. This is what will happen to

companies unless managers accord the same priority to the collective task of rebuilding the credibility and legitimacy of their institutions as they do to the individual task of enhancing their company's economic performance.[9]

The aristocracy, the church, the state, and now the corporation: Each one in this great succession of absolute powers faced attack in turn. Fortunately, the corporation had an army of management theorists at its disposal to orchestrate its defense, to supply the "credibility and legitimacy" that it needed to remain atop the social order.

This search for legitimacy was the true goal of the "business revolution." This was the reason why, regardless of the school or consultancy with which a given management writer was identified, and regardless of whether they specialized in "leadership," "strategy," "marketing," or one of the other established subdivisions of the field, a reader in the nineties could be fairly certain of what sort of evidence they would marshal, what authorities they would cite, what conclusions they would draw, and what vision of the good society they would endorse even before opening the volume. Above all else, one could be sure that they would use the language of market populism—of democracy and popular consent as revealed by the mediums of exchange—to describe the operations of the corporation. Whatever recommendations individual gurus might make regarding the structure of the workplace, the management literature of the nineties almost universally insisted that its larger project was liberation, giving a voice to the voiceless, "empowering" the individual, subverting the pretensions of the mighty, and striking mortal blows against hierarchy of all kinds. Even as the lot of the worker deteriorated and political candidates came to resemble one another ever more closely, the American business class, having ascended to new levels of social dominance, was announcing that democracy was thriving in the nation's factories and office buildings. Captains of industry were they no longer: Now they were the majestic bearers of the popular will, the emancipators of the common man.

Management theory thus grew hotter, louder, and more strident in direct proportion to the enfeeblement and disappearance of any countervailing power. Unions declined; management theorists assured us that the new, freewheeling, employee-worshiping world of work would not need them anymore. Big government declared itself "over"; management theorists told us that markets made the best government anyway. As corporations conquered the planet, management theory told us why the new world of work would be a pleasant one, a fulfilling one, a soulful one, and even if it wasn't, why it was that you could do nothing about it.

The real result that management theory of the nineties aimed to secure, then, was not so much quality as quiescence; submission to the corporate agenda both in the workplace and in politics. And measured according to this standard, the management theory of the nineties— even with all its bullshit, its fads, its jargon—worked exceedingly well. It was thanks at least in part to the hyperbolic prose of Tom Peters that so many of the downsized agreed that what had happened to them was right, was necessary, was justified; it was thanks to the revolutionary crowing of *Fast Company* that so many left the parking lots of their former employers in such an orderly fashion, talking confidently about their impending careers as "free agents." Even more tellingly, in a decade when unemployment fell as low as 4 percent—making management extremely vulnerable to demands for increased wages—union organizing and strike activity remained mired at their lowest levels in seventy years. That America was able to endure the wrenching upward redistribution of wealth that it did in the nineties with only small, localized outbreaks of social unrest must be chalked up, at least in part, to the literature that explicitly sought to persuade the world of the goodness and justice of that redistribution.

Bogue Millionaires / Cool Millionaires

To the extent that the business revolutionaries can be said to have revolted against anything, their target was the organizational theory known as "scientific management." This was the system by which a company was broken down into its component operations, from coal-shoveling to marketing, each of which were then analyzed and ratio-nalized in order to maximize the efficiency of the whole. Whether or not they have heard of scientific management's leading theoretician, turn-of-the-century engineer Frederick Winslow Taylor, virtually every working American knows what it entails and the nature of the world it built. Scientific management was the way of the vast bureaucracies, the great corporations of the 1950s, the elaborate systems of rules and discipline by which those organizations worked. Taylorism (as the theory was also known) was the way of the expert and the engineer, who studied and reordered human relationships as rationality dictated. It was also a central element of the consensus culture of the Cold War years. For some, managerial capitalism was even more than that: It was the zenith of American civilization. In the celebrated 1977 business history *The Visible Hand,* Alfred D. Chandler traced the rise of scientific management within various productive enterprises over the course of the nineteenth and twentieth centuries, leading finally to the greatest accomplishments of enlightenment—the incredibly complex flow charts of the Du Pont and U.S. Rubber companies.

For all its productive achievements, scientific management was not a democratic set of arrangements. On the contrary: Taylorism was explicitly sold as a way to strip skilled workers of their knowledge and power, and turn control of the productive process over to more trust-worthy professional managers. It was no coincidence that American companies adopted scientific management at the very moment when American labor radicalism was at its peak: Each development fed the other, with laborers outraged by the prospect of being reduced to automatons, and capitalists desperately searching for a means to bring their increasingly restive workforces under control. According to the findings of one high-profile congressional inquiry of the time, while scientific management was productive, politically it constituted "a reversion to industrial autocracy," effectively shutting down "democratic safeguards" in the workplace and denying workers what few independent means they had of bargaining for wages or seeking fair treatment.

The obvious solution to the problem of arbitrary and authoritarian management was organized labor. This was clear even to a believer in scientific management like Walter Lippmann. "Without unions industrial democracy is unthinkable," he wrote in 1914. "Without democracy in industry, that is where it counts most, there is no such thing as democracy in America. For only through the union can the wage-earner participate in the control of industry. . . ."[10]

It never got quite that far, of course, not even in the 1940s and 1950s, when union membership was at its all-time peak. Corporate managers always retained the prerogative of managing. But the dramatic union organizing campaigns of the 1930s combined with the regulatory and welfare provisions of the New Deal did indeed do much to democratize the distribution of corporate profits. Strong unions helped to build the great middle-class society of which mid-century social theorists were so proud; they were also responsible for humanizing productive processes. And once unions had fought their way into the workplace, management discovered that they brought a distinct benefit to them as well: By attaching their own, more democratic structure to the otherwise authoritarian corporation, unions lent corporations a certain legitimacy that they could not otherwise have achieved. This could be extremely useful in an age when the threat of taxation, regulation, antitrust, and even national control waited always in the political wings. With unions on board, however, and with a distinct place in the corporation for even the lowliest worker's voice, the corporation ceased to be the terrifying dictatorship that had once so alarmed Americans. Now it had at least the appearance of being a democratic organization, a normal part of American life.

But while some corporations learned to cohabit peacefully with labor—to this day Chrysler makes great efforts to publicize its relationship with the United Auto Workers—for the most part American management just waited for the right time to retaliate. That time finally came in the 1980s. When President Reagan permanently replaced the striking air traffic controllers in 1981, it was a signal to executives nationwide that the federal government would no longer protect union activity with the zeal of earlier administrations. While hiring scabs was once looked upon as morally repugnant, now it had the endorsement of the highest authority in the land. The suddenly commonplace use of permanent replacements, the increasing ability of companies to relocate easily to Southern states where unions were weak, and the shameful state of American labor law combined to tilt the playing field decisively against organized labor.[11] So difficult did it become for unions to win strikes that companies in the nineties actually sought to provoke them, bringing in a scab workforce immediately and thus carving themselves a shortcut to that most coveted of contemporary management ideals, the "union-free workplace." Organized labor shrank predictably under these assaults. By 1999 it could count only 9.4 percent of private-sector workers within its ranks.

The destruction of the labor movement in the eighties and nineties was a disaster for economic democracy, precipitating the massive reconcentration of wealth that so marks our time. But smashing their working-class enemies also brought the old problem of legitimacy back to the corporation. Having rooted out the institutions of workplace democracy and simultaneously ascended to a level of power that made eighty-year-old warnings of "industrial autocracy" seem prescient, how was the corporation to persuade its employees and the larger public that it was still a respectable citizen, a power worthy of deference?

Management theory had the answer. As it happened, labor unions were not the only ones to decry the horror of Taylorism. In fact, early management theorists had developed a critique of Taylorism of their own that ran parallel to the emerging union movement, sometimes even closely parroting it. While most early management consultants were timing workers with stopwatches and writing handbooks spelling out exactly how all company shovels were to be swung, a dissenting "human relations" school charged that Taylorism suppressed crucial aspects of productivity. Scientific management, these consultants argued, had no place for loyalty, emotion, or initiative. And yet by taking those less tangible human factors into account, critics asserted, even greater productivity gains could be realized. The first important piece of evidence for this perspective was developed in the 1920s by Harvard Business School professor Elton Mayo, who had been observing workers at AT&T's Hawthorne telephone assembly plant in Cicero, Illinois. Something surpassing strange was said to have happened at Hawthorne: In a routine study to determine the correct amount of lighting for a particular assembly room, researchers found that productivity increased whether they turned the lights up or down. Mayo concluded in his massively influential 1933 book, *Human Problems of an Industrial Civilization,* that the critical factor in situations like this was not lighting or some other technical workplace variable but simply that workers worked better when they thought they were being paid attention to, when their labors were appreciated. The seemingly incontrovertible evidence Mayo adduced for this "Hawthorne effect" led to all manner of corporate "personnel counseling" programs, company unions, and other sponsored social activities for workers.

Management theorists in the fifties and sixties took this critique of scientific management one step further. Taylorism may have reduced blue-collar workers to automatons, but it had even more far-reaching consequences for the higher operations of capitalism. Books like William H. Whyte's *Organization Man* and Douglas McGregor's *Human Side of Enterprise* charged that the bureaucratic, rule-bound corporate format was turning Americans into conformists and was actively discouraging initiative, entrepreneurship, creativity, and, most important of all, consuming. As new, more decentralized forms of organization began to take hold and as the broader American culture increasingly turned against conformity, new corporate thinkers were able to blame the Taylorist corporate establishment for everything from soulless suburbia to the disasters of the Vietnam War, managed as it was by Robert McNamara, former CEO of the Ford Motor Company. *Up the Organization,* a particularly harsh 1970 critique of corporate practice, actually went as far as to identify the new, creative businesses with the nation's Vietnamese enemies, struggling like them against an insane bureaucratic production machine.*

Regarded from this historical perspective, the partisans of the "business revolution" are simply the latest adherents to the "human relations" tradition. Little of what they demand is very new: Like their predecessors they are against order, bureaucracy, and hierarchy, and in favor of more human relationships between managers and workers, whether they wear white collars or blue. What's "revolutionary" about the management theory of the nineties is that the opposing school all but disappeared. True, Taylorism was still in full effect on shop floors, in sweatshops, and in back offices worldwide; and true, a handful of motivational speakers and writers still peddled a sort of inner Taylorism or "personal efficiency" to an army of insecure executives (most notably Stephen Covey, whose 1989 book, *The 7 Habits of Highly Effective People,* along with its platoon of sequels, was still selling briskly in 1999), and their role in the culture

---

*The Vietnam War continued to serve management theorists as a particularly fertile source of imagery and metaphor long after it ended. *In Search of Excellence,* perhaps the most representative literary work of the Reagan era, Tom Peters and Robert Waterman asserted that the American defeat in Vietnam was attributable to "our obsession with body counts . . . and our failure to understand the persistence and long-time horizon of the Eastern mind," thus making it an allegory for the nation's current problems at the hands of Japan. In the nineties, Vietnam continued to be an obligatory reference of the genre, a timeless lesson in creativity and foresight vs. hierarchy and accountancy. Gary Hamel and C. K. Prahalad cite the superior management strategies of North Vietnam explicitly in *Competing for the Future* (1994), while Peter Senge refers to the Vietnam debacle obliquely in *The Fifth Discipline* (1990). Even Newt Gingrich, who rode the bitterness of the Vietnam defeat all the way to the top, insists that the Vietnamese did more than beat the American army: They "destroyed" the "orderly world of [former secretary of defense] Robert McNamara," and with it "the liberal model" of the Great Society. With the business revolution in full swing in the late nineties, corporate minds were again drawn to the combination of ass-kicking and essentialized otherness that the war offered, with Oracle's Khmer Rouge reference and the way venture capitalists had of referring to themselves as "VC." As late as 1997, Tom Peters was still telling the world that "my passion is the destruction of everything that McNamara stood for."[12]

of capitalism should never be minimized. But in the public discussions of the nineties between the thinkers, writers, and consultants responsible for imagining how the corporation should be organized, nearly all[13] cleaved to the "human relations" school. Alfred Chandler's depiction of the great bureaucratic corporation as the crown of creation would in the nineties seem the most wrongheaded conclusion imaginable. In the nineties nobody spoke out for the top-heavy corporation; nobody sought to justify the great flow charts of the industrial era.

As this debate dried up, business writing entered a period of rhetorical hyperinflation. The conflict between good, new, humane management and bad, old, scientific management was not just the correcting of an error, it was *a class struggle*, a workplace uprising as stirring and as meaningful to the imagination of the Age of Clinton as the sit-down strikes had been to the Age of Roosevelt. Rooting out the vestiges of Taylorism wasn't just a matter of greater productivity; it was the forward movement of democracy itself; it was an uprising of the dispossessed; it was economic justice finally brought home to the workplace. In industry as well as on Wall Street and in politics, the Market and the People could be seen marching shoulder to shoulder, smashing their common enemies and raising the standard of populism over the citadels of elitism.

In this case, however, the people marching righteously into battle against the elites were the country's highest-paid management consultants and CEOs—in short, the very people who had damned and double-damned the last round of workers' triumphs in the thirties and forties.

Tom Peters and *Fast Company* were not the first corporate populists to denounce Taylorism. Since the days of Elton Mayo the clear-eyed men of corporate America had been telling the country that the clash between management theories was the real class war, the only industrial struggle that really mattered—and that all that collective bargaining nonsense the unions were pushing was but a dangerous dead end. A nearly perfect expression of this notion can be found in the 1937 movie *Stand-In,* the tale of a cold, bespectacled management consultant who is sent by his evil Wall Street master to evaluate a Hollywood studio he owns. The consultant, played by Leslie Howard, simply cannot fathom the intuitive workings of the dream factory. He lives only for mathematics, he does not dream when he sleeps, and he is obtusely insensitive to the advances of a pretty but unaffected starlet. He even teaches himself to dance by inventing a mathematical system for the operation. He is a man without soul. Most despicably, he speaks of the studio's employees as "units," as "cogs in a machine," and is responsible for the studio's sale to a new owner who immediately sets about breaking the place up and liquidating its assets.

The film is filled with classic thirties-populist scorn for capitalists—the Wall Street banker is shown griping bitterly through his own birthday party while a legion of yes-men smile and sing ingratiatingly—but it understands the battle against those capitalists in a novel fashion. When the Leslie Howard character finally undergoes his obligatory change of heart (now he spouts soulful remarks like, "the only thing that matters is that a man be true to himself") and contrives to return the studio to its rightful bosses, he finds he must rally the studio's workers. Now, though, they have been transformed into a marching proletarian horde, girding themselves for class war. They brush him aside with the epithet "white collar," trample him underfoot, and pelt him with tomatoes. But the newly besouled consultant persuades them to see it differently. The division between capital and labor is a false one: Since many of the workers own shares in the company, and since other stockholders are also fellow workers like "bricklayers" and "streetcar conductors," justice can be had simply by appealing to the stockholders. Convinced that the real conflict is between good, humane management and bad, scientific management, the marching workers take matters into their own hands and rudely toss the studio's cold-blooded new owner over a tall fence.

For anyone who actually remembers the industrial conflicts of the thirties, *Stand-In* must seem a pleasant but wildly misdirected representation of those struggles. Were it to be remade today, however (and Hollywood repeatedly appeared as an industrial ideal in the works of nineties management theory), it could stand alongside MCI's "Great

Time or What" commercials as one of the great statements of our ebulliently populist mood. In the thirties, to construe the conflict between management styles as anything like class struggle would have been to invite derision; to make the same claim in the nineties was to put oneself well in the mainstream of orthodox economic thinking.

This, then, was the business revolution. As each of the forces that once checked the expansion of the corporate worldview surrendered, succumbed, receded, or withered away—and as executive salaries, along with profits, embarked on their long climb heavenward—it dawned on American business thinkers that they had entered a revolutionary time, and that the revolutionaries, for once, were them.

The Horror of Management

Scientific management was anathema to organized labor in the early years of the century, but it never really sat well with the truest believers in capitalism, either. Of course, the capitalists' problem with Taylorism was of an entirely different nature: What annoyed them about management was not its brutal effects on workers but its implications for economic government. If experts could successfully restructure a factory in a more efficient way, what was to stop them from restructuring an entire economy in a more efficient way, or—God forbid!—restructuring an entire economy in a more democratic way, or a more fair way? The success of scientific management clearly suggested that government intervention and maybe even government planning were legitimate pursuits.[14] Management theory thus brought business a nasty ideological contradiction along with increased efficiency.

This is one of the reasons the free market faithful have long suffered from what might be called a horror of management: Obviously, the corporations they loved could not simply go without management or do without planning, but when the logic of management and planning was embraced by anyone outside the corporation it became instant anathema. Resolving this contradiction would be another of the central goals of the "business revolution." CEOs made for rightful and good managers, the revolution's leaders would proclaim; labor unions, regulatory boards, and government bureaucrats were incompetent, meddling cynics. The critical matter was finding the little twist by which the concept of management itself could be seen to embrace one and exclude the other. After all, owners could not simply shout, *preserve our profits!* and expect the rest of society to heed them.

The solution was market populism. The new, "revolutionary" corporation would adopt the populist language of its archenemy, the labor movement. But it would change the language subtly. While the labor movement has always equated "the people" with "the workers," the management theorists of the nineties sought a new "people" whose demands would simultaneously legitimize the corporation and call the power of everyone else into question.

The "people" on whose behalf the new management theorists agitated were better known as the "market." Only by answering the demands of the market, they argued, did an organization answer to the people, become a legitimate part of the democratic life of the nation. Not only were the workplace ambitions of government and unions thus automatically illegitimate, but the corporation itself could be seen in an entirely new light. By integrating the market into their operations, executives would become fairer, kinder, better at listening. They would have to "marketize" their operations, as Tom Peters put it in 1992; recognize the market; cooperate with the market; allow the market to organize their shop floors.[15]

To those accustomed to thinking of the market and the corporation as essentially one and the same, this talk of "marketizing" the firm probably seems very strange. But in fact, according to strict definition, the corporation shields within its walls a sort of command economy in miniature. Executives don't bargain with workers each time they want a form filled out or a bolt attached to a chassis; they order the employees to do so.[16] This internal efficiency of the corporation is the rationale for vertical integration, in which companies grow to encompass all manner of discrete economic operations that the market can't be counted on to provide in a predictable or timely manner. This is the meaning of Chandler's title, *The Visible Hand*: Managerial expertise is what gave America its unprecedented prosperity, not the fickle "invisible hand" of the market.

That the Taylorist corporation is not a perfect creature of the market is, for all practical purposes, an economic technicality, a curious quirk that, while embarrassing to certain business ideologues, cannot ever really be resolved altogether. But for the "business revolutionaries" of the nineties, it was like a revelation from on high, the key to everything that was wrong with American economic life. Of course! *The corporation wasn't capitalist enough!*

Thus Tom Peters, who emerged from the "quality" movement of the eighties to become a sort of Marat of the business revolution, spent the nineties exclaiming in ever more forceful terms that the imminent demise of the old Taylorized, hierarchical firm was to be a millennial liberation for humanity. In his 1992 book, *Liberation Management,* he named the new categorical imperative that was freeing everybody: *"blasting the violent winds of the marketplace into every nook and cranny in the firm."* There could be no more respite from the demands of the Market (Peters sometimes insisted on spelling it as one would the name of the Almighty); from now on Its demands would apply to each and every one of us. He told of how companies set their divisions to competing with each other; how they forced their in-house printing departments to match the prices of independent operations; how one company sometimes referred customers directly to line workers; how some newspaper reporters were actually freelancers. As he wrote in his 1997 tract, *The Circle of Innovation,* "Market fitness tests are becoming the norm . . . fast . . . for every internal service (HR, accounting) and every one of us (IF YOU CAN'T SAY WHY YOU MAKE YOUR COMPANY A BETTER PLACE, YOU'RE OUT). I.e., the Market (capital "M") will decide!"[17]

In this regard Peters was certainly right: Markets were indeed putting many people "out" in the nineties. And one market in particular—the American stock market—was doing the lion's share of the work. The phenomenon known as "downsizing," or massive white-collar layoffs, was a direct response to the pressures of the stock market.

As financial journalist Doug Henwood puts it, "By 1993, it was clear that the quickest way to add 5 points to your stock price was to lay off 50,000 workers."[18] The mechanism that made this great change possible was the stock option. Before the 1980s the interests and goals of corporate managers had been, theoretically at least, very different from those of shareholders. In the nineteenth century owners and managers had usually been the same person; in the twentieth century, though, according to the classic text on the "modern corporation," one found "owners without appreciable control and the control without appreciable ownership." Since managers back then did not have large stakes in the companies they managed, they had little incentive to perform the sort of stunts that would bring about the short-term appreciations that are Wall Street's greatest joy in life. Since they were a professional group in their own right, there was every danger that, "out of professional pride," managers might pay workers too much or produce goods of too high a quality. The answer devised in the eighties was to compensate managers in shares as well as salaries. This now-standard practice ensured that managers would forevermore see things the shareholders' way, would stop at nothing to deliver the ever-ascending price curve that became such a symbol of the nineties. Granting options to top executives changed the class dynamics of the corporation dramatically: Not only did the uppermost managers of the nineties now receive compensation packages that towered over those of their predecessors, but as Wall Street placed a very predictable value on layoffs and downsizing, CEOs often saw their own pay rise in direct proportion to the number of employees they could expel from the firm.[19]

This equation was the origin of many of the big management ideas of the decade: The corporation "delayered," throwing off entire levels of management; it "disaggregated," ridding itself of its extraneous operations; it embraced "flexibility," making it easier to replace career employees with (zero-benefits) temps; it "outsourced" every possible piece of work to the lowest bidder; it "reengineered" its various processes in a less labor-intensive way; it "disintermediated," using new technology to cut out middlemen and move "back office" jobs to wherever wages were lowest. Almost everybody who worked for corporate America during the decade has a tale to tell along these lines: the downsized workers hired back as temps to do their old jobs; the contracts lost because management kept laying off and rehiring the workforce; the once-prestigious companies that were downsized so senselessly they fell apart; the CEOs who, as payment for having engineered these disasters, collected instant riches. Top managers were enriched in proportion to the amount of power and security that workers lost: This is the single most important point one needs to know to understand corporate thought in the nineties.

This was the real reason the old-style corporation was doomed. It was a settlement imposed by Wall Street, not by management theory. The guru's duty was not to oversee the change but to legitimate it, to explain why the new, "marketized" corporate form was in fact the ideal productive model, the source of efficiency as well as democracy. Their books were crowded with heroic downsizers and colorfully imagined but radically minimized corporate forms.[20] Thus Tom Peters gushed rabidly in 1997 about a Swedish CEO who, putting this logic of the Market triumphantly into effect, managed to get rid of nearly 98 percent of his white-collar workforce. Peters sang the praises of a new sort of organization in which every single job (or, as he put it, "E-V-E-R-Y-T-H-I-N-G") was outsourced.[21]

Most people, upon hearing what Peters' Market had in store for them, would probably reply, "Then the Market be damned." Management theorists, though, live and breathe to prevent such a response. Whatever else they might do, their most important task is to reassure us—the downsized, the laid off, the temp workers, the consumers—that the new way is all for the best.

The market, acting strictly on its own, they told us, gave the corporation all the democratic legitimacy it required. For markets were the natural enemy of privilege, the destroyer of pretense, the greatest social equalizer of all time. Only with Galbraith's "countervailing powers" dismantled and with markets totally in control could America finally enter the promised land of industrial democracy.

Elitism Was the Crime

Douglas McGregor, the influential business writer of the 1950s, first hit upon the notion that the most fruitful way to classify organizational theories was not according to the societal results they yielded but rather by the version of human nature that informed each one. "Theory X" ideas, which according to McGregor encompassed nearly all existing corporate practice, placed little faith in the intelligence or motivation of employees, imagining them as recalcitrant slackers whose every hour had to be regimented and ordered. Adherents of McGregor's "Theory Y," on the other hand, were more optimistic about the workers under management's command, believing in their commitment to the job and their capacity to do things on their own.

When McGregor's ideas appeared in book form in 1960, it would have been extremely strange for a business writer to have charged his "Theory X" colleagues with "elitism" or to have called for workplace "liberation" or a management "revolution" or any of the rest of it. And yet in "Theory X" and "Theory Y" lay the seeds of today's market populism.[22] Like their counterparts in political commentary, management writers of the 1990s were discovering that all industrial ideas could be usefully boiled down to their core implications about the People. As in the populist political rhetoric of the age, nineties management theorists vigilantly crusaded against "elitist" ideas and language, savaging the hierarchs of old, the privileges of the executive washroom, the class distinctions implied by multilayered hierarchy. Following the new, more "democratic" management theory, of course, the American corporation actually yielded *less* democracy than in the past, rapidly transforming the country back into a land of haves and have-nots. But for the gurus and their followers, what mattered was not a democratic society but correct *attitudes* toward other people.

The central villain in the literature of the business revolution is the great, hierarchically organized corporations in whose malign service we are all thought once to have worked. As these corporations were not pure products of market forces, management theorists felt perfectly free to attack them using all the fiery rhetoric of workerist populism. In Peter Senge's formulation, the traditional corporation was an "authoritarian hierarchy"; its leaders smothered initiative, they stifled the individual, they were sexist and racist, they hadn't a clue about what went on in the world, and they spent their weekends playing golf with their former fraternity brothers, who in turn committed the same offenses against democracy at their corporations.

"No shit," working-class readers would probably respond. "So managers are assholes." But working-class readers weren't the ones launching this attack: It was the theorists of management themselves, going after their own fans in the most insulting language they could muster. And their characterization of old-style management as a bunch of prigs appeared almost everywhere in American corporate culture in the nineties. One example from among thousands: In commercials for PSI Net these wretched old-style managers are shown raging against the Internet, a collection of tired white men in dark suits who age visibly as the commercial progresses (one of them slumping to the dusty conference table with a clunk) and who insist petulantly that their rank should allow them to give the consumer what *they* think is right.

According to the business revolutionaries, the particular quality that distinguished old-style managers was *elitism,* that combination of class snobbery, intellectual certainty, and willful defiance of nature, of the People, and of the market that so imbued each of the various demon figures of market populism. Tom Peters, for example, seems to find elitism and simple human snobbery behind every corporate practice he opposes. Discussing those retrograde figures who resist his proposal to "outsource everything" (a proposal that was, as it happened, far more vocally opposed by union workers who were at the very bottom of the corporate hierarchy than anyone else), Peters unleashed this indictment of the old economy: "The underlying assumption: Regardless of the nature/complexity/uniqueness of the problem/any problem, the best resources . . . on earth . . . live on our 14th/26th/17th/5th/etc. floor. What shocking arrogance!" Managers refused to outsource all work simply because of personal moral arrogance: Absurd as it might seem, this was an intellectual tactic of considerable power. It was also pretty much in universal use, spanning the discipline from strategy to marketing and from corporate spiritualist to hardened empiricist. Even Gary Hamel and C. K. Prahalad, commonly thought to be the most realistic and serious-minded of the popular management theorists, were capable of declaring at times that moral issues of management outweighed more earthly ones, insisting in their highly regarded 1994 book *Competing for the Future* that "in the battle for the future," "elitism," "convention" and a host of other old-economy qualities will be far greater "enemies" of corporate success than the hostile trade practices of foreign powers.[23]

The greatest moralist of the business world, though, is Peter Senge. In his long-running battle against the "traditional authoritarian hierarchy," stretched out through two sequels to his original 1990 bestseller, *The Fifth Discipline,* Senge has managed to embrace just about every bit of daft pop liberationism to cross the national consciousness since the sixties. Stressing that the most needed corporate reform was not organizational but a matter of "restructuring how we think," Senge has led his readers in a mighty questioning of authority. For him the greatest problems of the world derived from the pretensions to "certainty" mounted by leaders and CEOs, and also from the deluded belief of the rest of us that somebody, anybody, had "the answers." We must abandon the dictatorial "controlling organizations" of the Taylorist past, Senge exhorted, where all decisions and "learning" came "from the top"; we must turn ourselves resolutely away from our "great man" idea of leadership, our "obsession with the hero-CEO" (which Senge diagnoses as "a type of cultural addiction"). We must do these things because believing in great men means *not believing* in the agency of the People, means accepting "the point of view that 'common people' are powerless to change things."[24] The good manager *believes* in the common people; whether he pays them properly is another question.

To show just how much the great men suck, Senge provides us with story after story in which leaders make colossal blunders by failing to understand the semi-mystical forces of the market and the universe (many of the most egregious of these offenses against nature were, naturally, committed by the activist government officials of the 1960s). The virtue that Senge presses upon readers most forcefully is intellectual humility, which is bound up in some mysterious way with faith in the "common people": We must stop trying to find "the absolute final word or ultimate cause" for things, stop trying to force our own schemes on nature and the market.[25]

For Senge the market—or, as he calls it, "reality" or "the system"— is a place of arcane but unalterable patterns. *"The system has its own agenda,"* he states emphatically. To help us align ourselves with it Senge piles on a catalog of even more cosmic advice, extending the checklist of managerial error to include such misdeeds as "anthropocentrism," which he defines as "seeing ourselves as the center of activities"; "linear ways of seeing," which is a mistake since it means ignoring the circles and cycles through which the world actually works; and using the English language, which Senge warns us against in the strongest terms, declaring that "all causal attributions made in English are highly suspect!" All of which are driven home with an endless pitter-pat of quotations from the Bhagavad Gita, Sufi tales, explications of Chinese symbols, and fawning remarks about the wisdom of the East and of simple unaffected indigenous peoples generally. In fact, Senge seems to have bought just about every academic-sounding critique of Western civilization to have trickled down in recent years. He even starts out his 1999 sequel, *The Dance of Change,* with that old chestnut about the bias of the Mercator map—*it made Europe look big!*[26]

Some management authors, pushing the envelope of inventiveness, understand the revolt against arrogance and expertise in which they are participating as a great historical event. It was a vast public enlightenment, not the destruction of organized labor or the grasping demands of Wall Street, that precipitated the "business revolution" and brought the modern, sensitive corporation into existence. To hear British guru Charles Handy tell it, from the Enlightenment up to the 1980s, West-

ern leaders and owners *thought they knew.* They thought they understood how things worked, and believed that man could control the
world around him. They lived in a fool's paradise of "certainty." They
were convinced, he wrote in a 1994 essay, that "greed was good" and
that "we knew how to run organizations." But those smug master narratives toppled spectacularly to the ground when the stock market
crashed in 1987 and heroes like Ivan Boesky went to jail. Only then
was Western Civilization forced to reconsider, to come to terms with
the "Chaos, Creativity and Complexity" that "science" was putting "at
the heart of things."[27] Out of this rethinking, Handy recollects, came
his own great contribution to the business revolution, the change-
worshiping 1989 book *Age of Unreason.*

Handy's unacknowledged historical template seems to be the great
questioning of religion by science that we ordinarily associate with the
nineteenth century; other management authors prefer to understand
the dawn of the "business revolution" as a replaying of the more familiar cultural revolt of the 1960s. Kenneth Hey and Peter Moore, authors
of the 1998 book *The Caterpillar Doesn't Know,* describe the big shift
of the late eighties as a general disillusionment of "the individual" with
"institutions." For Hey and Moore the key events were the 1986 space
shuttle explosion and the long string of popular movies in which government and industry were depicted as corrupt. Americans wised up,
they began to doubt the good intentions of their rulers, and only then
did the business revolution happen. According to this strange but oddly
commonplace interpretation, people finally grew disillusioned with big
government only during the Bush presidency and promptly began to
search for meaning in the voluntary simplicity movement, in "alternative," in books about the soul, in books about angels. And corporations,
responding with their usual obedience to the needs and desires of their
employees and consumers, promptly remade themselves from simple
profit-maximizing organisms into "communities of meaning." Suddenly
enlightened, they began to allow casual Fridays. They began to let people work from home. The revolution was under way.[28]

As the revolt against corporate arrogance was given an imaginary historical dimension, so it was also given an equally fatuous pedagogical dimension. This was particularly noticeable in the handful of books that focus on "learning" as the most important organizational remedy (as opposed to say, reengineering, or future-remembering, or one-to-one-ing). Here the still-hated educators of the author's childhood and the even more deeply despised intellectuals of the present are used as symbols of the arrogance of wrongful authority exercised by bad managers. Charles Handy, who maintains a refined, subdued tone regardless of the subject at hand, gets positively worked up when he contemplates the smug certainty of the intellectuals he's come across. He recalls with particular horror the rote memorization by which, he asserts, they like to teach things, a method that implies "that all problems had already been solved, by someone, and that the answer was around, in the back of the book or the teacher's head." Handy understands this sort of pedagogical certainty, this "ape your elders" way of learning, as a pillar of the very "status quo" that the "business revolution" is here to overthrow. Accordingly, he applies to those who are thought to use it the strongest epithets he can dream up: "bad academics," "intellectuals," "pundits," "ignorant" professors, "bigots."[29]

Anti-intellectualism is, of course, a commonplace of "New Economy" thought: In nearly every field we will examine, market populists were advising Americans to drop their futile efforts to figure the world out and to submit humbly to the will of the market. After all, the "experts" had misunderstood everything from productivity to stock market valuations. In management literature, though, the anti-intellectualism had to walk an extraordinarily fine line: On the one hand, business executives have long harbored a special animus toward academics, who not only exclude business from the canon of legitimate intellectual inquiry but seem always to be forming blue-ribbon commissions and setting up government bureaucracies in order to rein in free enterprise. On the other hand, management theory relies quite heavily on its own aura of expertise: Taylorism had billed itself as a "scientific" discourse,

a movement of experts, and no group of authors is fonder than management theorists of boasting about their academic credentials. The
key, then, was to batter traditional academia for some supposed pedagogical infraction while suggesting that the new corporation would
bring with it a more enlightened method of teaching. Thus Arie de
Geus, the erstwhile celebrator of *The Living Company*, accused academia of conspiring against learning itself by endorsing a pedagogical
model in which people are simply filled up with knowledge by their
professors, and then don't ever learn again. Internet guru Don Tapscott, speaking to an audience of telecom executives in 1999, blasted
the technique of "broadcast learning," the system by which those idle
professors enforced their hierarchies: "I'm a teacher, I have knowledge.
You're a student, you're an empty vessel. Get ready, here it comes." Fortunately, Tapscott announced, the "new generation" would no longer
stand for this, "because they're growing up interactively." And even
more fortunately, the market was stepping in to serve those inquiring
young minds, smashing the elitist teachers just as it had the elitist
managers, with innovative corporate schools like Motorola University.[30]

Labor on the March

Just as the literature of Wall Street was defined by a curious rivalry
with the legacy of Franklin Roosevelt, with the remnants of the New
Deal, and with the welfare state, so the "business revolution" moved
in a similar parallel to the great uprising of the CIO in the 1930s.
With unions having been pushed out of the "New Economy" picture
and with collective bargaining now off the table for most workers,
management literature insisted that it was time for the *real* democratization to begin. The market would revisit each of the issues of
the thirties and deliver a resounding victory for workers on every
count. The "business revolution" was thus a sort of class revolt, the
dawning of a new era of popular industrial democracy, a labor movement that management could cheer for. Workers weren't *victimized* by

downsizing and job insecurity; these were things they *wanted*, things they fought for, things they needed in order to realize their full humanity, to escape from the corporate conformity of yesterday. Thrown out on the free market, workers were discovering that they could bargain with management all on their own and win every time; that they could move from company to company as they saw fit, looking for the job that suited them best. They could demand the salary and benefits of their choosing. They could bring their weird pets to work. They could play extreme parlor games right there in the bullpen. They could work from home if they wanted. They could even wear jeans in the office.

For most workers, of course, the nineties were anything but a time of joyous, bubble-riding exuberance: Real wages declined for most of the decade along with job security and benefits. Workers were considerably worse off in the nineties than they had been in the sixties or seventies. But if all you read was management theory you would have missed this. The management literature of the 1990s was concerned almost exclusively with the dramas of white-collar life and the tribulations of the entrepreneur. And as the problem of corporate autocracy was now redefined as a matter of "elitism," "hierarchy," and "certainty," it was this latter group—the zany "change agents" and makers of wow—who were raising the real challenge to entrenched interests. The entrepreneur, by virtue of his or her close relationship to the market, was the true embodiment of the "common man." It was on their sassy shoulders that the populist mantle now descended. In one of his rare references to blue-collar workers, Tom Peters claimed that, in the privileged terms of the populist lexicon, the dot-com millionaires and the working class had switched moral positions—even stretching this absurd argument so far as to apply the populist keyword "parasite" to describe the very folks ("people who lift 'things' ") who once made up the People's Party. "When I began working as a management consultant at McKinsey & Co. in 1974," he wrote in 1997, "we" (the professional service people—accountants, lawyers, consultants, ad agency denizens) were considered PARASITES . . . living off the sweat of real people's brows.

Times have changed. And how!

The nerds have won! Bill Gates is the richest man in the world! It is the Age of Brainware. Now . . . the people who lift "things" (the . . . RAPIDLY . . . declining fraction) are the new parasites living off the carpal-tunnel syndrome of the computer programmers' perpetually strained keyboard hands.[31]

"Cynics" might wonder how being the richest man in the world gave one a claim to speak with the vox populi, but the logic of Peters' ecstasy is hard to miss: Management were the producers now; workers the "parasites." The populist tables were turned at last.

Meanwhile the CIO, that old bearer of the populist flame, slowly disappeared from the corporate imagination it had once haunted, replaced by a much friendlier sort of "CIO," a "chief information officer" who dealt in the new forces of liberation said to be sweeping out the exploitative practices of the hierarchical past. With our workplaces opened now to the cleansing winds of the marketplace, business theorists convinced themselves that for once they were on the side of the common people, united with them in righteous war against hierarchies and old-economy relics of all kinds.

Even as America became a society of enormous social inequality, partisans of the "business revolution" insisted that class was disappearing altogether. As Tom Peters put it, in the new, market-driven corporate order, workers were not merely "empowered," they were "businessed," promoted automatically into "real, whole businesspersons," self-responsible monads prospering on their own. Charles Handy went as far as to say that, under the new conditions, "everyone is a worker," so "we should stop talking and thinking of employees and employment."[32]

And with the market having neatly abolished the age-old problem of social class, the shimmering promise of economic democracy could now be made out on the horizon. Again it was Charles Handy who pushed this idea to its limits, describing the downsized, postrevolutionary white-collar workplace in his 1994 book *The Empty Raincoat* as a realization of "what Marx once dreamt of," since "the 'means of production,' the traditional basis of capitalism, are now literally owned by the workers because those means are in their heads and at their fingertips."[33]

In the imagination of the nineties, the towering figure at the head of the grand parade of industrial democracy was the "knowledge worker," a sort of white-collar superman for whom nearly any act of workplace revolution was feasible. According to a panelist at a 1999 discussion sponsored by Sprint on the glory and promise of the "New Economy," so great was this "knowledge worker's" powers that he had somehow managed to reverse the traditional relationship between employer and employee. "They come to you and they are trained and they know what you need and maybe you don't even know what you need," he told the audience. "So the demands from them to you in terms of financial independence, they have so many choices—where they can go to live and where they want to live and that changes the hiring equation."[34] Clearly management would have to do whatever it took to keep such a worker pleased—or else that proud proletarian would just reenter the job market, that zealous protector of workers' rights.

Of course, it doesn't always work that way, and someone arose from the audience to tell the panel how he, a black social worker in Chicago, had found employers as difficult as ever, regardless of his facility with knowledge and ability with computers. To solve his problem the assembled experts took off immediately for the land of market-populist fantasy: The market will deal with those employers most severely! "If those bosses, those supervisors, don't take advantage of your skills," an executive on the panel warned, "then you're probably better off elsewhere and that company is going to die. It's going to be overrun by somebody from somewhere—there's no choice about that."[35] There was no need for anything like collective bargaining or state intervention: The market would stamp out racism all on its own!

An even more telling document was a 1998 knowledge worker story that *Fortune* magazine chose to advertise with the words, "Yo, Corporate America!" The knowledge workers were not only said to be protected by the market, they were dictating the terms of the employment relationship to management. "Companies are no longer in the driver's seat," the magazine's writer opined. "Employees are in control now." Fortunately for companies, the things the young turks were demanding turned out to be exactly the same things that revolutionary businesses were already giving them: They were through with loyalty, rules, long-term jobs, and hierarchy. And in addition to being "well paid and well fed," they wanted an entirely new type of workplace—one that, quite by chance, looked a lot like the sort of disorganized, creative workplace that Tom Peters had been celebrating since 1992: The new knowledge workers were demanding "a job that's cool," where they wouldn't have to wear ties or even suits, where they could walk around in bare feet, where they could drink beer, where they could play with their pets— this last being a phenomenon that *Fortune* focused on with a curious singularity ("Yo, Corporate America! I want a fat salary, a signing bonus, and a cappuccino machine—oh, and I'm bringing my bird to work."). That this was a full-blown labor uprising there could be no doubt: One group of young knowledge workers even threatens a walkout if they aren't allowed to bring a refrigerator into the office. But this was the kind of workers' action that sent *Fortune* into paroxysms of ecstasy, not outrage—the fridge fringe even got their photos in the magazine, goateed and posing goofily for the camera. This was the myth of the "business revolution" in a nutshell: Whatever was changing in the workplace was changing because the People, through their agent the market, were changing it. Companies would no longer have to offer stable employment because workers these days were just too cool, too hip for that sort of square 1950s arrangement. *Fortune,* which had spent decades leading the fight against the traditional labor movement, wished this workers' uprising the best.[36]

So powerful was this fantasy of the omnipotent "knowledge worker" in the corporate imagination of the decade that even the casualization of the white-collar workforce could be understood as just another victory for those militant new proletarians. Charles Handy, who invented so many happy analogies for the new-style corporation in which most work is outsourced and most "employees" are temps, was by 1989 already setting up downsizing as a victory for the downsized, as some sort of populist fait accompli to which the corporation was being forced to accede. "Organizations have to get used to the idea that not everyone wants to work for them all the time even if the jobs are available," he wrote. "The ways of the core [the central, full-time corporate employees] cannot and should not be the ways of the flexible labor force, for while some may hanker after full-time lifetime jobs, many will not." Extending the logic only a little further, it became plain to Handy that, in the freewheeling new corporate world, most of us have *chosen* our class position. "Temporary work," for example, "is a choice" for many people. Even the unemployed can be held accountable for their fate, Handy wrote, since their real failing is in lacking the "urge or energy to turn that wheel of learning," in having failed to embrace uncertainty, unreason, change, and all the rest of it.[37]

As with so many other issues, *Fast Company* took this notion of worker agency the furthest. The way other management writers told the story of the nineties, it had at least been clear that companies *wanted* to shed many white- and blue-collar jobs; in *Fast Company's* version, "Free Agent Nation," a knowledge worker "Declaration of Independence" written in 1997 by former vice presidential speechwriter Daniel H. Pink, the larger corporate motives never come up at all. What had been "downsizing" was now "free agency"—it was *our doing,* a testament to the honesty, independent-mindedness, and intelligence of average people. Each of the various independent contractors whose tales made up Pink's story were said to have chosen "free agency," usually out of an overriding moral disgust with corporate life. One self-employed woman complained about the lack of "leadership" at her old company; another told Pink he just couldn't be himself as an employee; a third accused her former coworkers of being "fake, plastic"; and Pink himself recalled "wingtips that felt like vises and neckties that seemed like nooses." "Free agency" thus fit nicely into the familiar narrative of corporate horror—the conformity, the fakeness, the hierarchy—and individualistic rebellion that had tantalized middle-class America since at least the sixties. As an agent for software engineers told Pink, "This is the summer of love revisited, man!"

Other paradigms of workplace democracy were hinted at: Pink talked to a former labor organizer with all manner of thirties-style street-cred who seemed to believe, gratifyingly, that thirties-style labor strategies were no longer useful. Pink himself, though, preferred the symbolism of the American Revolution, with white-collar workers as the good guys. By becoming independent contractors, he asserted, "citizens are declaring their independence and drafting a new bill of rights." Free agents were "demanding" that work be fulfilling; they were "gladly swap[ping] the false promise of security for the personal pledge of authenticity"; they had "reversed the organizing premises of work in America." In the ringing "Declaration of Independence" that accompanied the story, Pink wrote, "we, the working women and men of America, declare ourselves free agents."

Or maybe getting to wear what we wanted to work was only a superficial sort of freedom. Maybe "free markets" actually had little to do with liberty for most of us; maybe all this talk about "free agency" was a delusional effort to convince ourselves that the casualized workplace demanded by Wall Street was just a great new path to personal fulfillment. That is the clear, if unintended, message of the late-nineties writing of Harriet Rubin, the woman who founded Currency Books in 1989 and who then left in 1997 to become what she called a "soloist," setting down the tale of her "free agent" adventures for readers of *Inc.* magazine. While the resulting story was meant to be inspiring, readers less inclined to see the magic in the jargon of the business revolution must have found its combination of pomposity, sycophancy, and self-pity simply horrifying. Although Rubin never made it clear exactly what a "soloist" does, her diary-like tale suggests that her goal as a "free agent" was simply to befriend the very, very rich and pander to their untrammeled egotism. (To help them, as she puts it, "rethink their legacy,

their place in history, now, while they are at the peak of their powers.")
Another goal seems to be to test whether someone can actually live
their life entirely according to the bad ideas that she helped to transform into cliché during all those years she worked on manuscripts
about learning organizations, one-to-one futures, and challenges to the
corporate soul. Can she do it? She certainly tries. She tells how she began "interpreting uncertainty as opportunity." She glories in the fact
that "the old rules—corporate rules—don't apply." She complains
earnestly about the problem of insincerity and how, in ordinary jobs,
she would "end up squeezing my skills into an off-the-rack costume."
She declares that, as a free agent, she is on "a quest for identity" and
speaks of the need to create "an authentic role for myself." She compares going solo to being an artist and "mixing my own paint." She
busts out with a little workplace feminism as well, imagining herself as
a pioneer "girl guru." She even recalls the youthful "dreams" of the sixties. All of which is to help her suck up to some young winner of the
dot-com lottery and help them "plan their legacy."

Naturally the presiding deity of Rubin's world is the market. It is the
force that has made these wondrous CEOs so very, very rich and that
also promises to let Rubin find her true self. It is the surpassing mystery which she plans to make a career out of explicating. And navigating its dark paths is, of course, her field of expertise. One passage from
her *Inc.* journals manages to bring it all together: The market as source
of divine wisdom, the necessity of networking, the power of the great
names, the famous CEO as the distant object of everyone's desire, and
the frantic, superstitious slinging of management theory cliché by the
desperate and the redundant.

> I decide to let the market tell me what it wants from me, and in a few
> days I get an invitation to have lunch with Andrew, a successful invest-
> ment banker. Andrew heard about me from George Stephanopolous,
> whom I don't know, who heard about me from someone else. Andrew
> wants to meet me because he thinks I have access to top CEOs. An-
> drew admires Barry Diller, who gets investors to commit lots of money

to his ventures because they think he's a visionary. That's my cue! I tell Andrew that the best way to get access is not to use intermediaries like me but to become a visionary himself.

This, then, is how Rubin strikes her blows for authenticity, for her own immutable identity, for womanhood, for the sixties generation, for the workers of the world, even—by hanging out at Davos, Switzerland, and at Sun Valley, Idaho, assisting the richest men on the planet to pass themselves off as "visionaries."[38]

Benevolent Dictators

While the workers of the world were learning to understand downsizing as an opportunity to search for personal authenticity and a jovial billionaire to attach themselves to, the managers who remained behind at the old corporation were also discovering that they would have to change their ways. The new manager—the figure who would let the market sun shine in on the old-style hierarchy—would be an instinctively fairer, more enlightened creature. While the old-style corporation had been "authoritarian," the new, marketized firm would be, by definition, a house of democracy, of freedom, of justice.

The theorist most responsible for persuading the world that "democracy" is the appropriate metaphor for the hacked-down corporation is the previously mentioned Peter Senge. Of course, his definition of democracy is a little odd. Forget equality, justice, and majority rule: What democracy is about was the same thing markets are about—humility. Listening patiently to other voices, respecting the opinions of other people, and never getting too far above oneself. And, as Senge points out in *The Fifth Discipline,* this sort of democracy is on the rise, being pushed ever onward by a new sort of manager, a market adept who is also a person of deeply democratic principles, who abjures the top-down ways of old for a system in which everyone has a voice and can contribute to the advance of what Senge calls the "learning organization." This is to be the polar opposite of the hierarchical dictatorship. Not that the democracy of the "learning organization" involves schemes for leveled pay scales or one-employee-one-vote or anything like that: What makes it so distinctive is that it runs by "dialogue" rather than proclamation. It is staffed with enlightened executives who will "listen" rather than simply dictate, who virtuously refuse to hold any idea more strongly than any other. The ideal type that emerges from *The Fifth Discipline* and its sequels is a figure of deep philosophical humility, a person who does not simply apply his or her own judgments but who instead solicits the contributions of his entire team. The wisest among us, Senge writes, "live in a continual learning mode. They never 'arrive.'" They remain "acutely aware of their own ignorance, their incompetence, their growth areas." Senge returns again and again to this notion of the humble nonjudgmentalist, saluting those executives who realize that "nobody has the answers," who achieve "the state of being open," who "suspend certainty." They are tolerant capitalists. They have learned to share. As he puts it in his 1999 sequel, *The Dance of Change*, the enlightened manager is "more comfortable with differences of opinion. They understand that their personal view doesn't necessarily represent the absolute truth, that other people will see things differently, and that everyone's assumptions are open to inquiry." In the learning corporation, managers do not exploit their charges, but instead "provid[e] the enabling conditions for people to lead the most enriching lives they can." They forgive mistakes and reward experimentation. They expect employees to "challenge the status quo."[39] Markets demand openness and tolerance from those who seek profit; markets insist that all people be empowered and that all opinions be respected. The only thing that markets seem to have no tolerance for—aside from the old-style industrial behemoth—are doubts about the beneficence of markets.

This is a doctrine that, once launched by Senge, was heartily seconded by just about everyone writing about business in the nineties. Describing one of his many antihierarchical corporate models, Charles Handy envisioned a new corporate "culture of consent" in which agreement replaces command and a "post-heroic leader" who functions more like a teacher than a traditional corporate autocrat, leads his charges in a life that is "one long teach-in." Significantly, Handy compares this new figure's duties to the populist gestures of various politicians, specifically "Clinton with his town meetings." Arie de Geus, a longtime Shell executive who made regular guest appearances in the works of Peter Senge before striking out as a guru on his own, imagined a similarly democratic arrangement when he insisted that, in the age of information, "judgment, on behalf of the company, could no longer be the exclusive prerogative of a few people at the top."[40]

Anita Roddick, the sensitive entrepreneur who likens her Body Shop cosmetics stores to schools, is a virtual embodiment of this new democratic ideal. She claimed in her 1991 memoirs to employ a version of "democracy at work" so advanced that she reports having had a difficult time convincing workers to question her authority sufficiently. Although she made it clear that employees were to "challenge the rules, to question the status quo," she points out that this is not enough, that entrepreneurs would have to "encourage lèse majesté from your staff, by hollering and hooting, by what you wear, by the language you use, by taking the symbols of authority and challenging them all the time." Evidently this is such a tall order that at one point Roddick even complains of difficulties finding employees nonconformist enough to be able to deal with "the idea of a company being quirky or zany or contemptuous of mediocrity."[41]

Naturally Tom Peters says it best. Not only is his model manager "liberated as hell," but this figure shuns absolutely the autocratic ways of the hierarchy. "Barking orders is out," Peters writes in *Liberation Management*. "Curiosity, initiative, and the exercise of imagination are in." Peters' books of the nineties were filled with zany entrepreneurs and layer-flattening CEOs. He extols the toleration, nay, the *encouragement* of mistakes and wars with his every sentence against centralization, order, hesitation, rules, propriety, balance, and consensus. "There is always the danger that big, successful companies become arrogant," he quotes the CEO of clothing manufacturer Hugo Boss as saying. "They start to think they know the right answers, which is never true because there are no right answers. If you deal with contemporary art, it'll teach you very fast that there are many answers and some of them are wrong and right at the same time."[42]

Some more au courant management authors even extended their horror of authority and of closure into the formal literary framing of their thoughts. Senge and his collaborators invited readers to write in the margins of *The Dance of Change*. Arie de Geus announced that he had discovered the four defining characteristics of long-lived corporations, but immediately pointed out that these four statements were "not answers," they were "the start of a fundamental inquiry." The 1998 celebration of "change" entitled *BLUR* was said to be "much more than a book"; it was a "window into a conversation," an "organic exchange of opinions" in which the authors were by no means authoritative. "We are not offering the ultimate word on our topics," they wrote, just "a starting point." A few pages later they instructed readers to "be critical," to "join this conversation" and to "help us better understand what we've written." Some might see in all this a virtuous acknowledgment of the "death of the author" school of literary criticism of the 1980s; others might note that, by a curious twist of "New Economy" fate, the "authors" of *BLUR* in fact weren't its authors: A notice in my copy of the book identifies their employer, the Ernst & Young consultancy, as the holder of the copyright.[43]

The Uses of Bolshevism

It will probably surprise no one to learn that when the business revolutionaries needed a symbol of ultimate evil with which to compare the practices they detested, they reached—just as had generations of backlashers, red-baiters, and America-Firsters before them—for the Soviet Union. Anticommunism has, after all, been the driving force of American conservatism for many, many decades; the demise of the ultimate evil Communist state could hardly be expected to prevent the great thinkers of business civilization from using its memory to redden their enemies. On the contrary, the Soviet Union's collapse and breakup only enhanced its usefulness as a business metaphor. Those who could be connected with it in any way were not unpatriotic or treasonous (and what did those terms mean after "the twilight of sovereignty," anyway?), but failures waiting to happen, organizations getting ready to seize up due to bureaucratic inertia, just as had their Moscow-based comrades in market-defiance.

What will astonish those unfamiliar with the field are the people and organizations that the young turks of management theory chose to compare to the commies of old: the great American blue-chip corporations. The fact that Dow, IBM, McDonnell-Douglas, General Motors, and their brethren had all been stout cold warriors would be of no avail in the red-hot free market cauldron of the business revolution. To the latter-day red-baiters of management theory, those organizations' size, their bureaucracy, their hierarchy, and their individuality-suppressing dress codes pointed to one obvious conclusion. The same market-populist logic that killed Communism would soon kill them as well. So just as the heirs of Joe McCarthy had long maintained that the main battle against Communism was the fight against liberals, pinkos, and softies right here among us, so it was that by the end of the nineties the "lesson" taught by the fall of the Soviet Union was almost entirely a domestic one: that the big, arrogant corporation was doomed.

This line of reasoning was already something of a shibboleth by 1992. It was in that year that conservative journalist Peter Huber declared to readers of *Forbes* that it was "market forces and the information age" that had beaten the Soviets and would soon force the dissolution of "America's largest economic organizations." "If you've grown accustomed to a sheltered life inside a really large corporation," he advised, take care: "The next Kremlin to fall may be your own." In his massive 1992 volume, *Liberation Management,* Tom Peters did his part to send this fairly workaday analogy into metaphor hyperspace: What united Communism and the traditional corporate model, it occurred to him, was *arrogance.* After all, he wrote, weren't traditional American corporations, just like the recently collapsed "totalitarian states," simply "a hubristic [sic] exercise in 'controlling everything that exists?' " Peters went on to draw an explicit parallel between the USSR and IBM (then a favorite "old economy" punching bag), and asserted that "most [American] companies, like the old Soviet economy, are still guided by comprehensible master plans that shrivel the human spirit [and] delay useful signals. . . ."[44]

Latter-day red-baiting was not a uniquely American literary strategy. Charles Handy, the British guru, took a look back at the Cold War in his 1994 book, *The Empty Raincoat,* and agreed that the enemy had been within all along. While "we were preoccupied with our common enemy in communism," he wrote, we "conveniently ignored the fact that many of our largest organizations were run in a similar totalitarian way."[45] By 1998, with the business revolution in full swing and the fall of Communism having been enshrined as the one and only history lesson required by the new order, management authors began to make spectacular claims for the red-smashing power of their pet theories. To the Jacobin authors of *BLUR,* for example, it was perfectly obvious that the fall of Communism discredited not only "the entire concept of a centrally planned economy," but also Western companies that rejected the authors' own shrill version of the antihierarchical, antitradition formula. After all, they observed, "Managerially, much of the West runs its corporations like the Soviets ran their economy," complete with that trademark Red "command-and-control approach" and guidance provided by a "centralized decision-making body like the Politburo." In fact—and even though they were writing almost ten years after the event—they could now divulge that it was the very phenomenon of really fast, really excellent change which they had identified as "BLUR" that was the *real* winning factor in the Cold War, the thing that finally made Ivan throw in the towel. And for those Americans who clung to Commie ways at the pinnacle of their arrogant corporate hierarchies, they offered this word of warning: "If you're not adaptable, BLUR will get you, too. Organizations that fail to replace bureaucracy and regulation with internal markets and other adaptive features—companies that resist BLUR, in other words—will fall like the wall and the Soviet economy. Discredited, laughed at, in rubble."[46]

But populism remained a language of the left, even when it was spoken by captains of industry and former speechwriters for Ronald Reagan. So even as the management thinkers of the nineties indulged in their casual red-baiting, they also imagined themselves filling the historical role of the traditional victims of red-baiting: the American left. Like the labor movement, they sought to bring democracy to the workplace; like the better-known lifestyle movements of more recent vintage, the gurus struggled to allow every citizen to "be" him- or herself. Business was bringing together the races. Business was abolishing war. Business was building a multicultural society. Business thinkers and industry leaders shared a deep concern for the environment and enjoyed intuitive friendships with whales, dolphins, orphans, and the peoples of the Third World. That their solution for pretty nearly every one of these problems was some variation on the libertarian prime directive—get out of the way and let the market work its magic—never seemed to impede this glamorous self-image. Peter Senge, for example, announced that, as government has clearly failed to solve the country's social problems, it would be up to business—that is, to the new, "decentralized, nonhierarchical" businesses being dreamed up by people with "radical corporate philosophies"—to "improve the injustice that exists in the world."[47] Talk about legitimacy! Maybe it was the noncorporate world that needed to show why *it* existed.

The figure who best captured the pseudo-leftist imagination of the business revolution was Anita Roddick, the leader of the early-nineties "socially responsible business" movement, and a consistent recipient of guru praise throughout the decade.[48] Roddick herself added considerably to the torrent of prose hailing her good works, publishing a volume of memoirs in 1991, penning leftish columns for the London *Independent* newspaper, and producing a series of pamphlets in which she exalted the figure of the "activist" and contemplated the glory of "empowerment." Roddick involved herself enthusiastically in the American culture wars, pounding the religious right for its real and imagined transgressions, but her greatest contributions were to the ideology of market populism that would eventually supplant those battles. For her there was a natural and obvious link between business and "activism," this latter a calling that Roddick seemed to regard as second only to sainthood. Both pursuits led to "empowerment," both required heaping doses of nonconformity, and both involved wise investing and careful shopping. Her own company, which she sometimes spoke of as a political movement all its own, even sold a brand of cologne for men called "Activist."[49]

Roddick's own views of corporate practice, however, are well in the mainstream of "business revolutionary" thought. Like nearly every other high-profile corporate personality in the nineties, Roddick was a vociferous opponent of traditional corporate practice, relating in her 1991 memoirs how she outmaneuvered such typical villains as the "pinstriped dinosaurs" of the London financial world and the wrong-headed professors of the Harvard Business School. She denounced corporate "arrogance" and "the tendency of many big companies to treat their workforce like children." More importantly, Roddick embraced the trademark leftist critique of the cosmetics industry, using it to blast her competitors. "It is immoral to trade on fear. It is immoral constantly to make women feel dissatisfied with their bodies. It is immoral to deceive a customer by making miracle claims for a product. It is immoral to use a photograph of a glowing sixteen-year-old to sell a cream aimed at preventing wrinkles in a forty-year-old." The Body Shop, by contrast, would be something considerably more than a store. It would be "a force for social change," "a communicator and an educator," for she, Anita Roddick, "soul trader," was in "into the consciousness-raising business." Hence the store's well-known identification of itself with all manner of noble causes and its peculiarly hectoring advertising style, in which enormous sans-serif emphatics exhort readers to do all manner of good. But Roddick is much more than a businesswoman with leftist politics. According to her own testimony the Body Shop actually *is* leftist politics all on its own; a merchant of "the politics of human rights" as well as of soaps and shampoos. "We dedicated our business to the pursuit of positive social and environmental change," she wrote in 1997, "and got on with becoming an activist organisation pursuing it." Her advance through the malls of America was not just commercial success but the onward march of reform.[50]

What makes the whole thing plausible is Roddick's jackhammer authenticity. While other cosmetics outfits manipulate women with deceptive advertising, the Body Shop deals in "the real." Her stores "radiate passion," her children speak "from the heart," her autobiography is packed with photos of her interacting ingenuously with all manner of massively authentic Third World peoples, duly dressed in their tribal costumes. She even informs readers that she flies first-class only so she can strike her blows for the People more effectively upon arrival. (Those who criticize Roddick, by the way, are routinely dismissed as "cynics.") No troublesome complexities or excursions into gray areas are allowed to detract from her unquestionable goodness: She's against cruel, mean things happening to animals and to distant peoples. She thinks we shouldn't waste so much paper and plastic and glass. She's opposed to nuclear war. On issues of workplace democracy Roddick reiterates the standard "business revolutionary" line, although with a curious twist. While she has stated quite clearly that unions have no place in a nonexploitative workplace such as her own, Body Shop spokesmen have also responded to union demands for recognition by playing the "radicalism" card—not accusing unions of being dangerously pink but insisting that the Body Shop was simply too radical for unions![51]

To be sure, Roddick and the "socially responsible business" movement suffered damaging blows in 1994 when a series of articles pointed out that the company had behaved in most circumstances just like any other enterprise would, that its politics were mainly a "greenwashed" brand image meant to appeal to sensitive consumers, that in fact it sourced a smaller amount of its materials through its much-vaunted "Trade Not Aid" program than customers might have believed.[52] But while this temporarily burst Roddick's media bubble and dented her credibility, the larger suggestion that free markets had little place for democratic values never caught on. The "business revolution" just grew louder and louder, ever more convinced of its strange faith that democracy and acquisition went hand in hand. By 1995, shortly before MCI would declare that business was in the process of conquering all of the various oppressions of the universe, the movement produced *Fast Company,* its own glossy magazine, a publication dedicated to the curious proposition that subversives make the best businessmen.

Guided by the belief that "the new business paradigm is economic democracy" and embracing the language of "revolution" with a fetishism reminiscent of the late 1960s, *Fast Company* would dedicate its pages not to the establishment companies followed by *Forbes* and *Fortune* but instead to the exploits of "business activists" and "corporate radicals." The magazine's premiere editorial was a manifesto for the "business revolution," hailing the forces whose "convergence overturns 50 years of received wisdom on the fundamentals of work and competition," and announcing that the corporate upheavals of the 1990s were "as far-reaching as the Industrial Revolution."[53]

While you might worry about your future in an economy that seemed built only to enrich CEOs, *Fast Company* was able to summon story after story of zany workplace liberation. Early issues offered tantalizing glimpses of a "dis-organization" (a maker of hearing aids, mundanely enough) which inhabits an "anti-office" where "all vestiges of hierarchy have disappeared"; related the saga of how a perfectly successful trouser manufacturer decided to implement "the most dramatic change program in American business," rooting out "resistance" and reorganizing itself utterly because . . . well, because it seemed like the thing to do.[54]

Virtually every article in those early days seemed to contain some denunciation of order or recipe for subverting holdovers from the "old economy." There was the story about a Texas computer services company that "consciously accelerates time," with devices such as an instructional video set to music by REM, reverse dress codes, and "culture cops" who punish employees "when they talk the language of the old world of business." There was the confession of a former business reactionary, including anecdotes of how his hierarchical ways inhibited revolutionary behavior among the white-collar rank and file. There were uplifting scenes in which retrograde executives were taken "through a personal reinvention process to show them new ways of leading."[55]

And there were stories of workplace innovation so far-fetched that one wondered how they could be set down on paper. A 1996 article entitled "The People of Hewlett Packard v. The Past" described how that company used a replica of a courtroom confrontation to stimulate a business meeting and the friendly and creative means by which it "killed off" an entire division: by staging "a full-scale New Orleans-style jazz-band funeral, designed to help the division's people deal with the emotional loss and the prospect of moving to other jobs." The company believed it was helping its employees to "celebrate transitions," to break those rules that used to bind us to one career and one job. "All possibilities come from endings," *Fast Company* quoted one executive as saying. "One career is finishing and another is beginning."[56]

In addition the editors went to great lengths to unearth at least one seemingly progressive operation per issue: an African company that recycled its waste; the Whole Foods supermarket chain, which was thought to represent the "future of democratic capitalism" with its hip "team members," which is what it called its employees. Not only were such companies loved by the people who worked for them, but they were also powerhouses of profit. The free market worked just as well in the realm of political economy, the magazine contended, as it did in the realm of making and trading things. Left to its own devices the market would not only make us rich, it would give us a just society to boot.[57]

Thus when *Fast Company* profiled cool executives or derived workplace wisdom from people like Hunter S. Thompson or Bruce Springsteen, it was not just ripping off rebel culture but explaining the breathtakingly grand cultural-economic shift which its editors imagined to be taking place and in whose forefront they endeavored to place themselves: as the *Wall Street Journal* described the magazine's basic idea, "Business was overtaking politics as a force for social change." The revolution whose anthems *Fast Company* was so reverently composing was nothing less than the replacing of civil society by business culture. "Corporations have become the dominant institution of our time," one of the magazine's writers insisted, "occupying the position of the church of the Middle Ages and the nation-state of the past two centuries." Corporations were becoming society, and the hip businessman knew it.[58]

Fast Company's totalitarian streak could sometimes grow quite pronounced. The cover of its first issue announced the new dispensation with two rather terrifying aphorisms—"Work is Personal" and "Computing is Social"—that summed up its vision of society as something that existed within and between the office complexes of the world and the upscale suburbs where the world's change-agents spent their down time. These declarations were offered up not as developments to be resisted but as principles of revolutionary liberation (one can easily invent others along the same lines: "boss is love," "office is home," "temps are rich"). When human and political values were mentioned in the magazine, it was usually not for some inherent quality of their own, but because they brought us into alignment with the spirit of the market and the corporation. One article on the solemn subject of leadership, for example, pointed out that "self-discovery" is an essential business practice, and that "if you want the kind of performance that leads to truly exceptional results," you must embrace a sort of corporate tao: "You have to be willing to embark on a journey that leads to an alignment between an individual's personal values and aspirations and the company's values and aspirations."[59]

Far from frightening readers or sparking popular movements to limit the insane ambitions of the corporation, *Fast Company*, like the business revolution, did just the opposite. It prospered fantastically. By decade's end it boasted a circulation of some five hundred thousand;

according to *New York Times Magazine* writer Tom Vanderbilt it also boasted twenty-five thousand readers who were so dedicated to its pronouncements that they joined local discussion groups referred to as "cells."[60] And it had become a fat magazine indeed, bulked up to more than three hundred pages a month by the advertising of New Economy startups eager to add their amens to the editors' visions of progress through benevolent corporate dictatorship.

While it was true that unions had been rolled back so comprehensively that economic democracy basically ceased to exist, *Fast Company*, along with an entire industry of social thinkers, energetically assured Americans that they had nothing to fear. The market, if we would only let it into our hearts and our workplaces, would look after us; would see that we were paid what we deserved; would give us kind-hearted bosses who listened, who recycled, who cared; would bring a democratic revolution to industry that we could only begin to imagine.

In 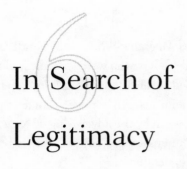Search of Legitimacy

How Business Got Its Soul Back

Corporations like to refer to themselves as "families."
Shouldn't it be the other way around?
　　　　　　　—Advertisement for Merrill Lynch, 1999

What Does Management Literature Manage?

Having established the corporation as the ideal vehicle for economic democracy, as an institution worthy of the respect and obedience of its employees, the management theory of the nineties moved to its second great project of legitimation: Informing readers of the corporation's rightful place in society. Having addressed us as employees, it now proceeded to speak to us as citizens. Here, too, misapprehensions born of the democratic impulses of the past needed to be cleared up. Did, for example, the state really have the right to tax or regulate or control or (heaven forbid) break up the corporation, as people seemed once to have believed? And here, too, the solution arrived at by the management theorists was to announce that the corporation, as a creature called into existence by the market, was of a special and even a superhuman nature. In fact, the corporation was democratic in a way that transcended our limited understanding of the term. The correct attitude when in its presence was childlike awe.

To make such points the gurus would have to wander pretty far afield from the practical matters of workplace theorizing. And this expanding of the discipline's purview became more and more noticeable as the decade went on. While earlier generations of gurus had mainly pondered efficiency or "excellence," the thinkers of the "business revolution" gradually became freebooting social theorists, producing an elaborate body of conjecture in which all premises, all disciplines, all arguments, and even all prose styles were permitted but in which only one conclusion could be arrived at: The new corporate way is the right way. Management literature, in other words, became a glorified form of public relations.

Not that management theory was ever entirely free from the imperatives of corporate publicity. Under scrutiny, even its greatest scientific moments turn out to be tainted with PR. Take the legendary Hawthorne experiments, the scientific bedrock on which stands the human relations school and market populism generally. In a detailed 1991 examination of the social and corporate context in which Elton Mayo came to his famous conclusions, historian Richard Gillespie shows that even before the experiments were conducted, AT&T had been an outspoken champion of "employee representation" schemes, its executives generating endless talk about the "human" corporation and "democracy in business." Hawthorne folklore always presents the experiments' central finding—that workers respond well when they are treated properly—as a surprise or accidental discovery; in fact, it fit quite well into AT&T's existing theory of workplace relations.[1]

Nor did AT&T's "democratic" corporate ideal arise from purely humanitarian motives. As Gillespie points out, the corporate rage for "employee representation" in the twenties arose directly from the series of bloody and highly visible confrontations with unions in the preceding decade—and from the public outrage that always followed. The early leaders of the "human relations" management school were explicitly concerned with minimizing worker discontent and preempting union organizing efforts. AT&T had its own unique corporate problems to worry about as well. It was, of course, a monopoly, and in that age of enthusiastic trust-busting AT&T went to great lengths to persuade the public to think of it as a lovable, democratic organization. In addition to its humanitarian relations with its workers, it emphasized its vast number of stockholders, presenting them—as business ideologues continue to do today—as evidence of the company's public-minded-ness.[2]

Mayo's own presentation of the Hawthorne "findings," moreover, showed him to be a deeply committed ideologue. He specifically pro-posed enlightened management as an alternative to (if not a way of staving off) government intervention in the economy. Furthermore, ac-cording to Gillespie, this advocate of worker-friendly management me-thodically discounted workers' own thoughts about the Hawthorne events as the irrational babbling of children and understood their oc-casional assertions of independence as evidence of a pathological "bol-shevism." Mayo was altogether typical of the human relations tradition of business theory. By the late thirties, after unions had achieved a de-gree of power in the workplace, these consultants still understood it as their duty to limit that power.[3]

Whether Taylorist or humanist, theories of management were sold as a way of defusing class conflict while keeping control of the shop floor firmly in the hands of the owners. As a tool of "nonviolent social control," management theory is, as Barbara Ehrenreich has argued, a close relative of public relations, another profession born at the same time to achieve roughly similar goals.[4] In historian Roland Marchand's massive 1998 study of the public relations industry, the commonalities between the two fields are made spectacularly clear. As Marchand points out, nearly every one of the massive campaigns of "institutional" advertising mounted by the great corporations before World War II was launched in order to counter some potentially costly critique or other. AT&T, in those days one of the most hated corporate powers of all, took center stage: It responded to its poor public image not only by emphasizing the humane management practices symbolized by the Hawthorne experiments but also with an intensive and long-running public relations campaign. For decades, AT&T countered public suspicion by describing itself as an unusually public-minded enterprise, a uniter of peoples, an "industrial democracy," a provider of a "universal service," an "annihilator of space," a "Main Street" fixture—themes recycled endlessly in the breathless business writing of the Internet-addled nineties. The campaign was considered a resounding success for public relations in general: When the antitrust showdown finally came in the 1930s and AT&T emerged unscathed, admirers credited its thirty-year public relations effort with sparing the company from the regulatory deluge.[5]

But whether it was AT&T, General Motors, Republic Steel, or Goodyear mounting the PR blitz, and whether the particular obstacle being anticipated was government- or union-related, Marchand insists that each campaign was part of a single overarching endeavor: "the corporate quest for social and moral legitimacy." The most commonplace criticism of the great business organizations coming to dominate American life at the turn of the century, he reminds us, was that while they had been legally defined as individuals, they lacked "soul." They were arrogant behemoths without conscience or accountability, upsetting the lives of millions and disturbing the rhythms of American life simply to enrich a small coterie of robber barons. Corporations were nobody's friend.[6]

The effort to make corporations everybody's friend, to create what Marchand calls "corporate soul," became an important objective of corporate speech. The effort brought employment to an army of admen and public relations experts. It yielded thousands of advertisements, house magazines, and worlds' fair exhibits testifying to the essential humanness of the corporation. The corporation portrayed itself as a public servant and a friend of family life. It bathed itself in small-town sentimentalism, clothed itself in the garb of the plain people. It gave up the arrogant self-interest of the Vanderbilts and Fisks for a ringing species of cultural populism. It became one of us.

Although Marchand discusses the project of corporate soul-creation mainly in terms of formally sponsored speech, one can clearly see it beginning to seep into the nascent field of management theory. And in the age of the "New Economy" consensus, of the sexy merging and blurring of so many once incompatible fields, management theory and PR have become virtually indistinguishable. While public relations seeks to personalize or humanize particular industries or corporations, management theory does so for the (new style) corporation generally, informing us of the freedom that is to be ours when the dictates of the market are finally followed to the letter. Both exist to rationalize corporate behavior. The publisher of *Fast Company* describes his magazine as "a religion"; the cognoscenti now use the term "evangelist" to describe what used simply to be called a "guru." The role of the wise is not merely to help corporation folk in their quest for efficiency, but to preach, to proselytize, to convert.[7]

Management theory's new role as PR becomes even more apparent when one looks to the corporations that have the most to fear from a revival of labor or an activist federal government. Just as the most hated monopolists of the turn of the century became the most enthusiastic patrons of institutional advertising and human-relations management theories, so the most enthusiastic corporate leaders of the "business revolution" are people like Bill Gates, who has written two books of management theory and whose company runs commercials proclaiming that its monopolistic reach is (like AT&T's in the 1920s) just a way of permitting you to "go" anywhere you desire. In fighting the antitrust suit of the late 1990s, Microsoft's lawyers and spin doctors were joined by a host of management theorists, all of them rallying to the company's defense in op-eds and full-page ads across the land. When it finally became apparent that Microsoft would be judged a monopoly in November 1999, its official reaction (according to the *Wall Street Journal*) was to roll out even more management theory, to ratchet up its populist rhetoric, to launch a new campaign celebrating the "personal empowerment" that the company is said to permit, and to tag its persecutors as noxious "advocates of centralized control."[8]

Wherever one turns, the same curious logic seems to hold true: The corporations most praised by the gurus for their sensitive and tolerant and listening management styles seem to be the companies with the most skeletons in their closet. Jack Welch, the CEO who has transformed General Electric from a manufacturer into a service conglomerate, probably represents the clearest-cut case of a manager who has done the bidding of Wall Street at the expense of what used to be called his "stakeholders." Through an endless program of layoffs, downsizing, outsourcing, and move-em-south deindustrialization, Welch managed to deliver miraculous rewards to his shareholders and poverty and unemployment to many of the towns and people who used to work for him. According to the glowing accounts of Welch's deeds in management literature, however, his really important accomplishment is the series of employee rap sessions he inaugurated. Known as the "Work-Out" program, it brings together workers and managers to discuss their differences (with the help of a management consultant, of course) in what the company called "town meetings," adding yet another layer of meaninglessness to what was already the most abused populist cliché of the decade. The company has also generated such mysterious entities as "RAMMP teams" and a "Six Sigma" program. The fact that a few years before "Neutron Jack" had been enthusiastically terminating the same people he was now "empowering" doesn't seem to have confused anyone: The combination of soaring share price, democratic rhetoric, and prominent employment for an array of consultants has made Welch one of the most admired CEOs of the decade, hailed by Tom Peters as a "Charter Member of the Lunatic Fringe."[9]

Similarly, Shell Oil, well-known to readers of management literature as the birthplace of the "learning organization," is equally well known outside the guru community as a reliable friend of dictators the world round, garnering extra credit in the mid-nineties for its entanglements in a particularly nasty episode in Nigeria. AT&T, a compulsive consumer of new management theory, singlehandedly provoked the biggest wave of anticorporate feeling in the decade when it laid off forty thousand employees one day in 1996.[10] The list could be extended indefinitely.

When Roland Marchand recounted the long cultural struggle of the corporation to create a "soul" for itself, he was describing a fundamentally defensive operation. "The soulless corporation" had been one of the sharper arrows in the quiver of the Populist, trustbuster, muckraker, New Dealer, and labor leader, and in establishing their metaphorical personhood, corporations were simply fighting the larger battle against regulation and unionization by slightly more abstract, more poetic means.

No one has seriously charged a corporation with "soullessness" for many years.[11] Like all clichés, the phrase died of its own success. And yet the corporate response that Marchand studies—the efforts to prove that companies were just as human as the rest of us, that they were "good neighbors," small-town fixtures, "folks"—lived on as if by some logic of its own. Now, though, the corporation was on the offensive, noisily establishing its "soul," its personhood, and hence its legitimacy even as it downsized the ranks of its blue-collar employees, smashed the company towns to which it had once sworn eternal loyalty, outsourced every possible job, and reintroduced Americans to the grotesque social formations of the nineteenth century.

While "creating the corporate soul" had been, in the period Marchand studies, the province of advertising and PR, in the nineties it became the duty of management theorists. And they took to it with a directness and a philosophical conviction that would have boggled the minds of the hardened PR men of the thirties. The efforts to prove that a corporation could be, in some profound sense, as human as the rest of us began in earnest with the very first shots of the business revolution. As early as 1990, Peter Senge was insisting that the hallmark of the good corporation, what he calls the "learning organization," was that it had a "spiritual foundation." It was a place where individuals underwent some sort of enlightenment regarding their role in the universe, the market. As such, the relationship between this "learning organization" and its workers must be considered "sacred" rather than "instrumental." Under no conditions should they be blasphemed with anything as logocentric as a contract. Thus Senge suggests that the corporate practice of signing contracts with workers be abandoned in favor of "covenants," which are nonbinding but which "reflect unity and grace and poise." As if to silence the guffaws of any working-class readers who have somehow made it far enough into *The Fifth Discipline* to encounter this passage, on the very next page Senge shifts to the subject of "cynicism" and how to prevent people from scoffing at these high-minded ideas when once they are put into effect in the workplace.[12]

But it was not until the 1994 appearance of the bestseller *Built to Last,* a study of companies that had prospered for long stretches of time, that the corporation's essential humanness became one of the reigning clichés of the decade. As the book's subtitle, "Successful Habits of Visionary Companies," transferred onto the corporate entity the attributes ("habits") that previous motivational literature had reserved for "highly effective people," the book's central argument transferred to the corporation the metaphysical property once thought to be uniquely human. What distinguished "visionary companies" was a "core ideology," a set of "values" that never changed, regardless of who directed the company or what went on in the broader economy. While some companies were interested only in profit, the "visionary" corporations came up with mission statements, declarations of principle, "idealized view[s] of its self-identity," theories about "the *why* of business." And what mattered, the authors insisted, was not the specific content of those statements of purpose, but how truly the companies believed. The visionary company had a sort of spiritual authenticity: "[The company founders] articulated what was inside them—what was in their gut, what was bone deep. It was as natural to them as breathing. It's not what they believed as how deeply they believed it. . . . Again, the key word is *authenticity.* No artificial flavors. No added sweeteners. Just 100 percent genuine authenticity."[13]

Although *Built to Last* had compared "visionary companies" to cults, it did not use the word "soul." That came later, most notably in a slim

1996 volume entitled *Redefining Corporate Soul.* Here the logic of corporate personhood was explained in the familiar terms of middle-class man's personal search for authenticity: Just as the questing organization man had to get in touch with his true self by stripping away the layers of conformity he had accumulated over the years, so corporations had to develop a *"here-and-now contact with their own authenticity—their corporate soul."* Again the key is a truthfulness of spirit, a sort of deep dedication to some great purpose, not just a superficial commitment to the guru du jour—"just *talking* globalism or quality or teamwork or reengineering doesn't cut the mustard."[14] Just as day-traders must learn humility in order to profit from the market's fluctuations, so executives must really *believe* in the eternal goodness of the market: CEOs must outsource soulfully; when they move the plant to Mexico the deed has to come from the heart.

But leave it to the sentimental Charles Handy to come up with the most far-fetched statement of corporate personhood. In *The Hungry Spirit,* his 1997 effort, he declared that corporations need "to know what their *telos* or consuming purpose is, for they, too, are hungry spirits at heart, seeking for the meaning in all their striving." Fortunately, Handy had already resolved their quest in his 1994 blast at the problem of conformity, *The Empty Raincoat.* The purpose of the corporation, he had declared then, was not just to make a profit, but to *live:* "We might call it the existential company." God may be dead but the corporation lived on, free to find its own purpose and act as it saw fit here on earth. The "existential company," as he proudly defined it, was something that "exists in its own right," that "has a life and a future of its own." Within a few years, of course, the notion had been elucidated at book length. Arie de Geus argued in 1997 not only that "the company is a living being" (like humans, companies learn, they have identities, they have relationships, they grow, and they die) but that it was *a higher order of living being* than a human: It could potentially live for hundreds of years, if not forever.[15] A Japanese robot manufacturer, quoted in a popular management text, put the matter well when he said, "I see the company as an infinitely growing child. I will die, but it continues to live, and my responsibility is to see to that. And I want to continue to build better and better robots." Not only was the corporation a happier sort of human than us mortals—living forever as a child, an angelic being of learning and innocence—but it was actively and rightfully working to replace us inferior beings with machines.[16]

The argument was even more potent when merged with that other subject of business mysticism, the brand. Like its soul, a company's brand was thought to have something to do with its innermost identity. Brands were eternal as well, generally believed to be the one aspect of a company that would allow it to weather the tumultuous waves of "change" that everyone thought were coming. Great significance was attributed to brands by the business revolutionaries: Brands were the intangible magic that separated the good corporations from the bad; brands were trust; brands were a promise; brands were a subtle negotiation between consumer and corporation; brands were a conversation; brands were the anvil of democracy, the place where the relationship between corporation and customer was hammered out; brands were democracy itself. The brand, readers of management literature were told, was the correct way to think about nation-states; it was the correct way to think about politics; it was the correct way to think about history.

The other shoe did not take long to drop. Between the head-swimming concept of the "corporate soul" and the awesome power believed to inhere in the brand, it was not long before someone proposed that corporations, what with their brands and all, were in some crucial way *more human than us*. It was *we* who should be modeling *ourselves* after the artifacts of business life. Naturally the honor fell to Tom Peters, whose essay "The Brand Called You" appeared in the August/September 1997 issue of *Fast Company*. For Peters it was an unusual excursion into the personal-motivation and -grooming side of the management-lit trade; for the rest of us it was a terrifying glimpse of the coming total-corporate state, a sort of *Dress for Success* rewritten by Chairman Mao. "Today brands are everything," Peters wrote, and he wasn't kidding. The brand was the idea to which everyone was gravitating, every business surrendering. So pervasive are brands, Peters observed, that we inhabit a "new brand world," a place where brands appeared everywhere, explained everything. Turning to the logo-ridden clothes we wear, Peters chants, "You're branded, branded, branded, branded."

It would not do to try to resist this "new brand world": Peters told us that it was "inescapable." The correct response was to internalize the logic of branding. "It's this simple," he wrote: "*You* are a brand. *You* are in charge of your brand." You had what amounted to total freedom when it came to promoting your brand/your self. If you turned out to be good at branding you could even "establish your own micro equivalent of the Nike swoosh," by which you could "put yourself in a great bargaining position for next season's free-agency market." But you had no choice about the larger context. Since we now inhabited a funky democratic free-for-all in which long-term employment was laughed at as "indentured servitude" and the reactionary "Generals" (General Motors, General Mills, General Electric, General Dynamics) were to be forgotten, all of we "free agents" were on the job hunt forever, not just two or three times in our lives. The price of all this freedom? Eternal vigilance about the way you present Brand You. And remember—we're watching! "Everything you do"—Peters mentioned the way you talked on the phone, the way you did e-mail, whether or not your "brand You business card" had "a cool-looking logo"—"is part of the larger message you're sending about your brand." What's more, we were advised to check in every so often with the presiding deity of this "new brand world," the Market, in order "to have a reliable read on your brand's value." Perhaps sensing that the "new brand world" he is evoking was neither free nor attractive, Peters closed the essay by hinting at a different sort of incentive: "Start today. Or else."[17]

Symbolism I: The Corporate Naive

One of the most remarkable management texts to appear in 1998 was *Orbiting the Giant Hairball,* which publicists described as "originally self-published and already a business cult-classic." The idea of DIY business lit is admittedly a strange one, but the most striking feature of *Orbiting* was its curious determination to render the various themes of the business revolution in the manner of children's books. The book's author, Gordon MacKenzie, a "corporate holy man" at Hallmark Cards, touched briefly on just about every one of the main themes of the decade: the importance of creativity, the perils of conformity, the nature of true learning, the problem of soul, the need for authenticity, the company as a living thing, and the horror of the conventional authoritarian corporation (the "hairball" of the title, in case you were wondering). But the theme that really dominates the book is the purity and innocence of children. Childhood is the thing that the old-style hierarchical corporation tames and destroys, the thing we in the business revolution must struggle to retain. *Orbiting* opens with MacKenzie visiting an elementary school and pondering how the students' "creative genius" was systematically suppressed as they grew older; it ends with a fantasy about the "masterpiece" that God commissions each of us to paint as infants, but which project is hijacked by "society" and turned into a conformist paint-by-numbers. The vast majority of the illustrations, which are placed randomly on almost every page, are done in a faux-naive style—glorified stick figures, big dots over the 'i's, a feigned ignorance of perspective—that carefully mimics the scrawl of elementary-school doodling. The appropriate attitude of a nineties-style corporation man, it suggests, is one of childlike wonder.[18]

And just about wherever thinkers were pondering the corporate condition in the nineties, they were coming to the same conclusion, settling on the same palette of imagery to describe the proper way of imagining the new-style corporation. In the works of Charles Handy, children come up again and again as a model for the true and unaffected style of thinking that all good corporations should embrace. The same is true for Peter Senge, who entitled a chapter of *The Fifth Discipline*, "Rediscover the Child Learner within Us." Business evangelist Guy Kawasaki instructs his readers on the critical task of standing up to experts by reprinting an entire children's book from the 1940s in the pages of his 1999 management text, *Rules for Revolutionaries*. Even the hardened strategists, Hamel and Prahalad, suggest that a good way to guess at future developments in industry is to assume "a childlike innocence."[19]

This superior wisdom of children could sometimes take on quite a menacing form: Not only were the very young thought to be spectacularly smart, but they were supposed to have little patience for the old-economy ways of their elders. Like the Internet, with which they were said to enjoy an unusually close and understanding relationship, children were sometimes understood as a furious and vengeful force, sweeping out the patriarchs and hierarchs of old with extreme prejudice. Business theorist Don Tapscott, speaking at the panel discussion mentioned above, attributed to the people he called "the kids" a preternatural power of commercial judgment, ready to nail a company instantly if its ads made claims that its products didn't back up. These "kids" had zero tolerance for old ways of corporate organization; they were "authorities on the big revolution that's changing business, commerce and learning, entertainment, government and the firm. . . ."[20] Leave it to Tom Peters to take this argument a m-i-l-l-i-o-n steps further. Kids RULE! Companies *must have them!* And F—K those meddling feds who say otherwise! "Forget federal and state child-labor laws," he froths in *The Circle of Innovation*: "If your information systems/information technology operation doesn't have a 'senior executive' under the age of 15 . . . or at least under 25 . . . you're in trouble."[21]

Let us give Peters the benefit of the doubt here and assume that he is not really planning in some dark and underhanded manner to actually secure the repeal of child-labor laws. Even so, the business revolution's fascination with the innocence of children remains astonishing. In institutional advertising the fanciful connection between the "New Economy" and the nobility of children ballooned into a full-blown aesthetic, a corporate naive style. Whenever some point about the fundamental benevolence of the new corporate order needed to be nailed down, companies were sending a boy to do The Man's job: MCI using a tiny tot to tell the world that they were abolishing space, that "there will be no more there"; Merrill Lynch filming a ten-year-old girl wandering through Berlin and South Africa in order to symbolize the birth and innocence of the "New Economy"; Lockheed-Martin introducing a new generation of fighter planes by showing a child regarding one with wonder; KPMG/Peat Marwick using a conversation over a five-year-old's lemonade stand to illustrate the magic of outsourcing in the age of the Internet; Agilent using slo-mo footage of children swinging on an old tire near a white picket fence to boast of how it inspects computer chips; or International Paper and Union Camp, who chose to announce their 1999 merger with gravitas-grabbing black-and-white footage of two kids playing together—and to explain the timeless significance of the event with an announcer of no more than eight: "Can the combined ideas of two innovative companies also change the way we look at things? Can it unite into something greater? Can it make all our lives better? It can and it will."[22]

It was IBM, though, that won first prize for the most egregious use of the corporate naive. In a purely business-to-business campaign that ran in the summer of 1999, the company dubbed its various Unix servers "the magic box." In each ad this "magic box," black and enigmatic like the monolith in *2001* (or the object on the cover of Led Zeppelin's *Presence* album), is shown as an object of worshipful contemplation by a child. Here a tot stares up at a black box before a baroque building; there one leans against a black box sprouting incongruously from Central Park; in a third picture a group of uniformed Japanese children join hands in a ring as they celebrate the black box that has landed in their schoolyard. Although the fine print lets you know all you need to know about the computer's technical features and runs through a respectable array of business-revolution jargon ("bandwidth," "knowledge management," "delivering shareholder value," "growing a business"), it's the clumsy, childlike big print that makes grandiose claims for the product's nobility: "The magic box brings people together"; "The magic box is always there for you." In one corner of an eight-page "magic box" ad that ran in the *Wall Street Journal*, stick-figure drawings help us understand how "business people use the magic box to send e-mails to other business people and their mothers" and also how "entrepreneurs use the magic box to compete against their former bosses." Mommy, can I please outsource the job now?[23]

In an age when preserving the innocence of children served as the justification for everything from disastrous ATF assaults to the impeachment of the president, there were of course any number of efforts by various political factions and social movements to capture the brand image of the child for their own cause. The "business revolution," though, had especially good reasons to identify itself so hamhandedly with innocence. On the most obvious level, children symbolized the way they wished Americans to regard them and the "New Economy" in general. To understand industrial enterprise as a child—or, even better, to think about industrial enterprise from a child's perspective—was instantly to deny its calculating side, its brutal, monopoly-seeking, lock 'em out, send-in-the-goon-squad nature. To portray a manufacturer of attack jets as the beloved companion of a small boy may turn the stomachs of some viewers, but the ad's makers no doubt believed it humanized the company in question in the bluntest, most direct manner possible. Children also made an ideal symbol for the new order because they lack long memories: For children everything is future; there are no encumbering recollections of a different way of doing things, a more democratic scheme that someone once proposed. What's more, children *believe;* they believe with endearing faithfulness even in the most outlandish fabulisms—an attribute that served the masters of the "New Economy" extraordinarily well as the stock bubble of the late nineties transported them to the heavenly reaches of billionaire-hood. As they could plainly see from up there, the new corporation was on the side of the angels.

Symbolism II: People of the Market

In 1904, and to great public fanfare, the Heinz food company moved the "little house" in which it was founded via riverboat to its corporate headquarters in Pittsburgh, where it could be depicted in advertising and gaped at by plant visitors. According to historian Roland Marchand, this was a spectacular instance of an early-twentieth-century publicity strategy in which old houses and original factories were used as emblems of a company's personableness and trustworthiness. In 1999, Hewlett-Packard, one of the marquee names of the New Economy, launched an advertising campaign featuring the humble old-fashioned garage in which the company had started. In its exemplary down-homeness the garage symbolized the "simple rules" that animated business generally. (One of "the rules of this garage," naturally, is "no bureaucracy.") In some spots this magic edifice, this "garage that invented an industry, that reinvented work" is shown popping up all around the world, a globe-trotting holy relic, revealing its weathered slats to the people of Prague, of Paris, of Beijing, before returning to Wall Street, where its simple wooden frame can rebuke the haughty granite towers where power used to reside.

From humble garages to great montages, the corporate speech of the nineties made enthusiastic use of the visual language of populism. A particular favorite was the panorama of differentness, the old Norman Rockwell technique in which the many different faces of working America were shown united in prayer, in patriotism, or in plenty. In the vehicles of market populism, though, the working class was replaced by bearers of a more convincing authenticity: The peoples of the world, their glorious differentness united in allegiance to whatever product or service was being promoted at the time. "New Economy" darling Cisco Systems, one of the most committed patrons of this populist style (and, for a time, the company with the greatest market capitalization in the world), promoted its services in the late nineties with a series of commercials in which a succession of small children from all over the world soberly read a testimonial to the Internet. While the kids—and the distinctly exotic adults who appear in other Cisco spots—are supposed to represent a cross-section of the world's peoples, their unsmiling faith in the goofy promises and even slightly threatening programs of the "New Economy" puts one distinctly in mind of *1984*, with its noble child informers.

American management theory first became a believer in non-

Western ways during the eighties, when Japanese industrial achievements so astonished the business class. Perhaps it wasn't that odd,
then, for Charles Handy to assert in 1989 that Japan was also well
ahead of us in the sensitivity race, viewing management as "a continual process of self-enlightenment" in which senior executives enjoyed
"sitting with their subordinates, *listening* to them, not talking at them."
The next year Peter Senge found traces of the new managerial style
among a whole array of faraway peoples. Suspending assumptions, for
example, is something that Senge claimed could still be found among
"primitive" peoples (he singles out the North American Indians), but
that had been "lost to modern society."[24] For Anita Roddick the wisdom
and authenticity of indigenous peoples had a much more direct business use—it was to be the commodity in which her Body Shops would
deal. Roddick went to great pains to let consumers know how she traveled the earth, researching the hair- and skin-care practices of Third
World peoples—and also to contrast the loathsome products of her
competitors with the earth-friendly ways of her pals, the people. *Which*
people didn't seem to make a great deal of difference to Roddick: All
indigenous people seemed to be alike, in her telling, in being "natural
people," the "caretakers of the earth," folks of "innate wisdom" whose
very company is "nourishing for the soul." What Roddick offered them
was a sort of soul-transaction: She took an interest in their minuscule
enterprises, they in turn "help to protect us from the perils of gigantism
and the inhumanity of big business." They would help the Body
Shop—and, by extension, its customers—"keep our soul."[25]

The ethnic essentialism of Roddick and Senge blended easily into
the corporate multiculturalism that one saw so much of in the mid and
late nineties. Ethnic diversity, the guru community agreed, automatically gave a company *intellectual* diversity, endowed it with an inherent
creativeness that would allow it to approach its problems in fresh and
unusual ways. In 1990, Senge had asserted that Shell Oil's multiculturalism (or, more precisely, its Dutch and British biculturalism) had
been the critical factor in enabling it to weather the OPEC shock of

the early seventies; by 1997, Tom Peters was describing himself re-
coiling in horror from the "Old White Males" who still ran so many
businesses—and who could never quite figure out why they had such
problems with innovation.[26]

So far, so harmless. But this stuff could easily turn crackpot. And
in some precincts of the "business revolution," one encountered
some pretty bizarre ideas. *Tribes,* a 1992 book by "business trends analyst" (and Democratic think-tanker) Joel Kotkin, gives the standard
critique of elitist hierarchy a racial edge by accusing "Anglo-Ameri-
cans and European capitalism in general" of suffering "from the
growth of corrupt and lethargic elites, a loss of competitive will, rising criminality, decay in basic values such as thrift, and the importance of hard work." The West was getting soft. Fortunately, Kotkin
finds that certain Asian peoples are basically Calvinists by a different
name, bringing with them wherever they wander "a common ethos of
discipline, work ethic and frugality." The successful Asian immigrants to the US and Britain upon whom Kotkin focuses are thus
even better attuned to the market than the tired Protestants they
live among, outhustling and outcompeting them. Market values, of
course, are universal, but while the common people of Asia still pay
them proper reverence, the Americans and British, decadent from
decades of top-down coddling by government or corporation, have
turned their backs on the Way.[27]

There was also a simple ideological reason for executives and management thinkers to believe in a unique Asian attunement to the market. If it was true, then it automatically settled by sheer force of
numbers any residual debate about the market's identification with the
people. "Asia" was a constituency so vast that it outnumbered any possible coalition of menacing trade unionists, Naderites, and environmentalists. This is why management theorists were sometimes so
desperate to declare themselves bowled over by the newfound prosperity of Southeast Asia. Tom Peters' 1997 "New Economy" nightmare,
The Circle of Innovation, began with a horror-homage to Kuala

Lumpur, where the jackhammers kept him awake all night and where some of the tallest buildings in the world drove home the lesson that, thanks to Asia, the coming of the business revolution was irresistible.

Some ethnicities, though, were less equal than others in the eyes of the business revolutionaries. The French, as already noted, were consistently used in "New Economy" writing to symbolically bring together the welfare state with the snobbery long attributed to them by American prejudice. Naturally they appeared in the TV commercials of the American nineties as figures of unbelievable affectation, inveighing pretentiously against snowboarding in a commercial for American Express or turning up their noses at some wonderful deal being offered by one of the long-distance companies. Even certain Asian nations could sometimes fall victim to such negative stereotyping. Consider the fate of the Japanese, who went in the guru mind from being a people of innate management ability to a people so backward and conformist and big government-y that they risked missing out on the "New Economy" altogether. Japan was in a slump, and business commentators were quick to identify the problem as a cultural one: Lack of initiative, creativity, risk-taking.[28] An IBM commercial strikes the perfect essentializing note: A group of Japanese organization men, dressed identically in dark suits and white shirts, are seated around a monstrous table in a *Dr. Strangelove*-like war room. They are, ironically, exactly the sort of conformatrons that management commentators earlier in the decade had imagined IBM executives to be. With this spot, though, IBM deftly passes the hot potato of wowlessness on to a distant people: One of the Japanese junior executives, it seems, can't get the valves cheap enough—and he is so ashamed! The elder-statesman CEO, no Peters-esque celebrator of mistakes, shows his displeasure in a typically patriarchal way. "But they're our only supplier," whines the fuckup, who (the viewers all know) has been screwed not by his own inability but by the rigid workings of the inflexible, top-down Japanese economy. "What about Mitchco?" pipes another young exec—he's found some funky, down-home American valve-maker by using . . . *the Internet*.

What was most attractive about the business revolution's new, globalized vision of the common man was that this *populi* had no *vox* at all except for that of its corporate sponsor. Removed by thousands of miles from the target audiences of the "business revolution," this People was entirely voiceless except when they were summoned up by MCI or Cisco Systems or Archer Daniels Midland, on which occasion they could always be counted upon to support management's latest scheme. The superiority of the new form would become increasingly obvious as the old populist subject, the American working class, their wages battered by equal measures of Reaganism and Clintonism, finally erupted, turning to the sort of confrontational attitudes and actions that would culminate on the streets of Seattle in November 1999. In the clash of populisms that inevitably resulted, friends of the corporate way sought again and again to trump the workerist populism of labor with the even higher octane populism of the market, charging protesters with seeking to deprive the vastly more numerous people of the Third World of the ability to make a decent living. Writing in the *New York Times,* Thomas Friedman offered a particularly memorable version of this formula, declaring that under no circumstances did unions (which were, after all, "afraid of the future") "represent the world and the poor." The masses as well as the virtue of "the downtrodden" were all on the other side, an arrangement that Friedman described in this classic market populist formula, relayed from an official of the Egyptian government: "The truth is, most of the world's population was *inside* the conference room in Seattle, not outside."[29] They had the guns *and the numbers, too,* baby! This was a rallying cry that rang virtually unchallenged through the mainstream media in the weeks after the Seattle showdown. There were few better demonstrations of the universality of the market populist consensus in all of the nineties: Charles Krauthammer and Michael Kinsley, writing in *Time,* said the same thing as Friedman. So did the editorial page of the *Wall Street Journal. The Economist* added its voice to the choir. And writing in *Newsweek,* foreign policy expert Fareed Zakaria made the same point as well. While demonstrators claimed to speak on behalf of "the downtrodden of the world," he sneered, "the downtrodden beg to differ." As people from "developing nations" could tell you, "Western workers . . . are rich and privileged by any standard." That the market was bringing them down a peg or two in order to elevate the humble "indigenous people" of the Third World was just an indication of the market's fundamental fairness, its kindly desire to help the downtrodden. And the downtrodden knew what a friend they had in markets.[30]

The Church of Change

For other journalistic commentators on the Seattle events, opposing free trade was more than an act of racist contempt for the Third World; It was a pathetic effort to halt the inevitable. That the gentlemen of the fourth estate were able to perceive the march of history so plainly, were able to distinguish so confidently between what was inevitable and what was hopeless, must also be chalked up to energetic efforts of management theory. For the gurus "inevitability" was a special concept, a weapon in the development of which much had been invested. This was the heavy artillery, to be rolled out in workplace or public situations when talk of the "corporate soul" or the wisdom of children or the luminous liberation of the New Economy failed to get results. There was, of course, an obvious contradiction here—how can we really be "free agents" or "empowered" or "liberated" if we are in the tight grip of inevitability?—but what matters in PR is not consistency but getting the job done. And "change," the business theorists' favored term for the mechanical processes of history they saw unfolding, most certainly got the job done.

"Change" is derived, of course, from "progress," that staple of the reassuring business literature of years past. But "change" is far sterner stuff: "Change" has no time for soft notions like uplift or the common good. "Change" is not a benevolent doctrine. On the contrary: Management theorists wield "change" like a weapon. "Change" cleans out resistance. "Change" blasts through the defenses. "Change" levels the city blocks. "Change" means "do it or die."

Theorists often characterize "change" as a "dance," but a more accurate term, given the way they describe it, would be "doomsday device." Their readers may well be prosperous functionaries of a social system that has conquered the world—in fact they almost certainly are, as many of the works in question acknowledge in their first pages—but without fail nearly every management text asks him to imagine himself on the receiving end of the unpredictable, man-made calamity that is, we are assured, just around the corner.

Change was also thought to have a historical dimension. Management theorists generally agreed that, up until a few years before, Americans inhabited a world where change didn't change much. Things were stable; things moved slowly; we enjoyed "certainty." Charles Handy wrote in 1989 that change used to be predictable but that now it is "discontinuous": He asks us to wrap our brains around the head-swimming notion that "change is not what it used to be." Gary Hamel and C. K. Prahalad, two of the greatest celebrators of change, write in their highly regarded 1994 book, *Competing for the Future,* that people used to understand the future as simply a "linear extrapolation of the past."[31]

Ah, but now things were *really* changing. Tom Peters opened his 1997 book, *The Circle of Innovation,* by invoking what he believed to be "planetary economic, social, and political upheaval on a scale—and at a pace—unprecedented in human history." We are accustomed nowadays to hearing such remarks and thinking, "Right, the Internet. It changes everything, doesn't it?" But the church of change was well-established among management theorists years before they began to notice the Internet. In 1989, Handy was already comparing the "change" of our time to the experiences of the Incas when the conquistadors showed up. *The One to One Future,* a 1993 book by consultants Don Peppers and Martha Rogers that hails the rise of individualized marketing through fax machines and direct mail, begins by declaring that "we are passing through a technological discontinuity of epic proportions," a "paradigm shift" that will unleash "cataclysmic changes." In 1994, *Competing for the Future* held that we are on the verge of "a revolution as profound as that which gave birth to modern industry." In more recent years, of course, the rhetoric has only escalated. *The Dance of Change,* a 1999 compendium of big thinkings on the subject, has by its fifteenth page referred to "change agents," "change agendas," "change initiatives," "change programs," "top-down change" (which is bogus change indeed), "inner" and "outer change," "deep change processes," "significant change," and has settled on one term as more meaningful than all others: "profound change." To illustrate the failure of rival theorists' "change programs," the book's authors offer what may be the most pointless graph in the entire history of business thought: Without benefit of notation, figures, or sources we are shown how an arrow marked "Time" bucks and subsides on its way to the future while another marked "Potential (unrealized)" ascends tragically to the heavens.[32]

Adherents to the "charlatan" school of guru-interpretation might see this constant invocation of "change" as a fad, as something no more profound than Dodge's use of the slogan, "We're changing everything." Or they might see it as a simple trick to sell more books: "Change" means that what you thought—and what yesterday's theorist told you to think—is all wrong and worthless; "change" means you need a new guru. They would be at least partially right. "Change" gives an entire cottage industry of "futurists" and "market intelligence analysts" something to do. A good example is the 1999 book *Net Worth,* published by the prestigious Harvard Business School Press, in which some three hundred pages are filled with imaginary solutions to imaginary problems that we are assured will arise sometime in the near future. Add to that a series of speculative constructions about the way businesses will compete in the future, the problems they will run into, and the sure-thing development that will force every business everywhere to completely rethink what they do, and the message is clear: "Senior managers" are going to have to change even more than they thought.[33]

By the end of the decade "change" had nearly become an article of worship. The title metaphor of the 1998 book *BLUR*—variously described as "a meltdown of all traditional boundaries," "the acceleration of business in every respect," and "momentous shifts" driven by "elements of change" that are "based on the fundamental dimensions of the universe itself"—is treated with the reverence ordinarily reserved for God. "BLUR" is spelled in capital letters throughout the book; it is said to be visible only to the true believers; it is thought to be constituted by a "Trinity" of factors; and we are repeatedly warned that "BLUR" has the whole world most securely in its hands: "Don't think you'll ever slow down BLUR, let alone bring it to a halt," write the prophet-authors, Stan Davis and Christopher Meyer. "Its constant acceleration is here to stay, and those who miss that point will miss everything." "BLUR" is also something of a jealous god, they warn: "Ignore these forces and BLUR will make you miserable and your business hopeless." Or, more bluntly, "Don't try to beat the BLUR. Join it."[34]

The management theorists of the nineties may have fantasized about executives as revolutionaries, as artists, as anthropologists, as innocent little children murmuring happy little nursery rhymes about corporate mergers. One fantasy that it did not indulge, though, was of executives as historians. Quite the contrary. Management theory expresses a virtually unanimous hostility not only to "the past" itself, but to just about any of the operations of memory. I have heard this particular shibboleth voiced most bluntly and directly by a retired football coach before an audience of adoring corporate types: "History is for cowards and losers" was his trademark tag line. Hamel and Prahalad, whose badmouthing of "the past" is only slightly more sophisticated, argue that "a company must work as hard to forget as it does to learn," that "a company must be willing to jettison, at least in part, its past," and actually entitle a section of their book "Unlearning the Past," an operation in which, they winningly relate, little children must serve as our models. Remembering, meanwhile, is said by Charles Handy to be an operation of the despised professoriate ("Endlessly they rehearse the past"—as opposed to "little children," whose true and unaffected learning is so inspiring) and the unemployed, who haven't embraced uncertainty and change and all the rest of it and instead want only to live in the good old days.[35]

"Change" is good for management theorists because it so thoroughly muddles the crucial issues of inevitability and agency. "Change" allows management thinkers to have it both ways: The big changes are made by market forces beyond our control, but still we must make our own changes to be in compliance with the big ones. We have no say in the matter and yet we are responsible for our own failings—which could double as a thumbnail description of life in "New Economy" America.

But most importantly of all, "change" does the trick when "democracy" doesn't. "Change" is what downsized you, not Jumping Jack Welch. "Change" is rocking the world—and so, by extension, are management thought and the corporations that embrace it. This is the reasoning that gives rise both to the most common confusion in change-thought—whether "change" is a prime mover in its own right or whether it is something that corporations have caused—and also to the colossal arrogance and autodeification that so permeates business culture. "I Am Superman," shouts IBM. Make way for *Business 2.0,* as the title of one hopeful new management magazine described our age. All of history is merely prelude to us, now, the makers and movers of this most glorious changealicious moment ever.

Moving with the Cheese

As I am writing this section, the great new metaphor and universal solution that is catching on among au courant managers, being cited and discussed everywhere, is "cannibalism." Or to be precise, auto-cannibalism. As the cover of the August 1999 issue of *Fortune* advises us, "Cannibalize Yourself." One can guess why this metaphor has the appeal it does—it rings of primitive, close-to-the-earth authenticity; it breaks rules and taboos; it sounds scary and ferocious—but the particular corporate practice it designates seems neither commendable nor sane. What it seems to mean is this: As the corporation can no longer be permitted to shield us from the "violent winds of the marketplace," companies must set their different departments, divisions, and branches to struggling with one another just as fiercely and as rabidly as if they were real-world competitors. We must "cannibalize ourselves" because *this is what the market demands we do.*

Auto-cannibalism is hardly the looniest idea out there. Tom Peters (naturally) has come up with an even more frightening aphorism. "**DE-STRUCTION IS COOL!**" he announces in the opening pages of *The Circle of Innovation*. He suggests that corporations create the position of "Chief Destruction Officer" and tells readers to learn this line: "DE-STRUCTION IS JOB NO. 1." A little later he informs his long-suffering students of his new "B-I-G IDEA":

> "It's easier to kill an organization than to change it. big idea: DEATH!"[36]

Peters has spent twenty years taversing the giant arc from excellence to celebrating "craziness." Anita Roddick, a favorite of his, once proclaimed that "there is a fine line between the delinquent mind of an entrepreneur and that of a crazy person." Maybe, at long last, we should start to take Peters and Roddick at their word. Maybe what the "business revolution" has enthroned is not democracy but madness. Examine *The Circle of Innovation* closely, its eighty-four-point typefaces, its continual use of the hectoring all-caps style, its compulsive parentheticals, its bombastic exhortations ("Say [SHOUT] YES to BRAND!"), its incomprehensible diagrams—and its insistence that its lessons apply not just to one business or two, but to all businesses, to the entire world. As a description of the tormented inner life of the white-collar class, it has a certain merit. But as a prescription for the common good it borders on the obscene.

Why would anyone choose to live in such a world? Why would we abandon the controls over corporate doings we have constructed over decades, surrender the limited power we have to compel companies to behave in accordance with the standards of humanity, give up the security of collective bargaining—such as it was—when this panorama of madness and destruction and waste is what business offers us in return? We do it because we believe Tom Peters is right when he says, *"You have no choice."* There can be no democracy on these questions.

But of course there can, and we do. Regardless of what they say in the MCI commercials, the way of the soulful, downsized corporation is not mandated from on high. We can always replace their insane talk of "liberation management" with the real instruments of industrial democracy. Unfortunately, the "business revolution" is determined to prevent us from doing so. For those who dare to organize in the workplace the gurus have nothing but the loftiest sort of contempt. Regardless of how they go about attributing some fine spirituality to the new-style corporation or how they applaud the sensitive, "listening" CEOs at their helm, the management theorists of the nineties regard unions and collective bargaining as fundamentally illegitimate, worthy of neither consideration nor respect. The authors of *The One to One Future* may celebrate "collaborative" communication, but they draw the line at union officials, who just don't seem to realize that "progress is inevitable." Even the sensitive Peter Senge only mentions labor unions as opponents of quality circles, people who "fear that the new openness will break down traditional adversarial relations between workers and management. . . ."[37]

Talk to many of those blue-collar workers and you will discover that they are quite right to fear the "new openness." Great displays of soulfulness by top management, they find, often go hand in hand with a species of shop-floor Taylorism so advanced and concentrated as to be almost inhuman. Management talks of the liberating power of "craziness"; workers get a life so regimented and rationalized that I have even heard rumors, from blue-collar workers whose sensitive managers put them on twelve-hour rotating shifts, of deliberate corporate plans to wear them out, shave a year or two off their lives, and thus save millions in pension outlays. In their experience, talk of empowerment, participation, and reengineering is followed automatically by an intensification of management demands. A more accurate rendition of the relationship between the fine democratic phrases of the "business revolution" and the fates of actual workers can be found in a 1996 *New York Times* article on the age of information at one Ohio company: After detailing events of the last ten years in which countless unionized, Rust Belt workers lost their jobs to nonunion workers in the South who are paid a little more than half as much, the newspaper printed without comment the CEO's astonishing explanation. Those people had to go because the company was becoming more open and was "empowering" its workers! " 'Unionism is going down because corporations have changed their views,' he said. 'We empower our people now. They work in teams with shared responsibilities. It's not management versus the workers in the plants now. We're all one for our shareholders.' "[38]

Unionists and hardhats may have been useful in the early backlash days, when it seemed like the longhairs might threaten the very basis of American capitalism. But the tables were turned now: In the "business revolution" it was the lifestylers and the altrockers and the soul-searchers who knew the ways of God and the Market, and it was the poor, deluded hardhats who desperately needed to be suppressed, to be convinced of their historical irrelevance.

Not that you will ever read about any of this in the madness-celebrating literature of management theory. To get an accurate understanding of what's happening on the shop floors of America you must turn to a different sort of business literature, a kind of writing that is heartfelt even without the Sufi wisdom, the meditations on the yin and yang, or talk of the corporate soul. I have in mind a three-hundred-page 1994 volume by labor writers Mike Parker and Jane Slaughter called *Working Smart,* a discussion of the effects that empowerment, reengineering, and corporate democracy programs have on the lives of workers, both blue- and white-collar. Unlike *Redefining Corporate Soul,* with its creamy, high-grade stock and delicately metaphorical dust jacket illustration, *Working Smart* is printed on standard-issue Xerox paper and features only its title on the cover. Unlike the works of Tom Peters, with their page-burning typefaces and creative use of blank space, *Working Smart* is laid out with an eye to saving money, its text crammed desperately onto the pages and its diagrams simply photocopied from other sources. It features no musings about the wisdom of children; it has inspired no commercials for IBM, MCI, Merrill Lynch, or Microsoft. You can't even buy it on Amazon.com. This is the cultural exile to which the literature of labor has been sentenced.

It is a sobering, infuriating read. In practice, as it points out, post-Taylorism generally means *intensified* Taylorism; workplace democracy means getting workers to make efficiency suggestions—efficiency suggestions that invariably lead to layoffs or speedup. Here, in this age of corporate liberation, is what daily life is like, according to the company manual, for UPS delivery workers:

> . . . the pen is kept in the left shirt pocket (for right handers) and never left with the clipboard or placed in another pocket. . . .
> Turn ignition switch off and remove the key with one hand; engage the emergency brake with the other.
> Release the seat belt with one hand and obtain the clipboard as you rise from the seat.
> Walk with a brisk pace (a brisk pace commands attention).

Every new theory, new buzzword, new movement, new consultant seems here merely to offer another means to the same goal: fewer workers, more output. Or, depending on your perspective, more work, smaller payroll. What is an intellectual playground for an entire class of consultants and gurus is, for the vast majority of working Americans, a living hell of surveillance and degradation in which every emotion is faked and every response anticipated.[39]

Perhaps it is best, then, that the book by which the management theory of the nineties be remembered is the asinine and chronic bestseller, *Who Moved My Cheese?* While the book's repetitive, infantile story, its Dick-and-Jane-sized typeface, and its home-computer-generated graphics initially cause the reader to suspect that he has mistakenly picked up a book written by a child and vanity-published by doting parents, it quickly becomes apparent that the oversized typeface and pointless, page-hogging illustrations are merely a device to push the thing to a barely respectable ninety-four pages. And yet within these slim covers—and even slimmer intellectual parameters—the author, serial management writer Spencer Johnson, is able to pull off a work of breathtaking obscenity, to both call for childlike innocence before the gods of the market and openly advance a scheme for gulling, silencing, and firing workers who are critical of management—and also to incorporate *into the book's very plot* a thinly disguised pitch for a whole array of *Who Moved My Cheese?* spin-offs and sequels. The mysterious-sounding title metaphor turns out to refer to four allegorical workers (not wanting readers to miss any of his genius nuance, Johnson eventually just informs us that the characters are symbols for different worker personality types), two of them "littlepeople" and two of them mice, who spend their days racing through a maze in search of cheese. As the cheese materializes in the same place every day, they become complacent. Then the cheese disappears. They never do find out "who" moved it or why, as this is simply a part of the unknowable beyond (this is "change"); the important question is, how do the characters react to their cheese being moved? Naturally, the blue-collar workers, i.e., the mice, are accustomed to looking for new work; they "did not overanalyze things," they react well to "the inevitable," and they promptly take off in search of "new cheese." The two "littlepeople," however, "ranted and raved at the injustice of it all," believing that they were "entitled" to their cheese. This is supposed to be transparently foolish; in fact, even to wonder about the logic of the cheese's movements or to ask the title question *Who Moved My Cheese?* is to commit workplace error of such magnitude that management can rightly "let" workers who are given to such thoughts "go." So while one of the "littlepeople" remains stubbornly at the place where he last sighted the cheese, the other sets off through the maze again, running the rat race, but finding along the way that job insecurity is good for his soul and composing a number of pithy observations about adapting to "change" that he writes on the walls of the maze—much like the pithy management sayings that adorned so many office walls in the 1990s.[40]

Alone among management texts, *Who Moved My Cheese?* goes one step further, proceeding to boast of its own powers as a tool of labor pacification. After the mice/maze allegory is concluded, Johnson switches over to a conversation among full-sized white-collar characters who marvel at the usefulness of his parable and eagerly apply it to their own lives. They realize, in the uninflected enthusiasm that we remember from the elementary school filmstrips of the 1950s, that they must drop their "arrogance" and learn to do as the unthinking blue-collar mice, who "kept life simple" and didn't question "change." One of the humans, though, is a manager of some kind, and he has a different use for the story: It seems that he and his colleagues were "changing" their organization, and some workers were "resisting." So he applied "the Cheese Story" to his workforce and found that its allegorical powers worked wonders! Those who had been fired learned to relish their new situation ("there was New Cheese out there just waiting to be found!") and those who were permitted to stay stopped "complaining" and bowed to management's new scheme. The book ends, appropriately, with an order form giving details on making bulk purchases.[41] Thus did social class, the supposed enemy of market populism, make its triumphant return. While most of us must "adapt to change," others get to make change; while most of us are expected to smilingly internalize management theory, to learn our place in the world from vapid fairy tales, others buy the insulting stuff in bulk in order to cram it down the throats of thousands who have the misfortune to toil in the bigperson's insurance agency or box factory.

Will the time ever come, Americans might well ask, when *we* get to move *management's* cheese? When the people, "little" though they might be, acquaint society's erstwhile cheesemasters with this "inevitable" fact: That there is no social theory on earth short of the divine right of kings that can justify a five-hundred-fold gap between management and labor; that can explain away the concentration of a decade of gain in the bank accounts of a tiny minority. "Change," like the American corporation itself, is the product of argument and social conflict. We have as much a role in it as the "change agents" on high, whether they ask our opinion or "listen" or not. But it is to forestall and sidetrack that version of "change" that management theory exists: The corporation, it teaches us, is capable of resolving all social conflict fairly and justly within its walls.

And yet what the "New Economy" desperately requires in order to restore a sense of justice and fairness is not some final triumph of the corporation over the body and soul of humanity, but some sort of power that confronts business, that refuses to "move with the cheese." Because it's not going to matter much to the people on the receiving end of the "business revolution" whether the guy who downsizes them is wearing a blue serge suit or a nose ring.

The Brand
and the
Intellectuals

*Advertising is a means of contributing meaning and values
that are necessary and useful to people in structuring their
lives, their social relationships and their rituals.*

—*from a British pamphlet introducing account planning*

So much depends upon . . .

What is this thing called brand? Wherever one wandered in the gleaming mansions of the "New Economy" one heard about its awesome powers. It was the brand that lifted the stock valuations of the people's bull market, quietly filling the pockets of the faithful. It was the brand that stood like a rock while all other aspects of industry were tossed to the winds of "change." Companies could reengineer themselves; entire industries could delayer down to the essential core; whole workforces could be cut loose, chopped down into "units of one," but the brand remained solid and unyielding despite it all. The brand was hailed as the model for personal life; as the model for urban rebuilding; as the model for national identity. According to some the brand was even the single greatest factor in geopolitics. Now that the market had seen fit to move manufacturing to those lands whose populations could be made to work for next to nothing, what distinguished the United States from what used to be called the "developing world" were its brands. We had brands. Other people didn't.

They made for quite an impressive edifice, these theories of the brand, a great monument of "New Economy" thought that had only one flaw. Americans hated brands. Or, to be more precise, they hated the advertising through which brands were built. While the rest of the business world talked of brands as a sort of economic Old Faithful, coming through on schedule regardless of circumstances, the leaders of the advertising industry spoke of crisis, of failure, of collapse. The public no longer believed. America was, as the principals of the Kirshenbaum and Bond agency put it, "in the midst of an epidemic of cynicism." The people had learned to distrust advertising, to change channels, to scoff and guffaw, to look beyond the surface. The brand-building industry couldn't even maintain a solid front itself. Marketing theorists like Peppers and Rogers of *The One to One Future* turned savagely on Madison Avenue, charging their colleagues with imagining "customers and marketers as adversaries," with using "the language of war" to plan their haughty assaults on the public mind. Meanwhile the public, the old reliable mass market, was coming apart at the seams, splintering into thousands of tiny, reclusive groups. On top of that, by century's end the average American was exposed to an estimated one million commercial appeals per year. Only the most extraordinary sort of ad could cut through this "clutter" to deliver its brand payload, and its success would merely escalate the brand-building arms race. Advertising had wandered into an overproduction crisis all its own, churning out so much cleverness and sloganeering that it was in danger of choking the world with branding, precipitating the "cataclysmic shakeout" predicted by Internet marketer Seth Godin in 1999.[1]

But just as the democratized, soulful corporation had arisen to resolve the problems of the hierarchical, elitist corporation, so a new breed of marketing thinkers proposed a new conception of the brand. To think of the brand as a static thing, as a rock of Gibraltar or one of the great books, was to miss its dynamic nature. The brand, according to the new cognoscenti, was a *relationship*, a thing of nuance and complexity, of irony and evasion. It was not some top-down affair, some message to be banged into consumers' heads. The brand was a conversation, an ongoing dialogue between companies and the people. The brand was a democratic thing, an edifice that the people had helped build themselves simply by participating in the market. The brand, in short, was us.

Naturally the construction of this new, more democratic brand universe required an entire new army of advertising people, men and women of learning and subtlety who could adjust the brand's every nuance to accommodate our views, our side of the discussion. In July 1998, I traveled to Boston to spend a few days in the company of these people upon whom so much depended. They call themselves "account planners," and while their field was then a relatively new addition to the organizational flowcharts of Madison Avenue, account planning had already captured the imagination of "New Economy" enthusiasts everywhere. Its orderly sounding name notwithstanding, Planning was insurrectionary stuff. Not only was it identified with the most creative and innovative of advertising agencies—the sorts of places where future-envisioning change agents were always making heroic revolution on the old rules—but Planning promised to restore legitimacy to the brand. Its every advance hastened the achievement of full consumer democracy, that free-market utopia where each empowered customer would make his or her voice heard in the great public agoras of shopping mall or Internet, participating in a system of choice vastly more complex, more lively, and more interactive than the sterile two-party plebiscites of our industrial past.

People's War on Bummer Brands

One of the first things I learned after arriving at the Westin Hotel in Copley Place, just across the street from the Boston Public Library, was that one does not come to a gathering of account planners dressed in a gray flannel suit. I had hoped to make myself inconspicuous by wearing the stereotypical adman's costume of the American 1950s; I accomplished exactly the opposite. Not only were a majority of the Planners female and a good number of them British, but I appeared to be the lone square in an auditorium full of high-budget hipsters. The women were in tight white synthetic T-shirts stretched over black brassieres, in those curious oblong spectacles that were the style then, in hair that was bleached, bobbed, and barretted after the Riot Grrl fashion. The men, for their part, wore four- and five-button leisure suits, corporate goatees and had pierced noses. One group of Planners periodically donned bright red fezzes while another set wandered around the proceedings in camouflage. During breaks between speakers, the house stereo played an inoffensive techno soundtrack. The sight of so much visible extremeness did what it was no doubt intended to do: It threw me into instant and compound self-doubt.

Another thing I learned right away was that 1998's Account Planning Conference was nowhere near as "radical" as 1997's. There were fully 750 people at the gathering, a number that seemed to startle everyone. The previous year's conference drew around 500 planners; a year before that it was an intimate affair of only 300. In 1998, Planning still had about it the air of a youth subculture that was on the cusp of going mainstream: It began in Britain in the corporate-revolutionary days of the 1960s and until quite recently was followed by only a handful of American initiates. But in the late nineties, as talk of corporate revolution once again blazed through the nation's office blocks, even the less tuned-in agencies were setting up planning departments, a fact that seemed vaguely to annoy several younger Planners I spoke to. One of these actually warned me against "fake planners," agency opportunists who claimed membership in a movement that was obviously in its ascendancy, but who in reality knew no more about the mystery and mission of Planning than they did about Altaic verb conjugation. No one actually came right out and complained that Planning's newfound popularity in the American hinterland meant that it has lost its edge or sold out to The Man, but the feeling was definitely there.

What permitted Planning to infiltrate the world of American business with so little notice, I suspect, was its name. The term "account planning" seems to have been designed to disguise the profession as just another unremarkable component of the old Taylorist order, just the usual paper-shuffling corporate mandarins who pass their days parsing pie charts or securing some raw material or other. But nothing could be further from the truth. While we had an extensive corps of management theorists and op/ed writers to tell us how perfectly the market reflected our desires, the Planners were the foot soldiers responsible for actually doing the job, for seeing to it that business knew our needs and desires. This was where the market populist rubber hit the road.

Back in the Taylorist days, maybe, it was possible to say that a brand meant, simply and unproblematically, what its makers said it meant. But in this age of public skepticism and heightened sensitivity to every subtle shading of the advertising form, it is hardly enough simply to dream up a pleasant-sounding jingle and a sleek-looking logo back at corporate headquarters. A brand's meaning is as complex and as contested and as socially constructed as, say, gender, and it was the job of account planners to monitor and study the brand's relationship with us in its every detail. As corporate figures of every kind were learning to understand markets as the ultimate democratic form, as an almost perfectly transparent medium connecting the people with their corporations, Planners functioned, or believed they functioned, as interpreters of and advocates for the popular will. Planning thus turned out to be virtually the opposite of what its name implies: Planners were the vanguard of economic democracy, at least as it's understood today, the lively and irrepressible voice of the people against the cold pronouncements of corporate rationality. I heard again and again over the course of the weekend how advertising people must change their ways to acknowledge the democracy of markets, how they must learn humility and abandon their arrogant, top-down ideas of the brand, how they must "talk to consumers," initiate an "agenda-free discussion," and "let consumers direct your plan." And to assist them as they went in search of the common man, Planners used any number of audience research techniques. Over the course of the weekend I heard about getting at the "essence of the brand" with the help of tools like "beeper studies," "fixed camera analysis," "shadowing," "visual stories," brainstorming sessions with celebrities, and, of course, focus groups, which some Planners seemed to invest with an almost holy significance.

Even more than it resembled a youth subculture, Planning seemed like postmodern cultural radicalism come home to Madison Avenue complete with all its usual militancy against master narratives and hierarchical authority, its cheering for the marginalized, its breathless reverence for the cultural wisdom of everyday people, and its claim to hear the revolutionary voice of the subaltern behind virtually any bit of mass-cultural detritus. Only one thing was wrong: These enthusiastic, self-proclaimed vicars of the vox populi were also, almost to a man, paid agents of the Fortune 500.

It was appropriate that the Planners were addressed on the first day of their conference by Geraldine Laybourne, introduced as someone "known for creating incredibly profitable media brands by always putting the consumer first," but more familiar as the former head of Nickelodeon. A woman who confessed to having "epiphanies" during focus group sessions and who referred to target demographics as "constituents" for whom she aimed to "make life better," Laybourne seemed to embody market populism's combination of concentrated corporate power with an effusive, philosophical love for the little people. She described for us the bleak world of TV programming before the dawn of Laybourne, back in the top-down days when one of her former employers "believed you should shout down a pipe" to reach your audience. The Planners murmured scornfully at this tale of corporate arrogance: They knew that the key was listening, respect, dialogue, interactivity—and they also knew what was coming next. The audience would have to talk back. Laybourne described the focus group where the breakthrough happened:

> [W]e asked kids a very innocuous question: "What do you like about being kids?" And in four different rooms, with these kids who were

ten years old, we got a barrage of stuff back. "We're afraid of teenage suicide, we've heard about teenage drunk driving, we've heard about teenage pregnancy, we're terrified of growing up, our parents have us programmed, we're being hurried, we don't have a childhood."

Laybourne, no doubt, sensed a breakthrough every bit as momentous and people-empowering as the Hawthorne experiments, when the elitism of scientific management yielded to the lovable logic of human relations.

So I stopped the research and I said, "Just go in and ask them what Nickelodeon can do for them." And in all four groups: "Just give us back our childhood." . . . And that became our battle cry. That became our platform.

Now, with childhood back in the hands of its rightful owners, with access to *Rugrats* and the eternal return of *Bewitched* assured in perpetuity, the demographic battle lines had been drawn and fortified. The people's brand squared off against the top-down brands. "We were clearly on the side of kids," Laybourne continued, "clearly their advocate, and we were never going to turn our backs on them."

But the work of empowerment-through-listening went on. There were other demographics to liberate, and Laybourne told the Planners how she and her new organization, Oxygen Media, were preparing to launch a new entertainment brand for women, a group that sounded just as lovable in Laybourne's telling, as misunderstood, as monolithic, and as desperate for accurate media representation as kids. While the exact nature of the programming and even of the medium to which Laybourne's new brand was to be affixed was still a mystery at that time, she did show a clear affection for the Internet, which she described as a living embodiment of her notion of democracy through marketing. She also took great pains to assert that this vision of the Internet as democracy incarnate—despite having already become a cliché from incessant repetition in all media—was utterly beyond the constricted comprehension of the pipe-shouting authoritarians "who are running the big entertainment companies." Growing audibly indignant, Laybourne switched into protest mode, railing against the arrogance of those who "think that they can put a structure on this thing."

> But the Internet is an organism, and they are trying to put mechanisms on top of an organism. *It won't work.* It's too powerful. Once people taste freedom—this is the United States of America, we've got that in our blood. This is a revolution that will be led by kids, primarily, and I hope women as well.

But while the kids got ready to turn the world on its ear, others were surely going to find the new regime distasteful. No revolution is complete without reactionaries, real or imagined, and so Laybourne let us know where she and her new brand drew the line, stopped listening, and started excluding—namely at Southern Baptism, which had recently made the subjection of women an official element of its credo. "I don't think that our brand is going to appeal to those Southern Baptist men," she remarked tartly. The ad execs erupted in laughter and applause.[2]

Readers familiar with the logic of mass marketing might find Laybourne's hostility to Southern Baptists a little odd. Baptists are the largest Protestant denomination in the country; shouldn't their sheer numbers (as well as their streak of consumer militance) cause a sales-minded executive to pause before writing them off altogether? But in dissing the churchgoing squares, Laybourne was in fact following a well-established brand-building strategy, one thoroughly explained a few years before by French advertising executive Jean-Marie Dru in a book called *Disruption.* Asserting that mankind had entered a new era in which the value of brands mattered far more than any material factors, Dru argued that successful brands would have to invent some high-profile scheme for identifying themselves with liberation; they would have to identify and attack some social "convention" (one of those "ready-made ideas that maintain the status quo"); and would have to align themselves with some larger "vision" of human freedom. From a longer perspective what Dru was proposing was the colonization by business of the notion of social justice itself. For a brand's vision to succeed, Dru wrote, it must be "audacious," it must be "made of dreams," a quality he illustrated with quotes from various figures of the historical left. So just as the left's terminal retreat in the nineties paved the way for the pseudo-progressive fantasies of the "business revolution," so it also left in its wake a whole array of glamorous and unconventional cultural niches ripe for corporate occupation. The brands that would prevail, Dru seemed to believe, would be those that identified themselves with some former aspect of radical politics.[3] In the nineties we would have brands for social justice rather than movements.

Dru did not invent this strategy: He merely described what was going on in advertising as the decade unfolded. Benetton was working to equate its brand with the fight against racism, Macintosh with that against technocracy; similarly, Pepsi owned youth rebellion, while Nike staked a claim to "revolution" generally. Even as unthreatening a brand as the humble Duncan Yo-Yo could be moved to smash "convention," running a commercial in 1999 in which young people in various postures of rebellion flipped off the camera while a voice-over sneered, "Give us the finger; we'll give you the power." The Christian Right was, of course, outraged.[4]

But in the revolution against convention, hierarchy, and arrogance that embroils the republic of business, Dru and Laybourne were but moderate and slow-moving Girondins compared to the Jacobins of the British St. Luke's agency, which dispatched Planner Phil Teer to the conference to inspire his American comrades with tales of upheaval and progress at "the agency of the future."[5] While white-collar workers in América, a land unfamiliar with degrees and shades of leftist politics, tend to imagine the "business revolution" as an analogue of the demands for better representation found in the Declaration of Independence, corporate thinkers elsewhere have a much broader palette of social upheaval to choose from. And St. Luke's was said to be nothing less than a syndicalist advertising agency, its ownership shared uniformly by each employee and its chairman paid only as much as its lowliest copywriter. Significantly, Teer came to advertising only after working as a critic of the tobacco industry, and this actual leftist experience bestowed upon him a credibility that not even Laybourne's focus group epiphanies could match. His irreverent, self-effacing way of talking won the instant enthusiasm of the audience. He showed slides containing the word "fuckin'." He spoke in a thick Scottish accent, which, he acknowledged, made him difficult for Americans to understand but which also demonstrated the progress of the revolution: "It used to be, a year ago, we always sent nice, middle-class Oxford-educated, public school boys to talk at conferences for St. Luke's." Surely this was the real thing at last.

Teer did not disappoint. He spent an hour fervently extolling the artistic idealism that burned at his agency and tersely proclaiming the slogans of the business revolution. "If we stop exploring, we'll die," he told the Planners. "Work is leisure," read one of his slides. "Transform people," insisted another, flashing on the screen while Teer recounted the liberation of the admen, the story of the security guard who now "dances to jazz funk as he does his rounds," the former suit-wearing executive who had become "a shaven-headed DJ." Not only had St. Luke's freed its employees to participate in the subculture of their choice, it had also invented such boons to productivity as "hot desking," a system in which people worked wherever they wanted in the company's unstructured, loft-like office. "Abolish private space, and you abolish ego," Teer proclaimed. "[Collective] ownership abolishes demarcation and hierarchy." Even agency performance reviews had been revolutionized (the chairman was reviewed by a receptionist) along the lines of the criticism/self-criticism sessions once fashionable on the Maoist left. But this was advertising, and the people of St. Luke's were less interested in smashing the state than in "killing cynicism," that pernicious anti-brand feeling.

Finally, Teer paraded before the Planners the results of all this defying of boundaries, upending of hierarchy, abolishing of order, and democratization of ownership: A set of TV pitches for the biscuits of Fox and the furniture of Ikea. Not surprisingly, the ads produced by syndicalist admen turned out to imagine the brands in question as the contested terrain of social conflict. For furniture maker Ikea, St. Luke's dreamed up a cultural revolution in which the women of England rose up against chintz, a symbol of the old order as loathsome as cold desks or middle-class public-school boys. "Chuck out that chintz, come on, do it today," ran the jingle, sung to acoustic guitar accompaniment. The Planners boisterously endorsed the call for People's War on chintz with waves of enthusiastic cheering.

I do not want to imply that the Account Planning Conference was a hotbed of social discontent, a meeting of some new, energetic, well-funded, and spectacularly well-connected Socialist International. As it happened, in the same year I went to the Planning gathering I also attended several conferences of the actual political left, and the differences are worth remarking. The word "revolution," for one thing, came up at these affairs about as often as did talk about "hot desking." Usually they were held in university classrooms or decrepit hotels. There was less blithe enthusiasm and more hissing, booing, interruption, and accusation. Attendees were generally older, squarer, poorer, and less white than the Planners. Sometimes they fell asleep during plenary sessions. Interaction with officers or institutions of state or national government was extremely rare.

But after the Planners had talked enough chaos and upheaval for one day, they descended on gleaming polished escalators past the Palm steak restaurant, the fountain pen boutique, and the Westin's indoor waterfall, and were ferried by buses disguised as trolleys across town to the Massachusetts Statehouse, where they were welcomed by a platoon of faux soldiers dressed in Revolutionary War uniforms and ushered up to one of four or five open bars dispensing microbrews and Maker's Mark.

"*Anyone* can make an identical product," one adman told me as we relaxed in a gallery of patriotic artifacts from Boston's heroic period. "*Why* do we choose one over another?" I listened to assorted rumors about Red Spider, the mysterious Scottish planning consultancy whose representatives conducted an extremely exclusive all-day training session at the conference. I was told by one Planner that your company's check had to clear the bank before Red Spider would even leave the UK; by another that Red Spider never distributed anything written down; by a third that their instruction took a mystical master-to-acolyte approach; by a fourth that their instruction took a simple fiction-writing-seminar approach; and by a fifth that in fact Red Spider *would* distribute things that were written down, it's just that the guy who was supposed to bring the written materials got sick.

Most Planners were former graduate students from the social sciences, a woman from a Chicago-area agency told me. It's "Margaret Mead meets the Marlboro Man." A man from one of the more creative New York agencies informed me that Planners were outsiders in a Peyton Place industry, both ethnically and institutionally.

"That's the *mystique* of the Swiss Army Knife," came an earnest voice from a nearby table. "Now, when you put that on a sweat-shirt. . . ."

Ritual, Romance, and the Brand

The most telling fact about account planning was that its practitioners did not speak of it as a job or a workaday division of agency labor. The Planners I met referred to what they did—and almost universally, it seemed—as "the discipline." The academic pretensions that the word carries are intentional: Even casual talk at the conference was suffused with a language that, while not academic jargon per se, was meant to imply familiarity with academia, with other "disciplines," with realms of learning and expertise that lay far beyond the usual narrow purviews of Madison Avenue. While other branches of the "business revolution" reviled the pretensions of mainstream academia, in Planning the exact opposite attitude seemed to prevail. Wanting desperately to assure the world that they knew what they were doing—that this branding stuff was both too complex for the uninitiated and yet easily mastered by experts—Planners grasped for the legitimacy of conventional academia the way their brethren in other corporate departments hankered for MBAs and consumed volume after volume of management theory.

A number of senior Planners, I was told, held advanced degrees in various, very sophisticated fields. I heard rumors of mysterious advertising specialists called "trendologists." One Planner told me how "my insight on the meaning of [a brand] came from evolutionary psychology." Another compared the goings-on at his agency to the intellectual freedom and self-questioning that takes place at university. A third answered a question about Planners' constant talk about "chaos" by informing me, simply, that "it's big in many academic disciplines." Geraldine Laybourne told us that "this whole planning process" she undertook prior to launching Oxygen made her "feel like I've been in graduate school." And again and again I came across the word "ethnography," used sometimes to describe what was normally called "market research" and on other occasions as a handy, compact definition of the discipline itself.

The only bona fide PhD I came across at the conference, however, was Rick Robinson, a social psychologist whose speech introduced the Planners to E-Lab, the Chicago-based consultancy he headed. Robinson littered his talk promiscuously with juicy bits of academese. He repeatedly reminded the assembled admen of his postgraduate credentials, implied that he spoke both German and ancient Greek, read a quote from Clifford Geertz (in which Geertz himself quotes Max Weber), and asked us not to confuse a book he wrote with a similarly titled one by Aldous Huxley. He described a brainstorming session in which "way too many people with advanced degrees were sitting in a small room for too long," told us about "theories of narrative behavior" and prefaced one story by remarking, "if this is Perception 101, I apologize."

But there was no need to apologize. In some benighted Zenith or Gopher Prairie, perhaps, solid citizens still railed against the devils of "deconstruction" and cursed the "tenured radicals" who had distracted our youth from their ancient and rightful concerns with forward passes. In the world of the brand, however, the esoterica of cultural studies and anthropology were the name of the game. The St. Luke's agency, for example, doesn't merely make ads; it has also invented an entire theory of contemporary culture it calls "Sensorama" and for which the agency's website supplied a full-blown intellectual pedigree, citing Nietzsche, Merleau-Ponty, and various aspects of postmodernism.[6]

There is a distinct difference between the jargon-slinging of academia and that of advertising, though—and not solely in that one is a sincere effort to grapple with reality while the other is simply a convenient way to appear authoritative before clients. There is also a profound gulf in tone and intention between the two. As the St. Luke's website put it, "Sensorama" (their house theory) was different from postmodernism (the academic version) in that the admen rejected "cynicism, irony and apathy." Building and burnishing the brands that made our country great was an altogether different venture from trying to understand the social world. What Planners did was far more an exercise in imperialism than in learning.

This distinction became clearer and clearer as E-Lab's Rick Robinson continued with his talk. It was helpful to think of the brand as a myth, Robinson counseled, as a primal, transnational tale of hero and archetype. Unfortunately, though, most brands had no Homer to collect them into one volume: they were related to consumers haphazardly ("disparate" and "distributed" were the terms he actually used, meaning that a company's thirty-second commercials didn't always dovetail with, say, consumers' actual experience of the company's products), permitting all sorts of misinterpretation and errant readings. And so Planners, whose job it was to transform these bits and pieces into what Robinson called "a mythic whole, a narrative whole," must sometimes call in the heavy intellect to put things right.

Enter E-Lab, which, as its promotional literature put it, "specializes in providing a deep understanding of everyday experience through a variety of innovative, ethnographic methods." Robinson described some of them for us: questioning people about products while they're actually using them, mounting cameras in stores or homes so the ethnographers can observe exactly how we go about buying coffee or watching TV. As Robinson showed us slides from the latter operation, distorted and grainy like surveillance-camera views of bank robberies or convenience store holdups, his language of benign academic interest seemed to morph into a language of imperial control. A brand's myth is everyday experience for consumers, he noted, and "if you can understand experience, you can *own* it."[7]

This rather startling remark was the closest anyone at the conference came to the sort of sales-through-domination language that was once such a standard part of advertising industry discourse. It has now been fully forty years since Vance Packard used a bookful of such manipulative talk to send the industry into a public-relations tailspin from which it has never really recovered. In those days advertising executives were in the habit of comparing themselves to scientists: They were "engineers of consent," (as one famous title had it) masters of applied psychology who were as certain of which sales pitches worked and which didn't as the lab-coated Authorities who peopled their works. In the sixties, and partially in response to the tidal wave of doubt whipped up by Packard's accusations, admen changed their minds: Now they were artists, temperamental geniuses whose intolerance for order and hierarchy was shared by the insurgent consumers they imagined clamoring to purchase all those cars, cigarettes, and air conditioners. These days, though, with the media world grown as fragmented as the American demographic map, the sales fantasy du jour is anthropology.

It is important to distinguish this professional fiction of the Planners from more standard corporate anthropology, all those practical efforts to increase productivity by studying shop floor behavior or avoid "insensitivity" when building a new factory in some distant locale and convincing the locals to work in it for some nominal consideration. Those varieties of corporate anthropology require real anthropologists, formally trained scholars who, the literature on the subject warns, tend to bring all sorts of troublesome "values" to the job with them. What I saw at the Account Planning Conference, however, was pretty much just the opposite: Planning preserved the troublesome attitude while largely jettisoning the expertise. The adpeople I met were as much anthropologists as their forebears were scientists when they donned white lab coats or sat for the cameras before a bookcase full of Encyclopedia Britannicas. What Planning took from anthropology was attitude alone: The anthropologist's status as a "technician of the sacred" (in the phrase of Northwestern University's Micaela di Leonardo), a retailer of the authenticity that consumers so crave these days.[8]

The anthropological fantasy seemed tailor-made for market populism, and particularly for Madison Avenue's curious version of it. Whatever advertising did, whatever research it required, whatever markets it had to penetrate, it could now do so in the democratic language of sensitivity and empowerment. There were plenty of weighty ideological benefits as well: To understand the relations of production and consumption as "rituals" is—like understanding them as "cheese" that is "moved" by some deity's unseen hand—to remove them from the great sweep of history and enlightenment altogether, to put them beyond criticism. To understand demographic groups as tribes and admen as sympathetic observers is both to ennoble the relationship between the two and to encourage the plutocratic populism of which Geraldine Laybourne was so fine a specimen: marketers as advocates for the "constituency" at hand. The people in the office blocks are professionals; the rest of us are mere subjects. They will study us and feed us and take care of us as best they can; they will manage our portfolios and shower us with cheap electronics, but for us actually to criticize—or worse, interfere in—their work is unthinkable.

The discipline of account planning is periodically swept with buzzwords and weighty-sounding ideas. In 1997 it was "chaos," but the notion carried enough power and academic cachet to make it unavoidable in 1998 as well. In fact, "chaos" now seemed to boast two distinct schools of elaboration. Like the management theorists arguing about "change," adepts of a happy chaos foresaw opportunity everywhere while others theorized a pessimistic chaos in which extinction lurked around every corner. Either way, account planning was touted as a crucial navigating tool, a compass without which clients would either (depending on your interpretation) fail to profit from chaos or fail to avoid chaos's pitfalls.

Ted Nelson of the Mullen agency cleaved to the happy chaos camp. With a series of slides depicting fractals, the growth of musical genres, and a tangled landscape of strip mall signs, he impressed upon a small audience in a hotel conference room that "life is getting complicated." Clearly brands that were "based on consistency" were, like the master narratives invented by all those dead white males, in for some pretty rough debunkings; meanwhile, brands that dared to acknowledge and accept chaos could prosper. Nelson's guidelines for achieving this profitability sounded a lot like the humility before the rhythms of the market that were pushed by management thinkers and investment gurus: "Embrace other traditions," he said, "recognize that there are other disciplines." And "surrender control," smash egotism, don't think about "where do I want to go, but where will consumers give me permission to go." As Nelson got carried away with his subject, "chaos" began to sound less like an unavoidable state of affairs and more like an ultrademocratic utopia that Planners had to work desperately to bring about. Until the day that planning was practiced as he counseled, Nelson cautioned, "the existing paradigm will not be subverted."

Others understood "chaos" differently, as something closer to "evasion" or, simply, the "cynicism" that was denounced by so many of the conference's dominant paradigm subverters. For all their zealous consuming, Americans were also notoriously suspicious of advertising. Even though we had built an economic boom out of consumer debt, we had also killed Joe Camel and made best-sellers of books that purported to find secret messages encoded in the ice cubes in liquor ads. Confronting that resistance, that "cynicism," that towering doubt— confronting it, measuring it, and finding a way around it—was, ultimately, what Planners were charged with doing. The Brand needed to be brought home to the People, understood as a friend and a real-world ally rather than a shouting exploiter or a high-handed manipulator.

No brand had enjoyed more success at this operation over the years than Nike, with its ubiquitous swoosh and its creepy soft-totalitarian Nike Town shops in the big cities. At the same time, no brand had suffered as much for its accomplishments. In the wake of revelations about its labor practices and its unpleasant encounters with Michael Moore and *Doonesbury*, Nike had gone from signifying athletic excellence to symbolizing everything that was wrong with the "New Economy": multi-millionaire athletes, starvation wages in Indonesia, ubiquitous logos, creepy soft-totalitarian shops in the big cities. So it was inevitable, perhaps, that as the Account Planning Conference drew to a close, we were all brought together into one room to hear two dramatic accounts of Nike's recent travails and of the heroic work of the Planners to whom the company turned to rescue its fortunes.

One day, Nike decided to sell special shoes for skateboarders. But there was a problem. Not the obvious problem of whether or not skateboarders actually required special shoes, but the problem of skateboarders being "cynical" and thinking Nike wasn't cool. As Kelly Evans-Pfeifer of the Goodby, Silverstein agency told the story, the problem when Nike "decided to get into the skateboarding market last year" was that "skateboarders did not want them there." Skateboarding, it turned out, was "an alternative culture" populated with difficult people who "don't really like this attention they're getting from these mainstream companies. They're very wary and cynical about these companies attaching themselves to the sport or trying to get into it." The cultural task that faced the Planners was not to decide whether this hostility was deserved or warranted, but to liquidate it: "The objective for the advertising was not to reach a certain sales goal, but rather it had a more basic, grassroots task, which was that it needed to begin to start a relationship between Nike and skateboarders, and make skateboarders think that it wasn't such a bad thing that Nike was going to get involved."

Nike had originally wanted the agency to "start a relationship" by making commercials featuring superstar skaters doing tricks at skating arenas, but the Planners at Goodby saw through that in a second: the thing to aim for was authenticity, not celebrity-worship. And the way to achieve this was to study "real" skaters, who do their tricks on the outdoor walkways, planters, and banisters of corporate America. Having done their research, what the Planners found was that skaters believed they were the victims of a culture war all their own, that they were persecuted unjustly by intolerant cops and suburban city councils. The key to bringing skaters into the brand's fold, then, was to transform Nike from an enemy into a sympathizer, to take up the skaters' side of the battle, "to acknowledge and harness all those feelings of persecution." The ads that resulted asked, amusingly, what it would look like if other athletes were harassed and fined the way skaters so routinely are. They ran in skating magazines and during "The X-Games," and, according to Evans-Pfeifer, they effected a sea change in the way this particular subculture regarded Nike. In focus groups done to test the commercials, she told us, skaters "came in completely hostile to Nike: 'Nike's the Man, they don't know anything.'" But, post-viewing, it was found that their perceptions had changed: "They said, 'God, man, that's totally coming from a skater's view. That's awesome that that's going to be out there.'" This was a campaign with "grassroots objectives," she reminded us, and it garnered "grassroots results." As evidence of this popular cultural shift, she recalled a scene at the X-Games, when the power of the Nike commercials, shown on nearby Jumbotrons, was enough to bring the action to a standstill. The Nike 800 number, ordinarily a conduit for complaints, she said, began to receive a shower of congratulations: One skater asked for a copy of the commercials to show during his court date. Then Evans-Pfeifer displayed the cover of the May 1998 issue of *Big Brother,* a skateboarding magazine, and proudly related to us the campaign's crowning victory: In an issue denouncing "corporate infiltration" of the subculture, the publication singled Nike out for praise.

Another team of Planners from the same agency, Pamela Scott and Di-

ana Kapp, described how they took on an even heftier bit of cultural lifting for Nike. They began their presentation by reminding us that "Nike
has been stewing in a bit of negativity for the last couple of years," a "negativity" which, by 1997, tainted even the coveted minds of teenagers. "We
realized that there was a distance, and certainly a disconnect that [young
people] were experiencing with the brand," the Planners told us. Again
that dread cynicism was tearing people and their brands apart! And again
the ad execs turned to a reliable cultural tool to battle it. Forgetting for the
moment about "making shoes fly off the shelves or a soaring increase in
sales," the planners rolled up their sleeves and prepared to "address this
negativity by re-injecting authenticity and credibility back into the brand."
To make their advertisements effective, Scott and Kapp needed to find a
sport as distant as possible from Nike's traditional advertising approach,
discredited now with its excesses of money and celebrity. So, becoming
convinced along with just about every newspaper, magazine, and lemon-
lime soda pop in the land that women's basketball was the ne plus ultra
of sporting authenticity, a new world as yet unsullied by the market's
touch, they set about studying high school girls' basketball and packaging
it into an elaborate pitch for the Nike brand. The two ad women narrated
for us how they embarked on an ethnographic fact-finding tour through
the South, "inner-city Philly," and other regions where authenticity could
be mined cheaply and plentifully. Somewhere, though, their scientific de-
tachment became tourist-like giddiness and they related with the enthusiasm of a post-vacation slide show how they encountered all manner of
curious "rituals" among the girl-athletes they found and how they came
across "the most unselfconscious laughter you've ever heard"; they played
a recording of an exotic-sounding high-school cheer and showed us black-
and-white photos of serious-looking teenagers staring past the camera like
dust bowl farmers in a Dorothea Lange picture. And then they told us
how they went about putting that authenticity to work for Nike.

As high school league rules forbade the agency to use an actual high
school team in the ads, the agency invented a replica team to reenact
the love of sport that the Planners had witnessed on their tour. A group

of high-school-age girls was duly recruited and dispatched to basketball camp, where they were assigned to "build their own sisterhood,
that we could reflect, with great authenticity." The squad was dubbed
the Charlestown Cougars, and we watched the intentionally low-bud-
get-looking commercials that documented the Cougars' arduous, un-
sung way to fictitious state championhood. The commercials stretched
to push all of our authenticity buttons: The timeless black-and-white
imagery, the heroic slow-motion at crucial points, the unpolished
voice-overs, the women's voices humming church spirituals in the
background. Consumers found all this authenticity convincing, we
were told. We heard of website hits and plaintive messages from real-
life high school girls. But the campaign shouldn't be judged merely in
terms of Nike sales, the adwomen told us, for the ads were much more
than that. They were about "raising consciousness" as well. They
worked not merely commercially, but "to build role models for young
girls." The campaign "validated who they are in their sport." The audience of Planners erupted once more.

I confess: The way the word is used in marketing literature, I am an extremely "cynical" person. I doubt advertising. I scoff at brands. I do not
believe that Macintoshes make you "think different" or that Virginia
Slims help you "find your voice." And yet I was stopped cold by what I
can only call the cynicism of Nike's approach. As nearly everyone
knows by now, Nike is an outfit with a certain reputation for New
Economy–style exploitation. They learned long ago that it was more
profitable to move production of their shoes to the union-free and
largely invisible Third World, where they could enjoy maximum "flexibility" and, thanks to some of the most barbaric regimes on earth, pay
their workers wages so small that it is difficult for Americans to understand how they stay alive. Having done that, though, Nike then proceeded to do pseudo-anthropological studies of the very Americans
whose world has been shattered by the departure of operations like
theirs to the lands of the "open shop"—and to produce gritty commer-

cials celebrating the authenticity of our poverty, our alienation, our earnest search for redemption through sport.

None of which concerned the Planners at anything more than a personal level. Labor unions don't hire account planners. They don't run commercials during the Super Bowl or even the X-Games. Neither do the unorganized workers of the Third World. One of the basic premises of the "New Economy" is that a good amount of industry is now more mobile than workers: Manufacturers can close a factory here and open another one there at the drop of a hat; they can use the Internet to instantly "outsource" virtually any kind of record-keeping work to the poorest countries on earth. Just as important, though, is their command over the culture in which we are sentenced to live while we stay put in Chicago or Kansas City. We can't evade the authenticity-fantasies of Nike any more than we can move to Guatemala to follow our old jobs: They blare not only from the commercials during halftime but from the uniforms the athletes wear, from TVs in airports, from the sides of cereal boxes.

I do not mean to imply by any of this that Nike's campaigns are uniformly successful—the one targeting skateboarders, in fact, turned out to be a failure[9]—or that the brand-builders of account planning are the experts and the geniuses they claim to be. Clearly "charlatan" would be as appropriate a description here as it is in discussing management theory. But one can't help but marvel at the effort it would require to achieve a comparable level of visibility for the actual concerns, not just the authenticity, of working-class life.

When I was in graduate school in the early 1990s, it was a pedagogical given that the great shifting of scholarly attention that was then in its final stages—the turn from studying the masters of culture to examining the way culture was received and experienced, from the highbrow canon to everyday life—was a liberating development. Liberating not merely in the sense of scholarly opportunity, in that it was now permissible to study things (like advertising) that had formerly been considered unworthy: This stuff was *politically* liberating as well, a blueprint for the eventual undoing of all manner of cultural and social hierarchies. Certainly the new pedagogies had all the right enemies: undersecretaries from the Reagan or Bush administrations who saw the end of the world in the failure of new textbooks to pay sufficient homage to national heroes, newspaper columnists angered to derangement by the parade of sin at this year's MLA conference, Pat Buchanan, the Southern Baptists. As the culture wars got loudly underway, what was less frequently remarked were the sundry ways in which the newly populist rhetoric of certain disciplines shadowed the rhetoric of the culture industries, their techniques and assumptions coming to sound more and more like market research.

After one has sat through a spectacle like the Account Planning Conference, though, the confluence of the two becomes difficult to ignore. The admen I spoke to were about as deeply interested in the care and maintenance of "master narratives" as they were in collecting the five-foot shelf of Harvard Classics. In advertising, the branch of business that has warred the longest and most ferociously against obsolete values, the ritual smashing of old orders—and ritual mocking of old advertising styles—has become almost routine. Today's market-populist twist merely takes the long-standing trajectory one step further: Where ads were once openly manipulative, relying on the raw assertions of stern-sounding authority figures, many of them work today by hauling authority off to the gallows and invoking instead *you* in all your youness: your desire to be you, your longing for authentic non-advertised experience, your suspicions of authority, and, most of all, your heightened sophistication towards the big authoritarian sell.

If I can be excused for appropriating one of the planners' favorite buzzwords, I would like to propose a "convergence theory" of my own: That what emerged in the nineties beneath all the Sturm and Drang of the culture wars was a distinct consensus between business and its putative opponents, a consensus in which massive abuse of the language of popular consent masked a repugnant politics of enrichment for some and degradation for millions of others. It was a consensus in which even the most radical-sounding pedagogies seemed to feed ever more directly into the culture industry, in which it no longer surprised anyone when, as at my own alma mater, ad agencies like Ogilvy & Mather trawled for anthropology PhDs (they are interested, they specify, only in ones with "no ideological or moral objections to consumption/materialism"). Gingrich and Clinton were shaking hands; the Labour Party was abandoning its age-old disagreements with the Tories. Wherever one looked, it seemed, the opposition was ceasing to oppose.

New Consensus
for Old

Cultural Studies from Left to Right

George was touched by the Fair. He stood one night with
Charles Nolan, watching the crowds of the Midway, and
dreamed aloud: the people had done all this! It was "of the
people, by the people, for the people!" The lawyer argued:
"No, most of the money was subscribed by rich men. The people had nothing to do with designing the buildings." The economist pulled his beard and sighed. Anyhow, the people were
enjoying it. . . . Perhaps the Kingdom of God was a little nearer.
—*Henry George's visit to the 1894 Columbian*
Exposition, according to Thomas Beer (1926)

Closing Down the American Mind

In matters intellectual the populist impulse burned across the nineties
like a prairie fire. Having spent the seventies and eighties railing against
busing, "secular humanists," the Panama Canal giveaway, "permissive-
ness," tax-and-spend liberals, the "special interests," those insidious flag-
burners, and a shadowy "new class" that controlled the nation's media,
the leaders of the backlash now turned, for their final, most spectacular,
most inflammatory act, on the egghead. To be sure, the backlash had carried a nasty strain of anti-intellectualism since its birth in the aftermath
of the campus revolts of the sixties, but open war on academia as an institution only commenced with the spectacular success of Allan Bloom's

cranky 1987 best-seller, *The Closing of the American Mind,* and the media frenzy three years later over the hideous campus phenomenon known as "political correctness." While the humanities had once been a placid world in which quiet men in tweed gently pondered the great books, it had somehow become a hotbed of subversion where outrageous foreign theories were taken seriously, where the "great books" were the object of politically motivated disrespect, and where tyrannical, hyper-sensitive minorities erected preposterous speech codes to lord it over the children of middle America. The equation was almost too good to be believed: The most elitist and affected profession of them all—and what red-blooded American doesn't hate know-it-all teachers?—could now be linked not only to the left but to an unbelievably offensive left, a left that was almost totalitarian in its smugness. "Political correctness" was backlash gold. Get a load of their hilarious jargon, their far-fetched interpretations, their preening radicalism! In the "tenured radicals" of the humanities, the right saw a nineties version of the "limousine liberal" stereotype of the seventies, and columnists, politicians, think-tankers, and even the president stumbled over one another in the rush to compare "political correctness" to the attitudes of Nazis or Communists, to dredge up frightening tales of good, humble faculty humiliated by brainwashed students or assaulted by Marx-mad colleagues.

Looking back on the anti-academia furor of the early nineties, though, one is struck by how widely the PC critique missed the mark, by how poorly it described what was actually going on in the humanities, and above all by its doleful tone of national decline. This is not to say that campus speech codes weren't outrageous—they sometimes were. And it is not to deny that many professors in English departments considered themselves "radicals"; on the contrary, by the mid-nineties even the most mainstream scholars in certain departments gloried to speak of their own "radicalism." But then, so did arch-capitalist *Wired* magazine. So did Tom Peters. So did Warner Lambert, the maker of Bubblicious bubble gum, which introduced a flavor called "Radical Red." And who gave a damn about defending the "great books" or halting our national decline or warding off deconstruction's challenge to Western Civilization when the Dow was soaring towards 12,000, when the American way was triumphant over all the world, and when the capitalists themselves were fantasizing about the total jettisoning of the human past, about the irrelevance of national borders, about the dawning of a "New Economy" in which the science and wisdom of all the disciplines and all the centuries was as useless as medieval astrology?

Of course, getting it right was never the object of the "PC wars." Winning elections was. And, with those elections won, the right lost interest in deploring the professors and moved on to new fantasies, new populisms, borrowing freely now from the "radical" theories of the humanities as easily as they had Nazi-baited the "politically correct" a few seasons before.

The greatest trouble to confront the humanities in the nineties was not the blustering of the backlash right but the economic crisis facing the recent graduates of its PhD programs. So heedlessly did certain departments hand out doctorates in the eighties and nineties that before long a massive oversupply of qualified job-seekers was on the academic market. This generation of an enormous reserve pool of labor coincided with the adoption of modern management techniques by university administrations, which were learning to bust faculty unions and achieve greater "flexibility" by farming out more and more education work to underpaid graduate students and "adjunct" professors, the academy's version of the zero-benefits temp. As the resulting state of affairs palpably eased the workload of traditional tenured faculty, they had little interest in cutting back the number of PhDs granted or in forcing more humane labor policies on their employers.[1]

The results were catastrophic. Anyone who spent any time in academia in the last ten years has heard the horror stories, tales far more destructive in their consequences for higher learning in America than even the most grotesque culture-war anecdote about loose accusations of "lookism" or disprespect for "dead white males": Of new PhDs teaching entire courses for fifteen hundred dollars per semester, putting together four or five such jobs at different colleges in order to make a living wage, preparing materials and commuting frantically between lectures to deliver quality knowledge to students who couldn't give a damn. In 1995 an advertised tenure-track job in a history department was rumored to have attracted six hundred applications; in 2000, I heard of an advertised tenure-track job in an English department that had actually drawn a thousand desperate young PhDs. Writing in 1997, Cary Nelson, one of the few tenured scholars to address this subject with an appropriate level of outrage, offered up an infuriating montage of the various humiliations inflicted on job-seeking PhDs he knew during the nineties, and wrote that "with many college teachers looking more and more like migrant factory labor—lacking health benefits, job security, retirement funds, and any influence over either their employment conditions or the goals of the institutions they work for—the ideology of professionalism seems increasingly ludicrous."[2]

Nowhere on the American scene was the New Economy myth of the all-powerful "knowledge worker" more clearly and more demonstrably wrong. The young PhDs of the 1990s found themselves transformed by the workings of the free market not from hapless organization men into fully souled businesspeople, but from professionals into casual laborers, their bargaining power determined not by their knowledge or ability or any of the rest of it but strictly by the age-old laws of supply and demand. No quirky pets at work. No ecstatic reeling round the keg while theorizing the new order. No lofty ultimatums to employers about exactly how much in wages and options they would need to ensure their presence. Not even any health care. What was destroying academia wasn't deconstruction; it was the market.

And in doing so the market was not only proving itself to be disastrous as a principle of social organization, but also an unmitigated ingrate as well. For market populism owed a great deal to the scholarly innovations of the nineties, and particularly to those departments where the market was working its worst depredations.

The Importance of Being Studly

The prominent sociologist Herbert Gans had been writing about popular culture and its audiences for some twenty years when he published his 1974 book *Popular Culture and High Culture,* a 159-page summary of his thinking on the subject. The volume is now twenty-five years old, and it builds on arguments Gans had been making since the fifties, but if not for a number of bad calls and an obsolete jargon it could just as easily have been written yesterday, so reliably does it predict certain dominant scholarly concerns of the nineties. For Gans, as for so many academic writers about culture, the long-standing American debate over high culture and mass culture was really a broader clash between elitism and populism, between the snobbish tastes of the educated and the functional democracy of popular culture. Gans began the book by rejecting the idea "that popular culture is simply imposed on the audience from above," that a malign culture industry is able to tell us what to think. In fact, he argues, audiences have the power to demand and receive, through the medium of the market, the culture of their choosing from the entertainment industry, and—in what would become in the late eighties and nineties the trademark gesture of academic cultural studies—Gans hammers the critics of the entertainment industry as nabobs of "elitist" taste "unhappy with [recent] tendencies toward cultural democracy." Those who criticize the structure of the media machine are themselves the real elitists, obnoxiously assuming they know what is best for the world. The real issue of cultural debate is whether or not the critic believes in the intelligence of the audience, and for holding audiences in inexcusably low esteem Gans singles out mid-century critic Dwight Macdonald and Herbert Marcuse, late of the famous Frankfurt School of Marxist social theory.[3]

Up to this point Gans seems to have anticipated with uncanny accuracy the issues, the preconceptions, and even the particular villains of academic literary and cultural criticism of the nineties. But his streak of prescience ends abruptly when he predicts that the elitist mass culture critique he identifies with Macdonald and Marcuse would stage a triumphant return in the very near future. Gans comes to this odd prediction by connecting the mass culture critique, as a theory that celebrates the transcendent worth of a canonical education and good taste, with the interests of intellectuals generally: When their "status" is under attack or in decline, they revert naturally to the old elitism, dreaming up all sorts of highbrow bushwa about art and culture in order to reinforce the hierarchies that support their exalted social position. But when respect for intellectuals is on the rise, they can lighten up, make peace with middle America, and read USA Today along with the rest of us.

This is almost exactly the opposite of what happened in the nineties, when the humanities came under the fiercest attack in generations. True, certain aspects of academic professionalism seemed to grow more and more pronounced with each assault from the right: Think of the clotted, ciphered academic prose—a reliable source of amusement for journalists throughout the decade—that seemed to knot itself more egregiously still with each blustering culture-war tirade. What Gans got wrong was that the object of all this credential-flashing, sentence-mangling expertise was not the sanctity of high culture, but the opposite. The mass culture critique that Gans so abhorred did not reappear in the nineties; on the contrary, scholars joined journalists, politicians, and media moguls in pounding it relentlessly, in dispatching it off to that special oblivion reserved for intellectual anathema. In his influential 1988 book, Highbrow/Lowbrow, historian Lawrence Levine declared that the problem of aesthetic elitism—as represented by the consolidation of the high cultural canon in the nineteenth century—was in fact the central drama of American cultural history. By parading before readers a series of vignettes in which repulsive, upper-class Yankee snobs—each of them coupled carefully with their racist and otherwise offensive remarks—looked to high culture for a refuge from democracy, Levine sought to prove that hierarchies of taste were analogous to social hierarchy generally and to racism specifically. Naturally what the high culture patrons of the past set out to do was make audiences "less interactive," to transform them from "a public" into "a group of mute receptors." Historian Andrew Ross carried both the argument and the rhetorical strategy into the twentieth century in his 1989 volume No Respect, finding in virtually any iteration of highbrow taste a tacit expression of contempt for democracy.[4]

The signature scholarly gesture of the nineties was not some warmed-over aestheticism, but a populist celebration of the power and "agency" of audiences and fans, of their ability to evade the grasp of the makers of mass culture, and of their talent for transforming just about any bit of cultural detritus into an implement of rebellion. Although cultural populism appeared everywhere in academia, its best known and loudest proponents were the various celebrities of the rapidly growing discipline known as cultural studies—the "cult studs," to use the phrase of one starstruck reviewer. Like Gans, the cult studs tended to be unremittingly hostile to the elitism and hierarchy that older ways of understanding popular culture seemed to imply; they tended to see audience "agency" lurking in every consumer decision. They found seeds of rebellion and resistance emplanted in almost any of the culture-products once scoffed at as "lowbrow," and accordingly turned their attention from the narrow canon of "highbrow" texts to the vast prairies of popular culture. British academic Jim McGuigan has described this central article of the cult stud's faith as a formulaic "populist reflex," a moral calculus in which the thoughts, proposals, or texts in question are held up to this overarching standard of judgment: What does this imply about the power of the people? Accounts of popular culture in which audiences were tricked, manipulated, or otherwise made to act against their best interests are automatically " 'elitist,' " as the distinguished cult stud Lawrence Grossberg once put it (in a line echoed in almost every cultural studies essay or book I have ever read), because they assume that audiences are "necessarily silent, passive, political and cultural dopes."[5]

Generally speaking, cult studs did not frequently apply the term "elitist" to Hollywood executives or TV producers. This was a characteristic they attributed not to the culture industries but to *critics* of the culture industries, most notably the same gang of easy-to-hate Frankfurt School Marxists that so pissed off Herbert Gans. Cult studs tended to see in the work of Marcuse and fellow Frankfurter Theodor Adorno (who once, to his undying infamy, expressed a dislike for jazz) the very embodiment of the snobbery from which academia was only now recovering. In reaction to the uptight squareness of the Frankfurters, the cult stud community wastes no opportunity to marvel at the myriad sites of "resistance" found in TV talk shows, sci-fi fandom, rock videos, fashion magazines, shopping malls, comic books, and the like, describing the most innocent-looking forms of entertainment as hotly contested battlegrounds of social conflict. Their books teem with stories of aesthetic hierarchies rudely overturned; with subversive shoppers dauntlessly using up the mall's air conditioning; with heroic fans building their workers' paradise right there in the Star Trek corpus; with rebellious readers of women's fashion magazines symbolically smashing the state. As critic and cult stud Michael Bérubé summarized the discipline's focus in 1992, "It is always attempting . . . to discover and interpret the ways disparate disciplinary subjects *talk back*: how consumers deform and transform the products they use to construct their lives; how 'natives' rewrite and trouble the ethnographies of (and *to*) which they are subject. . . ."[6]

For the cult studs the national outrage over "political correctness" came as something of a godsend. Having argued that studying popular texts (movies, TV programs, comics) instead of the great books was a profoundly revolutionary operation—since it corroded all those snobbish aesthetic hierarchies that Levine had insisted were propping up a racist, plutocratic state—they now had definite confirmation that their doings were in fact deeply offensive to the power structure. The fact that the culture warriors of the right tended to pin the blame for PC on the demons of "deconstruction" rather than the cult studs themselves was a bit of a problem, but otherwise everything fit. Studying fashion magazines or communities of fans was the real revolutionary stuff, the first step in what would become an irresistible assault on the powers that be. The fury of the right was a stamp of authenticity, and cult studs enthusiastically signed up for the culture wars, identifying themselves as the real targets of the PC outrage and declaring their firm intention to go on subverting, to continue "fighting the power" by celebrating the counterhegemonic messages of TV sitcoms.[7]

For all their populism, though, the cult studs tended to be remarkably professional-minded. They were perhaps the least public group of intellectuals ever to come down the pike. This is something that goes far beyond an excessive use of difficult academic jargon. Cult studs were nominally interested in the films of King Vidor or Mexican comic books, maybe, but by far the most attractive subject (judging by the number of pages and books given over to it) in the cult-stud canon was cultural studies itself: where it came from, what its proper subject was, whether it even existed or not. Actual cultural interpretation invariably took a backseat in its texts to long-winded theoretical maneuverings. A good example is *We Gotta Get Out of This Place*, a 1992 book by Grossberg that is ostensibly about rock 'n' roll, but that begins by plodding through a remarkable 127 pages of theoretical hedging—paying homage to all the right texts; identifying and avoiding the errors of this school and that; situating itself with relationship to Foucault, Gramsci, Deleuze and Guattari, and, yes, Kant—before taking up "the political possibilities of rock." Other cult stud texts wondered endlessly about the nature of "disciplinarity" and the correct role of intellectuals in society, but seemed always to come to the same conclusion. Namely, that boundaries between disciplines were false and reactionary, and that, since cult studs often write on subjects not traditionally under the purview of the (English) departments by which they are employed, there was something really revolutionary about them. So urgently did cult studs believe that this point needed to be made there were actually several books dedicated to it, each of which made abundant use of the connected theme of cult stud as a figure persecuted for crossing disciplinary boundaries. One 1996 anthology, *Disciplinarity and Dissent,* began with a mournful evocation of those who fell victim to the scourge of disciplinarity in previous decades, moved on to tell the arduous history of cultural studies, recounted the expertise, "training," and "disciplinary exile" of each of the volume's contributors, and offered, in a curious move from persecution fantasy to oracular wisdom, this bit of credentialing advice: "For someone interested in sociology and cultural studies . . . it would not be helpful to study sociology at the University of Illinois at Urbana-Champaign or at the University of Wisconsin, but it might well be helpful to study it at the University of California at Santa Barbara."[8] This resolute institutional-mindedness set up a contradiction in cultural studies' populist terms so blatant that it made possible excruciating moments like the one recounted in 1995 by Richard Hoggart, one of the British founders of the field, in which a "distinguished scholar from England" who was giving a paper at a cultural studies conference in America found himself "interrupted by a group of women graduate students who mounted the platform and demanded access to the microphone."

> They objected, they said, to any more "so-called experts" being allowed to speak from the rostrum when they had not been invited to do so. They demanded equal rights on the ground that their opinions were, as a matter of principle and fact, as good as anyone else's; to have only "established specialists" giving papers was "unacceptable academic elitism."[9]

The core features of the cult-stud approach can be brought into high relief by contrasting the discipline's founding American text, the massive *Cultural Studies* anthology of 1992, and the slightly less gigantic *Mass Culture* anthology of 1957, a standard assigned text of an earlier era which also took on the then-novel subject of popular culture. While the older book was organized by the different industries it covered, and while it lumped together essays originally published in popular magazines along with contributions to the *American Journal of Sociology*, the 1992 book was an impressively precise record of just about everything uttered at an academic conference that took place one heroic week in 1990. The central theme of the later book was not so much "culture" as its "study"; not the liveliness of "the popular arts" but the shimmering genius of culture's interlocutors. The book's size and weight made the message of its contents hard to miss: This is the cornerstone of a grand new professional edifice, complete with a language, purview, and theory that are uniquely its own. These days the earlier, more popular book is faulted (when it's remembered at all) for being an elitist showplace, a museum of the mass culture critique (it even included an essay by Dwight Macdonald), but the later, infinitely more populist volume seems to have been constructed without any concern at all for the reading public. It was only revised, its editors note, so that the participants in the conference could clarify their statements, fortify their positions.

But while the cult studs enshrined their brand of populism as the pedagogy of choice in the early nineties, hounding the mass culture critique from the field and establishing their notions of agency and resistance as interpretative common sense, neither Gans nor anyone else from the sociological school with which he is identified was invited to the victory party. Gans's 1974 book may have been a direct antecedent of the bumper crop of cult-stud monographs and anthologies issued by Routledge throughout the decade, but you will search those books in vain for references to Gans and his colleagues. This is especially curious given the cult studs' compulsive reciting of influences and intellectual genealogy. Gans was not mentioned in either the vast bibliography or the index of *Cultural Studies;* he did not appear at all in Patrick Brantlinger's 1990 history of cultural studies, in Grossberg's 1992 account of the history of cultural studies, in Stanley Aronowitz's 1993 account of the history of cultural studies, in Simon During's 1993 anthology on the history of cultural studies, in John Fiske's 1993 book on cultural studies and history, in Angela McRobbie's 1994 account of the history of cultural studies, in Jeffrey Williams' 1995 anthology on the culture wars and cultural studies, or in Cary Nelson and Dilip Gaonkar's 1996 anthology on academia and the history of cultural studies.[10]

NYU historian Andrew Ross, almost alone among leading cult studs, was willing to admit that the conflict between elitist dupe-theories and audience-agency notions that so characterized the scholarship of the 1990s had in fact been going on in the United States since the fifties.

He further concedes that the populist promontory held by him and his colleagues was one they inherited from sociologists of that era like Gans and David Riesman.[11] But even those cult studs who acknowledged the non-novelty of the populist reflex offered militant defenses of their discipline's uniqueness. Not on the grounds of its methods or theories, which drew on a range of preexisting influences, but on the grounds of politics. After all, they were the ones that the right was persecuting, weren't they? Cult-stud potentate Simon During fired the first shot in Routledge's 1993 offensive by distinguishing cultural studies from all other forms of academic criticism on the basis that it was "an engaged discipline," a proudly committed leftist pedagogy. And one must admit that this commitment was a sincere one. But the cult studs' radical chest-thumping also tended to draw attention to their distance from politics as it was experienced outside the academy.

The nineties were, of course, a time of populism generally in American culture. Even as the remnants of the backlash right rallied for family values and traditional culture, the corporate right was developing a market populism that identified the will of the people with the deeds of the market, that agreed with the cult studs on the revolutionary power of popular culture and the wonders of subjects who *talked back,* that gloried in symbolic assaults on propriety, on brokers, on bankers, on old-style suit-wearers of all descriptions. The populism of the microchip, not the populism of Pat Buchanan, was the truly hegemonic ideology of the "New Economy." And it bore at least a superficial resemblance to the pedagogical populism of cultural studies. Cult studs reveled in recounting their persecution by backlash right-wingers driven to apoplectic fury by their sassy questioning of aesthetic hierarchies; but as the backlash dried up, as its leading figures abandoned the field, and as it was supplanted by market populism, it made more sense to ask whether or not the politics of the cult stud were in fact as revolutionary as they seemed.

We might begin by asking about the curious absence of Herbert Gans from the swinging, resistance-filled world of the cult stud. One suspects the answer to this puzzle lay first of all in his politics: Although Gans was a refreshing voice of common decency on the question of welfare "reform," one senses that rallying to the defense of the welfare state was far too pedestrian an intervention for the new breed of radical. Certainly Gans was not forgotten because his books were out of print: On the contrary, many of them (most notably *The Levittowners,* his famous 1967 defense of suburbia) were still well known to nineties encomiasts of middle America like Alan Wolfe and Joel Garreau. Perhaps it was this appeal to the voices of moderation, and Gans's consensus credentials generally, that explained his absence from the cult-stud stable. Gans came from an intellectual generation that (to simplify ruthlessly) tended, in the face of a terrifying Cold War enemy, to downplay social conflict in order to emphasize a vision of a healthy and well-functioning national whole. In books like Daniel Bell's *End of Ideology* and Richard Hofstadter's *Age of Reform,* the consensus scholars (no studs they) portrayed dissent as disease; in public places like *Partisan Review* they more or less abandoned their adolescent leftism and enlisted in the American Century.

The cult studs could imagine nothing more reprehensible. The very idea of consensus was intellectual poison in the nineties, attacked ferociously by management theorists like Tom Peters and denounced as quasi-fascist in épater-by-numbers fare like the movie *Pleasantville.* In the works of the cult studs the consensus era comes off as a time of scholarly practice so degraded it is scarcely worth remembering. Patrick Brantlinger, for example, recounted how the discipline of American Studies (a slightly older rival of cultural studies) was founded in the years after World War II as a deliberate venture in national mythmaking and rips it as "an academic cultural chauvinism" whose "ultimate goal," despicably, was "social harmony." Lawrence Levine runs over the same story again in his 1996 book on the culture wars, tarring American Studies, in his characteristic connect-the-dot style, as nothing less than premeditated intellectual collaboration with the Cold War state. Nelson and Gaonkar remember it as a "McCarthy-era pact [with "state power"] guaranteeing silence and irrelevance from the humanities and collaboration from the social sciences. . . ." By contrast, any proper cult stud is out to develop, as Henry Giroux once put it, "a radical politics of difference," to revel in cultural and identity fragmentation, to pose boldly on the ramparts of the culture wars, to provoke and savor the denunciations of half-witted fundamentalists.[12]

Given such a gloriously transgressive, decentering present, it seems simply inconceivable that the cult studs should have anything to do with Gans and his consensus crowd. No, they must have an intellectual lineage more in keeping with their status as the ne plus ultra in counterhegemony, and so when the occasion arises (as it does so very, very frequently) to track their pedigree, the cult studs nearly always find themselves to descend not from the plodding drayhorses of American sociology but from the purest-blooded of barricade-charging European stallions.[13]

Still, the ghost of consensus will not rest. We may hear of how the cult studs stand on the front lines of political confrontation; we may gape at the wounds inflicted by the reactionaries upon their noble corpus; but we cannot help noticing that the noise from the front sounds a lot like somebody shaking a big chunk of sheet metal just behind the curtain.

What Business Culture?

While there is no denying that a number of very vocal right-wingers are annoyed by the cult studs' assaults on hierarchy (and maybe even by their war on "disciplinarity")—and that in this sense the champions of the popular do indeed "fight the power" as they like to believe—it is also worth pointing out that they share with their foes the same imagined bête noir. In February 1999, Moral Majoritarian Paul Weyrich fixed the blame for the demise of "Judeo-Christian civilization" on the same gang of sneaking German reds so demonized by the cult studs (Weyrich singled out Herbert Marcuse in particular). But leaving aside the lunacy of the backlash right and comparing the populist reflex to thinking of the corporate right, one finds the cult studs' particular species of transgression transgresses a lot less than all their talk of "radical politics of difference" would imply.

To an undeniable degree, the official narratives of the American business community of the nineties—as we have found them expressed by account planners, by management theorists, and by bull market ideologues—embraced many of the same concerns as the cult studs. They shared the cult studs' oft-expressed desire to take on hierarchies, their tendency to find "elitism" lurking behind any critique of mass culture, and their pious esteem for audience agency. There, too, from the feverish corporate democracy of *Fast Company* to the homely faith of the Beardstown Ladies, a populist reflex dominated the landscape. There, too, all agreed that Americans inhabited an age of radical democratic transformation, of multiculturalism and righteous subalterns; that we could no longer tolerate top-down organizational hierarchies; that no error outranked the moral crime of elitism, the belief of regulators, critics, and European bureaucrats that they knew better than the market or the audience. There, too, the language and imagery of production was being effaced by that of consumption; class by classism; democracy by interactivity, with the right of audiences to "talk back" to the CEO (through stock-holding) or the brand manager (through the focus group) trumping all other imaginable rights and claims. It was a world where listening executives joined forces with "change agents" to see to it that we were all "empowered," where the old-fashioned leftist suspicion of mass culture was used endlessly as evidence of a distasteful leftist "elitism" generally.

Unfortunately, it's difficult to discover what the cult studs themselves think about the parallel world of market populism. For all its generalized hostility to business and frequent discussions of "late capital," cultural studies failed almost completely to produce close analyses of the daily life of business. Convinced that the really important moment of production was not in the factory or the TV studio but in living rooms and on dance floors as audiences made their own meanings from the text of the world around them, the cult studs generally left matters of industry up to the business press. They seemed to not notice the antielitist and antihierarchical talk that so poured forth from boardrooms in the nineties. Cult stud Jim McGuigan attributes his colleagues' recurring avoidance of the economic to "a terror of economic reductionism," a pervasive intellectual reflex that, out of their aversion to the overly deterministic schema of an earlier Marxism, led cult studs to steer clear of the problem altogether. One wants to avoid reductionism, naturally, but why, wonders historian Eric Guthey, have "so many highly trained, intelligent and critical cultural scholars . . . chosen to overlook so completely the burgeoning corporatization of American culture?" At a time when corporations boast of being related to God and when Microsoft reminds millions of people every day of the meaning of domination, he asks, "Isn't this a bit like oceanographers refusing to acknowledge the existence of water?" Communications scholar Robert McChesney argues that the cult studs' weird silence on this subject is not so much denial as simple acceptance of market ideology.

> Perhaps the stupidity—and there is no better word for it—of some cultural studies is best shown by its stance toward the market. I have heard leading figures in cultural studies argue that the market is not the top-down authoritarian mechanism that political economists claim, where bosses force the masses to swallow whatever they are fed. To the contrary, they exult, the market is where the masses can contest with the bosses over economic matters; it is a fight without a predetermined outcome. One cultural studies scholar goes so far as to characterize the market as "an expansive popular system."[14]

Cult studs may style themselves radicals, McChesney argues, but many of them have no problem with the market, with what it gives consumers, with what it does to people's lives. And one can't help but wonder how different a decade the nineties would have been had the tidal wave of prose concerning fan communities, shoppers, and techno-enthusiasts been directed instead over the newly triumphant world of business; if the cult studs had chosen simply to ignore the moronic provocations of the Christian Right and focus their energies instead on a foe that was really worthy of their brilliance.

There are, of course, many species of cultural study that neither swallow the populist ideology of the free market nor suffer from rampant reductionism. Erik Barnouw, for example, while doing close readings here and there, still managed to spend a very distinguished career evaluating the broadcasting industry as a business enterprise granted specific franchises by the government; Roland Marchand dissected advertising and public relations with insights that arose directly from those industries' changing function in the world of business. In the works of the cult studs, however, both are treated to the same helping of oblivion as Herbert Gans. The editors of the original *Mass Culture* anthology published in 1957 arranged its articles according to industry and freely mixed analyses of culture as a business with studies of audience behavior. Routledge organized its massive *Cultural Studies* anthology of 1992 alphabetically by contributor's names; the book tiresomely pounds home the "talking back" interpretation almost without regard to the subject being evaluated.

And a Dreadlocked Libertarian Shall Lead Them

But the discipline of cultural studies is a constantly changing one. The optimistic, agency-affirming variety that has been the subject of this chapter so far was not, of course, what the discipline's founders had in mind back in Birmingham, England, in the late 1950s. Richard Hoggart's famous 1957 study of working class life, *The Uses of Literacy,* was affectionate towards its subject and refreshingly free of highbrow attitude and Marxist cant; at the same time it was distinctly pessimistic about the effects of the new forms of mass culture on the working audiences at which they were aimed. By 1995, when Hoggart published *The Way We Live Now,* he looked with exasperation at the endless claims to find subversion and resistance in every text, in every audience. What mattered most, he argued, was real-world political confrontation, not the ability of some subculture or group of fans to snicker behind their boss's back. Dismissing an American cult stud who had claimed of one group of subalterns that "the powerless, the people, are able to evade these structures and conduct a guerrilla warfare of resistance in which they win tactical victories which subvert the strategies of the powerful," Hoggart erupted thusly:

> Studies of this kind habitually ignore or underplay the fact that these groups are almost entirely enclosed from and are refusing even to attempt to cope with the public life of their societies. That rejection cannot reasonably be given some idealistic ideological foundation. It is a rejection, certainly, and in that rejection may be making some implicit criticisms of the "hegemony," and those criticisms need to be understood. But such groups are doing nothing about it except to retreat.

Fans may imagine democratic utopias using the materials of TV dramas or rock videos, but this does not alter their position in the world. "Not to give this fact its due importance," Hoggart concluded, "is to blunt the right instruments for change."[15]

An even more damning critique of the discipline came in 1996 when the scholarly journal *Social Text,* edited by Andrew Ross, unwittingly published a prank essay in which various cult-stud buzz-notions (the badness of "elitism," the progressive nature of interdisciplinarity, the artificiality of all boundaries, the need to cross borders, the call for an "emancipatory mathematics," etc.) had been liberally sprinkled over a preposterous premise—that physical reality was "a social and linguistic construct." In the media frenzy that followed, the cult studs only made matters worse by dropping their usual insistence on "playfulness" and the "pleasures of the text" (and whatever else it was, the prank essay was very funny) and making stern demands that the outside world stop laughing at once and treat this infraction of disciplinary rules with the gravity it deserved.[16]

As if to prove that they really did believe in reality, that they actually were interested in politics of the market as well as those of symbolic "poaching," in the years after the *Social Text* fiasco a number of prominent cult studs involved themselves in markedly down-to-earth political campaigns. Andrew Ross, for example, spoke earnestly on the plight of sweatshop workers, wrote trailblazing articles on exploitation in the dotcom industry, and assisted graduate students at NYU in their campaign for union recognition. Cary Nelson and Michael Bérubé both wrote with admirable forthrightness on the taboo subject of the crisis in academic labor. Stanley Aronowitz went back to doing work on labor unions. Some even suggested a rapprochement with the ideas of the long-hated Frankfurt School.[17]

And while many of the celebrity cult studs of the early nineties were turning to more earthly forms of political engagement, the discipline itself became more practical as well—although in exactly the opposite way. On some campuses cultural studies was becoming a more or less direct path into employment in the lucrative and fashionable businesses of TV, film, and advertising production. At Brown University, where the programs in Semiotics and Modern Literature and Society were merged into the department of Modern Culture and Media, the trend came into sharp focus. While the department's "mission statement" still proudly flies the interdisciplinary banner of cultural studies, questions distinctions between high and low, and makes the mandatory declaration that it is "not interested in producing . . . disdainful aesthetes," its approach to popular culture now includes teaching video production as well as postcolonial theory.[18] The pedagogy looked the same, but its object had changed. After all, one could hardly be a "disdainful aesthete" or a highbrow snob if one wanted to work as a script supervisor to James Cameron or produce episodes of *Xena the Warrior Princess*. What *would* help students interested in such a career were deep understandings of fan communities and audience "resistance"—precisely the issues raised by cultural studies. The point now wasn't so much to celebrate "resistance" as to work around it, preparing students to make commercials (like the Nike skateboarder spots) that flatter a subculture's paranoia or that use the more standard techniques of prude-dissing or let-you-be-you-ing to get, as the admen put it, *Under the Radar.* Maybe the corporate university and the academic left had something in common after all.

At the same time, the populist reflex was increasingly being used not by leftists but by a new round of neoconservative scholars who found in it a useful prop for the most rabid sort of free-market orthodoxy. Perhaps this development took the original cult studs by surprise. But in fact it was a surprisingly short walk from the active-audience theorizing of the original to the sterner stuff of market populism. While the cult studs may have insisted proudly on the inherent radicalism of their ideas concerning agency, resistance, and the horror of elitism, as these notions spread their polarities were reversed; they came across not as daringly counterhegemonic but as the most egregious sort of apologia for existing economic arrangements. Consider, for example, the extremely negative connotations of the word "regulate" as it was used in the cultural studies corpus: Almost without variation it referred to the deplorable actions of an elite even more noxious than the Frankfurt School, a cabal of religious conservatives desperately seeking to suppress difference. And then consider the strikingly similar negative connotations of the word as it is used by the *Wall Street Journal,* where it also refers to the deplorable actions of an obnoxious elite, in this case meddling liberals who assume arrogantly that they know better than the market. Both arise from a form of populism that celebrates critical audiences but that has zero tolerance for critics themselves.

Certain academics were capable of bringing the populism of cultural studies and the populism of the market together with breathtaking ease. Economist Tyler Cowen, for example, translated the populist reflex into an extended celebration of the benevolence of markets, wandering here and there over the entire history of art in his 1998 book *In Praise of Commercial Culture,* seeking always to prove that the market deserves the credit for all worthwhile cultural production. The market guarantees quality. The market guarantees diversity. And have you ever considered who pays the bills for all those artists? That's right: the market. As it turns out, the market maintains the strong record it does (over the centuries, according to Cowen's accounting, batting real close to 1.000) because it is indistinguishable from the people. And "an audience," he writes, "is more intelligent than the individuals who create their entertainment." Those who recognize popular intelligence are "cultural optimists," in whose camp Cowen puts himself, Gans, and a handful of leading cult studs, all of whom wisely believe in letting the people and the market make their decisions without interference.[19] On the other side, meanwhile, stands a motley group of critics united only by their shared "elitism," the conviction that they know best. From the Frankfurt School (who come in for severe chastisement) to the Christian Right, they are all "cultural pe simists," doubtful about the people's capacity to decide for themselves, skeptical about popular tastes, contemptuous of progress itself. As even the Nazis can be made to fit under such a preposterous definition of "pessimism," Cowen brings them in, too.

Advertising scholar James Twitchell crosses the bridge from cultural studies to market populism with considerably more diplomacy and style. In his 1999 celebration of consumerism, *Lead Us Into Temptation,* the debate is again about popular intelligence. Do intellectuals think the public is stupid or smart? Powerless and impotent or bursting with agency? Clearly, according to Twitchell, most culture critics fall into the former camp, seeing "the consumer as a dumb ox." Appearing in their usual role as the worst snobs ever are the Frankfurt School, who dared to criticize the makers of mass culture on the grounds that they sometimes tricked consumers, and that they, the arrogant professors, somehow knew better. Twitchell rejects such an argument—and also rejects Ralph Nader, Vance Packard, John Kenneth Galbraith, and presumably anyone else who has ever criticized corporate America—not because he wants to see corporate profits grow without the interference of the regulations that those men's work inspired (good heavens, no!), but because he loves democracy, he loves We the People. The fact is, he reminds us, audiences are active, not passive. "Watching television," he writes, "is almost frantic with creative activity." Consumers are *never* "duped," a point Twitchell makes three times in five pages; consumers are, in actuality, "the ones with the power, continually negotiating new sites for meaning." Twitchell does not write, "consumers will be the ones with the power once certain regulations are in place"; he asserts that they have the power *now*, as they have had it always, through the medium of the free market. So great is our wisdom and our agency that we don't just create some subcultural response to mass culture; *we create the mass culture itself!* By watching, by buying, we authorize all.

> I never want to imply that, in creating order in our lives, consumption is *doing* something to us that we are not covertly responsible for. We are not victims of consumption. Just as we make our media, our media make us. Again, commercialism is *not* making us behave against our "better judgment." Commercialism is our better judgment.

Strictly speaking, we may not have voted for the "New Economy," with all its grotesque inequality and its smashing of the local, but we have authorized its every act anyway, just by consuming. Turning to the globalization and cyber-economy of the late nineties, Twitchell writes in his conclusion that "we have not just asked to go this way, we have demanded." Consumerism is democracy, the veritable "triumph of the popular will." To criticize its workings is to express contempt for the judgment of the people themselves.[20]

Outside the academy the translation of cultural studies into market populism was even more pronounced. Granted, newspaper stories on the cult studs rarely manage to do much more than giggle at the spectacle of people with PhD's writing about Barbie and *The Simpsons,* but the cult studs' trademark language of audience agency and subversive subtexts seeped down to earth nonetheless. Journalists who absorbed the populist reflex could be heard calling on readers to rally around the communitarian teachings of the Teletubbies or wondering whether anyone even had the right to dislike the Spice Girls. More common was a simple injection of cult-stud theory into the usual industry PR: their war against hierarchy now turned up as a convenient weapon for stigmatizing industry critics as elitists; their fight against highbrow snobbishness became the logic of demographics. And while genuine cult studs almost never participated in this operation, still they did have an occasional role to play.

A revealing glimpse of this transformation in action could be found in the November 1995 issue of *Spin* magazine, a special issue "guest edited" by Jaron Lanier, a figure renowned in computer circles from Palo Alto to Prague for having coined the term "virtual reality." Over the years Lanier has become a sort of physical embodiment of the cyber-revolution's liberating promise, mixing copiously dreadlocked, in-your-face attitude with long-winded exegeses on the industry as a vast boon for human freedom. But whether it's the cover of *Civilization* magazine or a puffy profile in *Fortune,* Lanier's dreads seem always to be the focus of gaping admiration (granted, they are unusually full and healthy-looking for a white person of his age), establishing a rock-solid outsider credibility without messy argument.[21] Among other things, he had the honor of being one of the first to outline the position on the Microsoft antitrust trial that was soon adopted all across the free-market right, declaring from the authoritative heights of the *New York Times* op-ed page in 1997 that it was fruitless to even *consider* applying those second-wave antitrust laws to such superadvanced organizations.[22] Ordinarily, of course, Lanier's dreads are sufficient to certify that such ideas are not those of some hated hierarch, but occasionally better credentialing is in order. In *Spin,* therefore, he was paired with none other than prominent cult stud bell hooks, who evidently appeared solely to supply Lanier with a legitimacy that even his sturdy dreads couldn't muster. Hooks dutifully gaped at Lanier in terms only slightly less awestruck than those chosen by *Fortune:* "It strikes me how radically different you are, Jaron, from the prototypical image most people have of the nerdy white man behind the computers."

What hooks thought was "radical" was in fact strictly superficial. While the cyber-industry went from nerdy to dreadlocked, its libertarian politics changed not at all. On the contrary, the main function of its radical differentness was to give its defenses of Microsoft or its declarations from Davos a convincing populist patina. And yet cult studs like hooks showed surprisingly little ability to distinguish between antielitism as publicity strategy and the genuine article. Emblematic of this confusion is the oddly universal reverence for cult stud Donna Haraway, who is apotheosized with enthusiasm both in cult-stud circles and by *Wired* magazine, which quoted and name-checked her throughout the decade on a fairly regular basis. In her contribution to the landmark ur-anthology of 1992, Haraway declared herself a partisan of "socialism" but quickly distanced herself from "the deadly point of view of productionism," opting instead for a curious techno-environmentalism that emphasized not just human agency but that of animal "actants" as well. Haraway may have been a discerning reader of eighties-style corporate culture, cleverly analyzing in that same article a number of dry computer and medical advertisements, but when it came to the Web-based corporate fantasies of the nineties her critical edge seemed to disappear. "To 'press enter' is not a fatal error," she wrote, "but an inescapable possibility for changing maps of the world, for building new collectives out of . . . human and unhuman actors." Sure, the techno-culture of the eighties was a drag, but when it's an "inappropriate/d other" at the keyboard (a guy with dreads or, in Haraway's chosen example, a woman with a big cat perched on her head) everything was different.[23]

The society-wide confusion of market populism with broader human liberation comes into high relief when we make a hard right from the cyber-business press to the realm of high libertarian ideology. *Reason* magazine was formally dedicated to "free minds and free markets," but its most remarkable editorial achievement lay in a curious journalistic stunt performed over and over again in the nineties by a capable cast of writers: Our patriotic American belief in the intelligence of the common people, also known as consumers, was made to collide violently with the nose of whoever was besieging this month's corporation-in-distress. Agency, that cult-stud staple, was recast by *Reason* into the silver bullet of corporate defense. As it was used here, agency meant the people expressed themselves perfectly well through the market, through consumer choice; it meant that neither the government nor industry groups had any business protecting anybody from anything; best of all, it transformed those who criticized industry into the worst sort of (you guessed it) snobs and elitists, tacitly believing that the public were a collection of agency-deprived fools.

Like the works of Herbert Gans, *Reason* seemed never to come up in the monographs and anthologies of the cult studs. And yet one wishes that, if only to temper their endless culture war gasconade, the cult studs had somehow been required to take a peek beneath the publication's easter-egg colored covers. There they would have found a militantly pro-corporate right that, like consumer society itself, had no problem with difference, lifestyle, and pleasure; that cared not a whit for the preservation of disciplinary boundaries; that urged the destruction of cultural hierarchy in language as fervid as anything to appear in the pages of *Social Text*. There were even fairly exact parallels to the cult-stud argument. A 1998 *Reason* feature story by anthropologist Grant McCracken, for example, celebrated the "plenitude" of endless lifestyle diversity as "the signature gesture of our culture." After chewing out the usual right-wing culture warriors (Bennett, Buchanan, Robertson) and dropping the obligatory bomb on the Frankfurt School (Herbert Marcuse is also singled out for article-length punishment in the November 1998 issue), McCracken hailed the rise of "difference, variety, and novelty" and counseled his comrades to forget about suppressing the Other and to adjust themselves instead to the "inevitable." Declaring a democratic interest in even the oddest cultural novelties, McCracken informed his conservative colleagues, in a passage astonishingly reminiscent of Andrew Ross at his Saturday night worst, that

> line dancing provides an interesting and dynamic site for the transformation of gender, class, outlook, and, yes, politics. It is on the dance floor that cultural categories and social rules are being reexamined and, sometimes, reinvented.

Of course, the only thing that could make sense out of this world of endless differentiation was "the great lingua franca" of "the marketplace." It was capitalism that was breaking "the stranglehold of hierar-chies and elites"; it was the "consumer culture" that "is a cause and a consequence of plenitude."[24]

Other *Reason*ers cited the cult studs explicitly when making their trademark argument. Editor Nick Gillespie grounded his 1996 defense of the movie industry in the populist reflex as an established principle of legitimate social science, citing prominent cult stud Constance Pen-ley (best known for her work on pornographic fanzines in which the *Star Trek* characters get it on) as the authority for this most hallowed of culturisms: "All viewers or consumers have 'agency'; they *process* what they see or hear—they do not merely lap it up." Gillespie made the elusive-audience point again and again, bringing in cult stud Henry Jenkins for extra legitimacy, before moving on to the inevitable flip side: The elitism of the entertainment industry's critics. These were figures who believed that "viewers lack virtually any critical faculties or knowledge independent of what program producers feed them," that "the idiot box . . . turns viewers into idiots," that we were "robotic stooges," "trained dogs," "dumb receivers," "unwitting dupes." Not that they said any of this about us in public, mind you. These were simply *implied,* the obvious consequence of their "top-down conception of culture," their focus on "authorial intentions"—and the equally obvious and far more loathsome corollary, that "they know best," that "the viewer simply can't be trusted," that "regulation by the government" was in order.

Ah, but the market, the glorious, plenitude-permitting market, could make no such elitist presumptions. Not only did the market permit all the excellent examples of "resisting readers" that Gillespie found so very dope (of course he cites *Mystery Science Theater 3000*), but in the land of pop culture, "as with all market-based exchanges, knowledge, value, and power . . . are dispersed." The robots mock a lousy movie, ergo the government must leave Microsoft alone. Q.E.D.[25]

The *Reason* argument was remarkably flexible for all its simplic-ity. After looking through back issues I found it deployed on behalf of the advertising industry (we aren't fooled 100 percent of the time, you know), the tobacco industry (people choose to smoke cigarettes, you know), the gun industry (not all kids murder their classmates, you know), Barnes & Noble (people choose to go there, you know), Microsoft (choice incarnate, you know), and Jesse Ventura, whose election as governor of Minnesota gave our Mr. Gillespie an opportunity to explain his populism in historical detail, complete with passages about the affection felt by the good people of Minnesota toward corporations, and then this towering whopper, which came up as an explanation of, well, just about everything: "at the end of the Twentieth Century, 'money power'—indeed, power in general—is far more concentrated in government hands than in corporate ones."[26]

The same logic was also commonplace even further to the right. While the luminous names of Haraway, hooks, Jenkins, Penley, and Ross (along with the joys of the dance floor) may have been entirely unfamiliar to the fulminating Rush Limbaugh, their insistence on audience agency in the face of the culture conglomerates as well as their faith in democracy through pop culture and in the essential elitism of those who criticize it were as friendly and familiar to him as the winning smile of Ollie North. Rush's version of the populist reflex came across with particular vigor in his 1993 collection of witticisms, *See, I Told You So,* in which he referred to his own rise as an object lesson in the fundamental justice of markets, as in this rousing invocation of decentered power and audience agency: "Nobody put me in that [dominant] position—no network, no government program, no producer. You in the audience who have voluntarily tuned the dial to my voice—you alone—have caused my success." On the other side of the coin from the "magic of the marketplace," of course, were the high-handed, top-down, know-it-all regulators who wanted "to use this country as their grand laboratory experiment." But meddling liberals were just the tip of the hegemony iceberg: Even worse was the "sheer arrogance" of the elitists who believe that "people who listen to my show are just too stupid to tackle America's complicated problems." It wasn't long before

Rush wheeled out the Frankfurt School, this time in the person of Theodor Adorno, for its ritual thumping.[27]

Making History Just as They Please

For all the talk of cultural disintegration from one side, and of intolerance and persecution from the other, it is sometimes astonishing how much basic agreement lay beneath the stormy surface of the culture wars. However Americans fought over appropriations for the NEA, educated people everywhere seemed to agree on the perfidy of cultural elitism. And whether they simply ignored the world of business or actively extolled the corporate order, both sides agreed that our newfound faith in active, intelligent audiences made criticism of the market philosophically untenable. Taste was annexed to politics in the 1990s in a manner that trivialized both, leaving us with an understanding of "democracy" that referred increasingly to matters of accurate demographic representation, to a certain republican humility before the wisdom of the people. That left and right had entered into a new consensus was further suggested by the movie *Pleasantville,* where a scarcely believable smugness about the liberated present arose phoenix-like from the ashes of the old, gray flannel smugness. It may have been a consensus of masturbating moms rather than muffin-baking moms; of dreadlocked millionaires rather than horn-rimmed millionaires; of Kirk and Spock fisting rather than exploring new galaxies; of culture war rather than cold war, but it was as confident about the glories of life in these United States as any intellectual order has ever been.

If cultural studies had a unique intellectual virtue, it was a willingness to acknowledge its own failings, and in this chapter I have made liberal use of the work of several of the discipline's most prominent critics.[28] But in many other ways cultural studies looked, read, behaved, and legitimated just like its never-acknowledged consensus forebear. For all the cult studs' populist pretensions, the dominant tone of much of their writing was one of bombastic self-congratulation and vainglorious blaring—sometimes self-pitying, sometimes pompous beyond belief. Even more indicative of the hardening of a new consensus was the cult studs' strange fantasy of encirclement by Marxists at once crude and snobbish, a transplanted Cold War chimera that one found repeated in just about every one of the discipline's texts, that filled the e-mail signature lines of the academically stylish.[29] The point here isn't merely that the right and the cult studs used the same target for bayonet practice, but simply that their target is a straw man, that both groups ignore the facts of cultural life out of a misplaced anxiety over a cartoonish doctrine they imagine as both Teutonic and red, a horrifying cross between the nation's historical enemies. "Each generation is driven to theorize by the particular historical tendencies and events that confront it," Lawrence Grossberg and Cary Nelson wrote way back in 1988.[30] And yet while the cult studs fought the obvious fight with the Christian Right, they seemed almost completely to miss the history of their own era. Business publications were crowing in those days that the production and export of information was becoming the central element of the American economy; they saw the millennium in the conquest of the world by Monsanto and Microsoft. But up on the heights from which critical fire could have been brought to bear on their imperial parade, the self-proclaimed radicals were busy tying themselves in knots to avoid any taint of vulgar Marxism.

That is, I think, an optimistic take. What seems far more likely is that, as the politically committed drop by the wayside, cultural studies will evolve to a point where matters economic are simply defined away, where any transgression is as meaningful as any other, and where the new crop of cult studs can take the logical next step from academy to consultancy work for the growing number of hip ad agencies and ethnographic-based market research firms, celebrating the subversive potential of Sprite or the Catera without reservation or troubling doubt.

Consider in this regard the cult studs' marked complacency about their own role in the larger cultural economy. To be sure, the subject of the duties and responsibilities of intellectuals was one with which they were deeply, obsessively concerned: Andrew Ross, for example, brilliantly dissected the power of intellectuals to "designate what is legitimate" in his 1989 book *No Respect.* But in Ross's telling the cult studs themselves appeared only as a solution to this shameful historical condition. He did not consider what might happen when the corporate world outside the academy decided it no longer had any interest in the old-style markers of legitimacy and wanted only to hear about subversion and radical difference and the heroism of the change agent. After leading readers through a century of snobs and aristocratic Trotskyists, Ross concluded his story of intellectuals and popular culture by locating himself and his colleagues (the nonelitist "new intellectuals") on the high plateau of historical accomplishment where such behavior by academics was simply no longer possible.[31] This was a hopeful prediction but a wrong one, blindsided in just a few years by the fatal double irony of an academic radicalism becoming functionally indistinguishable from free market theory at exactly the historical moment when capitalist managers decided it was time to start referring to themselves as "radicals," to understand consumption itself as democracy.

These days, in advertising agencies and market-research firms worldwide, the gap between critical intellectuals and simple salesmanship seems only to shrink. With or without the assistance of the cult studs, American audiences are growing more skeptical by the minute; fashion cycles that once required years now take months; heroes of the age are despised by the people in spite of the best efforts of *Fortune* and *Time.* The intellectual task at hand is not just legitimation, it is infiltration, and suddenly questions like the oppositional or subversive potential of *The Simpsons* aren't quite as academic as they once seemed. Given the industry's new requirements, the active-audience faith of the cult stud becomes less an article of radical belief and more a practical foundation for the reprioritized audience research being done by the new breed of marketing experts, who can be found commenting lucidly on the postmodern condition in highbrow business publications like the *Journal of Consumer Research,* laying out plans to "reenchant" the brand with a "liberatory postmodernism," and warning advertisers to create with the active, emancipation-hungry consumer in mind. One day they're attentively following the Star Trek listserv or studying the counterhegemonic funeral wailing of the Warao people; the next they're inventing brands for a nation of alienated 7-Eleven shoppers and hegemony-smashing mallwalkers. Now *that's* interdisciplinarity.

Triangulation

Nation

Journalism in the Age of Markets

> I remember our pastor saying one time, "A cynic is a man
> who sneers, and a man who sneers is setting himself up to
> tell God that he doesn't approve of God's handiwork!"
>   —*Sinclair Lewis, "The Man Who Knew Coolidge," 1928*

Back to Normalcy II: The Theory

For all the adulation American economic thinkers heaped on "content
providers," that most heroic battalion of the "knowledge worker" army,
the nineties were in fact a time of humiliation and cataclysmic decline
for journalists. Americans have always reserved the right to complain
about their hometown newspaper, of course, to find it deficient or distorted or inaccurate in whatever way they chose. But between the rise of
new media, with its voice-of-the-people directness, and the increasing
appearance on TV of journalism's biggest names, pontificating like the
blowhards we always suspected they were, something changed. Our traditional skepticism toward the news seemed to mushroom. Journalists
faced a nasty legitimacy crisis, a sense of lost authority that in turn inspired a towering mass of journalistic confessions and self-examinations.

The news legitimacy crisis could be described in any number of statistical or metaphorical ways, depending on the reporter's requirements: Circulation was declining; Generation X was scoffing; other media were encroaching on the turf of network and newspaper; and journalists themselves were blundering wherever one looked, getting it wrong, falling for hoaxes, inventing hoaxes themselves. Then there was that terrifying statistical fact of nature, that mounting tidal wave of public disgust with the press reflected by poll after poll, by the popularity contests that journalists seemed always to lose—whether they were matched up against politicians, salesmen, phone solicitors, TV preachers, dogcatchers, prison guards, Mafia chieftains, computer moguls, second-story men, whoever. Journalists were at the bottom of the heap. They were sensationalists, distorters, and liars, Americans believed, as universally corrupt and untrustworthy as the elected officials with whom they were supposed to be perpetually at war. Their social position no longer secure, their power to shape public discourse no longer irresistible, and their traditional prerogatives now the right of any drudge who spoke html or knew how to run a photocopier, journalists were in danger of being demoted altogether, of embarking on that long slide from profession back to mere job. If the Internet was threatening to put the daily paper out of business, most of us couldn't wait.

To make matters worse, news-debunking became virtually a profession unto itself in the nineties, a booming shadow industry of watchdog magazines, radio hosts, online commentators, and freebooting critics, all of them bellowing with outrage and determined to undistort the media's distortions for the misinformed masses. The well-known mendacity of the press informed films like *Wag the Dog*. It gave every city its own media columnist, churning out news stories about news stories that were themselves about news stories. Even late-nineties advertisements for *Fox News,* the most degraded of news programs, announced that network news has gone too far, but that this network, by God, still believed in the consent of the governed: "We Report. You Decide."

Some charged that what made the news so loathsome was a liberal conspiracy. That journalists were kind to Castro because they secretly admired his regime. That the media showed photos of Ronald Reagan in a less than reverential light because they were out to undermine the great man's historical reputation. That reporters, editors, and publishers swallowed the Clinton line because they recognized him as a fellow member of the secretive "New Class" (a mysterious fraternity whose aims and deeds were the subject of excited speculation in even the most respectable conservative journals), engaged like them in the grand program of bringing the country to heel under its rightful elites.

What actually underlay many of the big changes in American journalism—and hence precipitated much of the public anger—was the deterioration of the few checks that had once constrained the business aspect of the news media. The "New Class" didn't transform most cities into one-newspaper towns; market forces did. TV news didn't get dumber and dumber and dumber because liberals wanted it that way, but because advertisers did. Broadcast news relied ever more heavily on factoids and split-second sound-bites because this left more time for commercials. Newspapers shrank what is infelicitously called the "newshole" (the space not taken up by advertising) because they made more money that way. They closed distant bureaus and recycled press release or wire service feed because it was cheaper. They learned to prefer cuddly human interest stories because strong opinions turned advertisers away. The big newspaper industry innovation that had everyone talking in the nineties was not the effort to reelect Clinton but the destruction of the "wall" between editorial and advertising, which paved the way for puff stories, puff sections, or puff supplements to help big advertisers. And, yes, there was a class aspect to all this, although not in the conspiratorial sense that right-wing media watchers seemed always to suspect. While once journalists had regarded themselves as functionally equivalent to blue-collar workers, now they fancied themselves professionals, far closer to management than to the guys who printed their words. Backlash media critics liked to point to this as the reason newspapers didn't pay God more mind, but it was also the reason labor reporting virtually disappeared in the eighties and nineties as well as the reason for the eerie editorial consensus on the great economic issues of the day—globalization, NAFTA, the "inevitability" of deindustrialization. As John Leonard, former book reviewer for the *New York Times,* put it recently, now journalists "have more in common with Henry Kravis and Henry Kissinger than [they] do with papermakers and deliverymen, or those ABC technicians who were so alone, on strike, on Columbus Avenue." Add to this the constant pressure exerted by advertisers interested only in reaching affluent readers, and you have a fairly concise picture of the forces driving the news media in the nineties. "The dumbing down, the demise of news is all about the hunger for advertising revenues and how that plays out in the newsroom," former *CBS Evening News* producer Richard Cohen wrote in 1997. "The real crisis in television news today is about corporate control and the emerging corporate culture."[1] What was killing journalism was also killing academia, killing organized labor: The market.

There is nothing novel about this critique. Pointing out the tension between market forces and journalistic integrity was in fact the main thesis of most media criticism for decades. "The function of the press in society is to inform, but its role is to make money," wrote A. J. Liebling, the greatest media critic of them all, many years ago. "The monopoly publisher's reaction, on being told that he ought to spend money on reporting distant events, is therefore that of the proprietor of a large, fat cow, who is told that he ought to enter her in a horse race."[2] In making this argument Liebling was not in the grip of some weird leftist economism, as certain critics of the nineties seemed to believe. He was well in the mainstream of American press criticism, echoing the verdict of bodies as respectable as the famous Hutchins Commission of 1946, which warned against increasing concentration of newspaper ownership. This was not Marxism; it was hardheaded journalistic empiricism. It was, in a word, obvious. To suggest in those days that the nation's newspaper publishers were excessively liberal would have been like announcing one's familiarity with gnomes and elves. Newspaper publishers were wealthy men often involved in nasty fights with union-minded employees; they made no secret of where their interests lay. They opposed Roosevelt by vast margins in the elections of 1936 and 1940; they opposed Truman by similarly large majorities in 1948. They provided a generous market for the services of ultraright columnists like Westbrook Pegler and George Sokolsky. Certain publishers like William Randolph Hearst, Frank Gannett, and Col. Robert McCormick (of the *Chicago Tribune*) tended not just to be conservative but downright loony.[3] Different though they were from the newspaper barons of our own day, the effect such figures' naked advocacy for the laissez-faire way had on public attitudes toward the press are strikingly familiar. "Anybody who talks often with people about newspapers nowadays must be impressed by the growing distrust of the information they contain," Liebling remarked in 1947. "There is less a disposition to accept what they say than to try to estimate the probable truth on the basis of what they say, like aiming a rifle that you know has a deviation to the right." The solution, Liebling believed, was for groups other than wacky, headstrong millionaires to start or gain control of newspapers. "I cannot believe that labor leaders are so stupid they will let the other side monopolize the press indefinitely," he chided.[4]

In the nineties, though, as the high councils of American journalism met to weigh their response to the ever-mounting public doubt, such solutions—along with Liebling's market-based critique—were simply out of the question. The problem wasn't the galloping influence of a newly unrestrained market; the problem was *attitude*. Newspapers didn't need to somehow counterbalance or question market forces; they needed to *stop criticizing*. The public mind had been poisoned by journalistic "cynicism," by journalistic "adversarialism," and unless these corrosive values were rooted out, they would destroy nothing less than the Republic itself. The nineties were a time of desperation in that Washington-based encampment of hypernormalcy that is the punditocracy, and the commentator class wheeled in formation to face its tormentors, issuing forth vast reams of journalistic wisdom, diagnoses of the malaise, and schemes by which American innocence might be recovered. In *Feeding Frenzy*, a 1991 compilation of lamentations by political scientist Larry Sabato, Beltway journalists could be heard regretting their "attack-dog" practices and their "adversarial" behavior. So many Beltway confessions of refusal to believe did Joseph Cappella and Kathleen Hall Jamieson summon up in their 1997 book *Spiral of Cynicism* that the authors' conclusion—journalists have *caused* the dread "cynicism" that stalks the land—seemed positively superfluous. It was a staggeringly arrogant notion, this idea of a public mind poisoned by an overdose of journalistic zealotry, and yet so glamorous did it sound that it was repeated virtually wherever the industry's legitimacy crisis was being discussed.* From Woodward and Bernstein to the less-than-civil Sam Donaldson to the packs of scandal-hunters on the trail of Di and Monica, journalists were the creatures responsible for destroying the happy consensus of yore, for making civility impossible, for wrecking our humble dreams of bipartisanship. The press, journalists admitted, was the reason we couldn't all just get along.[5]

To be sure, much that was worthwhile came of the decade's rage for journalistic mea culpas. In *Breaking the News* (1996), veteran editor James Fallows administered a series of much-deserved hidings to the various lights of the Washington press corps. He wrote intelligently about the changing class interests of journalists and their consequently skewed perspectives, and capably analyzed the bad reporting that dogged Clinton's failed health care plan. In *What Are Journalists For?* (1999), Jay Rosen, former media critic for *Tikkun* magazine, traced the evolution of American political journalism, the growing power of its celebrities, and its shameful performance in the 1988 presidential campaign, when its leading figures decided not merely to report on the candidates' transparent efforts to mislead voters, but also to comment constantly on how well they were doing at misleading voters. The story of the gradual emptying of content from politics—and of journalists' complicity in the operation—is a horrifying one, and Rosen tells it well.

---

*Unfortunately, it's also a wrong notion. A 1995 Times Mirror poll found that fully 77 percent of the public rated the honesty and ethics of public officials as low, while only 40 percent of journalists believed the same. If journalists were to faithfully represent the views of the public they served, they would have to become *more* cynical, not less.

But having landed these blows, each of these press critics proceeded to make the same curious error, blaming journalistic "adversarialism" for the great public disenchantment of the age. The problem with the press, they argued, was that it's too darn divisive. The media are too interested in finding fault, in tearing down rather than building up. And while this was clearly true on a superficial level—John McLaughlin and Fred Barnes did indeed make a great show of yelling at each other on TV—one could just as easily have pointed out that American "adversarialism" was only skin-deep, that the national press corps was generally not interested in raising fundamental challenges to the routine order of things. Bob Woodward, to whom journalism critics frequently refer as the most adversarial journalist of them all (mainly for his role in Watergate), is merely a close observer of power. While he has occasionally put politicians on the spot, he is hardly a doubter of the American order in the manner of, say, I. F. Stone. One can't help but feel that a more fruitful analysis of the intellectual failings of America in the nineties might have begun not with the media's "adversarialism" but with the across-the-board consensus that its sound and fury served to obscure. Such a study would zero in not so much on the staged acrimony of the Sunday talk shows as on American journalists' unbelievable ideological *smugness*, their cocksureness about the movements and ends of history, their reverence for free markets and global trade, their assumptions concerning the goodness of the advertised life and the absence of alternatives to the corporate order. It might have asked why it was that while other countries hotly debated whether to join the "Washington consensus," whether to privatize and deregulate, whether to permit genetically modified foods, our commentators seemed always to bury discussion under the language of "inevitability," under the assumption that business knows best. It might have compared the extremely narrow range of opinion represented on our op-ed pages to the wide-open debates that routinely sweep across the newspapers of countries like France, Britain, and even Canada. It might have inquired how it came to be that our journalists developed such a curious sense of their own independence when they were in fact, to all appearances, closer to the thinking of the elites of industry and government than their counterparts in almost any other land.

Consider, for example, the famous 1995 handshake between Bill Clinton and Newt Gingrich. This was Exhibit A for the authors of *Spiral of Cynicism*, the event that the cynical press just didn't get. For these critics the behavior of the press at the time was a moment of revelation: It was now time for reporters to change their mood and cover "civility" and "consensus"—and they didn't know how! They kept looking for a fight—but there wasn't one! Naturally, the authors told this story as a way of showing how the journalistic culture of "adversarialism" had gotten out of hand. But one could easily see it in exactly the opposite light. That the formal coming together of the two parties utterly flummoxed the press corps demonstrated not the destructiveness of "adversarialism" but the term's utter meaninglessness. Just because Democrats and Republicans got together hardly meant that journalistic questioning should cease; that cheering should commence immediately. Quite the contrary: Consensus sometimes deserves to be just as rudely debunked as conflict. And lord knows we could have used some well-aimed questioning, some "adversarialism," at that particular moment. After all, that handshake was in some ways the most important symbolic moment of the decade, the signal that the historical opponent to the business party was no longer interested in opposing. And we have had nothing but handshakes ever since, a constant party in the office towers and the nice suburbs while the people who voted for Clinton out of a desire for better welfare service and national health care were dropped off the media earth.

But finding grounds for debate that extended beyond what was considered legitimate by the two parties was most definitely not the object of mainstream nineties journalism theory. What was sought was a *cessation* of argument, a handshake and a consensus that journalists could call their own. Almost without fail the journalism critiques of the era follow the same weird trajectory, veering from scathing indictments of pundit idiocy to airy musings about civil society and its virtues. In place of cynicism, it was said, journalists must try hard and dedicate them-selves to service. They must build a "public journalism" that, in Jay Rosen's maddeningly vague terms, "clears a space where the public can do its work," which can "engage people as citizens," which could "help revive civic life and improve public dialogue."[6]

It certainly sounded quite noble, this "public journalism." But what, specifically, did it mean to apply democratic principles to the informa-tion industry? Were we not so blinded by the language of the market triumphant, the answers would be obvious: legislation to promote local control of newspapers, perhaps, or massive public subsidies to reduce the power of advertisers, or the breakup of the bigger media monopo-lies, or, at the very least, decent wages and working conditions for jour-nalists and pressmen. But public journalism, like so many other self-proclaimed reform movements of the decade, simply could not ad-dress itself to questions of institutional power. What its proponents meant by "democracy" was a kind of *cultural* democracy, a media pop-ulism according to which the industry's most vexing problem is the "elitism" of particular writers, their refusal to "listen" and their ten-dency to favor expert opinion over that of the people. What we needed was not a stronger wall between editorial and advertising, public jour-nalism maintained, but *more polls*. More focus groups. More "town meetings." What journalists had to do was learn to listen, to take into account the actual concerns of the public rather than the cynical urges of the self-centered writer. These were, of course, about as likely to of-fend journalism's conglomerate parents as would demands for, say, a more comprehensive astrology column.

But they were also perfectly in step with the market populism sweep-ing across other aspects of American life. So, having criticized the vari-ous Beltway boobs, the theorists of public journalism tended to indulge their middlebrow tendencies without reservation, returning again and again to the peculiarly naive formulation of democratic theory that al-ways characterizes market populism. Rosen, who was particularly given to grandiose fifties-era phrases like "the American experiment" and "our lengthy adventure in nationhood," argued that what journalists had to do was be "humble" before the public will, much like the all-American investors imagined by Wall Street and the new-style managers celebrated in the "business revolution." "Are we behaving as exemplary citizens?" he asked a gathering of journalists. Are we "listening well, working with others, claiming our rights as members of a community who also have a responsibility to the whole?"[7] Fallows seemed actually to believe that national discord was something invented by journalists; that social conflict was alien to American shores; and that, if only "elite journalists" would "listen" to the people rather than poison the democratic process with their "adversarialism," the few problems we faced would be quickly solved. He spoke heartily of one newspaper's "Public Life Team" ("We will lead the community to discover itself and act on what it has learned") and Rosen hailed the "People Project" launched by another (a combination average-folks documentary and "empowerment" initiative), both monikers so grandly meaningless that they could well be titles for superhero cartoon programs.[8]

However simplistic, this reduction of journalistic error to questions of personal arrogance, to an unfamiliarity with the ways of the people, struck the decade's populist sensibilities exactly right. The movement was especially popular with the nation's charitable foundations. The Philadelphia-based Pew Foundation took the lead in supporting the new journalism, setting up a "Center for Civic Journalism," and supporting and publicizing media projects with proudly populist names like "We the People/Wisconsin," the folksy "Front Porch Forum," and the "Leadership Challenge" mounted by (of course!) Peoria, Illinois. Journalists interested in the new way could read in Pew publications about do-it-yourself vox populi projects like "YOUtv," a bunch of cameras in public places that are explained as a way of "democratizing television," of giving "ordinary people access" to what is ordinarily an "elitist tool." In a Pew video entitled "Civic Journalism: A Work in Progress," the editor of a Colorado newspaper explained how the "same old" journalism wasn't working anymore and how he and his staff set about making it new. Barriers fell as the fourth estate learned about the wisdom and virtue of the common man: The newspaper "opened up (its) decision-making process, not just to the room, but to the community"; reporters discovered that convenience stores were "just as legitimate spaces in which to seek out the news and to cover it as a City Council meeting"; editors went in for "community conversations, facilitated focus groups, public listening. . . ."[9]

And before long, the language of public journalism had entered the mainstream. "Elitism" joined "cynicism" as the free-floating explain-all whenever some explanation was required for journalistic malpractice. From the embarrassing Stephen Glass episode (in which *The New Republic* and other magazines published fabricated stories) to the shameful Lewinsky circus, the errors of the journalistic "establishment" were attributed to its arrogance, its distance from the common folk. The news media were hopelessly out of touch, guided by their own ideas rather than those of the citizenry, always "widening the gap," as one hand-wringing 1998 *U.S. News* column put it, between their snobbish selves and "the rest of us."[10] As with so many other strains of market populism, public journalism seemed to understand critical judgment itself as an arrogant, undemocratic act. "Elitism," that cardinal democratic sin, was a quality that James Fallows repeatedly associated with hyperjudgmental figures like Novak and McLaughlin; the error of the "media Establishment" consisted of "talk[ing] *at* people rather than with or even to them." "Democracy," meanwhile, was a sort of eternal suspension of judgment, a process of endless "listening," "ambivalence," and virtuous deference to "the popular will." According to Jay Rosen, journalists had no business giving an arrogant thumbs-up or thumbs-down on everything our leaders did; they should instead be wondering constantly about who they were and whether or not they were correctly representing their constituency, the public, and asking the questions that the public would want them to ask. Rosen called his model of democratic journalism "proactive neutrality," a process of soliciting conversation with the public—"bringing people to the table"—but never "telling them what to decide."[11] According to this reform movement, democratic culture had no place for crusading or persuasion; by definition such efforts to impress one's own views on the community were acts of unpardonable elitism. No, journalists had to be neutral above all, flexible and content-free, their newspapers understood as community fixtures like a town hall or a fire department.

Like the cult studs ignoring the world of business, one can't help but feel that the leaders of the public journalism movement were making a fairly massive error of judgment. After all, they looked out at the America of the nineties, a place in which more and more aspects of public life were being brought under corporate control, in which the concentration of wealth was at a record level, in which no group or figure, public or private, dared challenge the authority of the market, and in which so many aspects of the general welfare were breaking down, and they declared that the real problem facing democracy was an excess of judgment. They earnestly argued that the thing to do in such circumstances; the answer to such acute and well-defined disorders, was to shut up, stop criticizing, and contemplate instead the majesty of The People.

Of course, if your objective was not so much democracy as restoring the legitimacy of a certain industry, such stuff seemed positively ideal. Here again, as in the world of management theory, a particularly blaring bit of watered-down thirties populism was offered up as a means of regaining public respect for journalism without calling into question any of the larger corporate developments of the era. The soft populism of public journalism was thus an easy compromise between the demands of the ever more corporate media and the alienated, hostile public: By giving even the largest info-conglomerates a human face it promised to dispel cynicism and yet keep those mergers coming at the same time.

Even worse than that, though, by putting its seal of approval on the trademark innovations of chain journalism—polls, demographic surveys, focus groups, "town meetings"—public journalism essentially embraced the market as an inherently democratic arrangement. The key to solving journalism's problems, its leaders maintained, was to understand editing as customer service.

Unlike other forms of market populism, though, public journalism did not fetishize "revolution," "rebellion," or the "subverting" of "dominant paradigms." As these terms had a meaning that is all too real in the history of newspaper writing, public journalism steered well clear of them, opting instead for a determinedly middlebrow formula that promised to keep journalistic creativity on a short leash and to guard against any outbreak of the old muckraking impulse. This is no time for conflict, it insisted, for journalism that called fundamental economic principles into question: This is a time for the cessation of questioning. Public journalism had no place for the more aggressive public-mindedness of figures like Upton Sinclair or Lincoln Steffens—or even for the idea that social interests might be in fundamental conflict. What it required was a sort of unilateral cultural disarmament. So in a business that was always schizophrenic, a place both of angry outsiders and the arrogance of the state, of protests and of platitudes, of rebellion and reassurance, public journalism came down solidly on the side of the latter: it was business poet Eddie Guest over H. L. Mencken, Roger Rosenblatt over Murray Kempton.

I do not doubt the good intentions of the leading public journalists. They were sincerely concerned about democracy. And surely one must acknowledge that any number of efforts described as "public journalism" have enjoyed signal successes: the *Kansas City Star*'s 1995 series on urban sprawl, for example, was an outstanding example of critical, community-minded reporting. But consider how neatly public journalism's dreams of a new consensus dovetail with the other great journalistic movement of the nineties—the corporatization of the news. Although both movements came to their conclusions through different logical routes, both insisted on almost an identical bill of reforms. Newspapers would have to "listen" more to their audiences, preferably through the standard marketing devices of polls and focus groups. Newspapers would have to redefine their coverage by demographic and excise the odd voices of those with funny (usually anticorporate) ideas they had come up with on their own. It is no coincidence that the most prominent practitioner of public journalism in the nineties was Mark Willes, the CEO of Times Mirror and publisher of the *Los Angeles*

Times. In addition to hosting town meetings and coming up with various schemes for encouraging average people to read the newspaper, Willes shut down the excellent *New York Newsday* for less-than-convincing bottom-line reasons and tried to boost the *Times*'s profitability by blowing down the wall between advertising and editorial, thus paving the way for all manner of lucrative synergies. Profit and populism went hand in hand. And although Willes' project was badly discredited in October 1999, when it was revealed that the *Times* had split the profits generated by a special Sunday supplement with the corporation that was the subject of the supplement, others cautioned against judging the paper too harshly.[12] All the *Times* was doing was using the proven democratic machinery of marketing to let the people of Los Angeles see themselves in all their glorious peopleness. And please understand: Elitists aren't those who run the world; they're those who criticize the CEOs.

Tycoon on a Bus: The Practice

If the rage for public journalism can be understood as a contest to shout "The People, Yes!" louder than the next guy, then the newspapers produced by the Gannett Corporation must be understood as the least cynical and the most civic-minded of them all. Certainly the company has made remarkable claims along these lines. In 1996, Robert Giles, then editor and publisher of Gannett's *Detroit News* (today he edits the more thoughtful *Media Studies Journal*), offered this definition of what public journalism meant to him: "It is a way to keep the reader's voice in our minds. We are constantly meeting with our readers, conducting focus groups to discover not only what broad areas they are interested in but what specifically is on their minds, what they want us to engage. What is it they want their newspaper to do?"

What their newspaper was doing at the time, specifically, was teaching its union employees a thing or two about the new market order on the streets of Detroit and Sterling Heights, Michigan. One could hardly argue that the bitter, long-running Detroit newspaper strike was the will of the Detroit public. After all, circulation fell off by a third at the strike's height. But for Giles it was just another object lesson in the principles of public journalism. To counterbalance the fact that the mayor of Detroit, the archbishop of Detroit, assorted congressmen, and a wide range of other civic figures supported the strikers, Giles mused how newspaper management was acting in the spirit of Martin Luther King, since it was the party that was really confronting the "established order." Rolling out his most powerful of weapons, he even argued that to support the strike was an act of *cynicism*.[13]

Unless you happen to be a worker on the receiving end of its flexibility strategies, or a reporter at a newspaper that competes with one of its products, it is unlikely that you've ever thought too much about Gannett, the nation's largest newspaper chain and publisher of *USA Today*. So well-camouflaged a part of the American landscape are its various newspapers that Gannett sometimes seems virtually invisible. And yet Gannett is precisely where those concerned about the future of journalism should be looking. Not only has the fervent "love of public" imagined by the theorists of public journalism here been refined to perfection, but in Gannett's hands it has also become an ideology of corporate power. An empire of uplift, an autocracy of interactivity, Gannett has fashioned over the years a perfect synthesis of market populism and corporate predation.

When figures from across the journalistic profession denounced "cynicism" in the nineties, Gannett newspapers were most definitely not what they had in mind. Generally speaking, Gannett products are filled with wire-service feed, with items about celebrities and photos of animals, with helpful page-one stories about how to store coffee (spotted in the *Louisville Courier-Journal*) or about how to avoid getting hurt while riding escalators (*Des Moines Register*).

In fact, prominent Gannettoids, as the chain's executives are humorously known, anticipated the nineties rage against cynicism—and the tendency to conflate criticism with "elitism"—by many years. Al

Neuharth, the charismatic founder of *USA Today* and the company's public face through the eighties (today he writes a weekly column for the paper and presides over the Freedom Forum, the organization formerly known as the Gannett Foundation), may have been the first prominent newspaperman in the nation to identify and blast "cynicism" and "elitism" as the industry's greatest problems. He was fond of lambasting the noxious elites "east of the Hudson and east of the Potomac," those purveyors of "intellectual snobbery," "pompousness," and "arrogance" who "think their mission is to indict and convict, rather than inform and educate." But *USA Today,* which he founded in 1982, was to be the home of something new, a "Journalism of Hope," in Neuharth's famous phrase, an embodiment of the new populism's refusal to judge: "It doesn't dictate. We don't force unwanted objects down unwilling throats." Gannett newspapers don't startle, shock, or use long words and difficult concepts. They offer consumers a pleasant product that is remarkably consistent from place to place and that emphasizes reader interaction and "good news."[14]

Critical stories about Gannett are fairly rare in the national media; when they do happen to appear, they seem always to revert to the most simplistic of denunciations. The company's literary products are dismissed as lowest-common-denominator stuff; its executives are hooted for their boorish tastes and faintly creepy corporate conformity. But to read Gannett in such a reflexively contemptuous way is to dismiss its very real and very significant theoretical contributions to American culture. Whatever else one might say about it, *USA Today* is arguably the nation's most carefully edited and highly polished newspaper; the way it looks and reads is the result of years of refinement and planning. Certain of its executives may be louts, but from the invention of coverage-by-demographic to color in the masthead to the pseudo-interactive style, *USA Today* charted the course that almost every paper in the country would follow in the nineties. And, of course, Gannett had a hand in developing the theoretical side of the business as well: the Freedom Forum has built a museum of the newspaper, it sponsors panel discussions featuring many of the great thinkers of public journalism, and it publishes the *Media Studies Journal.* While Gannettoids were not prominent participants in the nineties circus of media contrition, they joined quite naturally in the chorus of accusation. Each successive disaster to befall the Washington press corps—chased from the field by *Brill's Content* or James Fallows, humiliated by Stephen Glass, routed convincingly in yet another of those poll-driven popularity contests— was a little victory for Gannett, whose once-derided stand against "cynicism" and "elitism" now seems to be vindicated by every new whipping administered to the more respectable news institutions. *USA Today,* in fact, even sometimes took the lead in denouncing the newly vulnerable "media elite," deriding the reporters one op-ed writer calls "brainiacs," lambasting the folks Neuharth calls the "would-be Woodwards and Bernsteins (who) came off college campuses," and who have now so shamed their profession through their ignoble desire "to get rich and famous."[15]

Such sanctimoniousness is perhaps the ideal introduction to the series of painless contradictions that make up Gannett's trademark sensibility. In fact, according to just about everyone who has ever written about the company, Gannett's curious journalistic style seems to have been consciously invented to permit an extraordinary level of profitability. Realizing early on that owning the franchise in a one-newspaper town could be remarkably lucrative, the company has, since its beginnings, sought, bought, or created monopolies across the country. Since the "journalism of hope" requires little more than press-release rewriting and virtually mandates favorable coverage of local businesses, it can be done both cheaply and with an eye to cultivating advertisers. Critical observers have noted how Gannett routinely slashes both news content and news gathering staff at papers it acquires; how it constantly shuffles its editors about the country, preventing them from developing an affinity with a particular community; how it uses its immense power as a conglomerate to smash whatever competitors it encounters and its power as a monopoly publisher in many towns to soak advertisers. Superstitious profit-legends dot the literature surrounding the company: the armored cars in which each small-town paper's take is believed to be hauled off to Gannett headquarters in Arlington, Virginia; the "dobermans" (ferocious publishing executives) who can be dispatched across the country to put troublesome competitors out of business. Neuharth himself refers in his memoirs to the company as "a nonstop money machine" and approvingly quotes Wall Street figures who call Gannett "virtually an unregulated monopoly" and who note that its "management lives, breathes, and sleeps profits and would trade profits over Pulitzer Prizes any day." Observers of the company marvel at its over-sumptuous offices and the money-burning antics of its upper management. And while family-owned newspapers are lucky to make a 10 percent profit in a good year, Gannett routinely squeezes close to 30 percent out of its properties.[16]

The primary casualties of Gannett's corporate culture war are the cities in which the company does business. Richard McCord made this point thoroughly in his 1996 book *The Chain Gang*, recalling town after town where Gannett's intervention resulted in ruthless down-dumbing and the silencing of independent editorial voices. "Instead of providing central leadership," McCord says, "they just try to gauge the community and deliver something that will pass, and can be put out on the cheap." Gannett's ownership of the *Des Moines Register* and the *Louisville Courier-Journal*, two once excellent state-oriented newspapers that the company bought in 1985, yielded immense profits but disaster for local readers as each paper has recast its focus from rural regions to affluent suburban areas. One longtime *Register* columnist now compares the newspaper to a dead relative; when another newspaper owned by the family that sold the *Register* to Gannett was recently put up for sale, rumors that Gannett had put in the winning bid caused "concerns that approached panic" in its newsroom. In Nashville, where Gannett owns the *Tennessean*, the company bought the rival paper, the *Banner*, for $65 million in 1998 simply to close it down. Oddly, in each city the changes have been described as "inevitable," as though the triumph of "the journalism of hope" and Gannett's peculiar marketing logic required no more explanation than that.[17]

Another consistent victim of Gannett strategy is organized labor, whose wage scales can impede the astronomical profits that the company demands. "Gannett is among the most anti-union companies that we deal with," Linda Foley, president of the Newspaper Guild, told me in 1998. "They just do not believe that their employees should have collective bargaining rights." One can detect traces of this attitude in *The Making of McPaper,* an early panegyric of *USA Today's* beginnings by its former editor-in-chief Peter Prichard, who consistently describes union workers as troublemaking thugs bent on keeping "The Nation's Newspaper" from reaching its adoring public. One can see it more clearly in the company's policy of excluding employees "covered by a collective bargaining agreement" (as its 1997 annual report, entitled "Listening . . . Leading," puts it) from participation in 401(k) plans. And it came into particularly sharp focus in Detroit, where Gannett acquired the *Detroit News,* promptly ended years of competition by arranging for a joint operating agreement with the rival newspaper, and then squared off against its union employees, with disastrous results for everyone concerned—especially readers.[18]

But the point isn't just that Gannett practices a singularly vicious form of profit-seeking; this has been thoroughly documented elsewhere over the years, most recently and most comprehensively by McCord. What is remarkable is that it does so under such a proud populist banner. The company has seamlessly welded populism and plunder, covered its rapacity with an Up With People exterior. It is a uniquely American hybrid of opposites, combining a self-effacing, all-inclusive, antielitist editorial style with a shamelessly self-aggrandizing corporate culture and the no-nonsense kicking of worker ass. And in doing so Gannett virtually personifies market populism. It is the characteristic organization of the American 1990s, a machine that doles out misery to some but fantastic rewards to stockholders and CEOs; that seeks only to reflect us in our triumphant averageness; that whoops it up for the common people with the most reverent sort of populist rhetoric but actually brings cultural degradation home to the towns in which it operates. If the public journalists, the management theorists, the union-busters, and the bull marketers get their way, Gannett is what every aspect of American life will look like before long.

Although Gannett made grandiose pronouncements about its dedication to public journalism in the nineties, that movement's leaders generally remained silent about the company. (Jay Rosen, to his credit, explicitly distanced himself from Gannett in his 1999 book, *What Are Journalists For?*)[19] Shameful episodes like the Detroit newspaper strike were probably the reason why. But perhaps there was a larger reason as well. Gannett, in its typically ham-handed way, made the convergence between journalistic populism and market forces far, far too obvious. The conglomerate's practices might have posed the thinkers with a trickier question: Why are foundation millions required to theorize and legitimate an operation that the most ruthlessly profit-minded managers have found quite useful all on their own?

USA Today, Gannett's most visible product, is explicitly aimed at an audience of transient businessmen, the reading material of choice as one jets from sales meeting to sales meeting. But in a mix-up that speaks volumes about American culture of the eighties and nineties, it successfully cast itself as nothing less than the People's Newspaper, the folksy small-town read for a folksy, small-town nation. From its colorful page-one polls to its frequent use of the editorial "we," populist pretensions were an essential element of the publication's style. *The Making of McPaper,* Prichard's account of the publication's founding, begins with the story of how Neuharth decided on the paper's first day of publication to forgo a complicated story about an assassination in Lebanon and emphasize instead the death of Grace Kelly, the original "people's princess," thereby demonstrating, in Prichard's words, that *"USA Today* would be edited . . . not for the nation's editors, but for the nation's readers." Charles Kuralt, the *volksgeist* shaman of the official media, provided further populist credentials in the book's foreword by describing a Norman Rockwell landscape of honest Western towns dotted with omnipresent *USA Today* vending machines, each one bearing a "four-section, four-color gift from Al Neuharth." So you don't miss the point, Kuralt runs through a list of picturesque locales where he has purchased the paper ("the Holiday Inn in Klamath Falls," "the 7–11 store in Great Bridge, Virginia," "the last bus stop before the road runs out at Homestead Valley, California") and even brings in former Kansas governor Alf Landon for a cameo.[20]

But Neuharth himself takes the prize for populist posturing. Virtually every account of his life and deeds dwells on his midwestern background, his impoverished boyhood in South Dakota, his early efforts at a sports paper in that state, and the way his humble origins reflected those of his employer (in its early days Gannett had been an exclusively small-town chain). In his bizarre 1989 memoir, *Confessions of an S.O.B.*, Neuharth again and again attacks the nation's leading papers for their cynicism and negativity, describing their coverage of events in foreign countries, their strongly held opinions, and even their clamoring after Pulitzer Prizes as badges of class. The *New York Times,* for example, is said to have suffered from "intellectual snobbery," and the *Washington Post* to exude an "aura of arrogance." Neuharth himself, meanwhile, "declared war on the good old boys in our business," "said 'no' to the status quo," and won the plaudits of none other than Carter confidant Bert Lance, who was trotted out to enthuse, "This here Gannett is an all-American company, an all-American company." This narrative of Neuharth's career as class war against the quality newspapers seems to be repeated whenever he comes up for discussion. *USA Today's* account of his retirement, for example, dutifully describes him as a "nemesis of the newspaper elite."[21]

This zaniest of the press lords' populist tendencies took on a demented stridency in 1987, when he set out on an elaborate national tour called BusCapade. Ostensibly inspired by his conviction that the "national media" had "too much of an East Coast perspective," Neuharth began his tour at the most middling place in the land (a town in Missouri that was then the demographic center of the country), declaring that "people hereabouts are proud of being more middlemost than most of us." In the months of BusCapading that followed, Neuharth narrated for *USA Today* readers his Kuraltian wanderings amongst the people—chin-chinning with lots of just-folks, holding

plenty of "town meetings," and conducting polls wherever he went—
and led readers toward that iridescent goal of public journalists everywhere: "Understanding. Of each other. All across the USA." What this
meant in practice was that Neuharth wrote an installment of his column, "Plain Talk," from every state, celebrating each one successively
in ever more passionate terms. Most of his BusCapade dispatches
were organized around some state motto or song or other almanac-level
fact whose profundity Neuharth would consider in his usual truncated
style. Maryland, for example, struck him as being the place where the
national anthem had been composed: "Folks in Maryland think that
very appropriate. They consider their state a miniature of the nation.
'American in miniature,' says a slogan." Virginia, he wrote, is both "for
lovers" and "the Mother of Presidents." In New Jersey, he observed
that "Nickname 'The Garden State' applies." Kansans were said to "like
it at home on the range. Seldom is heard a discouraging word." Throw
in an occasional stray cliché like "Olympic dreams," a softball interview
with a governor or two, and some stories about local entrepreneurs and
industries on the rebound, and you've just about got it.[22]

Neuharth's BusCapade exploits bring to mind the emptiest variety
of American political demagoguery—one thinks of Richard Nixon's
foolish promise to visit all fifty states during the 1960 campaign and of
Bill Clinton's own 1992 series of BusCapades. Not only did Neuharth
serve as Clinton's "informal bus consultant" on these, according to
Business Week, but he was perhaps the only national newspaper columnist to regard Clinton's stunts as expressions of genuine populist feeling, a point which, he insisted in *USA Today,* the "media effete don't
understand." One might also understand BusCapade as a long-delayed
answer to "These United States," the famous series of articles run by
The Nation in the twenties in which an all-star cast of intellectuals and
eggheads flayed each state in turn for being the home of dolts, bigots,
boobs, and philistines. (Also as a delayed riposte to Ken Kesey's famous
bit of bourgeoisie-annoying on wheels: The music Neuharth chose to
blare from his bus's loudspeakers was not loopy, irritating rock but uplifting state songs, one for each state.) BusCapade, in other words, was

not merely a costly bit of idiocy on wheels, it was also an ideological assertion of undeniable significance. While those "effetes" who question the workings of capitalism might sneer cynically at the common folk, Al Neuharth, an eighties tycoon of the most garish variety, was sitting down at his honest manual typewriter and banging out little anthems of uplift for each and every one of us. Unlike the cranky documentary projects of the thirties, always proving that the corporate order was failing the common man, Neuharth took a turn in the country to do exactly the opposite: celebrate success. "While the experts are wringing their hands about what's wrong," he wrote at the tour's beginning, "the people across the USA are using their hands, heads, and hearts to make it right." The center—the market—*can* hold.[23]

The high point of BusCapade, in both Neuharth's and Prichard's accounting, was the moment in which Neuharth himself, polling and town-halling his way across the country in a valiant battle against media cynicism, received the tidings of entrepreneurial victory. A telegram arrived announcing USA Today's first-ever month of profitability, by coincidence, just as the Bus was Capading through Al's home state of South Dakota. The achievement thus became something of a market populist miracle: Local boy borne home on clouds of money. One can imagine the scene, depicted in heroic oversize in the National Gallery: "Annunciation of Profits in the Heartland." That is, one could have imagined it, had Neuharth not announced in his *Confessions* that the whole thing was a setup, that he had arranged to have the telegram sent to himself. Strangely, the founder of USA Today didn't seem to think this revelation cast any shade on the event. But pity poor Peter Prichard, whose account of a few years before solemnly gave the magical version of the event, even reproducing the (staged) telegram of glory.[24]

Phony as it was, the incident helps us get at the meaning of the market populism typified by Neuharth, Gannett, and the larger theories of public journalism. It was a populism in which "the people" weren't so much the hero as they were a symbol, an ideological figurehead for the larger democracy of the market. Neuharth's constant attacks on the "media elite," for example, seemed always to come back to questions of market savvy, in particular the idea that snobs are, by definition, poor entrepreneurs—a notion he shared with George Gilder and bull-market populists like the authors of *The Millionaire Next Door.* The newspaper "elite never really considered me an insider," Neuharth remarked at one point, just before relating how the publisher of the hated *Washington Post,* arrogant to the core, once lost a bidding war against him by "thinking her insider club membership would protect her interests." Within pages Al was besting her in yet another takeover contest, this time because she has foolishly sent "Ivy League reporters to Iowa to report on the farm economy," and thus misjudges the true heartland worth of the *Des Moines Register.* Similarly, Al explains that he beat out the *New York Times* in another deal simply because that paper's publisher was "elitist to the end."[25]

So closely is the market connected to the common people for Neuharth that it hardly seems contradictory when he turns directly, as he so frequently does in his *Confessions,* from celebrating the plainspoken ways of the heartland to an almost pathological boasting about the perks of power. With a certain pride he recounts his loudest acts of conspicuous consumption, rattling off the once-impressive brand names—the Porsche sunglasses, the Gulfstream IV jet (with shower), the uniforms worn by the crew of said jet, the Cristal champagne, the "beachside chapel" in his yard where he gave thanks, the luxury hotel suites in which he did business. Nor does Neuharth's dedication to the people and the "Journalism of Hope" with which they prefer to be addressed prevent him from writing his memoir as a diary of corporate megalomania. Stories are constantly interrupted so Neuharth can give an account of how somebody praised him or how he burned someone. He begins almost every chapter with a quotation about himself. And through it all, the only overt explanation Neuharth offers for his doings is the down-home logic of "having fun," or, better yet, "having a helluva lot of fun."

Neuharth's writing sometimes seems almost comically self-debunking. But his ideas deserve to be taken seriously nevertheless. As with the public journalism people, Neuharth believed that the decline of the American newspaper was a parable of fundamental democratic virtues. Elitism was what was killing newspapers; getting in touch with the common people through polls, focus groups, and town-hall meetings was what would save them. But what is "elitism," exactly? For Neuharth, who seems to hear the vox populi even when riding in his corporate jet, the term had little to do with its traditional connotations of economic power. Elitism was a sin committed by authors, not by owners. Elitism was nothing less than critical thought, a failure to properly suspend judgment. Tellingly, the pitfalls of elitism is a lesson that Neuharth chooses to put in the mouth of none other than Lee Kuan Yew, the Singapore strongman who made public gum-chewing a felony: "The more you judge others by your own standards," this beacon of the General Will tells him, "the more you show total disregard for their circumstances."[26]

In Gannett-land this suspension of judgment is called "listening" to readers, refusing to "dictate" to them. It is accomplished through a number of devices that allow journalists to understand the community for which they write (it is evidently assumed that Gannett reporters will not be reporting on places they know intimately). Polls not only appear every day in each section of *USA Today*, but they seem to hold a hallowed place in company lore. Prichard recalls how Neuharth discovered polling back in the sixties; how he used it to launch a new newspaper in Florida; and, most significantly, how a batch of market research appeared at just the right moment in 1981 and put Neuharth's arguments for launching a new national newspaper over the top. By the late nineties the idea of polling as democracy was so familiar to readers of *USA Today* that one of the paper's regular features—"Ad Track," a series of studies revealing how "key target groups" feel about various TV commercials—actually seemed to define consumer activism as participating in a focus group, as thinking about how you might best be sold running shoes or fruit drinks.

"News 2000" was the name of Gannett's comprehensive program in the nineties for "tailoring the content" of a newspaper anywhere in the country with the help of polling and focus groups. It was a theoretical program as well, informed by a vision of the news crisis that directly links the company's market populism with anti-intellectualism. A primary factor in the long decline of American journalism, one News 2000 document asserted, was that "some newspapers grew increasingly out of touch with their communities." They became "arrogant." Tragically, they "operated 'inside-out' with staffers deciding what news and information was needed by their community, often without a good sense of the concerns of the many groups comprising the community." The solution: Use focus groups, surveys, and "trend watchers" to help the newspaper conform more closely to the wishes of the public. Only then, with "two-way communication between residents and readers," could the Gannettoid in question "empower residents to improve their lives" and "help to establish newspapers as a 'member of the family' in their communities."[27] The 1997 Gannett annual report further defines the qualities of the non-cynical, non-arrogant newspaper: "positive stories," "stories that tell how new developments in the community have a positive effect on citizens and profiles that tell how local business owners have overcome obstacles."* Reading through Gannett's vision of the community- and owner-affirming newspaper, one can't help but think of the sort of writing that it would prohibit. From William Lloyd Garrison to I. F. Stone, what few transcendent moments American journalism can boast have each arisen from vicious, even violent conflict between an "inside-out" writer and a furiously intolerant "community," usually a "community" made up of precisely those "local business owners" who Gannett designated as the beneficiaries of its brand of empowerment. One also thinks of public journalist Mark Willes, whose brand of civic service encompasses both unprecedented dedi-

---

*The *Cincinnati Enquirer*'s fairly ferocious 1998 attack on Chiquita (a company whose chairman, significantly, once attempted a hostile takeover of Gannett) would seem an exception to this rule, were it not for the singular abjectness of the apology to Chiquita that the paper ran shortly thereafter.

cation to profit and what amounts to a war on critical thought itself. Soon after making his decision to tear down the wall between editorial and business at the *Los Angeles Times,* Willes announced that in order to make female readers "feel like the paper's theirs" it needed to come up with stories that were "more emotional, more personal, less analytical." Wherever newspaper moguls talked populism and profits simultaneously, it seemed, the practical results took the same form: A sort of corporate relativism in which tenaciously held ideas were the greatest journalistic error of all.[28]

What must be kept constantly in mind while pondering Gannett's ideal of the hopeful, happy newspaper, though, is that all this democratic talk goes hand in hand with a particularly adamantine species of corporate practice. Needless to say, Gannett's way of doing business is absolutely and utterly nonnegotiable, as subject to the public will as the coming and going of cold fronts. (Nor does the company's penchant for "listening" include tolerance for criticism: the *Nashville Scene* reported in 1998 that Gannett editors in that city tried to prevent critic McCord from speaking at a meeting of Nashville's Society of Professional Journalists).[29] There is an important distinction, though, between Gannett's market populism and the more organic journalistic populism of decades past: If we learn anything from the literature surrounding *USA Today* it is that superhuman efforts, both intellectual and physical, were required to put this most inoffensive of newspapers over. We read about the deeds of Neuharth's handpicked team of "geniuses" charged with inventing this masterpiece of mediocrity, about the tweaking of the prototypes and the response from the focus groups, about Neuharth's dictatorial leadership style, about his close editing of the newspaper's stories, about the people who couldn't take the rigorous pace and gave up. What was described was not merely the launching of a national newspaper, but the heroic forging of a new corporate ideology by a man who is simultaneously hard as screws and soft as flan, absolutely determined, with a Calvinist inner fire, to be other-directed.

Pro Patria et Pro Gannett: The Monument

"Freedom of the press," goes the old leftist saying, "belongs to those who own one." It is a cynical adage, to be sure, the scoffing negation of *USA Today*'s cheery polls and Al Neuharth's tendency to refer to even the "biggest media companies" with the possessive pronoun "our." And, as with all the other bits of cynicism so deplored by recent critics of journalism, it can have no place in the aggressively public-minded age into which "our biggest media companies" are leading us.[30]

Stamping out this and any other suggestion that journalism, properly practiced, might be guided by interests other than "ours" was the noble charge taken up by the Newseum, a museum of journalism that opened in 1997 across the street from the glass towers of the Gannett/USA Today complex in Arlington, Virginia. This latest Neuharth project was built by the Freedom Forum, of which the great man is "Founder" and former chairman; some official documents also list Neuharth as the Newseum's "Founder" so there is no mistake, while the executive director of the complex was until recently none other than Neuharth hagiographer Peter Prichard. Promising to transform Neuharth's deeds into history, his strange ideas into wisdom for the ages, the Newseum is the sort of project that will probably someday be mandatory for retiring megalomaniacs.

In keeping with Neuharth's peculiarly populist notions of his own greatness, the Newseum has banished the elitist devices of the traditional museum, all the formal traces of the patriarchal, the pompous, the pontificating. Its curving, open-ceilinged halls are filled with working video equipment, interpreters for the deaf, and computer stations on which people can try their hands at reporting.

An introductory Newseum filmstrip declares: "We're all reporters, because each of us tells stories." Mastheads from our hometowns help situate us on the "News Globe"; headlines from our dates of birth tell us who we are. The press is your pal, we learn. The press is you. In fact, the press is your memory, your consciousness, your conscience. Screens scattered throughout the history exhibits remind us of those journalistic moments—almost all of them disasters of one sort or another—that are increasingly all we have in common as a nation. Here Walter Cronkite announces the death of JFK; there Frank Reynolds briefly loses his cool while announcing the shooting of Reagan; and over in a corner falls a little hailstorm of emotional news moments from more recent years: an endlessly repeating pitter-pat of "We interrupt this program" and announcements that "Princess Diana [pause] has died"; an exciting hijacking and Baby Jessica caught in a well; glimpses of parents realizing that their daughter has exploded with the space shuttle, of the screen going blank as Scuds fall on Tel Aviv.

Strangely, almost every one of these episodes ranks, for less ecstatic critics, among American journalism's all-time lows. But at the Newseum there is no sense of shame or even acknowledgment of such criticism. Quite the opposite: Here these poignant moments of reporter-audience closeness are presented as the crowning glories of a centuries-long struggle against tyranny. It's a tendency one notices again and again here. While the Newseum's facade is all open-ended and egalitarian, the handful of serious points it makes are drummed down in a style so Whiggishly presumptuous that one might as well be learning about the advance of empire or the conversion of savages. The "News History Gallery," the museum's serious (and at times impressive) collection of historical artifacts, is as bombastic a tale of Progress and its millionaire heroes as anything invented by the commissars in their heyday. Beginning from the earliest colonial publications and taking us through the rise of yellow journalism and the twentieth-century tabloids, the gallery deposits us neatly before the USA Today exhibit ("The Newspaper is Reinvented"), the story of the media conglomerates, and the endless loop of Jessica, Challenger, and [pause] Diana, a fabulous now in which the emotional needs of The People are seen to efficiently. Just ahead lies "interactivity," the cultural-democratic New Jerusalem where authorial voice is finally dissolved in the ecstatic communion of journalist and audience. Pulitzer, Hearst, Neuharth, You.

Assuming you are among that vast majority of Americans who regard journalists with contempt, and can therefore see right through such stuff, the Newseum has an even more compelling narrative to offer: The heroic tale of the press as selfless champion of democracy, as an ever-advancing libertarian tide whose flow cannot be impeded and whose every move is a step forward for We the People. "Information is where liberty starts," intones the narrator of the introductory filmstrip, and the theme continues as one follows the glorious march of historical progress. Tyrants try to suppress press; but press suppresses tyrants. The invention of the moving-picture camera, for example, brings forth this astonishingly counterfactual remark: "The citizens now know they have a powerful ally in the hunt for the truth." But in the hands of the Newseum's curators, obviously concerned to make the point about the goodness of journalists as hard to miss as possible, the story rapidly descends from the enlightening—there is actually an exhibit on W. E. B. Du Bois' magazine *The Crisis*—to a mawkish obsession with the persecution of journalists, as though that alone were enough to establish their essential decency. A rather irrelevant quotation in which Thomas Jefferson mentions both "freedom of the press" and "martyrdom" appears on pamphlets and an outside wall. Scenes of Dan Rather in China are accompanied by the solemn observation that "reporters have been censored, jailed, sometimes killed for doing their job." One exhibit lingers libidinally over the physical dangers faced by reporters during the Gulf War (presumably as they were shuttled around in one of those closely chaperoned army pools).

Those who still doubt the democratic commitment of the press can visit Freedom Park, a collection of weatherproof souvenirs of The Struggle mounted next to a sidewalk outside: One relic each from the fights for women's suffrage, civil rights, and the battles against Nazis and apartheid, and no fewer than three from the war against Communism. None of them have much to do with journalism, of course, but T-shirts depicting the inspiring objects can be purchased in the Newseum store, along with copies of Al Neuharth's memoir, still clean and full-priced although published years before and readily available in thrift stores nationwide.

Whenever a Fortune 500 company (or its prodigal philanthropic stepchild) takes up public moaning about persecution, one is permitted a little skepticism. And the Newseum's historiography is suspicious stuff indeed, oblivious to vast regions of the American experience even as it goes out of its way to hail the achievements of just about every approved social or political struggle. As told by the News History Gallery, the march of liberty includes feminism and the civil rights movement, the fights against Hitler and Communism, dozens of individual battles against racism and sexism, and victory after victory for champions of free speech. It makes no mention—none—of the fight for the eight-hour day and for the right of workers to unionize, of the other various reforms won by labor in the course of the century, or of which side "our" friendly "media companies" were on in those struggles. And the closer one looks the more apparent this erasure becomes: William Allen White is lauded for opposing the Klan and for supporting free speech, but his Progressivism somehow never comes up. *The Masses* makes it into the museum because it was "banned from the mail for opposing U.S. participation in World War I," but the logic of its opposition is not discussed. The Newspaper Guild, which represents reporters and editors at any number of American newspapers, is mentioned only in a short bio of its founder, the popular columnist Heywood Broun. And "working class" is used almost exclusively as a demographic notation, as in its "relish" for tabloids and affinity for certain Hearst columnists.

The Newseum's consistent evasion of class is part of a more sinister reticence about the seamier side of the trade. The chronic journalistic problem of keeping editorial separate from business, easily the biggest journalistic issue in the nineties, is mentioned nowhere. The Ethics Center, where one may grapple with "the difficult choices faced by journalists every day" (typical dilemma: how to cover a wheelchair-bound president), fails to discuss how one might deal with the misdeeds of a local business that advertises in your paper. Even the exhibit on conglomerates, while acknowledging that the giant media companies have been criticized, invokes the tired The Press vs. Tyranny canard in this remarkable bit of casuistry: "Executives say the size of their corporations helps them stand up to governments that would control news." It's a view of liberty that consistently understands "freedom" as a thing wrung from an inherently repressive state by inherently liberating media corporations: That liberty might have an economic dimension, that the corporations themselves might sometimes be repressive and the state liberating is simply left out, as though contrary to the physical laws of the universe.

But then the goal here is hardly to mount a complex analysis of society. Like other Washington edifices, the Newseum is an exercise in patriotic instruction, an easily absorbed lesson in Why We're So Darn Good. The point isn't to condemn the state on a specific list of charges, but to drive home the underlying principle of recent press theory: We, too, are the state. You may despise us, and we may even be slipping into obsolescence, but the checking and balancing of the news media are as critical to the preserving of nice moderate moderation as are all those other purveyors of museums—from the U.S. Postal Service to the Supreme Court—on the other side of the Potomac.

Other troubled industries have also confronted their persecutors by symbolically comparing themselves to the state, but one exhibit at the Newseum manages to top them all in its desperate bid for gravitas. On a gray concrete bridge between the Newseum and the USA Today building stands the Journalists Memorial, a steel-and-glass monument to newspapermen, cameramen, and TV announcers killed in the line of duty. Like the Vietnam Memorial on the National Mall, its centerpiece is a bogglingly comprehensive tally of inscribed names, the sheer number of dead journalists impressing visitors with the magnitude of the Fourth Estate's sacrifices. Otherwise, though, it is the Vietnam Memorial's opposite: Colorful and fully above-ground rather than pitch-black and sunken, it immediately calls to mind the curiously durable inverse relationship, in public opinion, between the military and the press since the publication of the Pentagon Papers—or since the moment cynical newspaperman David Janssen dared to question John Wayne's war in *The Green Berets*.

Today, of course, the tables are turned: As Al Neuharth pointed out in a 1998 column, journalists are hated now while soldiers—always imagined these days as a cross between Schwarzeneggerian powerboys and victimized subalterns, kicking ass with a tear in their eye—are revered. Maybe Al came up with the idea for the Journalists Memorial (it certainly bears all the earmarks of a Neuharth project) in a poll-inspired epiphany, after poring one long, grim night over the figures that revealed how right-thinking Americans now hold not the long-suffering Nam vet but the reviled newsman responsible for losing that fine war—and maybe the idea of building the Cenotaph of the Fallen Scribe just flashed through his mind, like all his other bits of monumental aggrandizement must have done: the plan for the cross-country bus ride, the discovery that he needed to hire his own pollster, the stratagem by which he got astronaut Alan Shepard to take a copy of a Gannett newspaper to the moon, or the inspired decision to enclose with each copy of his *Confessions* a campaign-style button bearing his smiling visage and announcing both that you love *and* hate that darn SOB.

The Journalists Memorial also calls to mind the Tribune Tower in Chicago, where chunks of stone from other world-class piles (the Great Pyramid, the Taj Mahal, the Great Wall of China) stud its fake-Gothic facade and lend world-classness to a publication that, in Colonel McCormick's heyday, broke all existing records for abusive boorishness. The masters of *USA Today,* of course, are press lords of a different kind; they preside over a whirling interactive democracy in which The People have long since dispensed with the monoliths of high culture, and their symbolic needs are understandably different than those of the World's Greatest Newspaper. The Gannettoids don't need reminders of Glorious Pastness to sanctify their mission, but a colossal list of names, of martyrs from different faiths, countries, and centuries, all of them rounded up and plunked down a few steps in front of the USA Today building, as though this were it, as though 30 percent profits, full-color weather maps, a union-free workplace, and nationwide access to the staccato banalities of Al Neuharth were the great causes for which each of them died.

While examining the Journalists Memorial, I try to imagine what goes on here during the day, how the prosperous Gannettoids who inhabit these buildings must come out on this bridge to eat their lunches, how they must sit here next to this monument to the fallen and chew their focaccio and envy each other's company rings and cellphones and subtly rolled collars . . . and then it occurs to me: *It is day.* And yet there is nobody here. The sky is gray. The street is gray. The building housing the Newseum is gray. No pedestrians walk the streets; no faces peer out from behind the mirrored glass windows of the surrounding office blocks. So fabricated is the landscape that one can't even be sure when, exactly, one stands on terra firma: The people who do occasionally appear walk back and forth on enclosed pedestrian bridges where their tasseled loafers never encounter the elements; cars creep sporadically in and out of concealed underground parking garages; nearby a concrete church is built over a concrete filling station; and just a few blocks down from the Newseum lurks what must be the world's only underground Safeway, hewn from the solid concrete, its only entrance emptying into yet another parking garage.

It is a curious place for the nation's only monument to journalism's fallen. Why not New York or Chicago, where the frenzied babel of daily journalism gave rise to what little literature we have managed to produce; or at least Detroit, where one of the last great newspaper wars raged until none other than Gannett entered the scene and turned the war on the workers instead? How did it come to pass that this city— whose journalistic contributions have ranged from apologias for the exercise of imperial power to the invention of imaginary causes with which to tweak the middle Americans of the hinterland—is permitted to lay claim to the names of Elijah Lovejoy and Ernie Pyle? Maybe, though, the Journalists Memorial is less a monument than a funeral pyre, a symbolic flame of pink- and orange-colored glass wherein all those dead journalists, those prairie crusaders and abolitionist Jeremiahs, burn now for *USA Today.* Maybe Arlington is where journalism has come to die, in a place as distant as could be found from the urban maelstrom and the rural anger that once nourished it, within easy reach of the caves of state, sunk deep in the pockets of corporate power, here where busloads of glassy-eyed, well-dressed high schoolers from the affluent suburbs of northern Virginia can play anchorman on its grave.

To the Dot-Com Station

Whatever can be done, will be done.
If not by incumbents, it will be done by emerging players.
If not in a regulated industry, it will be done in a new industry born without regulation.
Technological change and its effects are inevitable.
Stopping them is not an option.   —*Andy Grove of Intel[1]*

One is tempted to add, "resistance is futile."
—Kevin Kelly, 1998[2]

The Wages of Reaction

If it was a bad decade for journalistic "adversarialism," the nineties were disastrous for more specifically critical traditions. Journalists learned to "listen" while intellectuals of all kinds were advised to let go the stubborn egotism of ideas and feel the market pulsate through them. Americans were warned that badmouthing the market—loose lips sink stocks!—could very well bring on crash, disaster, war. They were informed that the accumulated economic knowledge of the centuries, along with all our ideas about what democracy looked like, were as nothing to the "New Economy." And, as if to give concrete form to the market's hostility to ideas, the crisis in academic labor shredded the aspirations of an entire generation of young scholars.

But while it was bucket-kicking time for some ideas, it was a seller's market for others. If you were the lucky proprietor of a quirky new intellectual technique for reaching the decade's favorite ideological conclusion—that the market was the highest and the greatest and the most enviable form of human organization—then it was a great time to be in the intellectual business. The bookstores and the magazines blossomed with zany new meta-theories, each one purporting to explain how all of human history merely led up to the victory of the free-market "New Economy" over the government-laden old. George Gilder profited by describing class conflict as the battle between new money and old while Tyler Cowen divided us all up into cultural pessimists and cultural optimists.

But in this glamorous new marketplace of bad ideas, few could match the achievement of Virginia Postrel, editor of the libertarian magazine *Reason* and a contributor to *Forbes ASAP*. Hers was the provocative thesis that the great, transhistorical conflict of Business Man with his traditional enemies—critics and government regulators (she made almost no mention of labor unions, a fairly common oversight by 1998)—was in fact a titanic battle between "dynamists" and "stasists," between those who believe in the people and will let them do whatever they want (provided they do it through the market and with duly signed contracts); and those who think they know better and who thus favor a world ordered by technocrats. At least, that's how Postrel tells it. But so lopsidedly does she heap praise on her "dynamists" and shower abuse on her "stasists" that one feels they might more appropriately be labeled "saints" and "the worst assholes ever." The motley assortment of blowhard politicians, environmentalists, and griping naysayers who make up the "stasist" camp are not only elitists in the usual market-populist sense (they believe in expertise, they're skeptical of the market, and hence they're hostile to the tastes and preferences of the people), but they seem to have profoundly evil designs on the world. Postrel charges them with despising beach volleyball and with secretly wishing to "forever yoke the world's peasants behind a water buffalo." The stasist rogues gallery, it turns out, contains a truly astonishing assortment of hate-figures: Ur-regulator Louis

Brandeis, there for his sins against the railroads, is joined bizarrely with the southerners who passed Jim Crow laws. They are teamed up with the Unabomber, Jean-Marie Le Pen, the French in general, Robert Moses, and the grasping, ill-clad hairdressing regulators of New York State who so persecuted Vidal Sassoon back in the sixties. Pol Pot, making a cameo appearance as the greatest "stasist" of them all, is said to differ from other members of that monstrous fraternity—like the meddling legislators who passed affirmative action and who are mentioned a few sentences later—only in degree.[3] It is a scheme for understanding history so daft it's worthy of John Perry Barlow himself.

But Postrel's object isn't to understand the subtleties of history. Nor is it really to equate business with democracy, although that is, of course, an important theme. Her goal is to lay claim to the one idea that Americans hold in even higher esteem than democracy itself: the future. "The central question of our time," she writes, "is what to do about the future." Should we take the route of the fiendish "stasists," with their government regulation, their lousy clothes, and their killing fields? Or should we follow the "dynamists," those true believers in human promise? (who turn out when Postrel names them mainly to be captains of industry, management theorists, and Republican politicians.) The decision is easy to make; in fact, it's been made for us. We *can't* follow the "stasists" to the future, because by definition *that's not where they are going*. Since "the future" and "free markets" are essentially the same thing, to wish to restrain the latter is to set oneself fully against the former. "Stasists" are thus, in addition to all their other crimes, "enemies of the future."[4]

Readers who are put off by such casual slinging of Stalinoid accusation should know that Postrel's 1998 book, *The Future and Its Enemies* (for that was its title as well as its signature idea), was highly acclaimed by thinkers like Tom Peters and James Glassman, who would soon distinguish himself with *Dow 36,000*. It even earned Postrel a gig as an occasional columnist for the business section of the *New York Times*. Few in those exalted circles found it unseemly to hear a colleague arraign critics of business as "enemies of the future." By

1998 this was a style of accusation and of analysis that friends of the "New Economy" found perfectly comfortable, if not reassuring. That markets had a special connection to "the future" just as they did to "the People" was, if not a universal given of the late nineties, a proud conviction of the true believers.

Zeitgeist and Weltgeist

Usually this connection between the market and the future was explained by business thinkers in the language of technological and demographic determinism: The triumph of markets over everything else was not only democratic, it was "inevitable" because computers were growing faster and cheaper, because bandwidth was doing its miraculous tricks, because the kids just wouldn't stand for it, because globalization was so overwhelmingly, unthinkably, authoritatively global. That determinism of any kind flatly contradicted the everyone-will-be-free promise of the Internet and of market populism generally seems to have bothered no one. In fact, the two ideas were often connected rhetorically, in a kind of good cop/bad cop routine: The market will give you a voice, empower you to do whatever you want to do—and if you have any doubts about that, then the market will crush you and everything you've ever known.

In the "grand argument" in which business literature imagines itself engaged, "inevitability" served as a sort of logical atom bomb to be dropped on foes like unions, liberals, and environmentalists when conventional talk of "democracy" failed. It was a technique for putting over a backward social system through simple cocksureness about the future, a rhetorical maneuver we haven't seen so much of on these shores since the heyday of thirties-style Marxism and the appearance on bestseller lists of John Strachey's *The Coming Struggle for Power*.[5]

The tactic grew increasingly common toward the end of the decade. When economist Lester Thurow ran into narrative problems in his 1999 work of "New Economy" evangelism, *Building WEALTH,* he simply escalated right away up to "inevitability." Regardless of what you may think about genetic engineering, for example, it will "inevitably" triumph over its doubters; whatever reservations you might have about billionaire proliferation, "trying to defend" old standards of income equality "is impossible"; whatever those Europeans might think they're up to, they "will have to adjust to the realities of a global economy," as "wishing for a different game is a waste of time."[6]

Thus Thomas Friedman imagined the secretary of the treasury whipping it out to bring the prime minister of Malaysia back into line ("Ah, excuse me, Mahathir, but what planet are you living on? . . . Globalization isn't a choice. It's a reality.") and fantasizes how political systems the world over will be transformed by means of a "golden straitjacket" into replicas of our own.[7]

Thus the first sentence in Kevin Kelly's 1998 book, *New Rules for the New Economy*: "No one can escape the transforming fire of machines." The point of the book is that we must act at once to remake the world in the image of the Internet, but it's probably better to read it as a primer on the dark science of passing off really bad ideas—bad ideas that nevertheless happen to be making all your friends really rich— through mystification, superstition, and panic. "The net is our future," Kelly writes, "the net is moving irreversibly to include everything of the world," and, finally, this imperative: "Side with the net." That is, unless you fancy being run over by the freight train of history.[8]

To discover the origins of this strategy, though, we must turn again to George Gilder, fully transformed by the late nineties from griping backlasher into "radical technotheorist." Although Gilder bears much responsibility for launching the market-populist project, he also seems never really to have believed in its power to put laissez-faire across all by itself. Something much more intimidating would be required to suppress the liberal impulse, and all the way back in 1989 he set about finding it. So even as he was discovering that the microchip endorsed by its very architecture the class politics of the entrepreneur, he was also finding that the microchip revealed to mankind a number of new *laws of the universe*. In the mid-eighties Gilder had written that entrepreneurs "know the rules of the world and the laws of God"; by 1989 the entrepreneurs were writing the laws themselves, revealing them to the world through their intermediary, the Moses of the Microchip, descended from the heights of Sand Hill Road: "Moore's Law," "Metcalfe's Law," Gilder's own "Law of the Microcosm," and the awe-inducing "Law of the Telecosm," all of them as unrepealable as the old laws of gravity and of diminishing return.[9]

New laws of nature—*that specifically affirmed the politics of Gilder's beloved entrepreneur!* Now here was an idea to conjure with. Gilder could now simply inform us that we had either to bow to the free-market way or die. Not because he was still hostile toward those who doubted the market—good gracious, no!—but because there was simply no power on earth that could prevent the microchip from realizing its colossal market-populist ambitions. What Gilder called the "microcosm" was thus a foolproof device (literary if not factual) by which the imperatives of the free market could be made to triumph over all the peoples and all the ideas of the world. *Inevitably, inexorably, remorselessly, universally.* "The laws of the microcosm are so powerful and fundamental that they restructure nearly everything else around them," he wrote. And again: "However slowly theory catches up to practice, the microcosm will increasingly dominate international reality, subduing all economic and political organizations to its logic."[10]

But "subduing all economic and political organizations" wasn't enough for Gilder. Finally throwing caution to the wind he went all the way: "The logic of the microcosm" was becoming the very *"logic of history,"* getting set to deliver all of mankind to that luminous reverse communism in the sky where the state really does wither away and the dreams of the heroic soda pop bottlers and real estate operators who inhabited Gilder's earlier books would come true at last. *Inevitably* would the meddling feds lose control. *Inevitably* would labor unions decline into irrelevance. And *inevitably* would all the vaunted forms and receipts and regulations of the bureaucrat crumble like so much soggy paper.[11] Those who humbly imbibed the wisdom of the market profited immensely; those who arrogantly defied it declined in a slow death spiral that was encoded in the very weft of nature.

"These are not mere prophecies," the ever-humble Gilder wrote. "They are the imperious facts of life." Equipped with the microchip the capitalist is "no longer entangled in territory, no longer manacled to land, capital, or nationality."[12] The chosen of history but also free of history, free of corporeality, he is free of the laws of man and nature. He is pure idea, pure spirit, a god in his own right.

From New Times to New Economy

In Britain, where the "New Economy" was embraced in the late nineties as the miracle-worker that would snap the country out of its long decline, "inevitability" was put to much more rigorous uses. At the London think tank Demos, the thought of Gilder, Tom Peters, and Kevin Kelly was spun into the finest gold of "New Labour" industrial policy. For all its commitment to the Silicon Valley way, though, Demos was the kind of organization that would probably send old Gilder into a red-seeing rage. Martin Jacques, who helped to found the think tank in 1993, was an editor of both the Communist Party magazine *Marxism Today* and the 1989 *New Times* collection of essays that foreshadowed the periodical's termination. Geoff Mulgan, a writer who came with him from *Marxism Today,* served as director of Demos until 1998, when he began working for the prime minister. Charles Leadbeater, who contributed to both *New Times* and *Marxism Today,* is its reigning deep thinker, producing practical-looking policy booklets whose titles seem to return again and again to a mystic link between entrepreneurship and national identity (*Civic Entrepreneurship, The Rise of the Social Entrepreneur, The Independents: Britain's New Cultural Entrepreneurs,* and *Britain: The California of Europe?*). Both Mulgan and Leadbeater wrote much-celebrated works on the standard "New Economy" themes; Mulgan's book *Connexity* was published in the US by the Harvard Business School Press in 1998, while Leadbeater's book *Living on Thin Air* came out in Britain in 1999. The two men were very much the intellectuals of the "New Labour" moment: Demos held seminars at Downing Street, Mulgan became a member of Blair's "policy unit," and Leadbeater, who was once rumored to be the prime minister's very favorite political thinker, boasted blurbs from Blair as well as Peter Mandelson, the New Labour spinmeister, on the dust jacket of his book.

When I was a student the *New Times* group was a theoretical force to be reckoned with; their 1989 anthology was the product of a scholarly sophistication far beyond the ken of a midwestern kid like myself. And the various Demos publications initially inspired the same feeling of awestruck inadequacy. Again the authors spoke with an authority that seemed to arise from intimate familiarity with the massive, overwhelming forces that are remaking our world and determining our fates. The favorite label in the nineties, "New Economy," was slightly more specific than the older "New Times," and the grand historical themes which the Demos writers summon up—entrepreneurship, technology, and the market—were quite different from the big picture of 1989. Instead of Marx's dialectic they now had Moore's Law.

The head-swimming effect was the same as ever, though, with the Demos gang nimbly condemning "the conventions, laws, codes, and organizations we have inherited from industrial society" and tossing about the usual end-of-everything-you've-ever-known concepts like "the knowledge economy" and "weightless work." The reader reeled before the array of outrageous facts that were rattled off to show the obsolescence of the material world: The stock market valuation of Microsoft, the number of computers in a car, Nike's massive subcontracting network (*they don't make the shoes themselves!*). The "old economy" was not only "old," it was as dead and gone and forgotten and irrelevant as the five-year plans of the thirties. We can never go back.[13]

But if you read far enough into the works of Demos, you would discover that what the authors had actually done was simply round up various clichés from popular management literature and, adopting a tone of extreme historical righteousness, recast them as political advice. It was all there: The flattened, antihierarchical corporation as the way of the future, attacks on Taylorism, breathless praise for the "learning organization," the magic of "networks," even talk about "free agents." "Branding" emerged as the weightiest concept of all, the Demos solution to nearly everything that ailed Britain. Branding was what would survive as material industry dissolved into insignificance in the "weightless" years to come, they argued; branding was what justified companies' bizarre stock market valuations; branding was now something of a science; and what's more, building brands just happened to be what the British people were good at! In 1997, Demos actually suggested that the UK "rebrand" itself, purposely set about altering the world's perception of the country the same way that, say, Oldsmobile has tried to shake off its association with wealthy oldsters.[14]

Unfortunately, mixing high state seriousness with the inanity of management literature sometimes yielded some pretty stupid stuff. In *Living on Thin Air*, Leadbeater illustrated certain aspects of the rise of the "New Economy"—speedy entrepreneurs vs. slow moving big companies; cool brands vs. square brands—by comparing them to Princess Diana's struggle with the royal family and then taking an entire chapter to work out every absurd angle of this preposterous analogy. In a 1999 policy pamphlet titled *The Independents,* Leadbeater and a coauthor wrote a document that could easily pass as a parody of misguided think-tankery: Noting how important young creative rebels were to the British economy—the British music industry alone, another pamphlet noted, was the country's "strongest export sector"—they soberly, seriously, judiciously laid out a program by which cities could plan and develop thriving urban bohemias, "rebranding" themselves in an attractive manner and replacing dying heavy industry with colonies of profitable nonconformists. As if this spectacle of authorized dissidence and scientifically validated government schemes to promote "innovation in pop music" weren't enough, the pamphlet ended by soberly reporting a truly world-class bit of market idiocy: Like American towns bidding for a peripatetic NFL franchise, one dying Midlands city was finding its efforts to attract bohemians to its run-down former industrial district undermined by the even more aggressive boho-policies of *another* dying Midlands city only forty miles away![15]

In America, when leftists change sides and come around to the virtues of the business civilization, it is a privileged moment, a political set piece of great symbolic significance. Not only do we reward leftist apostates such as Whittaker Chambers and David Horowitz with undying literary fame or lifelong ideological sinecures, but we find in their movement from left to right an especially satisfying confirmation of the goodness of the corporate order. Having fought the market on behalf of the common people, on behalf of the workers, on behalf of equality, they now constitute living proof that the market is the true and correct protector of those noble causes. Their enthusiasm for capitalism is thus a special enthusiasm, an enthusiasm that somehow ranks above that of the poolside loungers at the country club or the traders in the Merc's pork-belly pit.

Demos offered a curious twist on this classic narrative. What they brought to the market wasn't so much the blessing of the workers, or even the sacred cause of equality, but the aura of "radicalism" itself. The value of this was obvious in a commercial climate like that of the nineties, when "radical," "subversive," and "extreme" were terms of approbation in everyday commercial use. Just as Diana was a different sort of royal than the queen, it was a different thing entirely when "radicals" approved of the market system than when Tories did. Demos's affirmations were worth something because Demos was cool. The Demos people wanted to build bohemia, not tear it down out of some misguided dedication to "tradition." They liked rock bands, they referred casually to rave scenes, they knew in which neighborhoods and even in which bars the cool people of Glasgow, Sheffield, and Manchester could be found. It was never very convincing when Tories talked about the creativity required for entrepreneurship; it was considerably more so when former leftist Leadbeater called for a "constitution which encourages experimentation, diversity, and dissent."[16] And it was infinitely more credible when a genuine revolutionary saluted the "revolutionary business model" of the hot advertising agency du jour than when *Advertising Age* did the same.

But it was in the eternal battle to uphold the truths of the market order that Demos really shone. While the world's telecom firms, software makers, and online brokerages fought an ideological bidding war, each one striving to top the others' association of the market with freedom, with democracy, Demos provided the theoretical ammunition. The democracy of markets was a fantasy that Mulgan, in particular, proved skillful in affirming. Writing in his book *Connexity,* he discredited the various traditional bête noirs of the business class—taxation and government economic planning—by linking them (and quite wrongly, especially in the American case) to "the era of absolute monarchy." He blamed not overweening, overpolluting, lying corporations for the vast tide of popular disaffection one found both in the UK and the US, but instead what he called "governmental hubris"—the bureaucrat's fatal impulse to fix everything. And he informed readers that "the upper classes in England resisted the telephone," thereby setting up communications technology as an automatic subverter of the power of "elites."[17]

Ah, but the Internet-empowered world of "connexity": Here was a place, Mulgan believed, where those hated "absolute hierarchies of culture" disappeared along with the "automatic respect" once paid to political leaders and aristocrats. Here was a land where the leftist dreams of yore were being swiftly accomplished, where new means of communication "liberate people from the bonds of settled agriculture and industry." In fact, so democratic were the market forces that gave us this wondrous "connexity" that Mulgan found it useful to reverse the traditional comparison: Electoral democracy was only democratic insofar as it operated according to the market principles of choice and competition.[18] (According to those standards, ironically, New Labour's much celebrated rapprochement with the market, as well as Clinton's "triangulations," could be understood as offenses against democracy itself, since they essentially deprived voters of any real political choice.)

Demos's greatest contributions were its thoughts on inevitability. Columnist Nick Cohen, who had some experience with the Demos crowd when they were briefly in charge of editing *The Independent* newspaper, recounts that "Leadbeater and the rest had lost their faith in socialism, but in their conversation you could still hear the sharp accents of Marxist teleology. . . ."

History was moving down the tracks; questioning the inevitable was pointless. After being given a long lecture in this vein, an old hand staggered out of an editorial conference. "These people used to go to Moscow and say, 'I've seen the future—and It Works!'" he bellowed. "Now they go to Singapore and cry: 'I've seen the future—and Gosh!'"[19]

Even in their dry policy booklets a tone of historical smugness seemed to be the Demos house literary conceit: Anthologies bore titles like *Tomorrow's Politics* and *Life After Politics;* blurbs asserted that "to read Mulgan is to read the future"; authors tended to slip nonchalantly into the future tense, to reason that, as "the future" will be requiring X, we'd better be doing Y in order to prepare. For Leadbeater, especially, all arguments about globalization and markets boiled down to questions of being in synch with our historical epoch. He began *Living on Thin Air* by warning that "we are on the verge of the global twenty-first century knowledge economy, yet we rely on national institutions inherited from the nineteenth-century industrial economy"; he made its narrative go by giving us hints of "what the knowledge-creating company of the future will look like." Strangely, Leadbeater also believed that the heroic entrepreneurs who populated his works shared his ability to predict the future. Thus he attributed the success of the great Bill Gates to his powers of "pre-cognition," his ability "to discern the emerging shape of competition . . . before everyone else."[20] It was as though the sage of Seattle had been by his side all along, from the days of *New Times* even, marching with the People as they advanced to meet their Future.

Looking back after ten years at the *New Times* anthology with which all this began, what impresses one most is the then-Marxist authors' powerful need to define the historical "epoch" that the Western world was then entering. In the book's introduction a name for the big change is suggested (the world was moving from "Fordism" to "post-Fordism") and leftists were warned of the dangers of being "overtaken by history." A "Manifesto for New Times" further noted that new ideas were necessary because "socialism has always claimed to speak for the future." Before it was anything else, according to this view, socialism was the custodian of historical periodicity, the movement responsible for understanding where we were going and what would have to be done when we arrived.[21]

Reading through the Demos books one can't help but marvel at the grip that historical determinism still held on the authors, even after its political polarities had been reversed. For Leadbeater and Mulgan, at least, it seemed to have drowned out every other consideration, every other value. They dumped the once-beloved working class, for example, like so much industrial slag, opting instead to cheer for the "cultural entrepreneurs." Does Marxism, like Jesuitism, leave its imprint on the soul even after apostasy?

Maybe, but a more likely explanation of the Demos shift is the same "New Economy" magnetism that sparked a brain drain in the world's consultancies and a gold rush in Silicon Valley, that sent everyone with even modest bullshit-slinging skills west to take their shot—any kind of shot—at that magic options/IPO combination. Forget the proletariat, forget the dialectic: Think NASDAQ. The only power worth considering in the world of the late nineties was the size of the rewards being handed out to the "New Economy" winners—the McMansions, the overnight 200 percent gains, the seven-figure bonuses. And the people from Demos were simply doing what they could—give 'em democracy! give 'em inevitability!—to ensure that the IPO Santa Claus made a stop in their country as well. For these were prizes for which we would gladly surrender anything, sink seventy years of social advance, lock up two million of our fellow citizens, send our heavy industry up in flames, *anything—just to keep that ticker spiking upward.*

The Pump and Dump Future

What does a capitalist ideologue do when she finds herself, by some twist of fate, driving the train of history? For some it is just another way to win that "grand argument" discussed in chapter 1. Virginia Postrel, who apparently can sometimes pick out "enemies of the future" by their personality type alone,[22] doesn't do so in order to hustle us (for I am named as one of those "enemies") off to reeducation camps, where we might be made more amenable to "plenitude," to beach volleyball, to popular music, and to the wacky "fun" enjoyed so abundantly in the office complexes of Silicon Valley. The point is, rather, to use "the future" as another weapon to pummel critics—costly, troublemaking critics—in the here and now.[23] For all Postrel's erudition, her writing sometimes reads less like a serious theory of politics than an extended new-business presentation to the nation's industrialists: These are the tools I can deploy on your behalf. With just a few references to "elitism," "the future," and the grand tale of "progress," we can put those dirty regulators and nasty critics back in their place.

But leave that battle to the true believers. Most readers of business literature just want to get rich. For them knowledge of the future is valuable only insofar as the seer can use it to make miraculous investments—the same golden promise that drives the plot of Hollywood movies dealing with time travel. And this is where capitalist inevitability has done its finest service, keeping the brokers busy and the mutual fund money flowing. Thus Rich Karlgaard, writing in the summer of 1999 as the publisher of *Forbes,* used "Moore's Law" and its allied principles to reassure investors suffering from cold feet:

> Hold the phone. The pace *can* go on. The physics of the Information Age is a sure bet. Chips *are* headed toward infinite speed at zero cost. So is bandwidth. The radical new software and e-commerce business models that will follow in their wake can only be guessed at. But their arrival is a sure bet. Zany zooms in the underlying power are locked in.[24]

Locked in. If, as John Kenneth Galbraith charged, runaway bull markets are propelled onward and upward by "incantation" of a particularly reverent sort, this was the incantation to top them all. That was no bubble on Wall Street: it was the future itself, generously whispering its secrets into the ears of the faithful and making us all wealthy beyond our wildest dreams.

Leave it to the great Gilder, the man who popularized the concept of "locked-in" progress in the first place, to come up with the most enterprising way to capitalize on this gift of prophecy. In 1996 he began issuing a pricy tip-sheet for investors anxious to cash in on the mad stock appreciations that theories like his had made possible. Here at last was the business end of Gilder's clairvoyance, what all his "laws" and "paradigms" and "inevitabilities" came down to in the end: Subscribers to his $295-a-year *Gilder Technology Report* could "grow rich on the coming technology revolution." As a mail solicitation for the newsletter promised, they would learn why "the Law of the Telecosm" would cause certain stocks to climb so rapidly that even Microsoft would be left in the dust. They would learn about "the Gilder paradigm," find out "why the bandwidth revolution is inevitable!" And for those who weren't sure about this Gilder fellow, the solicitation included the spellbound endorsement of his publisher, Tim Forbes: "I am convinced that the future as George sees it will happen."[25]

Strangely, the future as George saw it *did* happen, again and again. Not because of Gilder's psychic powers, but because the overheated stock market had transformed him from the man who talked to the microchip into the object of one of the long prosperity's most peculiar manias. "Listen to the technology," Gilder liked to say. "Listen to Gilder," chanted the rest of the world, logging on to his website on the day a new issue was scheduled to appear and desperately buying shares in whatever company the great man had touted. By the year 2000, financial journalists were discussing the "Gilder effect," the massive and immediate movement in a company's share price that the ideologue was capable of setting in motion with even the most indirect pronouncements. Novell, a maker of network software, saw its market capitalization leap by $2 billion one day in December 1999 after Gilder wrote favorably of it in his newsletter. When Gilder steered his followers towards Xcelera.com in February 2000, its price climbed 47 percent in one day; when he touted NorthEast Optic Network a month later, its price nearly doubled. And Qualcomm, which he had boosted for years, became one of the great bubble stocks of the late nineties, appreciating some *2,618 percent* over the course of 1999 as investors rushed to be a part of the future. And when Gilder pooh-poohed a technology, its makers discovered themselves on the wrong side of history in no uncertain terms, shunned by investors and their share price plummeting.[26] Having conjured the "New Economy" up out of the backlash mud, having transformed the lexicon of social class into the language of free markets, Gilder himself was now transformed into the archetypal character of the new era: The stock picker infallible, the bubble-blower as *philosophe*.

And perhaps the "New Economy" itself—this new order in which ideas trumped things—was nothing but the "Gilder effect" writ large, a colossal confusion of ideology with production, of populism with profit, of unprecedented good times for the rich with real social advance.

This Age of Incantation

The distant aerial view is one of the favorite conceits of the market-populist consensus. When human civilization is observed from far, far up, it occurs to several of the deepest thinkers of the nineties, a curious fundamental truth about us becomes evident: Life is in fact a computer. Everything we do can be understood as part of a giant calculating machine. The cars proceeding down the highways, the weave of our fabrics, even the fish in the ocean—all of us doing little sums, suspending judgment, surrendering control, participating in the hive mind. It's a Norman Rockwell image for the age of the Internet billionaire: The little people going happily about their business as tiny monads in the great swarm of humanity. From high up in the clouds, preferably from a seat in "business class," it can be seen that the "New Economy," the way of the microchip, is writ into the very DNA of existence.

I propose, though, that we imagine how all these things will appear from a historical distance rather than a high altitude. As the free money dries up and the euphoria cools off, as the pages yellow and the commercials get pulled and the websites are disconnected and the high-flying shares settle down for a thirty-year flat-line stretch at one-seventieth of their 1999 prices, we will look back at this long summer of corporate love and wonder how it was that we ever came to believe this stuff. We will shake our groggy heads and muddle on with our lives.

Unfortunately, though, we won't be able to shake off the material aspects of the "New Economy" quite as easily. The new era came with a real-world price tag, and the things we permitted to happen just so that we could live in its brilliant light for a few years are things we may never be able to undo or escape. In other lands where the advance of free trade is cheered on by our columnists as the greatest sort of empowerment, the battle to make the world safe for outsourcing has turned as bloody as any of our own nineteenth-century labor wars. In Colombia, recipient of a billion-dollar Clinton administration military aid package, union organizers have been assassinated every year in such numbers (around three thousand overall since 1987) that in 1997 they accounted for fully 50 percent of the trade union activists murdered worldwide.[27] Our political thinkers imagined our money frolicking open-mindedly through the economies of the world, chasing the best return without regard for color or creed. But what ensured those returns was not the "inevitability" of the microchip but the guns and the muscle and the hard unanswering face of economic power. Wherever one turned, old-fashioned coercion was the silent partner of "New Economy" ebullience.

Here at home the price was the destruction of the social contract of mid-century, the middle-class republic itself. Our portfolios may have appreciated graciously, but they did so only to the extent that we countenanced the reduction of millions to lives of casual employment without healthcare or the most elementary sort of workplace rights. We caught the tail end of the Qualcomm wave and pretended not to notice as sweatshops reappeared on our shores. We wondered like tots at the majesty of Cisco, at the generosity of Gates, and we stood by as the price of a good education for our kids ascended out of our reach.

The less tangible cost of consensus was the atrophy of the idea of conflict. Economic fairness, many of us came to believe, was something that just happened, that materialized at the mall like a new line of Pokémon products. Democracy was a thing served up to us like a

Happy Meal; it required no effort on our part. To be sure, it had a mysterious, counterintuitive quality to it: If we unilaterally gave up our power to compel humane treatment from the boss, like magic there would come some karmic payoff, some shower of money from heaven, some ten-bagger in Yahoo! If we acquiesced to the holy process of deregulation, to the tossing of millions of single mothers out into the labor force, we would one day stumble upon some vast picnic spread out just for our gratification by the Archer Daniels Midland Company or JDS Uniphase. Someday we, too, would be invited to help ourselves to the complimentary after-dinner mints. To board at our leisure.

But for others of us—the ones with no access to the Senator's ear or the hip ad agencies or the prime commercial time on CNBC—the nineties only sharpened the sense that something had gone drastically wrong. To the casualization of work, to the destruction of the social "safety net," to the massive prison roundup, the powers of commerce added the staggering claim of having done it all on our behalf. Out of the roaring chaos of everyday speech, they told us, they could hear the affirmations rolling up; from the chirped warnings of the car alarms to the screeching of the modems they could hear America singing. But the great euphoria of the late nineties was never as much about the return of good times as it was the giddy triumph of one America over another, of their "New Economy" over our New Deal. Though they banged the drum with a fervor almost maniacal, the language of the euphoria still rang so patently false, sounded so transparently self-serving that it threatened to collapse in on itself almost as quickly as it bubbled up from the talk shows and the celebrated think tanks. And in the streets and the union halls and the truck stops and the three-flats and the office blocks there remained all along a vocabulary of fact and knowing and memory, of wit and of everyday doubt, a vernacular that could not be extinguished no matter how it was cursed for "cynicism," a dialect that the focus group could never quite reflect, the resilient language of democracy.

Notes

PREFACE

1. I am following the description of the passage and effects of the Telecommunications Act given by communications scholar Robert McChesney in his excellent summary of the broadcasting industry in the 1990s, *Rich Media, Poor Democracy* (Urbana: University of Illinois Press, 1999), pp. 64–65, 75, 151. See also McChesney's article, "Media Mergers," *Newsday*, March 22, 2000, p. A53.

2. A 2000 Internet search for postings of Barlow's "A Declaration of the Independence of Cyberspace" found some 608 websites reproducing its ringing cadences. One place where it can be found is Barlow's own website:

http://www.eff.org/pub/Publications/John_Perry_Barlow/barlow_0298. declaration

3. Krauthammer, "Return of the Luddites," *Time*, December 13, 1999, p. 37. Friedman, "1 Davos, 3 Seattles," *New York Times*, February 1, 2000, A25.

4. Paul Krugman, "Workers vs. Workers," *New York Times*, May 21, 2000, p. 17. Krugman's attempt to blame apartheid on the labor movement was particularly monstrous, and reveals the extremes to which the nation's press was willing to go in its

battle against labor. In fact, elements of the American labor movement fought as hard to isolate apartheid as anyone else, and largely for the same reasons they fought against free trade with China: Free workers can hardly be expected to compete with workers who live under dictatorships or conditions of virtual slavery. For a particularly colorful example of the conflict between the American labor movement and apartheid, see Thomas Geoghegan, *Which Side Are You On?* (New York: Farrar Straus Giroux, 1991), pp. 27–29. The main purpose of the China free-trade bill was, of course, to reduce labor costs for American employers by permitting them to outsource work to people kept in bondage by one of the world's most notorious dictatorships. It aimed to take advantage of a regime every bit as murderous as South Africa's had been in the seventies. But on *that* maneuver Krugman had no calumny to heap or scurrilous comparisons to make: being an operation of the market, outsourcing was as natural as earth and sky.

Jagdish Bhagwati, "Nike Wrongfoots the Student Critics," *Financial Times,* May 2, 2000. As for that monotonous chanting, it is worth pointing out that a student journalist from Columbia University, where Bhagwati teaches, made almost exactly the same points as Bhagwati had two weeks later on the op-ed page of the *New York Times* (Jaime Sneider, "Good Propaganda, Bad Economics," *New York Times,* May 16, 2000, p. A31).

5. Thomas Friedman, "Senseless in Seattle," *New York Times,* December 1, 1999. The Canadian editor was Paul Jackson of the *Calgary Sun.* He made this point in an article that appeared in the paper on May 2, 2000, and returned to the subject again on May 6. As he insisted in his second story on the topic, "many of those involved in the protests may be well-meaning individuals who don't realize that shadowy figures are manipulating them and using them, as Leon Trotsky said, as 'useful idiots' and naive dupes."

Two weeks later, Friedman echoed this bizarre verdict from the respectable heights of the *New York Times,* labeling the union campaign against free trade with China a "jihad." "Winners Don't Take All," *New York Times,* May 19, 2000, p. A29.

6. It appeared in *In These Times* under the title, "It's Class, Stupid: How the Culture Wars Sank Populism," October 18, 1998, p. 24.

CHAPTER ONE

1. Byoir as quoted in Stuart Ewen, *PR! A Social History of Spin* (New York: Basic, 1996), p. 295.

2. "Talking the Future With John S. Reed," *New York Times,* December 20, 1999, p. C18.

3. George Gilder, *The Spirit of Enterprise* (New York: Simon & Schuster, 1984), p. 19. Gilder has also famously compared microchips to cathedrals. Owen Edwards in *Forbes ASAP,* October 7, 1996.

4. "The Market's Will Be Done" is the title of chapter 35 of Tom Peters' *Liberation Management* (New York: Fawcett Books, 1994). "The Nine Laws of God" are explained in chapter 24 of Kelly's 1994 book *Out of Control: The New Biology of Machines, Social Systems and the Economic World* (Reading, MA: Perseus, 1994). The comment of *Fast Company*'s publisher appeared in the *Boston Business Journal,* November 8, 1999. The "Internet Goddess" was Morgan Stanley analyst Mary Meeker. The "laying on of hands" line is found in the October 1999 issue of *Red Herring*, p. 117. Oddly enough, this is also where the GoTo ad occurs. The website where investors and startups meet in "heaven" is garage.com, the product of Guy Kawasaki. See the *Wall Street Journal*, May 14, 1998.

5. The television version of this commercial, featuring guitarist BB King, ran in the first months of 1999. The print version can be found in *Fortune* for July 5, 1999.

6. *US News & World Report* editorial by Mort Zuckerman, February 10, 1997, as quoted in Uchitelle, "Puffed Up by Prosperity, US Struts Its Stuff," *New York Times,* April 27, 1997, section 4, page 1.

7. Charles Handy, *The Empty Raincoat* (London: Arrow Books, 1995 [1994]), p. 129.

8. "The Inner Circle," *Red Herring,* October 1999. The "pundit" who is profiled is, of course, George Gilder; the "journalist" is John Markoff of the *New York Times;* the "academic" is Tim Berners-Lee of MIT.

9. Uchitelle, "Puffed Up by Prosperity."

10. Of course the Europeans were never quite persuaded to join in the celebrating. As the *Financial Times* reported, one European official said, "They keep telling us how successful their system is. Then they remind us not to stray too far from our hotel at night." *Financial Times,* June 23, 1997.

11. According to economists Lawrence Mishel, Jared Bernstein, and John Schmitt, authors of *The State of Working America 1998–99* (Ithaca, NY: Cornell University Press, 1999), this is true of 60 percent of the American workforce. p. 5.

12. The 475 figure appears in *Business Week*'s annual survey of CEO compensation, April 17, 2000. Figures for Japan and Britain are from the AFL-CIO's "Executive Pay Watch" Web site, http://www.aflcio.org/paywatch/ceopay.htm

13. Welch made nearly forty million dollars in 1997. These figures are given in a GE shareholder resolution from 1998 reprinted in *A Decade of Excess: The 1990s,* Sixth Annual Executive Compensation Survey, United for a Fair Economy/Institute for Policy Studies, p. 21.

14. The figures up to 1995 appear in *State of Working America,* p. 258. They are based on the Federal Reserve's Survey of Consumer Finances. Figures to 1997 are given in *Shifting Fortunes: The Perils of the Growing American Wealth Gap,* published in 1999 by the group United for a Fair Economy (Boston), p. 76. They are estimates derived from "Recent Trends in Wealth Ownership," a paper given in 1998 by NYU economist Edward Wolff.

15. Doug Henwood, "Boom for Whom?" *Left Business Observer (LBO)* 93 (February 2000), p. 4.

16. At times this was stated quite bluntly. A *Wall Street Journal* editorial for June 13, 2000, asserted that the stock market would only continue to do well if "the productivity gains associated with the New Economy are captured by capital, and not labor" (p. A26). A good example of how the beneficiaries of productivity growth were changing was the announcement, in February 2000, that productivity had risen at an annual rate of 5 percent during the second half of 1999, without any corresponding increases in wages, which caused the stock market to spike upward again. As Louis Uchitelle put it in his account of the story, "Workers, in effect, are producing much more without having to be paid more. . . ." *New York Times*, February 9, 2000, p. 1.

It is also important to mention that, before 1999, productivity increases in the nineties were in fact generally smaller than they had been in the past. This was a consistent point of embarrassment for "New Economy" enthusiasts, who believed that massive productivity increases were out there, that all we had to do to find them was alter the way we calculated the statistic. On this see financial journalist Doug Henwood's comments in *Left Business Observer*: http://www.panix.com/~dhenwood/Payoff.html

17. On temps, see Edward Luttwak, *Turbo Capitalism: Winners & Losers in the Global Economy* (London: Orion Business, 1999), p. 60. Luttwak reports that, in 1995, some 17 percent of American temp workers were actually working for their former employers—most without health or pension benefits, of course.

18. On prisons and worker discipline, see Christian Parenti's excellent and terrifying book, *Lockdown America* (New York: Verso, 1999), especially chapter 11.

19. Louis Uchitelle, "How Slow Can Your Paycheck Grow?" *New York Times*, February 20, 2000, p. 3.

20. On historic class mobility in the U.S., see the paper by economists Peter Gottschalk and Sheldon Danzinger, "Family Income Mobility—How Much Is There and Has It Changed?" (1997), available online at http://FMWWW.bc.edu/ec-p/wp398.pdf. See also the authoritative review of the literature on the subject by Doug Henwood, "Up & Down the Ladder," *Left Business Observer* #84 (1998). On comparative mobility in the U.S. and Europe, see *State of Working America*, p. 369.

Most of the optimistic accounts of increasing class mobility in the "New Economy" refer back to the authoritative-sounding work of W. Michael Cox and Richard Alm, respectively an economist at the Dallas Fed and a journalist. Their findings—that America is in fact the "land of opportunity"—appeared first in the 1995 annual report of the Dallas Federal Reserve Bank. They were repeated in *Myths of Rich and Poor* (New York: Basic Books), a 1999 volume in whose first sentence Cox and Alm saluted their own "courage" in "writing a good-news book" (p. ix).

Henwood, though, finds something quite different from courage at work in the two men's research. Cox and Alm's study, he charges, was "designed to make a point, and it stacked all the numbers its way." For example, Cox and Alm study income mobility by using individuals, not households, and they include in their research people as young as 16, who thus, as Henwood writes, "contributed vastly to mobility just by growing up." Furthermore, they demonstrate social mobility by showing growth in real incomes over time, not by comparing those real incomes to social averages. With their calculations adjusted for these factors, Henwood writes, some 43 percent of the population who were in the lowest income quintile in 1975 were still there in 1991, not the miraculous 5.1 percent cited by Cox and Alm.

21. Lewis: "The Rich: How They're Different . . . Than They Used to Be," *New York Times Magazine,* November 19, 1995, p. 69. Management Theorists: The work-burden of the rich is a theme especially emphasized by Charles Handy. *Wired,* January 1998, n.p.

22. There is a wealth of literature on this subject. Marisa Bowe of *Word* magazine records the following remarks of "a 34-year-old investment banker" at the height of the "Silicon Alley" IPO craze: "You take someone like Henry Kravis. Here's a guy who spent 40 years in New York, the grueling, big New York power banker thing, how pissed off must he be when these young guys and gals are doing I.P.O.'s and walking away with hundreds of millions of dollars—eclipsing his own wealth—and they're like in their 20's!" Bowe, "Envy Hits New York's Web Workers in the Greedy IPO Rush of '99," *New York Observer,* April 19, 1999. Also check out "Nothing Left to Buy?," a story about the class envy of those who made their millions in the eighties and must now look on while the nineties billionaires buy the luxury implements they cannot afford. *New York Times,* March 3, 2000, p. C1

23. Lester C. Thurow, *Building WEALTH* (New York: HarperCollins, 1999), pp. 14–15. As astonished to encounter this passage as you are, I searched Thurow's text for evidence that he was kidding, or that he was citing these attitudes in order to shock readers. I am sorry to report that he was not. Although these are clearly attitudes that Thurow believes are common to our time rather than eternal truths, he makes no effort to distance himself from them. So frequently does he lapse into his own vernacular affirmation of these wealth-worshiping pointers (see below) that the distinction melts away. It should also be pointed out, in Thurow's favor, that he does suggest that other interpretations of the "New Economy" might be possible. Unfortunately, he repeatedly turns his back on these and continues to elucidate the orthodox perspective.

24. Thurow, p. xiii. Thurow repeats the line, "It is the best of times for Americans" on page 17, again after citing evidence from the personal life of Bill Gates.

25. One of the *Wall Street Journal's* polls on this subject appeared on May 1, 2000, p. B1. *Time,* November 15, 1999, p. 29.

26. The British observer was Jonathan Freedland, *Bring Home the Revolution* (London: Fourth Estate, 1998), pp. 111, 112. The paperback edition of Freedland's book was reported by the *Times* of London to have been read enthusiastically by the well-known Americanophile Tony Blair (October 24, 1999).

27. *Wall Street Journal*, June 24, 1999, p. 1, my emphasis; Thurow, *Building WEALTH*, p. 199.

28. Thurow, *Building WEALTH*, pp. xiii, 33, 36.

29. Geoff Mulgan, *Connexity: How to Live in a Connected World* (Boston: Harvard Business School Press, 1998) p. 31. Mulgan cites one John Kao as the source of this law. The only other references to "Kao's Law" that I have been able to discover, though, appear in a series of speeches given in 1998 and 1999 by Lew Platt, chairman of Hewlett-Packard.

30. On Enron's record of contributions to the Bush, Clinton, and Blair administrations, the company's appointments of politicians to lucrative board seats, and other amazing forms of bullying, see Nick Cohen, "A Word About Their Sponsors," in *Cruel Britannia* (London: Verso, 1999), pp. 194–99. On Enron's TV commercials, see http://www.askwhy.com/mainf.asp. In one of them Enron comes very close to making the entire argument of this book in just thirty seconds. The spot depicts an electricity-industry spokesman using the A-bomb word, "Why?" against some stodgy old politicians who are refusing to deregulate utilities on the deluded and elitist grounds that they know what's best for everyone.

31. Luttwak, *Turbo Capitalism*, p. 25. Lanier: *Wired*, January 1998, p. 60. Lanier also declares that this unanimity "annoys" him, because markets sometimes crash. Friedman, *New York Times*, August 15, 1998.

32. Richard Hofstadter, *The Progressive Historians: Turner, Beard, Parrington* (New York: Knopf, 1968), p. 463.

33. Daniel Yergin and Joseph Stanislaw, *The Commanding Heights: The Battle Between Government and the Marketplace That Is Remaking the Modern World* (New York: Simon & Schuster, 1998), pp. 116, 389.

34. George Gilder, *Wealth and Poverty* (New York: Basic, 1981), pp. 97, 99, 105. This idea seems to be an extension of the belief in positive thinking as an instrument of personal achievement. "Upward mobility," Gilder continued, "is at least partly dependent on upward admiration: on an accurate perception of the nature of the contest and a respect for the previous winners of it."

35. Rich Karlgaard, "Get ready to defend the free market," *Forbes ASAP*, June 2, 1997, p. 13. Ellipses, et ceteras, and asinine remarks about class war in original.

36. On the culture wars as a skewed form of populism, see Chris Lehmann, "It's Class, Stupid," *In These Times*, October 18, 1998, p. 24. On the working class and the backlash, see Barbara Ehrenreich, *Fear of Falling: The Inner Life of the Middle Class* (New York: HarperCollins, 1989), particularly pp. 160–71. On the culture wars as a planned provocation by the right, see Michael Lind, *Up From Conservatism* (New York: Free Press, 1996), p. 3 and also chapter 6, "The Culture War and the Myth of

the New Class." The Lee Atwater quote comes from Lind, page 138. Speaking of Pat Buchanan, Lind writes: "He, more than anyone else, should have understood that conservative populism was not to be taken seriously, that it was merely a method of persuading white working-class voters to vote their prejudices rather than their economic interests."

37. Kenneth Auchincloss, "Fanfare for the Common Man," *Newsweek,* December 20, 1999.

38. *Newsweek,* April 27, 1998, p. 50. Samuelson was referring specifically to the stock market.

39. This early strain of market populism still thrives in some quarters. Writing in the *Wall Street Journal* in May 2000, *Car and Driver* editor Brock Yates imagined that one could see even in the debate over the SUV a playing out of class snobbery, with "pecksniffs" and "guilt-ridden rich kids" senselessly assailing the people's chosen car. Unfortunately, this was an extremely poor cultural terrain on which to stage a defense of the common man: The rage for SUVs began as a class phenomenon, first with the way-up-scale Range Rover, and soon involving SUVs made by Mercedes, Cadillac, and Lincoln. Brock Yates, "Pecksniffs Can't Stop the SUV," *Wall Street Journal,* May 17, 2000, p. A26.

40. John Keats, *The Insolent Chariots* (Philadelphia: Lippincott, 1958), pp. 46–48.

41. On Brand's career see David Stipp, "The Electric Kool-Aid Management Consultant," *Fortune,* October 16, 1995, p. 160. Brand, "We Owe It All to the Hippies: forget antiwar protests, even long hair. The real legacy of the sixties generation is the computer revolution," *Time,* March 22, 1995. The IBM ad ran as a four-page insert in the *Wall Street Journal,* February 23, 1999. Tom Freston, CEO of MTV Networks, in an interview with the *Wall Street Journal,* March 21, 2000, p. B4, ellipses and parenthesis in original. In the same interview Freston recounts how his company has actually used hypnosis as a market-research tool.

42. See the page-one story by G. Pascal Zachary in the *Wall Street Journal,* June 2, 1999, in which Singapore's decision to cultivate "nonconformists" in order to bring "creativity" to that authoritarian nation is described.

43. Gilder, *Wealth and Poverty,* pp. 96–97, 98, 101. The book devoted to the apotheosis of the entrepreneur was *The Spirit of Enterprise.*

44. Gilder, *Wealth and Poverty,* pp. 38, 90, 259.

45. Friedrich Hayek, *The Fatal Conceit* (Chicago: University of Chicago Press, 1988), pp. 90, 91, 100.

46. "What's the Matter With Kansas" appears in William Allen White's *Autobiography,* (New York: MacMillan, 1946) pp. 296–99. The Baer quote is taken from Frederick Lewis Allen, *The Lords of Creation,* (New York: Harper & Brothers, 1935) p. 91.

47. Ewen, PR! A Social History of Spin, pp. 74, 75.

48. Ibid., p. 294.

49. Ibid., pp. 355, 382.

50. Kevin Phillips, The Politics of Rich and Poor (New York: Random House, 1990), p. 7. Emphasis in original.

51. William A. Henry III, In Defense of Elitism (New York: Doubleday, 1994), p. 2. Henry's book begins to go wrong with its second paragraph and within a few pages becomes yet another culture wars battle cry, hammering cultural populism according to the standard "political correctness" script of the day.

52. Rush Limbaugh, "Voice of America: Why Liberals Fear Me," in Backward and Upward: The New Conservative Writing, David Brooks, ed. (New York: Vintage, 1996), p. 308. Rush Limbaugh, See, I Told You So, 1993, pp. xv, 165, 169. Rush Limbaugh, The Way Things Ought to Be (New York: Pocket Books, 1992), p. 162.

53. All this stuff, plus a salute to the project from Hillary Clinton, can be found on the project's website, http://www.favoritepoem.org/

54. Michael Kazin, The Populist Persuasion (New York: Basic, 1995), pp. 273, 277.

55. Jeffrey Bell, Populism and Elitism: Politics in the Age of Equality (Washington, DC: Regnery, 1992), pp. 3, 11, 12.

56. Bell did offer some rather unique historical interpretations: He cited the career of millionaire industrialist Mark Hanna as evidence of the GOP's move away from "social elitism" and towards the "urban working-class vote"; asserted that the People's Party "captured the Democratic party" in 1896 rather than the other way around; characterized Woodrow Wilson, whose administration assumed control of much large-scale private industry during World War I, as a faithful believer in free markets and minimal government intervention; and attributed the invention of the word "capitalism" to Karl Marx.

57. Brooks, Backward and Upward. Bartley, pp. 197, 198. "Philosopher-kings": Jeffrey R. Snyder, p. 255. Barnes, p. 115.

58. Fund: Backward and Upward, p. 321. On Perot and Bagby, see Rick Perlstein's devastating essay, "The X-Philes," Dissent, spring 1999. See also Bagby's book, Rational Exuberance: The Influence of Generation X on the New American Economy (New York: Dutton, 1998) and the website of her "Annual Reports," http://www.arusa.com.

59. Mr. Paul was speaking, naturally, on the subject of the Microsoft antitrust ruling, a favorite topic of market populism. Congressional Record, November 8, 1999. Among other things, Paul also asserted that only government can create bad monopolies; monopolies created by the market are beneficial to all. www.house.gov/paul/congrec/congrec99/cr110899.htm

60. Both quotes are found in Nick Cohen, "New Labour . . . In Focus, On Message, Out of Control," Guardian, November 28, 1999.

61. Cohen, "Goodbye, Mr. Chips . . . Hello, Mr. Fries," 1998, *Cruel Britannia,* p. 182.

62. Gingrich: on firing elected officials and "consumer-directed government," see "Newt's Brave New World," *Forbes ASAP,* February 27, 1995. On asking the corporations, see Newt Gingrich *To Renew America* (New York: HarperCollins, 1995), p. 71.

63. Gingrich, *To Renew America,* pp. 66, 108, 47, 74. On the "so-called business cycle," Gingrich's reasoning goes like this: Economists believe in the business cycle, so they make policies in anticipation of it, so they wind up causing it. Q.E.D.

CHAPTER TWO

1. Hitchens, *No One Left to Lie To* (New York: Verso, 1999), pp. 23–24.

2. The Mitchell story is told in Charles R. Geisst, *Wall Street: A History* (Oxford, 1997), pp. 163–65 and 178; the Barton quote is reported in Frederick Lewis Allen, *Lords of Creation,* p. 312. Mitchell's remark on soundness is found in Frederick Lewis Allen, *Only Yesterday: An Informal History of the Nineteen-Twenties* (New York: Harper Perennial, 1964 [1931]), p. 269.

3. On Mitchell's downfall see Geisst, *Wall Street: A History,* and John Kenneth Galbraith, *The Great Crash, 1929* (2d ed., Boston: Houghton Mifflin, 1961), pp. 155–59.

4. I do not exaggerate Nocera's intentions here. See chapter 3. Joseph Nocera, *A Piece of the Action: How the Middle Class Joined the Money Class* (Simon & Schuster, 1994), pp. 140–41.

5. As one of the most remarkable aspects of the "New Economy" consensus is the migration of what were once clearly, identifiably right-wing ideas to the center of the national conversation—and the tendency of right-wing figures to insist that they are, in fact, nice, trustworthy centrists, I offer the following list of overt right-wing signifiers. Wriston worked on the Reagan administration's Economic Policy Advisory Board and is an officer of the American Enterprise Institute and the Manhattan Institute. The big thinkings in his book are sourced to figures like George Gilder, Peter Drucker, Hayek, Martin Wolf, Jeane Kirkpatrick, and Rupert Murdoch, plus assorted articles from *Fortune,* the *Wall Street Journal,* and the *Financial Times.*

6. Walter B. Wriston, *The Twilight of Sovereignty: How the Information Revolution is Transforming Our World* (New York: Scribner's, 1992), pp. 61–62.

7. Ibid., pp. 9, 45, 170.

8. Ibid., pp. 46, 121.

9. Ibid., pp. 95, 107, 108.

10. Kelly, *Out of Control.* On Hayek, p. 121. Equation of market with robots and nature, pp. 47–48. Obsoleting the printing of money, p. 227. "Encryption," p. 209.

11. Ibid., "revolutionize," p. 186. Outsourcing and flexibility, pp. 190–91. Outsourcing company, p. 192. "Brahmins," p. 226. Benetton, "superorganism," p. 188.

12. Ibid., pp. 184, 202, 227, 257. The prediction concerning smart clothes appears on page 194.

13. On the problem of the productivity numbers, see Doug Henwood's comments in *Left Business Observer:* http://www.panix.com/~dhenwood/Payoff.html

14. Peter Schwartz and Peter Leyden, "The Long Boom: A History of the Future, 1980–2020," *Wired* 5.07, July 1997. The "long boom" story, widely regarded as Schwartz's manifesto, was more than ten thousand words long.

15. Ibid.

16. Yergin and Stanislaw, *Commanding Heights.* The quote about markets voting is from Yergin, "Going to Market," *The New Republic,* April 26, 1999, p. 52. On Yergin's admiration for Margaret Thatcher, see his *Wall Street Journal* op-ed, "The Revolution of 1979," May 3, 1999.

17. Yergin and Stanislaw, *Commanding Heights,* pp. 126, 137, 138, 328.

18. Wriston, *Twilight of Sovereignty,* p. 36.

19. Both of these comparisons are made in Friedman's 1999 book, *The Lexus and the Olive Tree: Understanding Globalization* (New York: Farrar Straus Giroux, 1999), pp. 39–40. On the professional athletes, see pp. 247–48.

20. *New York Times,* December 17, 1999, p. A29.

21. *New York Times,* December 1, 1999. On the AFL-CIO as sugar daddy of the opposition, see *New York Times,* February 1, 2000.

22. "Dupes," *New York Times,* December 1, 1999. "Afraid of the future," *New York Times,* February 1, 2000. Hostility to turtles, *New York Times,* February 1, 2000. On the air traffic controllers, *New York Times,* August 20, 1999. In Friedman's most labor-tolerant moods, he will acknowledge that bad employers exist and even express sympathy for those who toil in Third World sweatshops, but he goes on to insist that the way to rectify these abuses is through consumer enlightenment via the Internet, so that "activists" here in America can buy the right products. The problems of labor are thus left up to the consumer, like everything else: The key is "mobilizing consumers and the Internet," not organizing the actual workers in the sweatshops. Friedman presents this wildly impractical suggestion as "practical help . . . , not the usual moral grandstanding." *New York Times,* July 30, 1999.

23. Friedman, *The Lexus,* p. 66.

24. Ibid., pp. 87, 88, 141.

25. Ibid., pp. 298, 302, my emphasis.

26. Lewis, "Royal Scam," *New York Times Magazine,* February 9, 1997, p. 22; Wolf explicitly linked "hatred of markets" to "fear of foreigners." The speeches given in the

debate can be found at http://orwell.monde-diplomatique.fr/dossiers/ft/wolf.html. *Wall Street Journal,* September 20, 1999.

27. Among prominent publications and writers who weighed in with exactly this opinion one finds: the *Wall Street Journal* (which gets extra credit for accusing the protesters of First World elitism before the protests even happened), November 26, 1999 and December 2, 1999; Thomas Friedman, *New York Times,* December 1, 1999; Charles Krauthammer, *Time,* December 31, 1999; etc. etc. etc.

28. *New York Times,* February 10, 1998.

29. *Wall Street Journal,* January 14, 2000, November 8, 1999. The *Journal's* most ferocious stories on the Microsoft trial were penned by columnist Holman Jenkins. Good examples of Jenkins's outraged missives are found in August 18, 1999, and June 30, 1999, the latter being the same day the *Journal* ran a page-one story on a humble photographer who had become a millionaire by clinging to Microsoft shares for ten years.

30. A *Wall Street Journal* news story quotes as follows from an advertisement Monsanto ran in the UK in 1998: "While we'd never claim to have solved world hunger at a stroke, biotechnology provides one means to feed the world more effectively." May 11, 1999. Similarly, Gregg Easterbrook of *The New Republic* wrote that "the luddites" must be prevented from opposing GM crops, for it is "the world's poorest people who would have the most to lose." (*New York Times,* November 19, 1999, p. A31)

Interestingly, Thomas Friedman included a section in *The Lexus and the Olive Tree* describing the CEO of Monsanto as an avatar of corporate "democratization," since he had removed much of the company's hierarchy by using "E-mail, intranets and the Internet" to give "everyone on the front lines" the same information he himself had. See pp. 74–76.

31. George Melloan, "Technophobia Poses a Real Risk to Europe's Future," *Wall Street Journal,* June 29, 1999, p. A15. See also Michael Fumento, "Why Europe Fears Biotech Food," *Wall Street Journal,* January 14, 2000.

32. On PR in the UK: *Wall Street Journal,* May 11, 1999, p. A10; on Monsanto conference, *Financial Times,* October 7, 1999, p. 11.

33. *New York Times Magazine,* May 31, 1998, p. 36.

34. Ibid, p. 58.

35. *Wall Street Journal,* June 8, 1999, p. 1; June 22, 1999, p. 1.

36. Luttwak, *Turbo-Capitalism,* p. 6.

37. Roger Cohen, "For France, Sagging Self-Image and Esprit," *New York Times,* February 11, 1997, p. A1, A6; "France vs. U.S.," *New York Times,* October 20, 1997, p. A10.

38. *New Republic,* June 23, 1997, http://www.tnr.com/archive/06/062397/editors-

062397.html. *Wall Street Journal Europe,* November 23, 1999. Guy Sorman, "History's Dustbin: The Last Soviet Republic," *Wall Street Journal Europe,* March 27, 2000, p. 14.

Jonathan Lewis, "Khmer Rouge Ideas Spawned in France," letter to the editor, *Wall Street Journal,* May 11, 2000, p. A27. *The New Republic's* June 23, 1997, account of the French elections must rank among the most pompous pieces of writing in the entire "New Economy" period. Of those French elections the editors wrote: "It is so perfectly perverse, so perfectly comme toujours. So perfectly French. As the rest of the world shuts the door on the disastrous and dismal and discredited experiment of Marxism, the French, in the grand tradition that produced the reigns of Robespierre, Napoleon and Vichy, have regarded the political scene, examined the historical evidence, analyzed the current situation, discussed the future ramifications—and chosen precisely the most obtuse and suicidal course possible."

39. Thomas Friedman, "Parlez-Vous USA?" *New York Times,* February 26, 1997, p. A15.

40. Roger Cohen, *New York Times,* "concrete," September 19, 1997; others, "For France, Sagging Self-Image and Esprit," February 11, 1997, p. A1, A6. The line about the need to "nourish" the "French ego" is quoted from writer Marek Halter.

41. Roger Cohen, Stanford-educated businessman, February 11, 1997, p. A1; Yquem, "A Chateau Divided: Famed Yquem Riven by Family Feud," *New York Times,* July 12, 1997.

42. Roger Cohen, "France vs. U.S.: Warring Versions of Capitalism," *New York Times,* October 20, 1997, p. A10.

43. Cohen on Le Pen: *New York Times,* February 11, 1997. On Haider: *New York Times,* February 6, 2000, section 4, p. 1.

44. Roger Cohen, *New York Times,* October 11, 1997.

45. Kudlow, "What's More Important Than the Fed?" *Wall Street Journal,* August 27, 1999, p. A8.

46. George Gilder, *Microcosm: The Quantum Revolution in Economics and Technology* (New York: Simon & Schuster, 1989), pp. 113–14, 352.

47. Ibid., pp. 346, 369.

48. George Gilder, *Life After Television: The Coming Transformation of Media and American Life* (New York: Norton, 1994), p. 205. The book was first published in 1992, but this quotation comes from Gilder's 1994 "Afterword."

49. See, for example, Po Bronson's cover story about Gilder in the March 1996 issue of *Wired* in which remarks about Gilder's ideas are tempered with irritation at Gilder's more reactionary views: "One minute Gilder is defending the intelligence of the American public, and I want to cheer him. But then I recall that he just denied the existence of racism," p. 193.

50. On *Forbes ASAP*, I am quoting *San Francisco Chronicle* writer Tom Abate, who described the publication this way on June 4, 1998. On the counterculture: In *Microcosm*, Gilder states at one point that "the 1960s Berkeley revolt" was "against the mainframe," hence giving it some value (p. 41). In a 1998 issue of *Wired*, Gilder goes as far as to identify "Lennon and McCartney" as among the century's great forces of change. January 1998, p. 40.

51. Jon Katz, *Media Rants* (San Francisco: Hard Wired, 1997), pp. 8, 11, 38, 43.

52. Jon Katz, "The Digital Citizen," *Wired*, December, 1997, pp. 71, 72, 82, 274. The hot ideas of management theory that come up in the story are the notion that ethnic diversity enhances a company's productivity and the identification of "digital citizens" as "agents of change," both p. 72.

53. Frank Luntz and Bill Danielson, "Message to Politicians: If Digital Citizens Don't Back You, You're Going Nowhere," *Wired*, December, 1997, pp. 76, 78.

54. All of these except for the flatulent cartoon characters (which appeared on the cover of the November 1999 issue) come from *Wired*'s remarkable fifth anniversary edition, published in January 1998, pp. 42, 52, 62, 66, n.p., n.p., 90, 126, n.p.

55. In Ronald Reagan's famous speech to Moscow State University, May 31, 1988 (a speech written for him, oddly enough, by one Josh Gilder), he made the following Gilderesque statement:

"Like a chrysalis, we're emerging from the economy of the Industrial Revolution— an economy confined to and limited by the Earth's physical resources—into, as one economist titled his book, *The Economy in Mind*, in which there are no bounds on human imagination and the freedom to create is the most precious natural resource. Think of that little computer chip. Its value isn't in the sand from which it is made but in the microscopic architecture designed into it by ingenious human minds. Or take the example of the satellite relaying this broadcast around the world, which replaces thousands of tons of copper mined from the Earth and molded into wire. In the new economy, human invention increasingly makes physical resources obsolete. We're breaking through the material conditions of existence to a world where man creates his own destiny. Even as we explore the most advanced reaches of science, we're returning to the age-old wisdom of our culture, a wisdom contained in the book of Genesis in the Bible: In the beginning was the spirit, and it was from this spirit that the material abundance of creation issued forth."

As reprinted in "The Public Papers of the Presidents: Ronald Reagan," and found at http://www.idgop.org/docs/reaganm.htm.

56. Benjamin R. Barber, *Jihad vs. McWorld* (New York: Times Books, 1995), p. 243.

57. On this point see the fascinating book by Timothy Bewes, *Cynicism and Postmodernity* (London: Verso, 1997).

CHAPTER THREE

1. Stepping in as if on cue to make all this antiauthoritarian fantasy that much more believable, the chairman of the Securities and Exchange Commission—surely the king of the suits—actually denounced the campaign in May 1999. The ads were, of course, spunkily defended by business journalists, setting up a nice culture war in a teapot. Barbara Lippert, columnist for *Adweek*, pounded the SEC chairman, who had warned—so squarely!—that these campaigns might "create unrealistic expectations," by sneering, "Hello? It's known as advertising, which exaggerates reality in a comedic and entertaining way to make an impression, to get your attention." *Adweek*, May 17, 1999.

2. The thinking behind this campaign was discussed in the October 18, 1999 edition of *Advertising Age*.

3. *New York Daily News*, November 9, 1999. The newspaper quoted the magazine's "president" as making the following thirties-style remark: "It's all about individuals making a difference if they work collectively."

4. The REIT ad appeared on the op/ed page of the *Wall Street Journal*, June 16, 1999.

5. This particular ad appeared on the back cover of *The New Yorker* for July 5, 1999.

6. "From One Revolution To the Next," E*Trade 1999 Annual Report, p. 12. Is there any reason to bother pointing out that the descriptions attached to these "revolutions" are wrong? The famous Montgomery bus boycott in fact took place in 1956–57, while the most notable victory for feminism in 1973 concerned abortion rights, not "glass ceilings."

7. The correct figures for all "direct or indirect stock holdings," according to the Federal Reserve Board's Survey of Consumer Finances, were 31.7 percent of all families in 1989, 37.2 percent in 1992, 41.1 percent in 1995, and 48.8 percent in 1998. These figures include pension plans, 401(k)s, and mutual funds in addition to shares of common stock, and they measure households instead of individuals. Obviously for the rosiest version of the favorite market populist metaphor to have real legitimacy—the notion that through stock ownership We the People endorse the deeds of corporate America, voting on their actions and generally approving of what goes on economically—the stock in question must be voting stock, i.e., directly owned shares of common stock. Here, though, the figures were very different. In 1992, 16.9 percent of families owned stock directly, which number actually declined to 15.3 percent in 1995 and then rebounded to 19.2 percent in 1998. Meanwhile the popularity of mutual funds soared, going from 10.4 percent of families in 1992 to 12 percent in 1995 and to 16.5 percent in 1998. Among the wealthiest families, of course, these trends were much more pronounced. In the income bracket $50,000–$99,999, mutual fund ownership increased from 15.3 percent in 1992 to 20.9 percent in 1995; in the income bracket $100,000 or more, mutual fund ownership increased from 30.5 percent to 38 percent. (A particu-

larly revealing set of statistics in the survey is the median value of family holdings in stocks: While the amount in 1992 for each of the brackets less than the $100,000-per-year families falls between $4,000 and $6,000, the amount for the "$100,000 and more" category is $38,000.)

8. Friedman, *Lexus*, pp. 115, 142.

9. A good example of this ideological operation can be found on the op-ed page of the *Wall Street Journal* for September 3, 1999, in which James Glassman, he of *Dow 36,000* fame, dismisses the doubts of Fed chairman Alan Greenspan by noting that he had expressed similar doubts for several years now. Another can be found in the January 24, 2000, *Fortune* story "Has the Market Gone Mad?" in which the bearish statements of various Wall Street economists and strategists from several years before are paired with the same men's resignation statements and confessions of wrongness. Even more painful is the page one *Wall Street Journal* story of February 25, 2000, on ten years of erroneous fears of imminent downturns.

10. *Wall Street Journal*, editorial, August 11, 1999, p. A18. This was in response to revelations of unsavory practices at day-trading firms.

11. *Wall Street Journal*, March 25, 1996.

12. Thurow, *Building WEALTH*, p. 202.

13. Allan Sloan, "The Hit Men," *Newsweek*, February 26, 1996, p. 44. James J. Cramer, "Let Them Eat Stock," *The New Republic*, April 29, 1996, p. 24–25. Another interesting point: Cramer described the appreciation of share prices as "wealth they [the workers] created" simply by being fired.

Others advocated doing absolutely nothing to prevent debacles like the AT&T episode. Hailing the CEO of AT&T as "courageous," Harvard economist Michael C. Jensen and Perry Fagan announced in the *Wall Street Journal* that workers would just have to get used to lowliness in the New Economy. It was right, good, and moral that massive layoffs result in "increased profits and stock prices": after all, this was the demand of the "Third Industrial Revolution," and "without the private pain, most people will not change." *Wall Street Journal*, March 29, 1996, p. A10.

14. David Sanger, "Meet Your Government, Inc." *New York Times*, November 28, 1999.

15. Thurow, *Building WEALTH*, p. 207.

16. "How the Longest Boom Transformed Main Street," *Wall Street Journal*, January 25, 2000, p. B1.

17. "Of course, the biggest contributor to exorbitant CEO pay is stock options," write the authors of *A Decade of Executive Excess: The 1990s*, a 1999 publication by United for a Fair Economy and the Institute for Policy Studies.

http://www.ufenet.org/press/decade_of_executive_excess.html. See also "Share and Share Unalike," *The Economist*, August 7, 1999.

18. "Windfall" was the term used by the Associated Press (and reported in many urban dailies) to describe the mutual fund industry's support of Social Security privatization, November 14, 1996. The AP estimated privatization would reap the industry some $60 billion in fees, commissions, and administrative costs. In an article on the specious statistics used by the right-wing proponents of Social Security privatization, Doug Henwood points out that the figure could actually run up to $130 billion per year. *Left Business Observer* 87, December 31, 1998.

19. Advertisement for T. Rowe Price, *Forbes,* December 27, 1999. The footage occurred in TV commercials for the same company.

20. March 1991 is the date used by the National Bureau of Economic Research. It is given in "How the Longest Boom Transformed Main Street," *Wall Street Journal,* January 25, 2000, p. B1. In the 1994 book *A Piece of the Action,* Joseph Nocera gives January 18, 1991, as the starting date for the people's market. However, in a January 11, 1997, article in *Washington Monthly*—a curiously pessimistic and questioning article, given the views he expressed in *A Piece of the Action*—Nocera saw it extending all the way back to 1982. Others who give 1982 as the starting date include James Glassman and Kevin Hassett (see the *Wall Street Journal,* March 17, 1999, p. A26) and Diana Henriques, a business reporter writing in the *New York Times Book Review,* November 14, 1999.

21. Henry Adams, "The New York Gold Conspiracy," in *Chapters of Erie* (Boston: James R. Osgood and Company, 1871), p. 101.

22. "Speculation on a large scale," Galbraith wrote, "requires a pervasive sense of confidence and optimism and conviction that ordinary people were meant to be rich." Galbraith, *The Great Crash,* pp. 17, 21, 174.

23. Quoted in Nocera, *A Piece of the Action,* pp. 107–8. This line also appears frequently in Merrill Lynch advertising.

24. As William Z. Ripley, one of the financial industry's most thoughtful critics, summarized the dominant thinking of the twenties, the years since World War I had seen "a great incursion into the field of investment by the common people—corporate possession being shared by those of moderate and small means with the wealthy class. The movement has been called 'an economic revolution'—'the passing of ownership from Wall Street to Main Street.'" Ripley, *Main Street and Wall Street* (New York: Little Brown and Company, 1927), p. 116.

25. See, for example, the *Money* magazine cover story for August 1999, "Your Best Moves Now," p. 69.

26. In the twenties this notion sprang from the work of Edgar Lawrence Smith, author of *Common Stocks as Long-Term Investments;* in the nineties the belief that a reliable return awaited those who bought and held forever became one of the prevailing faiths of the age. Jeremy Siegel, author of the 1994 book *Stocks for the Long Run,* at

times came uncannily close to echoing Smith's strategies of the 1920s. The comparison between the two is made with uncomfortable accuracy by John Cassidy in *The New Yorker,* August 18, 1998. In the late nineties one even occasionally came across superimposed charts of RCA and AOL, or other representative indices of the two eras.

See also Chris Lehmann, "Boom Crash Opera," *Baffler* 10, 1997.

27. On Raskob: "Mr. Raskob's 'Poor Man's Investment Trust,' " *Literary Digest,* June 1, 1929, p. 88. "Everybody Ought to be Rich, An Interview with John J. Raskob," *Ladies' Home Journal,* August 1929. Although the article is signed by Samuel Crowther and titled "An Interview," the interviewer's voice does not appear in it.

28. Brooks, *Once In Golconda: A True Drama of Wall Street, 1920–1938* (New York: Harper & Row, 1969), pp. 22, 106–7.

29. Whitney quoted in Frederick Lewis Allen, *Lords of Creation,* p. 352.

30. Ibid., 186.

31. Geisst, *Wall Street: A History,* p. 213.

32. Galbraith, *The Great Crash,* p. 44. Parenthesis in original.

33. "Adam Smith," *The Money Game* (New York: Random House, 1967), pp. 43, 197, 198.

34. The edition of *Extraordinary Popular Delusions* to which "Smith" refers is that of 1932, which carried an introduction by financier Bernard Baruch, who so famously sold everything after receiving a stock tip from a shoeshine boy. After "Smith's" book appeared in 1967, *Extraordinary Popular Delusions* was reprinted in popular paperback editions in 1972 and 1980. In 1996, with a substantial new demand for business-related titles, it was reissued once more as part of publisher John Wiley's series of Investment Classics.

35. Roger Lowenstein, *Buffett: The Making of An American Capitalist* (Random House, 1995), p. 392.

36. Ohio representative Dennis Eckart, as reported by Ron Suskind in the *Wall Street Journal,* November 8, 1991, page A1.

37. *Forbes,* December 27, 1999. Raskob: p. 178; T. Rowe Price and FDR, pp. 6–7. The actual title of Raskob's infamous *Ladies' Home Journal* article was "Every*body* Ought to be Rich." Forbes gets it right on the inside of the magazine.

38. Although it was reissued in 1996, electronic searches of all articles published in the *Wall Street Journal* and *Business Week* found only two that referred to *Extraordinary Popular Delusions* in the period 1998–99 (one of these in a book review by Roger Lowenstein), while a search of the period 1993–99 found only eight. On the other hand, comparisons of the Internet stock craze to the tulipmania of the seventeenth century, one of the book's most memorable episodes, abounded in 1999 and 2000.

39. Brooks, *The Go-Go Years* (Macmillan, 1973), p. 5.

40. "Smith," *Money Game,* pp. 23–25, 198.

41. Nocera, *A Piece of the Action,* p. 241.

42. Peter Lynch, *One Up on Wall Street* (New York: Simon & Schuster, 1989), p. 13. On the seventh graders and investment clubs, Peter Lynch, *Beating the Street* (New York: Simon & Schuster, 1993), pp. 26–35.

43. Lynch, *Beating the Street*, p. 151.

44. Lynch, *One Up*, pp. 24, 32; *Beating the Street*, p. 27.

45. Lynch, *One Up*, p. 289; *Beating the Street*, pp. 40–43, 45. Chapter 20 of *One Up on Wall Street* is entitled "50,000 Frenchmen Can Be Wrong."

46. Lowenstein, *Buffett*, p. 236.

47. Lowenstein, *Buffett*, ellipsis and emphasis in original, pp. 159, 232, 247–73, 334. Buffett has family ties to other mutant strains of populism as well. While he himself is a notable supporter of liberal causes, his father, Nebraska congressman Howard Buffett, was one of the pioneers of right-wing populism, a fierce red-baiter, and a prominent early member of the John Birch Society.

48. "Uneasy Street," Randall Smith and Robert McGough, *Wall Street Journal*, November 18, 1994, p. A1.

49. These figures can be found on the ICI website, http://www.ici.org/ There is some confusion concerning ICI's numbers of mutual-fund owning households, as their methods of measuring seem to change periodically.

50. Stars on the way up: "Superstar Funds," a feature focusing on eight fabulous mutual funds and their managers, who are all portrayed in yellowish-tinted close-ups, *SmartMoney*, June 1995. Stars on the way down: "Odd Man Out: Why did bond-fund superstar Mark Turner hit the skids at Putnam? The story of what happens when a hot hand turns cold." *SmartMoney*, July 1995.

51. The first Cramer scandal involved a February 1995 *Smart Money* column in which he touted a number of stocks his hedge fund held. In fact, as his defenders have pointed out, Cramer routinely touts stocks he holds—the keys to his appeal are his exciting discussions of actual trading—but for some reason the column in question appeared without the usual disclosure statement.

52. Chernow, "The Bull Markets to Come," *Wall Street Journal*, August 30, 1993, p. A8.

53. Richard Thomson, "Spinster's long, lonely road to untold wealth," *The Times*, December 9, 1995.

54. Michael DiCarlo was ousted as manager of the Special Equities Fund in July 1998 after two years of poor performance, *Boston Globe*, July 2, 1998. *Business Week*: Suzanne Woolley, "Our Love Affair with Stocks," *Business Week*, June 3, 1996. Lowenstein: "Securities Blanket," *Wall Street Journal*, September 9, 1996. *New York Times Magazine*: Diane K. Shah, "Riding the Bull for a Day," *New York Times Magazine*, December 1, 1996. It should be noted that each of these stories was careful to note the risks that confront individual investors, and to include stories of market failures as well as successes.

55. Nocera, *A Piece of the Action*, pp. 11, 167, 168, 276.

56. Ibid., pp. 17, 114, 395.

57. Ibid., pp. 27, 288, 402–3, 405.

58. Ibid., pp. 167, 175, 228.

59. *Wall Street Journal* on Knoxville, June 19, 1996, on the rich, November 12, 1996; *Reader's Digest,* "You Can Make a Million," July 1996.

60. Thomas J. Stanley, PhD and William D. Danko, PhD, *The Millionaire Next Door: The Surprising Secrets of America's Wealthy* (New York: Simon & Schuster, 1996), pp. 15, 25, 192.

61. *The Beardstown Ladies' Common-Sense Investment Guide* (New York: Hyperion, 1994), pp. 30, 103.

62. *Money,* December 1996, p. 88. The Klondike portfolio seemed to adhere to the same general rules as the Beardstown one did, except they held, appropriately enough, Harley Davidson instead of Office Depot. Otherwise, many of the same issues: McDonalds, Gillette, PepsiCo.

63. "Even Leftists Have Servants Now," declared the headline of a *Wall Street Journal* story from June 1999; "The students of Mao have given way to the children of the Dow," announced comedian Ben Stein on the paper's op-ed page in February 1997, citing the interest of a number of his usually left-leaning colleagues in the doings of Warren Buffett. *Wall Street Journal,* June 23, 1999, February 5, 1997.

64. Nocera, *A Piece of the Action,* pp. 386, 391.

CHAPTER FOUR

1. For a devastating debunking of the privatizers' logic, see Doug Henwood, *Left Business Observer* 87, December 31, 1998, "Antisocial insecurity." It also appears on the LBO website, http://www.panix.com/~dhenwood/Antisoclnsec.html

2. Josh Mason, "Three Scenes from a Bull Market," *Baffler* 9, 1997, p. 93. The section that follows is indebted to Mason's article.

Thau's remarks are dated July 13, 1995. The full text can be found on the Third Millennium website, http://www.thirdmil.org/media/opeds/pips.html

3. My first clue that there was anything amiss with Third Millennium were Thau's oft-repeated denials of any kind of conspiracy between his organization and Wall Street, denials which he backed up by citing Wall Street's apparent failure to rally to his 1995 call and "invest" in the PR instruments he deemed appropriate. On Third Millennium's cooperation with Oppenheimer, see Rick Perlstein, "The X-Philes," *Dissent,* spring 1999, pp. 112, 113. On the massive amounts being spent on PR and lobbying for privatization by Wall Street, see Robert Dreyfuss, "The Real Threat to Social Security," *The Nation,* February 8, 1999. For Thau's denials of the massive amounts being spent on PR and lobbying for privatization by Wall Street, see "Social Security Reform: PR Slugfest,"

by Anne Willette, *USA Today,* February 18, 1997; *National Journal,* February 15, 1997, and *Crain's Investment News,* June 8, 1998.

4. The roster of Third Millennium's board of directors can also be found on its website, http://www.thirdmil.org/about/directors.html

5. See in particular Bagby, *Rational Exuberance.*

6. Perlstein, "The X-Philes," pp. 112, 113. These polls were also absurdly misguided, the exactly wrong sort of finding on which to base a debate over what ought to become of Social Security. In fact, as far as I have been able to determine, no Third Millennium poll asked whether Generation X or anybody else thought Social Security *should* continue to exist, whether, say, the rich *ought* to pay more for the maintenance of the society that has treated them so well. These choices, as Perlstein has noted, were always left discreetly off the questionnaire.

7. More generally, it was on the Social Security battlefield that one came across the most inflated versions of the decade's various market-populist myths, as each one was armored up and rushed into service against the big government foe. Here, for example, it is not unusual to hear it argued that the stock market will never go down again. Or to find Wall Street spokesmen desperately turning the populist tables on the New Deal and asserting that, in fact, state guarantees are a marker of paternalism and class arrogance while privatization is an expression of faith in the common people.

8. Heather Chaplin, "Baby Bulls," *Salon,* April 15, 1998. Chaplin offers what may be the most optimistic historical view ever of the bull market of the nineties, asserting that stock market returns have averaged a whopping 19 percent for a full fifteen years. She also gives one of the largest versions of the famous People's Market percentage: She cites the Investment Company Institute (a mutual fund industry group) to prove that "45 percent of people aged 18 to 30 invest in the stock market."

9. Jonathan Hoenig, *Greed is Good: The Capitalist Pig Guide to Investing* (New York: HarperCollins, 1999), pp. 83, 156, 227.

10. Hoenig, *Greed Is Good,* pp. xiv–xv, 7, 237.

11. Ibid., pp. xvii, xix. Italics in original. It is important to point out that while Hoenig proclaims himself a follower of James J. Cramer, his true model seems to be Ken Kurson, whose ideas and career trajectory he has followed with uncanny precision. Kurson also started out as a financial commentator by publishing a zine in which he made the same curious argument for money talk as "taboo," endorsed the same idea of investing as class conflict, and was widely heralded as a financial spokesman for Generation X. On Kurson see Josh Mason, "Three Scenes from a Bull Market," *Baffler* 9, 1997.

12. *Money:* Gen-X family, August 1991, p. 54; US standards of living, October 1991, pp. 86, 88, 148; middle class, October 1992, p. 102; Editor in Washington, September 1991, p. 7.

13. *Money:* Puff Daddy: The manager of the Van Wagoner Emerging Growth Fund, December 1999. The "King of extreme investing": Jeff Vinik, February 2000. Projected stock listings, eyeballs, distorted photos: December 1999. Richest people: March 2000. Caution: April 2000. Tanking stocks (Lucent): March 2000. Japanese family: March 2000. James Grant: June 1999. Sarcasm: March 2000, p. 27. Cool stock-flogging high schoolers: April 2000.

14. James J. Cramer, "Investor Nirvana," *Worth,* May 1997.

15. Gregory J. Millman, *The Day Traders: The Untold Story of the Extreme Investors and How They Changed Wall Street Forever* (New York: Times Books, 1999), p. 25.

16. David & Tom Gardner, *The Motley Fool Investment Guide: How the Fool Beats Wall Street's Wise Men and How You Can Too* (New York: Simon & Schuster, 1996), pp. 8, 10.

17. David & Tom Gardner, *The Motley Fool's You Have More Than You Think: The Foolish Guide to Investing What You Have* (New York: Simon & Schuster, 1998), pp. 8, 10. The comment about the broker's De Lorean is found in a Motley Fool junk e-mail sent on July 24, 1999.

18. Gardners, *You Have More,* p. 31. *TMF Investment Guide,* p. 14. *You Have More,* p. 71. The "ignorance and fear" line is found in the Fool website's "Welcome" board, which also includes sagacious advice about the wonders of compound interest. It should also be noted that the Fools' skepticism toward elites includes standard neo-conservative denunciations of higher education. They charge in one book, for example, that "in America's finer, greener universities . . . the notion of excellence and incentivization has given way to a soft, sleepy relativism." *TMF Investment Guide,* p. 62.

19. http://www.fool.com/portfolios/RuleBreaker/Spirit.htm A cardinal Foolish principle is the notion that good investors are also good people, that investing is somehow a primal test of character. "Warren Buffett's investment career, for instance," they write in *TMF Investment Guide,* "is not so much about balance-sheet analysis as Buffett's own humility, patience, and diligence," p. 18.

20. http://www.fool.com/portfolios/RuleMaker/RuleMakerStep6.htm This particular list of stocks is from *You Have More,* the Fools' 1998 book. A year later, the Fools decided they would be better served by having two different portfolios, one of which takes more risk—and endorses newer, chancier brands—than the other.

21. Gardners, *TMF Investment Guide,* p. 10. *You Have More Than You Think,* p. 279.

22. On this curious chapter in the development of the People's Market see the two *Fortune* stories by Joseph Nocera, April 15 and May 27, 1996.

23. James K. Glassman and Kevin A. Hassett, "Stock Prices Are Still Far Too Low," *Wall Street Journal,* March 17, 1999, p. A26, and "Dow 36,000," *Atlantic Monthly,* September 1999, p. 37. Emphasis is in both originals, of course.

24. James K. Glassman and Kevin A. Hassett, *Dow 36,000: The New Strategy for*

Profiting from the Coming Rise in the Stock Market (New York: Times Business, 1999), pp. 110, 111, 116. See also Glassman's telling exchange with Clive Crook of *The Economist, Slate,* April 28 and May 27, 1998.

25. Lawrence Kudlow, "The Road to Dow 10000," *Wall Street Journal,* March 16, 1999, p. A26; "What's More Important Than the Fed?" *Wall Street Journal,* August 27, 1999, p. A8.

26. David Futrelle, "Stock Splits: How the Dumb Get Rich," *Money,* June 1999, p. 177. "Hooray, U.S.A.," p. 39. Faith in the power of splits to lift share prices was derided as one of the cardinal delusions of small investors by "Adam Smith" in *The Money Game,* p. 200.

27. Andy Serwer in *Fortune,* October 11, 1999, p. 118.

28. "The market is saying you rattle your sword all you want," strategist Byron Wien told the paper, referring to Fed chairman Alan Greenspan, "you'll only affect the Old Economy stocks. The New Economy stocks *have transcended Fed policy*" (my emphasis). *Wall Street Journal,* February 24, 2000, p. C1.

29. *Time,* May 31, 1999.

30. I am referring here to Julian Robertson, Jr., the hedge fund manager, who abandoned the field in March 2000. *Wall Street Journal,* March 31, 2000, p. C1. On Buffett's woes, see "Has Buffett been a casualty of the 'new economy?'" by Charles V. Zehren, *Seattle Times,* March 10, 2000, p. C1.

31. *Wall Street Journal,* May 6, 1999, p. A1.

32. *Wall Street Journal,* July 19, 1999.

33. Jay Walker of Priceline was worth some ten billion dollars at Priceline's peak; a few months later his net worth had fallen to about six billion. *Wall Street Journal,* June 28, 1999, p. C1. But why do I scoff? According to Lester Thurow's calculus of social value, building a billionaire in this manner is one of the noblest deeds any society can perform.

34. Priceline's memorable TV commercials, in which Shatner performed a variety of self-mocking skits, were widely believed to have given the company a recognizable brand identity and were probably just as responsible for its success with investors as its famous business model. No one has explained, however, what camp and irony have to do with airline travel. See also the devastating article on Priceline in *Fortune,* September 6, 1999. It was *Forbes* magazine that referred to Priceline founder Jay Walker as a "New Age Edison."

35. Pierre Omidyar, quoted in *Time,* December 27, 1999, n.p. Here is how the magazine sidesteps both skepticism and hollow idealism as it applies the golden label "community": "'Community' is an overworked term, too often applied artificially to any motley of people who share a skin color, an income level or a set of political bugaboos. But from the limitless ether of cyberspace, eBay has managed to conjure up the real thing."

36. This story is retold in the *New York Times,* June 6, 1999, section 3, p. 9.

37. "Person of the Year: An Eye on the Future," *Time,* December 27, 1999, n.p.

38. See Henwood, *LBO* 89.

39. Summers: "The American Economy: Poised for a New Century," speech to the New York Economic Club, September 8, 1999.

40. John Simons, "For Risk Takers, System Is No Longer Sacred," *Wall Street Journal*, March 11, 1999, p. A12.

41. On TheGlobe.com's photogenic cofounders and their brief careers as media darlings, see Lessley Anderson, "The Selling of TheGlobe.com," *Industry Standard*, July 5–12, 1999. On the ugly aftermath, see *Fortune's* feature stories on "Dot-Com Ethics," March 20, 2000, p. 116.

42. *Wall Street Journal Europe*, May 12, 1999, p. 18.

43. *Washington Post*, April 7, 1995. A year later Cramer continued to bemoan the *SmartMoney* controversy, recounting in *The New Republic* how he "would like to help make money for others" besides those in his hedge fund, but how journalistic snobs would keep him from sharing the wealth. *The New Republic*, January 8, 1996.

Cramer was also prone to conflict-of-interest controversies going the other direction. In 1998 he famously slagged stocks he was shorting on CNBC, generating yet another instant uproar.

44. *SmartMoney*, October 1, 1997, p. 115.

45. *Time*, May 31, 1999, p. 106.

46. Y2K: TheStreet.com, January 3, 2000. Symbol: *Newsweek*, March 29, 1999.

47. Hoenig: *TJFR Business News Reporter*, vol. 12, nos. 18 & 19 (1999), p. 19. Kurson: "In Defense of James Cramer," *Salon*, March 12, 1999.

CHAPTER FIVE

1. As quoted in the *Wall Street Journal*, November 8, 1999.

2. Another amusing example of corporate coolness was the ad for The MegaPath Networks internet service provider in which a photo of a hippie, flowers duly in-hair, accompanied the never-stale slogan "Power to the People."

3. South Bend, Indiana, Columbus, Indiana, Centerville, Iowa, and the Hawaiian island of Kauai have reportedly embraced the "7 Habits" theories of Stephen Covey as their more or less official civic philosophies. Evidently the main thing this entails is reduced-price training for anyone who is willing at Covey seminars. The president of one Indiana town's chamber of commerce embraced Covey training as a solution to rampant "hopelessness and cynicism." Ellen Debenport, "Indiana City Finds Self-Help in '7 Habits,' " Minneapolis *Star Tribune*, March 13, 1996, p. 5E.

More recently, the business leaders of Jacksonville, Florida are reported to have pushed for a Covey makeover, actually suggesting that all 100,000 of the city's residents go through Covey seminars. Bruce Bryant-Friedland, "Seven Habits for Success," *Florida Times-Union*, April 6, 1998, p. 12.

4. Sumantra Ghoshal and Christopher Bartlett, *The Individualized Corporation* (HarperBusiness, 1997) pp. 244–45.

5. John Micklethwait and Adrian Wooldridge, *The Witch Doctors: Making Sense of the Management Gurus* (New York: Times Books, 1996), p. 12.

6. Thomas J. Peters and Robert H. Waterman, Jr., *In Search of Excellence: Lessons from America's Best-Run Companies* (New York: Warner Books, 1982), p. 96. *Thriving on Chaos,* Peters' second sequel to *In Search of Excellence,* begins with the words, "There are no excellent companies." On the first page of *Liberation Management,* Peters writes of *Thriving on Chaos,* "I don't think it was a revolutionary book" and admits on the next page that its suggestions wouldn't have helped you very much; xxxi–xxxii. He starts off *The Circle of Innovation* by announcing, "A lot of what I say here contradicts what I said 15 years ago" and that, "I admit it. I have often been (v-e-r-y) wrong," xxi. In fact, the book's very subtitle, "You Can't Shrink Your Way to Greatness," contradicts the loud cheering for teams and tiny corporate units that had characterized *Liberation Management.*

7. Richard Tanner Pascale, *Managing on the Edge: How the Smartest Companies Use Conflict to Stay Ahead* (Simon and Schuster, 1990), p. 19.

8. This particular Dilbert episode appeared in newspapers on September 5, 1999. On Dilbert's absorption into one workplace, see Tom Vanderbilt, "Gaudy and Damned," *The Baffler* 9, 1997, p. 15.

9. Charles Handy, *The Hungry Spirit* (London: Hutchinson, 1997), p. 157; Ghoshal and Bartlett, *Individualized Corporation,* pp. 279, 280.

10. On Taylorism, see David Montgomery, *The Fall of the House of Labor: The Workplace, the State, and American Labor Activism, 1865–1925* (Cambridge: Cambridge University Press, 1987), especially chapter 5, "White Shirts and Superior Intelligence." "Industrial Autocracy": *Final Report of the Commission on Industrial Relations* (Washington, DC, 1915), p. 223. Unions and democracy: Walter Lippmann, *Drift and Mastery* (Madison: University of Wisconsin Press, 1985 [1914]), p. 59.

11. The legal penalties for firing an employee because of her pro-union views are so slight that I have heard of business school lecturers who openly encourage their students to break the law and do so. Of course, the labor movement's own lack of imagination and outright complacency in the seventies, eighties, and early nineties must also bear much of the blame for its decline.

12. Peters and Waterman, *In Search of Excellence,* p. 45; Gary Hamel and C. K. Prahalad, *Competing for the Future* (Boston: Harvard Business School Press, 1994), p. 153; Gingrich: *To Renew America,* p. 113, Peter Senge, *The Fifth Discipline: The Art and Practice of the Learning Organization* (New York: Currency Books, 1990), p. 59; Peters made the remark about McNamara in an interview with *Reason* magazine, October 1, 1997. Peters voices similar sentiments in *The Circle of Innovation: You Can't Shrink Your Way to Greatness* (New York: Alfred A. Knopf, 1997), p. xxi. The business revolu-

tion is not uniformly sympathetic to communism, though. As we shall see, one of their favorite rhetorical strategies is comparing old management theories to Soviet-style communism.

13. The only important dissenters from this consensus, Michael Hammer and James Champy of *Reengineering the Corporation,* were often described as "neo-Taylorist" because of their concern with flowcharts and organizational hierarchy. But even they made a point of rejecting the most basic premises of Taylorism, writing that their goal was "reversing the industrial revolution," undoing each alienating, dehumanizing aspect of "Adam Smith's industrial paradigm—the division of labor, economies of scale, [and] hierarchical control. . . ." Hammer and Champy, *Reengineering the Corporation: A Manifesto for Business Revolution* (New York: HarperBusiness, 1993), p. 49.

14. This implication is quite clear, for example, in Walter Lippmann's 1914 book *Drift and Mastery,* where the professionalization of management is understood as a step toward conscious reorganizing of American economic life.

15. Tom Peters, *Liberation Management: Necessary Disorganization for the Nanosecond Nineties* (New York: Alfred A. Knopf, 1992), chapter 22: "Networks and Markets I: A First Look at 'Marketizing' the Firm."

16. See Ronald Coase, the economist who invented the classical theory of the firm, "The Nature of the Firm," *Economica,* New Series, Vol. IV (1937), pp. 386–405.

17. Blasting the Winds: Tom Peters, *Liberation Management,* p. 14, italics in original. Printing departments, line workers, reporters: *Liberation Management,* chapter 22 passim. "Market fitness tests": Tom Peters, *The Circle of Innovation,* p. 265, ellipses, parenthesis, and caps in original.

18. Doug Henwood, "A New Economy?" Speech given to the Friday Forum, University YMCA, Champaign-Urbana, Illinois, October 1, 1999.

19. The classic text is Adolph Berle and Gardiner Means, *The Modern Corporation and Private Property* (New York: Macmillan, 1932), p. 121. My account of the increasing use of options relies on Henwood's chapter on "Governance" in his book *Wall Street: How It Works and For Whom* (New York: Verso, 1997), pp. 254, 259, 266–267.

20. The management text that comes closest to differing from this trajectory is *Built to Last: Successful Habits of Visionary Corporations* (New York: HarperCollins, 1994), the 1994 best-seller by James Collins and Jerry Porras, which contradicts much of the rest of management theory in a number of different ways. The authors' central point is that a company's "core ideology" is what matters, not its dedication to profits. They even scoff at what they call "the profit myth," insisting that truly "visionary" companies are interested in more long-term goals. But they can't just walk away from it. Having downplayed profit, Collins and Porras then turn around and use those "visionary" companies' fantastic delivery of shareholder value as the ultimate proof of their excellence. The paradoxical moral seems to be that companies which concentrate on their "ideology"

rather than short-term profits will eventually do better for their shareholders than the companies that concentrate strictly on shareholder value.

21. Peters, *The Circle of Innovation*, pp. 160–61, 240.

22. Jeffrey Bell, the Republican political theorist, says it forthrightly: Taylorism was "the culmination of elitist management theory" while "a more populist management strategy" has begun to emerge in recent years. Oddly, Bell traces populist management to Japan rather than to McGregor. *Populism and Elitism*, pp. 21, 22.

23. Peters, *Circle*, p. 240. Ellipses and emphasis in original. Hamel and Prahalad, *Competing for the Future*, pp. 270–71.

24. Senge, *Fifth Discipline*, 69, 282, 340. Senge et al, *The Dance of Change: The Challenges to Sustaining Momentum in Learning Organizations* (New York: Currency, 1999), 11, 12.

25. Senge, *Fifth Discipline*, 58–59, 159.

26. Ibid., pp. xiii–xiv, 73, 78, 94 (italics in original). Mercator map: Senge et al, *Dance of Change*, p. 4.

27. Charles Handy, "Beyond Certainty," in *Beyond Certainty* (London: Arrow Books, 1996), pp. 13, 18.

28. Kenneth R. Hey and Peter D. Moore, *The Caterpillar Doesn't Know: How Personal Change Is Creating Organizational Change* (New York: Free Press, 1998), pp. 12, 144.

29. Handy, *The Age of Unreason* (Boston: Harvard Business School Press, 1989), pp. 9, 10, 57. The anti-intellectual epithets are found on pp. 56–63.

30. Arie de Geus, *The Living Company* (Boston: Harvard Business School Press, 1997), p. 56; Don Tapscott in transcript, "Conversations at the Intersection of Commerce and Technology, Chicago Conference, May 6, 1999," pp. 50, 51. Yes, Motorola University exists. See http://mu.motorola.com/AboutMU.html. See also Chris Lehmann, "Popular Front Redux?" *Baffler* 9, 1997.

31. Peters, *Circle*, p. 8, ellipses, parenthesis, and caps in original.

32. Peters, *Liberation Management*, p. 235; Handy, *Age of Unreason*, p. 25.

33. Handy, *Empty Raincoat*, p. 23.

34. Sprint "conversation" transcript, p. 18. In a curious typo, my copy of the transcript actually reads "irony equation" rather than "hiring equation." Go figure.

35. Sprint "conversation" transcript, p. 53.

36. Nina Munk, "The New Organization Man," *Fortune*, March 16, 1998. In the months to come, *Fortune* would commence a general attitudinal makeover, running record reviews and focusing on the various accessories of the Gen-X lifestyle.

37. Handy, *Age of Unreason*, pp. 73, 99, 100.

38. *Inc.*, August 1, 1998, and November 1, 1998.

39. Senge, *Fifth Discipline*, pp. 140, 142, 172, 282, 284. Senge et al, *Dance of Change*, 45.

40. Handy, *Age of Unreason*, pp. 162, 166; *Empty Raincoat*, p. 107. De Geus, *Living Company*, p. 18.

41. Anita Roddick, *Body and Soul: Profits with Principles—The Amazing Success Story of Anita Roddick & The Body Shop* (New York: Crown, 1991), pp. 135, 148, 227.

42. Peters, *Liberation Management*, p. xxxiii; *Circle of Innovation*, pp. 102, 119.

43. De Geus, *Living Company*, p. 9; Stan Davis and Christopher Meyer, *BLUR: The Speed of Change in the Connected Economy* (Reading, MA: Addison-Wesley, 1998), pp. xi, xiii.

44. Huber, quoted in Peters, *Liberation Management*, pp. 470, 479, 569.

45. Handy, *Empty Raincoat*, p. 130.

46. Davis and Meyer, *BLUR*, pp. 112, 113, 115, 116. The authors assert that BLUR is what killed the USSR on page 115.

47. Senge, *Fifth Discipline*, pp. 5, 15.

48. Roddick, the patron saint of "socially responsible business," is celebrated in many of the significant texts of the business revolution. Tom Peters devotes a section to her exploits in *Liberation Management* and refers to her again in *The Tom Peters Seminar* and *The Circle of Innovation*. She also comes up in Ghoshal and Bartlett's *Individualized Corporation*, in Hamel and Prahalad's *Competing for the Future*, and in both Charles Handy's *The Empty Raincoat* and *The Hungry Spirit*. Strangely, she is not mentioned in any of the *Fifth Discipline* books, the place one would most expect her.

49. The 1991 autobiography was entitled *Body and Soul*. Roddick's columns were collected into booklet form in 1997. The pamphlet series, of which I have only issue 2 (which seems to have been written largely by Roddick and was published in 1997) was entitled *Full Voice*. On the religious right: Roddick asserted in her *Independent* column for March 16, 1997, that in New Hampshire "the religious right has managed to have the word 'imagination' banned from use in schools." On activism and its properties, see *Full Voice*, issue 2. In a list of "Ten Ways To Be An Activist" that appears in that pamphlet, Roddick includes "Invest wisely" and "Go Shopping."

50. Roddick, *Body and Soul*, pp. 15, 110–11, 129, 225. Also, *Full Voice*, issue 2, 1997, n.p.

51. *Full Voice*, n.p.; Roddick, *Body and Soul*, pp. 131–32, 142, 192, 218. Unions and radicalism: According to a story to appear in *The Guardian* for September 3, 1994, "Body Shop said it had heard nothing from the union for three years, and suggested employees were more interested in joining organisations like Greenpeace and Amnesty. 'The unions are, frankly, a bit too conservative for some of our staff here. We're interested in rather more radical organisations,' a spokesman said."

52. The story that sparked the debunking of socially responsible businesses was "Shattered Image: Is The Body Shop Too Good to be True?" by Jon Entine, which appeared in *Business Ethics* in September 1994. See also David Moberg, "The Beauty Myth," *In These Times,* September 19, 1994. Entine's summary of his charges can be found online at http://www.animalconcerns.org/ar-voices/business_ethics.html

53. *Fast Company:* "Economic democracy," December/January 1997. Manifesto: November 1995, issue 1.

54. "Dis-Organization": Polly LaBarre, "This Organization is Dis-Organization," *Fast Company,* June 1996. Trouser manufacturer: David Sheff, "Levi's Changes Everything," *Fast Company,* June 1996.

55. Robert Bryce, "At BSG, There's Only One Speed—Faster," *Fast Company,* April 1996. Mort Meyerson, "Everything I Thought I Knew about Leadership Is Wrong," *Fast Company,* April 1996.

56. Eric Matson, "The People of Hewlett-Packard v. The Past," *Fast Company,* November 1995.

57. Charles Fishman, "Whole Foods Is All Teams," *Fast Company,* April 1996.

58. *Wall Street Journal,* June 7, 1996, p. B1. Richard Pascale, "The False Security of 'Employability,' " *Fast Company,* April 1996.

59. From an interview with leadership theorist Joe Jaworski by Alan M. Webber, "Destiny and the Job of the Leader," *Fast Company,* June 1996.

60. Tom Vanderbilt, "The Capitalist Cell," *New York Times Magazine,* March 5, 2000, p. 85.

CHAPTER SIX

1. Richard Gillespie, *Manufacturing Knowledge: A History of the Hawthorne Experiments* (Cambridge University Press, 1991).

2. Ibid., pp. 24, 26. See also Roland Marchand, *Creating the Corporate Soul* (Berkeley: University of California Press, 1998).

3. Gillespie, *Manufacturing Knowledge,* pp. 73, 181, 189–90, 196–97, 268.

4. Ehrenreich, *Fear of Falling,* 134.

5. Marchand, *Creating,* chapter 2 passim, page 86.

6. Ibid., p. 3.

7. The remark comparing *Fast Company* to a religion appeared in *Boston Business Journal,* November 8, 1999.

8. Microsoft's full-page ad in the *New York Times* ran on June 2, 1999. *Wall Street Journal,* November 15, 1999, p. A3.

9. On Welch's career generally, see Thomas F. O'Boyle, *At Any Cost: Jack Welch, General Electric, and the Pursuit of Profit* (New York: Vintage, 1998). On the company's

various empowerment and quality initiatives, see Jacquie Vierling-Huang, "Culture Change at General Electric," in Senge, *Dance of Change,* pp. 74–82; Tom Peters, *Circle of Innovation,* p. 479.

10. Micklethwait and Wooldridge call AT&T "a playground for the gurus" and offer a brief synopsis of the waves of theory-enthusiasm at the company, p. 10.

11. A Lexis-Nexis search of major American newspapers during the entirety of the 1990s yielded only two instances of the once common phrase, "soulless corporation." In both cases the term was used sarcastically.

12. Senge, *Fifth Discipline,* 7, 12–13, 144–45, 146.

13. Collins and Porras, *Built to Last,* p. 76.

14. Allan Cox with Julie Liesse, *Redefining Corporate Soul: Linking Purpose & People* (Chicago: Irwin Professional Publishing, 1996), pp. 29, 37. Italics in original.

15. Handy, *Hungry Spirit,* p. 157, *Empty Raincoat,* pp. 143, 145; de Geus, pp. 10, 201. De Geus does not write, "the company is LIKE a living being"; his assertion is most definite.

16. Handy, *Empty Raincoat,* pp. 71, 241.

17. Tom Peters, "The Brand Called You," *Fast Company,* August/September 1997. The article is also found at http://www.fastcompany.com/brandyou/start.html

18. Gordon MacKenzie, *Orbiting the Giant Hairball: A Corporate Fool's Guide to Surviving With Grace* (New York: Viking, 1998). MacKenzie is referred to as a "corporate holy man" on the book's back cover.

19. Guy Kawasaki, *Rules for Revolutionaries* (New York: HarperBusiness, 1999), pp. 169–72. The childrens' book is Crockett Johnson's *The Carrot Seed,* about a little boy who plants a carrot seed and believes that great things will come of it. Hamel and Prahalad, *Competing for the Future,* p. 82. They even come up with a number of cases in which executives compare their forward-thinking to the thought of children!

20. Sprint transcript, p. 35.

21. Peters, *Circle of Innovation,* p. 11. Ellipsis in original.

22. All of these commercials, with the exception of the MCI and Merrill Lynch spots, ran on CNBC during the period September-December 1999.

23. IBM advertisement in the *Wall Street Journal,* June 30, 1999, pp. A11–A18.

24. Handy: *Age of Unreason,* p. 156. Senge, *Fifth Discipline,* pp. 10, 371. Foreword to Arie de Geus, *The Living Company,* p. xi. "Primitive" is in quotes in original.

25. Roddick, *Body and Soul,* pp. 176, 179, 181, 206.

26. Peters, *Circle,* pp. 42–43. Peters' own thoughts on diversity (it's where "creativity" comes from) are found on pp. 376–78.

27. Joel Kotkin, *Tribes: How Race, Religion and Identity Determine Success in the New Global Economy* (New York: Random House, 1992), pp. 7, 102. On Asian migrants, see in particular chapter 4, "The New Calvinists."

28. A good example of the conformity-of-the-Japanese myth as it was commonly used to set up or contextualize a story can be found in the page-one story about a Japanese blues singer that the *Wall Street Journal* ran on May 4, 2000: "The audience of two-dozen Japanese in their 20s watches quietly. A head bobs, a toe taps; by Japanese standards, that's getting pretty raucous. In a nation that prizes calm and conformity, music about getting drunk on Saturday night and being shot by your common-law wife isn't for everyone."

29. Thomas Friedman, "1 Davos, 3 Seattles," *New York Times,* February 1, 2000, p. A25. The logic by which the government of Egypt can claim to represent anybody is not supplied.

30. Fareed Zakaria, "After the Storm Passes," *Newsweek,* December 13, 1999.

31. Handy, *Age of Unreason,* p. 5; Hamel and Prahalad, *Competing for the Future,* p. 5.

32. Peters, *Circle of Innovation,* p. xiii; Don Peppers and Martha Rogers, PhD, *The One to One Future* (New York: Currency, 1993), pp. 4, 6; Hamel and Prahalad, p. 27; Senge, *Dance of Change,* passim; graph, p. 7.

33. John Hagel III and Marc Singer, *Net Worth* (Boston: Harvard Business School Press, 1999), p. xi.

34. Davis and Meyer, *BLUR,* pp. 6, 7, 21, 107. The "trinity" of "BLUR," in case you were wondering, is made up of "Connectivity, Speed, and Intangibles."

35. Hammer and Champy, *Reengineering the Corporation,* p. 49; Hamel and Prahalad, *Competing for the Future,* pp. 59, 60, 61; Handy, *Empty Raincoat,* p. 57; Handy, *Age of Unreason,* p. 73.

36. Peters, *Circle of Innovation,* pp. xvi, 69, emphasis, caps, and lowercase in original.

37. Hamel and Prahalad, *Competing for the Future,* pp. 67–69; Peppers and Rogers, *One to One,* p. 365; Senge, *Fifth Discipline,* p. 99.

38. *New York Times,* July 7, 1996.

39. UPS manual for package car drivers, as quoted in Mike Parker and Jane Slaughter, *Working Smart: A Union Guide to Participation Programs and Reengineering* (Detroit: Labor Notes, 1994), p. 68.

40. Spencer Johnson, MD, *Who Moved My Cheese?* (New York: Putnam, 1998), pp. 32, 35, 38, 86.

41. Ibid., pp. 71, 82, 91, 92. My copy of *Who Moved My Cheese?* also came with a bookmark offering information on "Movie • Programs • Products."

CHAPTER SEVEN

1. Kirshenbaum and Bond: Jonathan Bond and Richard Kirshenbaum, *Under the Radar: Talking to Today's Cynical Consumer* (New York: John Wiley, 1998), p. 1. Peppers and Rogers, *One to One,* p. 54. "Cataclysmic shakeout": Seth Godin, *Permission Marketing* (New York: Simon & Schuster, 1999), p. 39.

2. Laybourne's confusion of audience research with empowerment is evidently quite convincing in certain circles. Oxygen Media's research arm, known as "The Pulse," is a joint project between Laybourne's organization and the screechingly progressive Markle Foundation. As the organization's website describes the project, "the Oxygen/Markle Pulse seeks to learn what women think and believe and to give voice to these findings through the media. We believe that research and the media, used together, can be powerful tools for change." http://www.pulse.org/whatweare.jsp. More examples of cooperation between the corporate media and the nonprofit sector are mentioned in the section on "public journalism" in chapter 9.

The willingness of putatively civic-minded foundations to assist the corporate media and would-be tycoons like Laybourne with their polling and demographic profiling must rank as one of the most staggeringly misguided aspects of the market populist consensus. Among other things, it illustrates the utter bankruptcy of the foundations' aspiration to serve as a counterbalance to corporate power: Far from critiquing the corporate imperium, such foundations have in fact internalized the transparently specious doctrine that audience research is done primarily in the interests of the audience, not the broadcaster, advertiser, or ad agency. What makes this more frustrating still are that thousands of deserving and even excellent anti-corporate projects go begging while the big foundations shower their progressive credibility—along with their money—on corporate liberators like Laybourne and companies like Gannett.

3. Jean-Marie Dru, *Disruption* (New York: John Wiley & Sons, 1996), pp. 56, 95, 214.

4. On the efforts of the American Family Association to persuade Duncan to withdraw this commercial, see http://www.afa.net/alert/aa991112.htm.

5. In the late nineties St. Luke's, with all its homegrown postmodern theory, its talk about ethical advertising, and its unordered workspace, exerted a strong fascination over the business revolutionary mind. The story of its heroic break from parent agency Chiat/Day (when that agency was taken over by conglomerate Omnicom) was told in one of the early issues of *Fast Company* (Stevan Alburty, "The Ad Agency to End All Ad Agencies," *Fast Company,* issue 6, December 1996); the agency was also described admiringly in Hey and Moore, *The Caterpillar Doesn't Know,* Charles Handy's *Hungry Spirit,* and in *Living on Thin Air* (London: Viking, 1999), British social theorist Charles Leadbeater's contribution to the literature of the "New Economy."

6. See http://www.stlukes.co.uk/STANDARD/senses/index.htm

7. Robinson is today "Chief Experience Officer" for a firm called "Sapient."

8. Micaela di Leonardo, *Exotics at Home: Anthropologies, Others, American Modernity* (Chicago: University of Chicago Press, 1998), p. 278. Di Leonardo's book is a comprehensive look at the way anthropological fantasies inform American popular and retail culture.

9. Skater resistance proved too powerful even for Nike. According to a story that

appeared in *Forbes* magazine for November 29, 1999, Nike suffered a massive backlash in skateboard zines despite its clever and humorous commercials. In that same month, Goodby, Silverstein lost the few Nike accounts they had handled as the client brought everything back to its longtime agency, Wieden and Kennedy.

CHAPTER EIGHT

1. On faculty unions, the key case was the "Yeshiva" decision of 1980, in which faculty at many private schools were ruled to be "management" and hence prevented from organizing by the provisions of the Taft-Hartley Act. See the *Chronicle of Higher Education,* January 21, 2000, p. A16. On the adoption of modern management techniques by universities, see the tongue-in-cheek proposal by Michael Bérubé, *Chronicle of Higher Education,* January 28, 2000, p. A64. See also Chris Lehmann, "Popular Front Redux?" *Baffler* 9, 1997.

2. Cary Nelson, "Late Capitalism Arrives on Campus," in *Manifesto of a Tenured Radical* (New York: NYU Press, 1997), p. 154.

3. Herbert Gans, *Popular Culture and High Culture* (New York: Basic, 1974), p. 52. Gans continued to work this vein at least into the 1980s. In his essay "American Popular Culture and High Culture in a Changing Class Structure," in *Prospects: An Annual of American Cultural Studies,* vol. 10 (1985), he extends his attack on theorists of mass culture to include Christopher Lasch.

4. Lawrence Levine, *Highbrow/Lowbrow: The Emergence of Cultural Hierarchy in America* (Cambridge, MA: Harvard University Press, 1988), p. 195.

5. Jim McGuigan, *Cultural Populism* (Routledge, 1992), p. 79. McGuigan's book is the source for my argument about cultural studies as a form of populism. McGuigan also points out that the "populist reflex" was, when his book was published, becoming "hegemonic" in the academy. McGuigan's critique of cultural studies as a too-optimistic form of cultural populism is now widely acknowledged by cult studs themselves. Acknowledging the critique, though, did not seem to change the discipline, and critics continued to assail cultural studies on these grounds throughout the nineties.

Lawrence Grossberg, *We Gotta Get Out of This Place* (Routledge, 1992), p. 65. I could discern no reason from Grossberg's text for the word "elitist" to be in quotation marks. Nevertheless, it is.

6. Michael Bérubé, "Pop Goes the Academy: Cult Studs Fight the Power," in *Public Access* (Verso, 1994), p. 138.

7. Although there was an immense flow of writing on this point, Stanley Aronowitz's 1993 book *Roll Over Beethoven* is particularly remarkable. In a chapter on the political correctness uproar he writes: "Cultural studies signified the refusal of a new generation of British and American intellectuals in the late 1950s and 1960s to observe the hier-

archy between high culture and the culture, in both the aesthetic and anthropological sense, of the working class and, most saliently, addressed the ideological basis of such distinctions. In the subsequent decades as new, emergent discourses developed into social movements, particularly of feminism and race, but also ecology and sexuality, and found their way into universities, cultural studies became one of the names for what became a virtual revolution in literary and cultural-theoretical canon." p. 25.

8. Cary Nelson and Dilip Gaonkar, "Cultural Studies and the Politics of Disciplinarity," in Nelson and Gaonkar, eds, *Disciplinarity and Dissent in Cultural Studies* (New York: Routledge, 1996), p. 13.

9. Richard Hoggart, *The Way We Live Now* (London: Chatto & Windus, 1995), p. 59.

10. Patrick Brantlinger, *Crusoe's Footprints*, (New York: Routledge, 1990), Lawrence Grossberg, *We Gotta Get Out of This Place*, (New York: Routledge, 1992), Stanley Aronowitz, *Roll Over Beethoven*, (Hanover, NH: Wesleyan University Press, 1993), Simon During, ed., *The Cultural Studies Reader* (New York: Routledge, 1993), John Fiske, *Power Plays, Power Works* (New York: Verso, 1993), Angela McRobbie, *Postmodernism and Popular Culture* (New York: Routledge, 1994), Jeffrey Williams, *PC Wars* (New York: Routledge, 1995), Nelson and Gaonkar, *Disciplinarity and Dissent*.

11. Ross, *No Respect: Intellectuals and Popular Culture* (New York: Routledge, 1989), p. 53. Jim McGuigan, in *Cultural Populism*, also maintains that consensus sociology has been "unwittingly echoed" by cultural studies. Andrew Ross has followed Gans in other ways as well, including actually moving to Disney's planned suburb of Celebration, Florida, much as Gans once moved to Levittown, New Jersey, in order to study the unfairly maligned suburbanites who lived there. On cultural studies' compulsive telling and retelling of its own "narrative of arrival," see Herman Gray in Nelson and Gaonkar, *Disciplinarity*, 1996, p. 205.

12. Brantlinger, p. 27. Lawrence Levine, *The Opening of the American Mind* (Boston: Beacon, 1996), pp. 88–89. See also John Fiske, *Power Plays, Power Works* (New York: Verso, 1993), p. 39.

13. Thus in a 1992 essay entitled "Pop Goes the Academy: Cult Studs Fight the Power," Michael Bérubé listed among the discipline's forebears Hoggart, Raymond Williams, E. P. Thompson, Louis Althusser, Juliet Mitchell, Antonio Gramsci, Ernesto Laclau and Chantal Mouffe, Pierre Bourdieu, and Michel de Certeau (Reprinted in Bérubé, *Public Access*, p. 141).

The willingness of those Europeans, especially the Birmingham School, to acknowledge American sociology is a different matter entirely. See Dick Hebdige, *Subculture: The Meaning of Style* (New York: Routledge, 1988 [1979]), pp. 75–79, and Ken Gelder and Sarah Thornton, eds., *The Subcultures Reader* (Routledge, 1997).

14. McGuigan, *Cultural Populism*, p. 40. Curiously enough, Herbert Gans has also

commented incisively on this very subject, decrying those postmodernists who, moti-vated by a curious revulsion against "long-gone vulgar and Stalinist Marxisms," insist on downgrading class as an analytic concept. Letter to *The Nation*, May 11, 1998. Guthey: Eric Guthey, "A Brief Cultural History of Corporate Legal Theory, and Why American Studies Should Care About It" (forthcoming). McChesney: Robert McChesney, "Is There Any Hope for Cultural Studies," *Monthly Review*, March 1996, p. 10. The un-named scholar McChesney quotes is Angela McRobbie.

Other academic critics go even further than McChesney. In a remarkable reading of the landmark 1992 *Cultural Studies* anthology, French literature scholar Stephen Adam Schwartz argues that the politics of cultural studies, to judge the discipline by its argu-ments rather than its chest-thumping vanguardism, is in fact "strikingly but not sur-prisingly content-poor, reducing in general to praise for transgression and well-meaning bromides about respect for 'difference.'" Unwilling to distinguish between Western democracies and more rigidly ordered societies, and concerned quite exclusively with "the possibility of expressing oneself" as "the rightful beginning and absolute end of all social and political life," cultural studies, Schwartz charges, is closely related to good old American libertarianism. Schwartz, "Everyman an Übermensch: The Culture of Cultural Studies," *SubStance* 91 (2000), pp. 116, 117, 118, 123.

15. Hoggart, *The Way We Live Now*, p. 186.

16. Alan D. Sokal, "Transgressing the Boundaries: Toward a Transformative Hermeneu-tics of Quantum Gravity," *Social Text* 46/47 (Spring/Summer 1996), pp. 217–52. A good account of the cult studs' humorless response to the prank can be found in Katha Pollitt's account of the incident, "Pomolotov cocktail," *The Nation*, June 10, 1996, p. 9.

17. See Andrew Ross, "Techno-Sweatshops," *Tikkun*, January–February 2000, p. 57. See also Douglas Kellner, "Critical Theory and Cultural Studies: The Missed Articula-tion," in Jim McGuigan, ed., *Cultural Methodologies*. (London: Sage, 1997).

18. http://www.modcult.brown.edu/info/intro.html. MCM is also just about the only department at Brown where one can imagine this book being read.

19. On the other hand, Cowen is reluctant to align himself with cultural studies too closely, perhaps because he mistakenly identifies it as a movement presided over by known Marxist Fredric Jameson. Cowen, *In Praise of Commercial Culture* (Harvard, 1998), p. 12.

20. James B. Twitchell, *Lead Us Into Temptation: The Triumph of American Materi-alism* (New York: Columbia University Press, 1999), pp. 14, 20, 21–26, 36, 39, 41, 46, 285, 286. Twitchell's exact words on this last point are: "To some degree, the triumph of consumerism is the triumph of the popular will."

21. *Fortune* also adds Lanier's skills with exotic instruments to the mix, commenc-ing its story about him with an anecdote of how he played "nose flute" at "the Kitchen, the famous avant-garde nightclub in downtown Manhattan." Ed Brown, "Technofile," *Fortune*, March 2, 1998, p. 194.

22. Jaron Lanier, "The Care and Feeding of Digital Behemoths," *New York Times*, October 11, 1997, p. A11.

23. Donna Haraway, "The Promises of Monsters," *Cultural Studies*, p. 327. The woman with cat that sends Haraway into a prose paroxysm is in a painting, a particularly heavy-handed bit of New Age allegory complete with zodiac symbols, a pyramid, and a white tiger; p. 328. *Wired:* Hari Kunzru, "You Are Cyborg," February 1997. Kunzru does acknowledge that Haraway is "harshly critical of techno-utopians, including some of those found between the covers of this magazine," but that doesn't seem to stop the magazine from continually reading Haraway's writing as the ultimate in techno-utopianism.

24. McCracken's story appeared in the August/September 1998 issue of *Reason*.

25. Gillespie's story appeared in the February 1996 issue of *Reason*. A more recent example of the confluence with the cult stud concerns is senior editor Charles Paul Freund's June 1998 *Reason* essay in which the Frankfurters are dissed yet again and a "culture . . . indifferent to elites and divorced from taste hierarchies" is trumpeted one more time. Freund concludes by saluting the "Birmingham School" for having "at least gotten in the schoolhouse door. A little more homework, perhaps, and the scholars will arrive at the answer which the audience itself found long ago." Meaning, of course, the virtues of "marketplace culture," where people find "opportunities for the liberation and satisfaction of their senses and their intellect."

26. Yeah, he said it. In the March 1999 issue of *Reason*.

27. Rush Limbaugh, *See, I Told You So* (Pocket, 1993), pp. xv, 20, 238, 335.

28. McGuigan, Kellner, During, Bérubé, Guthey, McChesney, Ross. See also Stuart Hall's talk about "institutionalization" in Grossberg, Nelson, Treichler, *Cultural Studies*.

29. I am referring here to a quotation of Raoul Vaneigem that seemed to appear everywhere in 1997 and 1998. "People who talk about revolution and class struggle without referring explicitly to everyday life, without understanding what is subversive about love and what is positive in the refusal of constraint, have corpses in their mouths." Vaneigem evidently came up with the ringing cadences of this proclamation thirty years before. Its enthusiastic repeating across the cultural studies left betokens a weird belief that there are a great number of people in America who "talk about revolution and class struggle," and that these people need desperately to be defied.

30. "Introduction: The Territory of Marxism," *Marxism and the Interpretation of Culture* (University of Illinois Press: 1988), p. 4.

31. Ross, *No Respect*. On legitimacy, p. 61. On the "new intellectuals" reaching the high plateau, pp. 230–31.

CHAPTER NINE

1. John Leonard, "Follow the Bouncing Ball," in William Serrin, ed., *The Business of Journalism* (New York: New Press, 2000) p. 203. Richard M. Cohen, "The Corporate Takeover of News," in Barnouw et al, *Conglomerates and the Media* (New York: New Press, 1997), p. 33.

2. A. J. Liebling, *The Press* (New York: Pantheon, 1981), p. 6.

3. Frank Gannett was founder of an organization called the Committee for Constitutional Government, which attempted to stir up a popular reaction against the policies of the Roosevelt administration. Directed by one Dr. Edward Rumely, who had been convicted of being a German agent during World War I, it was denounced in 1944 by Congressman Wright Patman as the "No. 1 Fascist organization in the United States." Among the group's list of notable accomplishments were the 1943 effort to suppress John Roy Carlson's best-seller *Under Cover*, a study of American fascism which detailed the group's doings (copies of a vaguely threatening letter from Gannett were sent to bookstores nationwide warning them against carrying the book), and the dissemination of the famous Lincoln Hoax, a list of ten moralistic libertarian arguments ("You cannot help the poor by destroying the rich," etc.) erroneously attributed to Abraham Lincoln which still crops up in right-wing circles to this day.

George Seldes, *1000 Americans* (New York: Boni & Gaer, 1947), p. 213; Kenneth Stewart and John Tebbel, *Makers of Modern Journalism* (Prentice-Hall, 1952), p. 335; John Roy Carlson, *Under Cover* (New York: E. P. Dutton, 1943); Morris Kominsky, *The Hoaxers: Plain liars, Fancy liars, and Damned liars* (Boston: Branden Press, 1970).

4. Liebling, *The Press*, p. 22, 23.

5. Larry Sabato, *Feeding Frenzy: How Attack Journalism Has Transformed American Politics* (New York: Free Press, 1991). Cappella and Jamieson, *Spiral of Cynicism: The Press and the Public Good* (Oxford University Press, 1997).

For the Times Mirror poll on public cynicism as well as a savage takedown of nineties journalism criticism, see Chris Lehmann's April 1997 essay in *Salon*: http://www.salon.com/april97/media/media970414.html

6. Rosen, *Getting the Connections Right: Public Journalism and the Troubles in the Press* (New York: Twentieth Century Fund, 1996), p. 1.

7. Fifties-era phrases: Rosen, *Connections*, pp. 3, 6. Humble: Rosen, *What Are Journalists For?* (Yale University Press, 1999), p. 117, "Listening well": Rosen, *What?* p. 261.

8. James Fallows, *Breaking the News: How the Media Undermine American Democracy* (Pantheon, 1996), p. 257. Rosen, *What?* p. 47.

9. YOUtv is detailed in the Pew Foundation's serial publication, *Civic Catalyst*, fall 1999. The transcript for "A Work in Progress" is dated 1998.

10. John Leo, "Hold the 'Wrong' Story," *US News & World Report*, August 10, 1998, p. 12.

11. Fallows, *Breaking the News*, p. 240. Rosen, *Connections*, p. 13.

12. On Willes as "civic journalist," see Ken Auletta, "Demolition Man," *The New Yorker*, November 17, 1997, and *Civic Catalyst*, winter 1999.

13. Giles' thoughts on Public Journalism appeared in the *Detroit News*, April 14, 1996, at the height of the strike. Giles' fantasies about Martin Luther King appeared in the *Detroit News* on March 10, 1996. "The civil rights movement sought to create change and reform," he wrote. "The newspaper strike seeks to resist change and reform." He also described the effort of replacement workers to "create a new, more efficient, and competitive order for the newspapers" as true "civil disobedience." King's son, Martin Luther King III, came to Detroit a few weeks later to support the strikers and denounced Giles' remarks as "the epitome of white arrogance." *Detroit Sunday Journal*, March 31–April 6, 1996, p. 1. Giles' talk of cynicism is recounted in Jack Lessenberry's column in the *Detroit Metro Times*, May 15, 1996. Lessenberry himself, a supporter of the strike, was the one Giles accused of cynicism.

14. Al Neuharth, *Confessions of an SOB* (New York: Doubleday, 1989), pp. 157, 255. On the "journalism of hope" and its differences from the snob journalism of "despair," see p. 258.

15. "Brainiacs": Samuel Freedman, *USA Today*, July 6, 1998, p. 13A. Neuharth: *USA Today*, July 10, 1998, p. 15A.

16. On these points see Philip Weiss, "Invasion of the Gannettoids," *The New Republic*, February 2, 1987; Richard McCord, *The Chain Gang: One Newspaper Versus the Gannett Empire* (Columbia, MO: University of Missouri Press, 1996); Neuharth, *SOB*, p. 178.

17. Interview with Richard McCord, June 23, 1998. Sig Gissler, "What Happens When Gannett Takes Over," *Columbia Journalism Review*, November/December 1997. The *Register* columnist is James Flansburg, he is quoted in the *American Journalism Review*, November 1997. The panic was at the *Minneapolis Star-Tribune*, which belonged to the same family that sold the *Des Moines Register* to Gannett; it was reported on November 14, 1997. $65 million was the figure reported by the *Nashville Scene*, June 4, 1998.

18. Interview with Linda Foley, June 29, 1998. Peter Prichard, *The Making of McPaper: The Inside Story of USA Today* (Kansas City, MO: Andrews, McMeel & Parker, 1987), pp. 200–202. There is a vast literature on Gannett's activities in Detroit. See *The Nation*, November 6, 1989, and November 25, 1996; Bryan Gruley, *Paper Losses* (Grove, 1993); *New York Times*, September 2, 1998; and every issue of the *Detroit Sunday Journal*.

19. Responding to a 1995 Gannett ad that stated "We believe in 'public journalism'—and have done it for years," Rosen argues that, since Gannett is clearly more interested in profits than in publics, it does not practice a pure or forthright version of the

faith. Still, he writes, watching them twist the meaning of the movement to their own uses was "part of the adventure of public journalism." *What Are Journalists For?* pp. 257, 261.

20. Prichard, pp. xi, xii, 7.

21. Neuharth, *SOB* pp. 240, 248, 255. Neuharth, "Saying No to the Status Quo," speech given to the National College Media Convention, November 3, 1994. *USA Today,* March 31, 1989.

22. Al Neuharth, "BusCapade USA," *USA Today,* September 14, 1987, August 14, 1987, August 21, 1987, August 7, 1987, July 27, 1987.

23. *Business Week,* December 21, 1992. Neuharth, "Plain Talk," *USA Today,* January 15, 1993. Neuharth, "BusCapade, USA," *USA Today,* May 8, 1987.

24. Prichard, p. 357, Neuharth, *SOB,* p. 301.

25. Neuharth, *SOB,* pp. 186, 187, 199.

26. Ibid., p. 274.

27. "Facts About News 2000," Gannett publicity document, dated 1991.

28. Mark Willes as quoted in the *Wall Street Journal,* May 1, 1998, p. A1.

29. *Nashville Scene,* March 5, 1998.

30. Al does this in *USA Today,* July 10, 1998, p. 15A.

CHAPTER TEN

1. As quoted in *Wired,* January 1998. Curious line breaks in original.

2. Kevin Kelly, *New Rules for the New Economy: 10 Radical Strategies for a Connected World* (New York: Viking, 1998), p. 77.

3. Virginia Postrel, *The Future and Its Enemies: The Growing Conflict over Creativity, Enterprise, and Progress* (New York: The Free Press, 1998), pp. xvii, 50, 114, 128, 171, 192. I have no idea why Postrel feels she must point out that the members of the "state cosmetology board" who antagonized the stylish Sassoon wore crappy clothing (one might even remark here that, from a certain perspective, polyester can be regarded as a liberator just as easily as Sassoon himself), but nonetheless she quotes a favorite source, anthropologist Grant McCracken, who celebrates Sassoon's victory thusly: "Some 30 years after his tangle with that angry little bureaucrat swathed in wash and wear, Sassoon's empire continues to grow." One wonders if Pol Pot might seem more of a "dynamist" when his stylish black cotton pajamas are taken into account.

4. Ibid., pp. xiv. Postrel equates the future with markets by pointing out that the enemies of the one are the enemies of the other, p. xv. She also defines the two "processes" (future and market, that is) in strikingly similar terms, cf. pp. xiv, 35.

5. The argument could be made that the entire "New Economy" literature is a descendent of Stalinist rhetoric. Francis Fukuyama, the foreign policy thinker whose 1989

article about the "End of History" ignited this feeling of world-historical infallibility among American intellectuals, based his argument on the interpretation of Hegel proposed by the Russo-French intellectual Alexandre Kojève. In 1999 the DST, the French equivalent of the FBI, announced that Kojève had in fact been a KGB agent for some thirty years before his death in 1968. Although this revelation has since been disputed by friends and biographers of Kojève, his fondness for Stalin was already well known. "La DST avait identifié plusieurs agents du KGB parmi lesquels le philosophe Alexandre Kojève," *Le Monde,* September 16, 1999; Dominique Auffret, "Alexandre Kojève: du trompe-l'oeil au vertige," *Le Monde,* September 24, 1999; Edmond Ortigues, "Pour l'honneur d'Alexandre Kojève," *Le Monde,* October 4, 1999; Daniel Johnson, "Europe's Greatest Traitor," *Daily Telegraph,* October 2, 1999, p. 22.

6. Thurow, *Building WEALTH,* 33, 45, 97.

7. Friedman, *Lexus,* p. 93. Imagining national leaders talking like hardguys to one another is one of Friedman's trademark conceits. Strangely, Friedman also makes a big fuss over the mountainously arrogant notion that affluence is a matter of a choice, since it has been so fully figured out by us here in America. Any country, it seems, can ditch their history, can ditch the shitty hand nature has dealt them and "choose prosperity" as easily as that (p. 167). In this respect the "New Economy" revolution is not as inevitable as was the dictatorship of the proletariat, since a country can opt not to don the "golden straitjacket" and remain mired in poverty. But if a country wants a decent standard of living, it has no choice.

8. Kelly, *New Rules for the New Economy,* pp. 1, 8, 73, 81.

9. Kevin Kelly describes Gilder in these words on page 52 of *New Rules.* He also describes the "Law of the Microcosm," whose provisions are described in chapter 2 (along with Moore's Law) as "Gilder's Law." "Metcalfe's Law," which Gilder revealed to the world in an article in *Forbes ASAP* ("Metcalfe's Law and Legacy," September 13, 1993) seems to be interchangeable with what Gilder calls the "Law of the Telecosm," which is defined thus in Gilder's 1992 work, *Life After Television:* the "total value" of n linked computers "rises in proportion to the square of 'n,' " p. 19. It should be noted that Gilder's fondness for "laws" and inevitabilities was not a passing taste: He stuck with it quite doggedly in his *Forbes ASAP* "Telecosm" writings in the nineties.

10. Gilder, *Microcosm,* pp. 319, 344.

11. Ibid., p. 369.

12. Ibid., p. 369.

13. Kimberly Seltzer and Tom Bentley, *The Creative Age: Knowledge and Skills for the New Economy* (London: Demos 1999), p. 13; Geoff Mulgan, *Connexity,* pp. 30, 223; Leadbeater, *Thin Air,* p. 38.

14. Mark Leonard, *Britain™: Renewing Our Identity* (London: Demos, 1997).

15. Leadbeater, *Thin Air,* pp. 19–23; Leonard, *Britain™,* p. 54; Charles Leadbeater

and Kate Oakley, *The Independents: Britain's New Cultural Entrepreneurs* (London: Demos, 1999), p. 74.

16. Leadbeater, *Thin Air,* 224.

17. Mulgan, *Connexity,* pp. 35–36, 168, 183.

18. Ibid., pp. 76, 44, 167.

19. Nick Cohen, "There is no alternative to becoming Leadbeater," *London Review of Books,* October 28, 1999, p. 33.

20. Mulgan, *Connexity,* back cover; Leadbeater, *Thin Air,* pp. viii, 80; Ian Hargreaves and Ian Christie, eds., *Tomorrow's Politics: The Third Way and Beyond* (London: Demos, 1998), p. 16.

21. Stuart Hall and Martin Jacques, eds., *New Times: The Changing Face of Politics in the 1990s* (London: Verso 1990 [1989]), pp. 12, 16, 452.

22. Postrel discusses "dynamism," "stasism," and their related personality types, as these were revealed to her by a friendly economist on p. xv of *The Future and Its Enemies.*

23. Postrel seems to have a problem generally with criticism. While she makes a great fuss over the tolerance of "dynamists" (see p. 142) and the intolerance of "stasists," the grand theme of the book is that "stasist critics," if left to do their criticizing, will ruin "the future" for all of us. Evidently criticism is of a different nature entirely when it issues from a "dynamist" and a "stasist": "Dynamists" always limit their criticism to questions of taste or contract violation, while whenever a "stasist" opens his mouth he is demanding, implicitly if not overtly, government intervention of the most loathsome sort. "Stasist criticism," therefore, is ipso facto intolerant, and must be beaten back.

24. Kelly, *New Rules,* p. 81. Karlgaard: *Forbes,* August 23, 1999. Emphasis in original.

25. Mail solicitation for *The Gilder Technology Report,* "A Joint Publication of Forbes magazine and the Gilder Group," dated "Winter 2000," collection of the author.

26. "Technically, Gilder's Words Carry Weight," *Wall Street Journal,* January 7, 2000, p. C1; Fred Barbash, "Market Guru Puts Acolytes on Wild Ride," *The Washington Post,* March 5, 2000, p. H1; Aaron Zitner, "Sage of the Berkshires," *Boston Globe,* March 20, 2000, p. C1; George Gilder and Richard Vigilante, "AT&T's Wireless Debacle," *Wall Street Journal,* May 1, 2000, p. A34. As for Gilder's personal holdings, the *Journal* reports, "He says he owns about seven of the companies on his list, and he doesn't sell."

27. See the various reports on Colombia produced by the International Confederation of Free Trade Unions. http://www2.icftu.org.

Index

Adams, Henry, 103
Adams, Scott, 177
Adorno, Theodor, 282, 303
advertising: academic pretensions of, 263–66; account planners, 254–72; agencies, 253, 260–62, 263, 264–66, 268, 269–71; anti-elitism tactics, 28–30, 51, 194; anti-French, 238; Ameritrade commercials, 143–44; Arthur Andersen consultants, 28; brands, 252–72, *see also* brand(ing); brokerage, online, 88–90, 136, 153–54, 157, 159–61; business-as-God, 4; business revolution and, 170, 172–73, 172n, 185n, 234, 261, 348; celebrating the New Economy, 5,16,

18; chaos theory in, 264, 267–68; Charles Schwab, 133–34; children used in, 232–34; consumption, and market populism, contradiction, 151; Enron's ads, 16; ethnic diversity in, 233–39; Fidelity, 119; humanness of corporations, 223–28; IBM, 3, 33–34, 67, 233–34, 238, 244; Internet as Messiah, 160; "Is this a great time or what?," 172, 187–88; Merrill Lynch, 134, 160, 172n, 220, 232–33; number of ads, public exposed to, 253; radical politics and social movements used in, 19–20, 260–62, 277; as reflector of popular sentiment, xiv; sales-through-domination, 266; serial